A HISTORY OF THE SOUTH

VOLUMES IN THE SERIES

I   THE SOUTHERN COLONIES IN THE SEVENTEENTH CENTURY, 1607–1689
by Wesley Frank Craven

II   THE SOUTHERN COLONIES IN THE EIGHTEENTH CENTURY, 1689–1763
by Clarence Ver Steeg

III   THE SOUTH IN THE REVOLUTION, 1763–1789
by John Richard Alden

IV   THE SOUTH IN THE NEW NATION, 1789–1819
by Thomas P. Abernethy

V   THE DEVELOPMENT OF SOUTHERN SECTIONALISM, 1819–1848
by Charles S. Sydnor

VI   THE GROWTH OF SOUTHERN NATIONALISM, 1848–1861
by Avery O. Craven

VII   THE CONFEDERATE STATES OF AMERICA, 1861–1865
by E. Merton Coulter

VIII   THE SOUTH DURING RECONSTRUCTION, 1865–1877
by E. Merton Coulter

IX   ORIGINS OF THE NEW SOUTH, 1877–1913
by C. Vann Woodward

X   THE PRESENT SOUTH, 1913–1946
by George Tindall

Volume III

THE SOUTH IN THE REVOLUTION

1763–1789

JOHN RICHARD ALDEN is professor of history at Duke University. He received his undergraduate and graduate training at the University of Michigan, where he was awarded the Ph.D. degree in 1939. Before assuming his present post, he was professor of history at the University of Nebraska.

Previous books have won Mr. Alden a high place among contemporary American historians. His *General Gage in America* (1948) and *General Charles Lee* (1951), both published by Louisiana State University Press, are fascinating rehabilitations of two "villains" of the Revolution. His *American Revolution, 1775-1783* is a volume in the *Rise of the American Nation* series edited by Henry Steele Commager. The American Historical Association awarded Mr. Alden the Beveridge Prize in 1945 for his *John Stuart and the Southern Colonial Frontier, 1754-1775*. He has also edited Christopher Ward's great work, *War of the Revolution*, and has written a number of articles and reviews for professional journals.

A HISTORY

OF

THE SOUTH

Volume III

EDITORS

WENDELL HOLMES STEPHENSON

PROFESSOR OF HISTORY
AT THE UNIVERSITY OF OREGON

E. MERTON COULTER

REGENTS' PROFESSOR OF HISTORY AT THE
UNIVERSITY OF GEORGIA

The South
in the
Revolution
1763-1789

BY JOHN RICHARD ALDEN

LOUISIANA STATE UNIVERSITY PRESS

THE LITTLEFIELD FUND FOR SOUTHERN
HISTORY OF THE UNIVERSITY OF TEXAS

1957

Designed by Robert Josephy

PUBLISHERS' PREFACE

A HISTORY OF THE SOUTH is sponsored by Louisiana State University and the Trustees of the Littlefield Fund for Southern History at the University of Texas. More remotely, it is the outgrowth of the vision of Major George W. Littlefield, C.S.A., who established a fund at the University of Texas in 1914 for the collection of materials on Southern history and the publication of a "full and impartial study of the South and its part in American history." Trustees of the Littlefield Fund began preparations in 1937 for the writing of the history that Major Littlefield contemplated. Meanwhile, a plan had been conceived at Louisiana State University for a history of the South as a part of that institution's comprehensive program to promote interest, research, and writing in the field of Southern history.

As the two undertakings harmonized in essentials, the planning groups united to become joint sponsors of *A History of the South*. Wendell Holmes Stephenson, then professor of American history at Louisiana State University, and the late Charles W. Ramsdell, professor of American history at the University of Texas, were chosen to edit the series. They had been primarily interested in initiating the plans, and it was appropriate that they should be selected to edit the work. Upon the death of Professor Ramsdell in 1943, E. Merton Coulter, professor of history at the University of Georgia, was named his successor.

Volumes of the series are being published as the manuscripts are received. This is the seventh published volume; it follows Volume VI. When completed, the ten-volume set will represent about fifteen years of historical planning and research.

AUTHOR'S PREFACE

MANY BOOKS have been written about the South, and many concerning the American Revolution, but this volume is the first to be devoted to the South during the era of the Revolution. It begins with the Peace of Paris of 1763 and ends with the establishment of the Federal government under the Constitution, these being the traditional limits of the Revolutionary time. The history of the South during that period is, of course, complex and many-sided; and the writer, traversing uncharted ground in selecting and organizing materials, has very likely failed to find ideal solutions to the host of problems of arrangement and emphasis which have confronted him. Indeed, it is not at all inconceivable that topics considered by some to be both relevant and important have actually been omitted, although it is certainly hoped that there are no serious lacunae.

The South of the Revolutionary epoch was not geographically the South of 1860 or of 1920, and but little is said in the following pages about that part of the later South which lies west of the Mississippi. In the days of the Revolution the Americans had not sunk root beyond the great river, were just then planting the states of Kentucky and Tennessee. In consequence, emphasis has been placed upon the development of that part of the modern South between the Appalachians and the Mississippi, and above all upon the history of the people of the old colony-states on the seaboard from Maryland to Georgia. Here there are four subjects which have demanded much attention: the role of the Southerners (not yet generally called by that name) in the struggle for independence; the rise of sectional controversy between North and South, which is as old as the nation; the internal reformation below the Mason-Dixon line that proceeded from the contest with Britain; and the part taken by the South in the making of the Federal union formed at the end of the Revolutionary time. Accordingly, the canvas is

ix

broad, and diverse persons and scenes appear upon it. Diplomats confer in Paris, and equally dignified Indian chiefs converse about war and peace with American emissaries in South Carolina; George Grenville pushes through the Stamp Act in London, and a mob frightens Marylander Zachariah Hood in New York City; woods warfare is waged on the Ohio, and British veterans engage American Continentals and militia in formal combat at Guilford Courthouse; frontiersmen angrily denounce Spain and her officials on the Mississippi while fifty-five gentlemen make the Constitution at Philadelphia.

Although extensive and intensive use of contemporary records has been made, the writer is heavily indebted to many scholars who have delved into Southern history, and he has tried to indicate his obligations in citations and bibliography. His errors in fact or opinion are, however, his own.

As the result of a seminar directed by Professor Verner W. Crane some twenty years ago, the author first felt the fascination of research in the early history of the South. Later he published a study of the Southern frontier in the third quarter of the eighteenth century which was soberly written and which may not have conveyed his enthusiasm to its readers. Now, after pursuing in the intervening years researches devoted more to the Revolution than to the South, he returns with pleasure to his first scholarly love. With the passage of time the author has become ever more convinced that a historian should present his findings as attractively as his materials, his abilities, and his energies permit. Much historical writing of great value, being intended for scholars and teachers, is not for the "general reader." Nor is this book directed toward that mythical being, but the author will be pleased if the many people who enjoy and profit from reading about the vicissitudes, the follies, and the triumphs of the past do not avoid it merely because of its form and language.

One does not write a book such as this without the assistance of many people. Helpful services and advice were contributed by Miss Susan Armstrong, Miss Jean M. Bigelow, Dr. Lester Cappon, Dr. Jack P. Greene, Miss Virginia Gunter, Dr. R. Don Higginbotham, Mr. Julian Metz, Dr. Edward Riley, Dr. Mattie Russell, Professor Richard L. Watson, and Professor Robert H. Woody.

Mrs. Joanne M. Ballard and Mrs. Edith Thornton typed the manuscript.

Dr. James H. Easterby and Dr. Benjamin Powell, by making manuscript materials easily accessible, offered aid of the first importance. Without the gracious support of the John Simon Guggenheim Memorial Foundation and of Duke University, which made possible uninterrupted research and writing during a fifteen-month period of 1955–1956, this volume would have been long delayed, and, conceivably, never finished.

My wife, Pearl Wells Alden, drew the maps for this book, and helped with innumerable other tasks connected with it.

A heavy debt of gratitude is owed to the editors of the History of the South Series, Professors Wendell H. Stephenson and E. Merton Coulter. Above all other obligations is that to Professor Stephenson, whose scholarship and meticulous editing arouse admiration. Without his labors the merits of this volume, whatever they may be, would be far fewer than they are.

J. R. A.

CONTENTS

PUBLISHERS' PREFACE		vii
AUTHOR'S PREFACE		ix
I	INTRODUCTION	1
II	PEOPLES AND THEIR PURSUITS	5
III	THE SOCIAL SCENE	26
IV	MR. GRENVILLE'S PROGRAM	45
V	CHALLENGE FROM THE CHESAPEAKE	64
VI	THE SOUTH FOLLOWS MR. HENRY	78
VII	THE TOWNSHEND CRISIS	99
VIII	ADVANCE INTO THE OLD SOUTHWEST	118
IX	SECTIONAL CLASH	143
X	TEA AND TRUMPETS	164
XI	EARLY AMERICAN VICTORIES	186
XII	SEPARATION AND UNION	207
XIII	A CHAIN OF DEFEATS	227
XIV	TRIUMPH IN THE FAR SOUTH	247
XV	THE SOUTHWESTERN FRONT	268
XVI	YORKTOWN AND THE PEACE	290
XVII	THE SOUTHERN STATES: POLITICAL RECONSTRUCTION	306
XVIII	THE SOUTHERN STATES: SOCIAL FERMENT	329
XIX	THE SOUTHWEST AGAIN	349
XX	TOWARD A MORE PERFECT NATION	367
XXI	THE SOUTH ENTERS THE NEW UNION	390
CRITICAL ESSAY ON AUTHORITIES		401
INDEX		427

MAPS AND ILLUSTRATIONS

	Facing Page
Henry Laurens	16
George Washington	49
The Governor's Palace, Williamsburg	81
The Old Southwest	121
War in the Carolinas	235
Sir Henry Clinton	240
General Horatio Gates	273
General Nathanael Greene	304
Thomas Jefferson	337
Charles Cotesworth Pinckney	368

CHAPTER I

INTRODUCTION

LONG after the din of the American Revolution had died away, John Adams, musing upon it in retirement at Quincy, said that it began in the minds of the Americans long before they came into bitter clash with Britain. Assuredly, shrewd John Adams was not mistaken; it commenced with the founding of the first permanent English settlement in America in 1607. The Englishmen who settled on the east coast of North America between Maine and Georgia became less and less English, more and more American with every passing day, the process of change being slow and almost imperceptible, the result startling and easily evident. It follows that the remotest origins of the Revolution are to be found in the South, in Virginia, in the impressions of the bold adventurers who landed upon the banks of the James River in the fifth year of the reign of the monarch for whom they named it.

But the South had far more to do with the Revolution than merely to supply the scenes where the metamorphosis of Englishmen and others into Americans began. From the lands between the lower boundary of Pennsylvania and Georgia's Altamaha River, from Southern Tidewater and Piedmont, from beyond the Blue Ridge and the Great Smokies, came soldiers and statesmen without whose courage and genius the patriot cause must have been lost. The new nation would not have been, without Southern devotion and sacrifice. The warriors of Maryland, Virginia, the Carolinas, and Georgia who fought at Boston, Quebec, Cowpens, and Eutaw Springs were no less heroic than their descendants of Chancellorsville, Gettysburg, Chickamauga, and Franklin. The names of Washington, Light-Horse Harry Lee, Francis Marion, George Rogers Clark, John Sevier, Isaac Shelby, Thomas Sumter,

1

William Moultrie, and Andrew Pickens will not be forgotten so long as military prowess is remembered. Nor did the Southerners fail to do their part in creating the new political and social order which arose with the Revolution. The civil exploits of Washington, Thomas Jefferson, James Madison, George Mason, John Rutledge, and the Pinckneys were at least equal to those of their Northern brethren.

To be sure, in the year 1763, generally recognized as marking the end of the colonial time and the beginning of the era of the Revolution, the boundary between Pennsylvania and Maryland did not separate sectional and sharply opposed antagonists, nor did there then exist that remarkable community of institutions, thought, and feeling which was afterward so evident in the Southern regions of the United States. It has been suggested, in fact, that before the Declaration of Independence there were actually four societies to the southward of the line which Charles Mason and Jeremiah Dixon surveyed in 1767, that there were before 1776 "Old Souths" rather than an "Old South." [1] Certainly there were in the era of the Revolution striking differences in economic and social structure between Tidewater and Piedmont in North Carolina, between Low Country and Upcountry in South Carolina. Moreover, even the words "South" and "Southerner" had not the meaning in 1775 that they later acquired. As late as the beginning of the War of Independence, New England was referred to as "the Eastern provinces," with the remainder of the Thirteen Colonies described as "Southern," that term including Pennsylvania and Pennsylvanians as well as Georgia and Georgians.

By the end of the Revolutionary epoch, however, the South had emerged as a section and the Southerners as a people different from Northerners. Divergences continued within the region below the Mason-Dixon boundary, but there was when Washington assumed the presidency a South at least loosely united, and one certainly distinct from a North in terms of climate, slavery, economy, social structure, and political viewpoint. As the War of Independence proceeded, the words "South" and "Southern"

[1] Carl Bridenbaugh, *Myths and Realities; Societies of the Colonial South* (Baton Rouge, 1952), vii–viii.

were increasingly applied only to the area and the people below the Susquehanna. That they were so used more and more commonly was not merely a matter of convenience; conflict appeared during the war between those who lived upon one side of the line and those who dwelt upon the other. In the Federal convention of 1787 accommodation of the jarring interests of South and North offered a perplexing and harassing puzzle, one which required solution if there was to be an American union.

Some may prefer not to include Maryland in the South, since western Maryland contained farms rather than plantations, produced wheat, corn, and livestock rather than tobacco, and was tilled by free whites rather than Negro slaves, or because Maryland was slightly more commercial, a trifle more urban than Virginia. There was a large degree of identity, however, in economic, social, and political structure between Virginia and Maryland.[2] It is a striking fact that the planters of the latter were as potent politically as those of the Old Dominion, and that the viewpoint and behavior of the two colony-states were similar in the Revolutionary epoch. In the South Carolina convention which ratified the Constitution of 1787 Charles Pinckney declared, "When I say Southern, I mean Maryland, and the states to the southward of her." [3] Pinckney doubtless had the right of it. To be sure, Maryland did not belong to the Southern South as did Georgia. But neither did Virginia. Certainly, the history of the colony-state founded by the Calverts is inextricably linked with that of the South, and it is convenient and helpful to deal with them as one.

In these pages Maryland and Marylanders will often appear. So will East Florida and West Florida and their white inhabitants, newly British in 1763, and also the Southern Indians, both groups playing roles in the course of Southern history during and after the era of independence. Something is said as well about the Spanish in Louisiana and the Floridas, since they likewise had their part in the rise of the South. Nor can the saga of the pioneers who

---

[2] "From every point of view except a political one, the Chesapeake tidewater was a single unit." Arthur P. Middleton, *Tobacco Coast; A Maritime History of Chesapeake Bay in the Colonial Era* (Newport News, 1953), 355.

[3] Jonathan Elliot (ed.), *The Debates in the Several State Conventions on the Adoption of the Federal Constitution* (Philadelphia, 1859), IV, 324.

moved across the Appalachians into Kentucky and Tennessee be ignored, for they added to the colony-states of the Atlantic seaboard the empire of the Old Southwest. The Negro, whose history in British America began with the first attempt to found an English colony on Roanoke Island, plays his part.

CHAPTER II

PEOPLES AND THEIR PURSUITS

IN THE year 1763 the region now known as the South was only partly settled by the English. There were few English homes beyond the southern Appalachian Mountains. Before the outbreak of the Seven Years' War in the upper Ohio Valley in 1754, some families from Virginia had crossed the height of land and had thrown up log cabins "on the waters of Mississippi." These, however, had been slain, captured, or forced back across the mountains during the war by hostile Indians. A few had probably returned to their trans-Appalachian clearings by 1763; certainly some families had done so by 1764. Except for this recent penetration by home builders and the journeys into it of hunters, explorers, and traders with the Indians, the southern Mississippi Valley was, so far as the English were concerned, an untouched territory. Indeed, there were then large areas east of the mountains in the Carolinas and Georgia inhabited only by Indians or vacant of humankind. The beautiful valley of the Shenandoah and southwest Virginia were still in process of settlement. The western portion of the Piedmont in the Carolinas and Georgia was as yet almost virgin land. Beyond the far-flung farms, villages, and plantations of the South, in the eastern approaches to the mountains, within them, and off to the west resided many Indian tribes, containing fifty or sixty thousand persons. Among these were five principal nations, the Catawbas, Cherokee, Creeks, Choctaw, and Chickasaw. Still farther to the west were the scanty settlements of the French along the Mississippi, and the even thinner Spanish population of Texas, imbedded among other Indian nations.

Even in the Southern regions long traversed by the English plow there was nowhere a congestion of people, nowhere a district which could be described as thickly populated, except by a Daniel Boone desiring neighbors no nearer than a "whoop and a holler." In the valley of the James River, where the English had broken the soil six generations earlier, there was far more of woods than there was of tobacco fields. Indeed, it may be said that almost the entire South was a forest, now coniferous, now deciduous, interrupted more or less frequently by small clearings or larger plantations. Save for Charleston, South Carolina, there was not a city in the whole South. The South was rural, its countryside, unspoiled by commerce and industry, in turn fertile and barren, drab and beautiful, rich and poor, tilled and untilled, peopled and empty.

More than 700,000 persons, not including Indians, lived between the Mason-Dixon boundary and the Altamaha in 1763, nearly one half of the population of the Thirteen Colonies. More than one third of the Southerners were to be found in Virginia; there were at least 150,000 Marylanders and as many North Carolinians; somewhat more than 100,000 people resided in South Carolina; Georgia, still almost undeveloped, contained about 13,000. At that time Negroes and mulattoes formed two fifths of Virginia's population, one third of North Carolina's and of Maryland's, towards two thirds of South Carolina's, and more than one third of Georgia's.

The Southern whites, then as earlier and later, were basically of British stock. The first settlers in Virginia and Maryland were English by birth, and many later immigrants came from England. By the end of the Seven Years' War there were many Germans in the colony of the Calverts and in the Old Dominion, pushing into the Piedmont and the Shenandoah Valley from Pennsylvania. There were also a few Roman Catholic Irish and Scots in both colonies. Then there were the Scotch-Irish, who came with the Germans and who entered the same areas, especially in Virginia. So much felt was the presence of this sturdy, intelligent, courageous, and contentious people that Charles Lee, that English officer who purchased a plantation in the Shenandoah at the beginning of the War of Independence and soon afterward became an American general, said that Virginia was neither an aristocracy nor a democracy but a "macocracy." The Scotch-Irish, chiefly descended from lowland Scots, with minor English and Irish admixtures, added materially, of course, to the British element among the Virginians. Hence it was that the Old Dominion remained very largely British in stock, and especially English. Virginia, except for her Negroes, was almost as overwhelmingly English in background as contemporary New England.

North Carolina was less English than the older colonies on the Chesapeake, but equally British. The first settlers between the Pee Dee and the Dan were English, and those who followed them were frequently emigrants from English towns and fields. Again there were many Germans, who had entered the colony both by way of its low-lying shores and from the north; and again the presence of numerous Scotch-Irish moving toward a warmer sun was a remarkable phenomenon. In North Carolina, however, there was a much larger Scottish element than in Virginia, for hundreds of Highlanders sought new homes in that colony after the collapse of the ill-fated rising of 1745.

The white people of South Carolina and Georgia as of 1763 were also of mixed origins, but dominantly English. The first comers to Charleston and its vicinity were English out of the West Indian islands, especially Barbados, and from the mother country directly. Those who followed were often English, from Old and New England and the West Indies. Scottish Highlanders settled in the region of Charleston as early as 1686, and French Protestants even before. Afterward came Swiss and Germans, a few Jews, and just at the beginning of the French and Indian War the ubiquitous Scotch-Irish. The French Huguenots had been very quickly assimilated, and South Carolina was conspicuously English in culture. Georgia, still a frontier colony, was not the seat of an advanced civilization. Its Scotch-Irish had not yet arrived in numbers, and it contained no considerable contingent of French Protestants. It was in essence a younger South Carolina.

The Southern whites grew rapidly in numbers during the era of the American Revolution, partly as the result of natural increase—families were so large that we should say, instead, unnatural increase—partly because of continuing immigration from

7

Europe, and also from other colonies to the northward. By 1775 they were hardly fewer than 750,000; by 1790 they numbered more than 1,200,000 persons.[1]

In this astonishing increase Maryland did not share equally with the other Southern colony-states. Partly this fact is to be explained by her relatively small area. Partly it proceeded from emigration by Marylanders to the lands of the other colony-states beyond the Alleghenies—hence to a degree arose Maryland's famous fight to place western limits upon all the seaboard states in the middle years of the War of Independence. There were about 115,000 whites in Maryland in 1763, something like 170,000 in 1775, and 217,000 in 1790.

The Virginians, expanding rapidly to the westward and occupying Kentucky, multiplied amazingly. Immigration from Europe continued, with interruption because of the War of Independence; there were large accretions of Scotch-Irish and Germans —and English—for the tide of settlers from Pennsylvania remained high until 1775; moreover, many Carolinians in their search for new lands moved northward and westward within the boundaries of Virginia.[2] In the year of Lexington and Concord there were 300,000 white Virginians; at the close of the Revolutionary period, in the first Federal census, there were over 500,000. Granted that there was heavy immigration, it is apparent that Virginia was the home of many mothers who nurtured nonpresidents. Indeed, travelers in the 1760's noted that the "buckskins," the plain folk, were astonishingly fecund, that they kept pace with the Yankees, even though the latter had a supposed advantage in the practice of bundling, that even the Virginia belles were "great breeders." Were one to judge by the scanty figures available, the Revolutionary soldiers of Virginia had offspring as fre-

[1] For data concerning Southern population, see *Heads of Families at the First Census of . . . 1790* (Washington, 1907–1908); Franklin B. Dexter, "Estimates of Population in the American Colonies," in *Proceedings of the American Antiquarian Society* (Worcester), new ser., V (1904), 39–49; Evarts B. Greene and Virginia D. Harrington, *American Population before the Federal Census of 1790* (New York, 1932), 123–86; Stella H. Sutherland, *Population Distribution in Colonial America* (New York, 1936), 169–270.

[2] Little is known regarding this migration. It is not likely that Carolinians moving northwest equalled in numbers the Virginians going southwest.

quently as their forebears. It was doubtless well for Virginia, the South, and the nation, that those who fought also fathered.

The North Carolina white population also almost tripled during the Revolutionary era, and in general for similar reasons. North Carolina gave to Virginia's Kentucky but received Virginians in her Piedmont and her Tennessee. By 1775 there were about 175,000 North Carolinians, in 1789 there were almost 300,000— this despite the fact that the state was the scene of bitter internecine warfare in the War of Independence, especially in the years 1780 and 1781.

Strange as it may seem, the white population of South Carolina apparently quadrupled between the end of the French and Indian War and the first inauguration of Washington. The close of the Anglo-Cherokee war of 1760–1761 brought the restoration of peace upon her western frontier, and the Peace of Paris of 1763 removed the Spanish menace from Florida. Then the Scotch-Irish, following the Calhouns, who had arrived in the colony as early as 1756, came into the Piedmont of that province by hundreds and thousands, settling fertile lands in the valleys of the Congaree, the Wateree, the Broad, and the Saluda rivers. As in Virginia and North Carolina, the Scotch-Irish were accompanied by Germans. Moreover, immigration continued from Europe. So 500 or 600 Palatine Germans, crossing the ocean with assistance from British officials and generous citizens of London, occupied new homes in Abbeville District in 1764; and near them in the same year settled over 200 French Protestants, who had been led to freedom and a new life in America by Jean Louis Gibert, and who had been encouraged and helped by the governments of Great Britain and South Carolina. By 1775 there were in the colony about 70,000 whites; fifteen years later there were 140,000.

Georgia proportionately grew at least as rapidly as South Carolina. Again the Peace of 1763, quieting the western and southern frontiers of the British colonies, permitted, stimulated immigration and occupation. At the beginning of the War of Independence there were something like 25,000 whites in the small colony; and in spite of civil and Indian warfare as well as the assaults of British troops after 1775, there were over 80,000 in the first Federal census.

9

Highly important in the Southern population was an element for most of which the Revolution had immediately no great meaning, the Negroes. For every three whites as of 1763 there were two human beings partly or entirely of African descent. There were about 300,000 blacks in the South at the beginning of the Revolutionary era; and although the Negro population failed to keep pace with the white during that period, there were about 650,000 of them recorded in the first United States census. In 1790, then, there were some 35 blacks to every 65 whites below the southern boundary of Pennsylvania.

The Negroes were, of course, usually slaves. Free men of African background were not unknown, but they were as a group unimportant. The Negroes, appearing in Virginia as early as 1619, were not novel in the Southern scene. Unwilling immigrants to the New World, they had formed the cargoes of thousands of slave ships sailing from the western shores of Africa to the eastern ones of America. In Africa they were of many tribes, of disparate stocks, and from various societies. By 1763 a large part of the Negro population was American-born, but the slave ships, from Liverpool, from Newport, from Charleston, were still bringing in thousands of slaves from both Africa and the West Indies, although the trade was soon to diminish, to suffer interruptions, and to come to an end in 1808 when the Federal government of the United States made the importation of slaves a criminal offense punishable by death. Only fractionally of African birth, the Negroes were not entirely of African stock, for intermixture between them and their white masters and neighbors began early and never ceased.

Virginia supplied a home, of sorts at least, for more Negroes than any other colony-state, about 100,000 in 1763 and three times as many in 1790; North Carolina and Maryland had far fewer, each approximately 50,000 in 1763 and slightly more than 100,-000 in 1790. South Carolina contained 70,000 and 109,000 at the same times; Georgia had about 5,000 at the beginning of the Revolutionary epoch and 30,000 by the first Federal census. If the figures available are correct—and except for those of the enumeration of 1790 they can be no better than approximations —the Negroes failed to increase in proportion with the whites during the time in which the American Union was founded. The interruptions in the oceanic slave traffic which came as the result of the War of Independence and adverse legislation by many states probably explain the discrepancy. Although the British and their loyalist allies carried away thousands of slaves during that conflict, it is obvious that the growth of the white population was partly checked by military casualties and exigencies and also by the emigration of the Tories, both of choice and by force. It will hardly be contended that white men entered into liaisons with Negro women before 1763 and after 1789, but not during the years between. Nor can it be asserted with confidence that the occasional unions of Negro men and white women which occurred in the colonial time ceased completely at the approach of the Anglo-American war.

Miscegenation was, of course, inevitable because of the youthful ardors of white men and the presence in large numbers of Negro girls and women who frequently could not resist the solicitations of white males.[3] In 1732 one white man who had been unable to live up to the principle that posterity should begin at home, who had been conquered by the charms of a Negress, philosophically and poetically explained his situation in the *South Carolina Gazette* of Charleston:

> *All Men have Follies, which they blindly trace*
> *Thro' the dark Turnings of a dubious Maze:*
> *But happy those, who, by a prudent Care,*
> *Retreat betimes, from the fallacious Snare.*
> *The eldest Sons of Wisdom were not free,*
> *From the same Failure you condemn in me.*
> *If as the Wisest of the Wise have err'd,*
> *I go astray and am condemn'd unheard,*
> *My Faults you too severely reprehend,*

[3] About North Carolina planters at the beginning of the War of Independence, Janet Schaw, a loyalist lady, said, doubtless jestingly: "As the population of the country is all the view they have in what they call love, and tho' they often honour their black wenches with their attention, I sincerely believe they are excited to that crime by no other desire or motive but that of adding to the number of their slaves." Evangeline W. Andrews and Charles M. Andrews (eds.), *Journal of a Lady of Quality* . . . [Janet Schaw] *1774 to 1776* (New Haven, 1921), 154.

11

More like a rigid Censor than a Friend.
Love is the Monarch Passion of the Mind,
Knows no Superior, by no Laws confin'd:
But triumphs still, impatient of Controul,
O'er all the proud Endowments of the Soul.[4]

Hence the blue-eyed, red-haired mulatto and less conspicuous persons of mixed blood.

Now something should be said about the third race in the South, the red men, a people usually neither enslaved nor subservient. They too mingled their blood with that of the whites, and to some extent with that of the Negroes. Beyond the borders of the American settlements dwelt the descendants of the first Americans, the warriors and their women and children of the woods and savannahs east and especially west of the Appalachian divide. Once they had occupied the seacoast as well as the interior, and they had been numerous enough and sufficiently warlike severely to limit English occupation, though hardly to prohibit it. The Indians on the coast had been unable, however, to unite in the defense of their lands; they had suffered from inferiority in weapons and discipline; they had been decimated by exposure to the white man's diseases, especially smallpox; they had been hurt by his rum, to which they became inordinately devoted. Except for a few who were more or less domesticated among the English colonists, they had been destroyed or driven inland. In the end their history would be repeated to the westward. But not immediately. At the close of the Seven Years' War there were between the Ohio and the Gulf of Mexico several Indian nations free and even formidable. Principal among them were the Catawbas, Cherokee, Creeks, Choctaw, and Chickasaw.

Least powerful of the five were the Catawbas, who could put in the field no more than three hundred warriors, probably even fewer. Long the target of attacks by the Iroquois and other forest enemies, they had dwindled in numbers. They had, however, cohesion, for they dwelt in a small area in the valley of the Wateree River at the northern limit of South Carolina. They were brave and loyal friends of the Carolinians, had protected

[4] Hennig Cohen, *The South Carolina Gazette, 1732–1775* (Columbia, 1953), 193–94.

12

their frontiers, had been valuable allies to the colonials in the harassing Anglo-Cherokee war of 1760–1761. They were semi-domesticated, for British officials had acquired preponderant influence in the choice of their principal chief, or "king." [5] They were not to be despised.

More numerous and less firmly under British hegemony was the Cherokee nation, the villages of which clustered in and about the southern Appalachians, occupying the present-day western parts of the Carolinas, northern Georgia and Alabama, and eastern Tennessee. There were four principal divisions of this attractive people, the Lower, Middle, Valley, and Overhill tribes, so named because of their locations from east to west. They had a single major chief, chosen from one distinguished family, who was referred to by the English as "emperor." His authority was far less than that indicated by his European title. It was largely based upon hereditary and personal prestige: he might lead; he could hardly force. The Cherokee nation was a confederacy rather than an empire. A singularly attractive people to British eyes, especially in the view of lonely traders who looked upon their girls and women, the Cherokee were entering upon the road to the white man's civilization. Their tall, slender men were slowly losing their savage ardor. Thinking about wrongs inflicted upon them by colonial traders and settlers, and goaded on by French agents, they had turned against their English allies in 1760 and had been rather severely handled in the struggle which followed. They were now chastened, but their 2,500 "gun-men" could still be dangerous foes.

To the south and west of the Cherokee were the towns of the confederacy of the Muskogee, or Creeks, as they were usually called by the British, in what is now Alabama, Georgia, and northern Florida. Of disparate stocks, the Creeks were even less a unit than the Cherokee. There were three groups of villages, the Upper ones, in north central Alabama, the Lower ones, to the eastward, and the Seminole towns, on the Florida peninsula. The last were moving toward complete independence; the inhabitants

---

[5] John F. D. Smyth, meeting the "king" immediately before the War of Independence, remarked that "his English name was Joe." John F. D. Smyth, *A Tour in the United States of America* (Dublin, 1784), I, 118.

of the Upper and Lower settlements frequently did not act in unison. The Lower towns had had an "emperor," but his influence had waned and the title was passing into disuse; the Upper settlements tended to accept the leadership of one chief, but in such degree that he had not been royalized by the British. The Creeks had long been bitter enemies of the Spanish and had severely limited their sway in Florida. They had not, however, definitely committed themselves as a group to either side during the protracted struggle between the French and English for empire in North America. They had profited from a policy of neutrality, had not suffered serious military defeat, had retained their pristine vigor; their 3,500 warriors could be formidable. In the year 1763 they were unhappy and sullen because the French and Spanish had departed, or were about to go, from St. Augustine, Pensacola, and Mobile, indeed from the whole region east of the Mississippi. They would not in the near future be able to play the Europeans against each other, would be dependent upon the British for guns, ammunition, clothing, and liquor.

To the west of the Upper Creeks, between the Alabama River and the Mississippi, resided the Choctaw, the most numerous and the least united of the Southern Indian nations. There were perhaps three Choctaw warriors to every two Creeks. However, three divisions, the East Party, the West Party, and the Six Villages, existed among them. They had no "emperor" and no "king." Moreover, as clients of French officials at New Orleans they had suffered from lack of guns and ammunition. Ill-organized and inferiorly armed, they had lost military prestige. With suitable weapons and a measure of leadership they might have been a power in the Southern forests.

North of the Choctaw in the valley of the upper Tombigbee River were the few villages of the Chickasaw, a people scanty by count but great in spirit. They had been for more than six decades allies of the British and enemies of the French Bourbons. Governor after governor at New Orleans, with the help of the Choctaw and other Indians, had striven to crush them, and had failed. So hard pressed had they been that some of them had fled among the Creeks and others to new homes on the Savannah River, but the majority had continued the struggle for existence and had ultimately triumphed. No more than half a thousand warriors could be collected from their compact towns, but the vigorous and brave Chickasaw were redoubtable and respected. For the "breeds," as they were known because of the various strains in the little nation, the immediate future was brighter because of the approaching departure of the French from New Orleans and the valley of the Mississippi. Yet the vanishing of the fleur-de-lis from the valley would surely lessen the flow of goods, arms, and friendship which had come to them from the British, since their military services, recently of the greatest value to their allies, would not be so sorely needed.

The year 1763 was a sharp turning point for all the Southern Indians. With the removal of the French from the eastern part of the Mississippi Valley, with their replacement at New Orleans and in the western half of the watershed by the weak Spanish (the transfer of authority being consummated in 1769), they all became almost entirely dependent upon British traders and officials for the guns, powder, lead, tomahawks, knives, clothing, and rum without which they could now hardly live. And they all, even the Chickasaw so distant from the Atlantic, were soon to see white settlements advance upon their towns, were all, though in differing degree, to suffer from the limitless yearnings of speculators and farmers for their lands. Some of them, especially the Cherokee and Creeks, would plot against and even attack King George's people. Rent by their own ancient feuds, Chickasaw versus Choctaw, Choctaw versus Creek, and Creek versus Cherokee; set against each other by shrewd whites; lacking unity even within their nations; ultimately requiring of the white man what they needed in order to survive—they could not in the last analysis effectively protect either their hunting grounds or their villages.

For the whites, the Southerners, the year 1763 brought easing of foreign and Indian menaces and a hopeful prospect. They were not dependent upon others who might withhold from them at will the necessaries of their way of life.

No land of cities, the South two years before Patrick Henry informed the Virginia House of Burgesses and George III that he preferred liberty to life was a country in which traffickers were few and tillers many. If it be true that trade and industry debase,

15

that "honour sinks where commerce long prevails," as Oliver Goldsmith, Thomas Jefferson, and many another man unaccustomed to counter or scythe have argued, the South was then largely free from their corrupting influence. Typically the Southerner was a planter or farmer; and the exceptional one who engaged in the businesses of processing and exchanging goods was commonly also an owner of soil and a husbandman, or employer of husbandmen.

The South then was not a land of cotton. Indeed, but little of it was grown, and the gins of Eli Whitney and other inventors were yet to be made. But if there was no Cotton Kingdom, there was a Tobacco Empire, also a Realm of Rice-Indigo, a Principality of Tar and Turpentine, and, off in the hinterland, even a small Cattle Country.

To be sure, the Southern economy of that time or of any other time since the founding of Jamestown cannot be described in terms of a few crops or products. The cultivated produce of the Southern soil was in fact highly varied. Everywhere were fields of maize, bringing directly little cash, but furnishing food for animals and men, and being ultimately in its own ways as important to the Southern people as rice, or even tobacco. Wheat was raised in all the colonies. Though of small importance in the deep South, in Maryland and Virginia it was a major crop. Indeed, as the War of Independence approached, planters and small farmers around Chesapeake Bay and to the westward were increasingly turning from the "smoke-weed" to wheat, which was consumed locally and also sold away as flour. Potatoes, Irish and sweet, unlike wheat, were eaten where they were grown. Like corn, they supplied a basic food. Other vegetables, especially peas and beans, were standard in the Southern diet. Rye and barley supplied the basic ingredient for whisky. Hemp, flax, and cotton were minor products. In the far South there had been and were dreams of grape, olive, and silk production; these dreams resulted in little silk, few olives, and not much wine.

Nor should it be forgotten that the raising of stock was universal. The horse was almost indispensable for tilling and for transportation on land, and few free families were without one. The lighter, swifter breeds, often developed from fine imported

HENRY LAURENS by Charles Willson Peale. Courtesy of City of Philadelphia, Department of Public Works

animals, were nurtured for racing, an extremely popular sport in the South, indulged in wherever there were fast horses and room for running. Herds of sheep were common, supplying the wool in linsey-woolsey clothing. Hogs were everywhere, munching upon corn or, more frequently, upon mast in the woods. If as the result of poor breeding and feeding they were scrawny rather than fat, still they furnished ham and bacon, and pork which could be salted and preserved over long periods. Cows, less numerous, served as a source of butter, milk, and especially meat. They were probably more frequently found in the long settled areas, but there were some remarkable establishments on the frontiers of the Carolinas which were the equivalents of the later ranches of the trans-Mississippi West. In the meadows and canebrakes of the Piedmont, after the disappearance of the Indian and the wild animals, before occupation by planters and farmers, grazed thousands of cattle. Fences rather soon destroyed such "ranges" and forced both cows and owners westward. They remained on the Piedmont long enough for the development of cowpens, though not of cowtowns. And, though no romantic Chisholm Trail appeared, there were long drives of lean cattle from the back country to Charleston, Petersburg in Virginia, Baltimore, and even faraway Philadelphia.

Fishing and hunting also had economic importance, and both were sports then as later. Fish were abundant both in coastal waters and in the lower reaches of the numerous rivers, and hardly less abundant above the fall line. Shad, herring, mullet, white perch, and trout crowded the rivers near Tidewater in their mysterious migrations; and they were so plentiful that herring were exported to the West Indies as well as imported with cod and salmon from northern waters. In the streams of the interior there were turbot as well as trout, these and other fish to be had almost by sinking a line. In the woods and savannahs adjacent there were herds of deer, which slowly vanished as settlements moved inland. Their flesh supplied venison, and their skins clothing as well as cash. Bears and many other animals had their uses; and everywhere there were wildfowl furnishing succulent food.

There was little mining, except for iron in Maryland, and iron and lead in Virginia. The coal beds and the iron deposits upon which Birmingham was built lay unknown in the western wilderness beneath the feet of Creek warriors and women; and the precious metals of the Appalachians had not yet been discovered.

Far above all other crops in market importance in the upper South, and a determining force in society and politics in addition, was tobacco. Once it had been used only for ceremonial purposes by the Indians. Becoming known to the white man, it was smoked and chewed increasingly in the American colonies, in the British Isles, in Europe, eventually almost everywhere on the globe. At length even the Eskimo would bring fox skins to Hudson Bay posts in the heart of the Arctic in order to enjoy its narcotic effects. The tobacco plant is easily grown. Assured of a market for tobacco and receiving at times excellent prices for it, Virginians and Marylanders had increasingly devoted themselves to producing it, often to their ultimate sorrow.

Tobacco culture was not confined to Maryland and Virginia. The very first settlers in North Carolina, moving southward from Virginia into the Albemarle region in the northeastern part of that colony, grew the plant, doubtless at first for local consumption. The later and far more numerous settlers from the northward at the middle of the eighteenth century likewise inevitably planted tobacco on the Piedmont of both Carolinas for their own use. The soils and climate of Albemarle and of the Piedmont were perfectly suited to its cultivation, and North Carolinians exported it in ever larger amounts. Their colony produced perhaps 2,000,-000 pounds of it in 1763, about twice as much ten years later, and was exporting 6,000,000 pounds annually soon after the War of Independence.[6] These figures are, of course, small when set beside contemporary ones for Maryland and Virginia. The great growth of the tobacco industry in North Carolina was off in the future. It never did become major in South Carolina. The cotton gin appeared just as the inhabitants of the Piedmont of that state were turning toward tobacco. Cotton-raising was accordingly more profitable, and they chose to supply materials for external rather than internal coatings.

Tobacco-growing was almost as seductive as tobacco-smoking.

[6] Charles C. Crittenden, *The Commerce of North Carolina, 1763–1789* (New Haven, 1936), 74, 161.

The profits in fortunate periods were large; and its planters tended to remember the fat years, to forget, or at least ignore, the more numerous lean ones. Moreover, the light and simple labors required to grow the plant and process its leaves could be easily performed by Negro slaves. There were many operations in tobacco production, but only one requiring remarkable mechanical or physical dexterity. Placing the tiny seeds in seedbeds of fresh soil, transplanting at the end of spring, additional transplantings after heavy rains, and cultivating by the hoe were routine tasks. Cutting off the top of the plant in order to encourage the growth of the leaves was a more delicate matter, one to be entrusted only to skillful hands. There followed various plain duties. The removal of the "suckers," which appeared after the severing of the top, and likewise of worms and their eggs from the nether side of the leaves, was a light summer duty. In late summer or fall, when the leaves began to yellow, the plant was cut at its base and allowed to dry in the field. Still later the leaves were placed upon lath and further dried in barns or out-of-doors, by artificial heat or by wind and sun. In the early spring the stems were stripped away, the leaves bundled tightly on moist days, to assure proper curing. At length they were packed tightly into hogsheads, so tightly that a hogshead usually contained a thousand pounds of tobacco, light, dark, or "lugs" (bottom leaves of inferior quality). Then the hogsheads were rolled or pulled by horses to a ship landing or possibly to the store of a country trader. All of these operations could be carried out by slaves under supervision. Besides, Negro women and children were able to offer assistance at various stages. A Negro slave could tend three or four acres of tobacco. Tobacco-growing had still another advantage: the field hand when not occupied by it was able to work in the wheat fields and corn rows, since the duties connected with these and with tobacco dovetailed rather nicely.

Small wonder that Virginia and Maryland exported vast quantities of tobacco, over 100,000,000 pounds annually immediately before the struggle for independence. The value of their crop, sent to London, Glasgow, and other ports, mounted to an annual figure near £700,000. Even so, tobacco planters had good cause for uneasiness, for they were commonly heavily in debt.

The cultivation of rice and indigo played much the same role in the economy of South Carolina and Georgia as did tobacco in Maryland and Virginia. Immediately before the War of Independence there were heavy demands for rice in Europe and the British West Indies, and planters of the far South strove, profitably, to meet those demands. Rice cultivation had begun in the South Carolina Low Country before 1700, and became ever more important as seed, methods of production, and markets improved. Until 1758 rice-growing was somewhat limited in scope because the planters had no better way to secure the large supplies of fresh water required than to dam streams immediately above the requisite rich and level lands, releasing the water as needed. In 1758, however, McKewn Johnstone developed a method of flooding that made possible the cultivation of rice on the large, flat flood plains of the rivers and streams adjacent to the sea. By a relatively simple system of levees, drains, and gates he was able to use the force of high tides to push fresh water upon such lands, and also to expel water when the tides were low. His system was promptly copied by other planters, and exportations of rice from South Carolina almost doubled by the year of Lexington and Concord.[7]

The physical toil involved in growing rice was neither little nor healthy. Much of the labor of planting, which took place from March to May, and of hoeing and harvesting, which were required in late August or September, had to be done in stagnant water or mud, and the worker in the rice field was accordingly exposed to disease. It was believed, conveniently, by whites who owned such fields that such toil was dangerous for whites but not for Negroes. Negroes were capable, under direction, of performing the various tasks required. Hence the rice plantation of South Carolina and Georgia became for the Negro a harsher equivalent of the tobacco plantation of Virginia and Maryland.

If a rice field survived flood from above, excessively high tide from below, the attacks of bobolinks, who were accustomed to spend September in gorging themselves upon rice as preparation for wintering farther to the south, and various other assaults, the

---

[7] Leila Sellers, *Charleston Business on the Eve of the American Revolution* (Chapel Hill, 1934), 156–57.

crop was harvested, dried, threshed by flails or the treading of animals, and husked. In these processes much of the rice was broken. By sieves the "small rice" was separated for the use of the Negroes and animals, or for sale in the British West Indies; the "middlings," or less damaged kernels, were reserved for the owners and other local whites; the rice, or undamaged kernels, was prepared for sale in Europe or the northern colonies. Put into barrels and sent by oxcart or boat to Charleston, Savannah, or another port, rice was shipped especially, by way of Great Britain, to Holland and Germany, where more than 60 per cent of South Carolina's production was consumed. It was also sent to Portugal, Spain, and Italy, and to New York, Pennsylvania, and Rhode Island. Thousands of barrels of "small rice" were sold in the British West Indies. At mid-century the average annual exportation of all grades of rice from South Carolina was above 60,000 barrels, twenty years later about 125,000 barrels. Since its price ranged from twenty-five to ninety shillings per barrel, the average being forty-five,[8] it is apparent that gross returns from the grain exported from South Carolina just before the War of Independence usually ran far above £100,000 per annum, and sometimes easily surpassed £200,000.

In the eighteenth and nineteenth centuries indigo, a plant which resembles asparagus in appearance, was the source of a rich purple dye much desired in Europe until it was superseded by artificial products. It could be efficiently grown both on the seacoast and in the interior of South Carolina and Georgia. A gang of plantation workers could raise simultaneously both rice and indigo, for the tasks connected with the growth of the two plants could be, and often were, alternated. Most of the indigo was grown on islands off the coast, although small planters well inland sometimes made good profits raising it.

Indigo cultivation in the Carolinas and Georgia was novel in the 1740's and almost unknown there after 1800. Until the famed Eliza Lucas came to South Carolina from Antigua, indigo production was largely confined to the West Indian colonies of France and Spain. The extraordinary Miss Lucas proved that the plant could be grown in South Carolina, and she distributed seed and

[8] *Ibid.*, 156–57.

helpful advice. In 1748 a Parliament which did not choose that the British people spend £150,000 per annum for foreign indigo began to pay a bounty of sixpence the pound for blocks of the dyestuff imported from Britain's American colonies. The result was an indigo boom in South Carolina and Georgia. The indigo produced in those colonies was inferior to the French and Spanish types, but governmental assistance assured a large, steady, and profitable market for it in the home islands, where the making and dyeing of cloth were major matters.

Ideally, indigo was grown on light, rich soils. Two and even three crops could be cut each year (six or more in the West Indies). If the crop survived grasshoppers and worms, the leaves of the plant were soaked in water, which absorbed the dye. This product was dried, pressed into small blocks, and put into casks for shipment. The labor involved was arduous and unhealthy, because of stagnant water used in the processing, hence better suited to Negro slaves than to free whites. Indigo, like tobacco, exhausted the soil, a fact which was of no great interest at the time. It was of the greatest moment, however, that during the years 1758–1775 the average exportation of indigo from that area was about 500,000 pounds, that there were a few years in which the figure reached 1,000,000, that Southern indigo at the end of that period brought in more than £200,000 annually in British markets, being second in cash value for the Carolinians and Georgians only to rice.[9]

It is obvious that there were indeed in the South a Tobacco Empire and a Realm of Rice-Indigo in the quarter century before the War of Independence. Was there then also a Principality of Tar-Pitch-Turpentine, in North Carolina? Certainly, the production of these "naval stores" did not dominate the economy of North Carolina as tobacco did on the Chesapeake, or rice and indigo in the deep South. The pine forests of the coastal plain of North Carolina supplied about one quarter of the exports of that colony and brought in something like £40,000 annually. The production of tar, pitch, and turpentine was therefore of great importance but was merely principal in an economy better bal-

[9] *Ibid.*, 166–68. For indigo culture, see Lewis C. Gray, *History of Agriculture in the Southern United States to 1860* (Washington, 1933), I, 290–97.

anced than those above the Dan River and to the westward of Cape Fear.[10]

The processing of naval stores in North Carolina was similar to the production of indigo in South Carolina in four major respects. Negroes performed most of the manual labor, under direction; the product was inferior; the market was the British Isles; only bounties given by a Parliament desiring an assured supply of stores for the British navy and merchant marine made good profit possible. Both the indigo planter and the entrepreneur of the pine forests to his eastward were recipients of British cash, were indeed rather dependent upon that cash if they had not other occupations or resources independent of indigo fields and coniferous timber.

In a Southern economy conspicuously producing raw and processed materials for export, manufacturing and internal trade were inevitably secondary. Indeed, there was little manufacturing beyond processing, and that which existed was devoted to supplying local needs. The making of linsey-woolsey clothing, rifles, kitchenware, tools, and many other items was directed toward use by the family or neighbors. There were, of course, flour mills upon the streams, blacksmith shops, and sawmills.[11] Numerous country stores were to be found in the villages, doing business both in barter and in cash. In the towns there were equivalent and more elaborate establishments, something crudely like modern department stores, printing shops, bookstores, haberdasheries, and the places of business of artisans. Taverns, ordinaries, and grogshops were plentiful everywhere, although good and clean commercial lodgings for the wayfarer were uncommon. Means of internal communication were inevitably confined by defective roads and ferries, but the many navigable streams offered easy avenues of transportation by boat, compensating to a degree for the difficulties of travel and trade by land routes.

External commerce, however, was relatively immense, and the

[10] Crittenden, *Commerce of North Carolina*, 53–58, 73, offers a very useful summary concerning the production and value of naval stores.

[11] In 1768 Lieutenant Governor William Bull of South Carolina reported that his colony contained only five "manufactories," three ropewalks and two houses "for baking and refining sugar." Bull to Board of Trade, September 6, 1786, Sainsbury Transcripts (South Carolina State Archives, Columbia).

men engaged in it were not inconspicuous, especially in Charleston. The Thirteen Colonies as a whole after the Seven Years' War annually sent products worth about £1,500,000 to Great Britain, which received the bulk of their exports. Well above two thirds of these products originated in the South, more than a third being loaded from wharves of Maryland and Virginia, almost a third from those of South Carolina. Tobacco, rice, indigo, naval stores, deerskins, provisions, and lumber were the principal exports. Imports of cloth, ironware, furniture, Negro slaves, wines, coaches, tea, and a host of other and diverse items were also on a large scale. The value of imports delivered in all the Thirteen Colonies was in 1768 something more than £2,000,000, of which about £1,000,-000 worth were absorbed in the South. Immediately before the War of Independence, Virginia and Maryland alone took in about £1,000,000 worth of goods and persons, and South Carolina half as much as Virginia and Maryland.

The merchant, he who engaged in commerce beyond the local, was less important in the Southern economy than in that of New England or Pennsylvania. Indeed, in Virginia there were few commercial magnates such as were commonly found in Boston or Philadelphia, for the planters of the Chesapeake often sold to and bought directly from merchants in the British Isles, many of whom maintained agents in Virginia. There were such men scattered in the ports of the Southern coast, but only in Charleston, which commanded the business of South Carolina, of adjacent parts of North Carolina and Georgia, and even of the Floridas, was there a group of middlemen whose operations were on a large and lucrative scale. There Gabriel Manigault and Henry Laurens were the counterparts of Boston's John Hancock. Engaged in local retail trade as well as oceanic commerce and also in land speculations and the operation of plantations, Manigault and Laurens were among the richest men in America.

Even in South Carolina the merchants and the traders were far less important in terms of wealth, and of course in influence, than the planters. Charleston, nevertheless, was not only the city of the South, but the fourth largest in the Thirteen Colonies. In small part the city grew because it was the provincial capital, also because prominent planters maintained residences in it. Commerce, however, was the great basis for its prosperity. Before 1775 as many as 400 ocean-going ships, averaging between 200 and 300 tons, annually used the ports of South Carolina, principally Charleston. At times Charleston harbor was thronged with such ships and with smaller vessels engaged in coastal and river traffic. The wharves and streets of the city throbbed with economic activity, and its population easily surpassed 10,000 persons, over half of whom were Negro slaves, before the day of Lexington and Concord. "This town," said Josiah Quincy, Jr., who visited Charleston not long before the shooting began, "makes a most beautiful appearance as you come up to it, and in many respects a magnificent one. I can only say in general, that in grandeur, splendour of buildings, decorations, equipages, numbers, shippings, and indeed in almost everything, it far surpasses all I ever saw, or ever expected to see, in America." [12]

No Southern city could claim to rival Charleston in the era of independence. Indeed, there was no other Southern port city in British America. Baltimore, Norfolk, Savannah, and Mobile existed, but the first three were no more than thriving towns, the last only a garrisoned outpost. Baltimore had begun to develop a great trade in wheat, and it was to prosper during the War of Independence. Norfolk, to a lesser degree, found sources of growth in the exportation of both wheat and tobacco. Savannah was more than a satellite of Charleston, but not much more. Wilmington was a small town, Pensacola, like Mobile, a military base.

Nor were there inland cities. The sites of Atlanta and Birmingham lay in the Indian country. There were, to be sure, many towns and villages in the interior not without significance. Frederick Town, Maryland, was attractive and prosperous, and had 2,000 people. Winchester in Virginia, though not so neat, was almost equally impressive. Salisbury in mid–North Carolina and Camden [13] in upper South Carolina were important communities, and Augusta was the depot of a flourishing trade in deerskins. The Piedmont had its local prides in population. But Charleston was the political, economic, social, and strategic center of the deep South.

[12] Josiah Quincy, *Memoir of the Life of Josiah Quincy, Jun.* (Boston, 1825), 95.
[13] Called Pine Tree Hill before 1768.

CHAPTER III

THE SOCIAL SCENE

A FAMILIAR and well-loved epigram has it that North Carolina was once "a valley of humility between two mountains of conceit." There can be no doubt that the North Carolinians generally, "lubbers," as William Byrd II called them, along with frontier folk and lowly whites everywhere, not to mention Negroes, were looked down upon by tobacco lords and rice-indigo magnates at the time of the Revolution. It is equally certain that the superiority of those same lords and magnates and their families, on the basis of wealth, education, manners, character, ability, and heredity, in varying proportions and emphases, was commonly conceded and frequently envied. Located near the shores of the Chesapeake, there was a true upper class, a group which was not quite the equivalent of a European aristocracy; in Charleston and the Low Country about it there was another upper class, newer, more tainted with trade, but possessing a larger portion of manners and charm, enjoying momentarily a sounder financial position, asserting equal claims with its Chesapeake counterpart to dignity and hegemony. Elsewhere in the South there was less pride, less culture, and less leadership.

At the time of the Revolution the great planters of Virginia and Maryland, located usually on Tidewater, but also occasionally on the Piedmont and to the west as far as the Shenandoah, formed a true American aristocracy, though hardly a genuine one according to European standards.[1] In Virginia and Maryland no

[1] Hence William Vans Murray of Maryland, no social leveler, could say in 1787, "there neither is in the United States an aristocracy, nor does there exist that ground for its ascendency, which hath usually been its foundation in other countries." William Vans Murray, *Political Sketches, Inscribed to His Excellency John Adams* (London, 1787), 61.

resident save Thomas, Lord Fairfax, born in England, was officially a lord—and at least some members of an authentic European aristocracy should bear lofty titles; there was no great planter
who was opulently rich—and persons of vast wealth were numerous among the aristocrats of contemporary Europe; relatively
few of the upper-class Virginians and Marylanders could prove
respected and gentlemanly ancestry through several generations
—and many European aristocrats could. The Carters, Randolphs,
Carrolls, and their kind had loftier social and economic stature
than English squires, lower standing than English families such as
the Wentworths, Stanleys, and Cecils.

Whether or not the European forebears of the First Families of
Virginia and Maryland were frequently of gentle birth is a question much canvassed. It would appear that the Chesapeake aristocracy arose principally from the English middle class, with
some ancestors of higher estate and as many, doubtless, of inferior
status. It is perhaps as idle to extol the antiquity of their superiority as it is to speculate about the origins of their means and the
meanness of their origins. Certainly membership in the select
portion of Chesapeake society was based upon property rather
than heredity. To be sure, substance and family superiority are
intimate associates rather than inveterate enemies. The possession
of wealth, however, was a sure key to the door of the élite in
Virginia and Maryland, as it was and is always and everywhere,
sooner or later. The man or woman of ample means was not long
excluded from the best circles, nor even from the occasional tri-
angular relationships among them.

Indeed, the Chesapeake aristocracy was then decidedly fluid,
accretions being frequent and welcomed. Although its members
highly prized and eagerly sought wealth in land, they did not
despise the proceeds of trade or mining, and engaged in the one
and the other. Nor did they look down upon persons who acquired
property, in whatever decent fashion, but accepted them, when
not obnoxious in terms of character or personality, as equals or
near equals. George Washington, who was born into a substantial
middle-class family rather than a great one, in his mature years
occupied an unassailable niche in that aristocracy; Horatio Gates,
the son of an English upper servant, but a military officer and late

in life the possessor of wealth, was *persona grata* in stately mansions; other men and women less known to history but of means, education, and repute in varying quantities similarly ascended the social ladder. Fluidity appears, alas, in another fashion, for the members of a Virginia family which had lost its money did "not now meet with so great respect, as . . . they formerly did." [2]

It may be said that the aristocrats of the Chesapeake were chiefly of middle-class antecedents and that they displayed some "bourgeois" qualities, but not that they were town dwellers. They did not reside in Norfolk, Alexandria, Dumfries, or Frederick Town, but upon their estates, in comfortable and often elegant mansions, of which several are happily preserved. Stratford, home of the Lees in Westmoreland County, Virginia, Sabine Hall, built by Landon Carter in Richmond County, the Nomini Hall of Robert Carter, the Gunston Hall of George Mason, the Mount Vernon of Washington were rural residences, their owners the masters of one, two, or several plantations. Handsome and imposing without, such mansions were often luxurious and beautiful within. Studding the landscape, sometimes at large intervals, they were the seats of elegance, culture, and power on both banks of the Potomac.

The patrician order of Virginia and Maryland, comprising no more than a few hundreds of families much interrelated by descent and marriage, had reached full flower at the day of the Revolution. Its men, often tall, slender, strong, graceful, and handsome, were splendid physically, fine specimens of the most imposing type of American manhood; its women were commonly extremely attractive in youth, although perhaps merely amiable and charming after their middle twenties, after bearing several children. Finely clad, poised, easy, polite, hospitable,[3] these gentlemen and their ladies formed an elegant country society. Against a background of retinues of Negro slaves they feasted, drank their Madeira, watched cockfights and horse races, played whist and

---

[2] Bridenbaugh, *Myths and Realities*, 16.

[3] Hospitality was almost a necessity. Said Landon Carter: "In virgia a man dyes a month sooner in a fit of any disorders because he cant have one soul to talk to." Landon Carter Diary, November 23, 1763 (University of Virginia Library, Charlottesville).

billiards, performed minuets, country dances, and jigs, conversed about the worlds of tobacco and politics, visited each other frequently and at length.[4]

It was not an idle and consequently vicious aristocracy, although the traveler Johann David Schoepf wrote in 1784 that the Virginia gentleman passed "the greatest part of the summer on soft pallets, attended by one or several negroes to ward off the flies, light pipes, and proffer punch, sangry, toddy, or julap." [5] Such sybaritic and parasitic persons were by no means unknown, but the typical great planter was a man occupied with private affairs of crops, slaves, lands, and business,[6] and with public problems as well. He had much leisure only when he neglected the duties which he owed to his family, his slaves, and his neighbors, who looked to him for leadership. The multifarious activities of a plantation required constant supervision; the Anglican Church, to which in Virginia he almost invariably belonged, demanded some attention and more support; the courts, local and otherwise, called him to service; the militia of his neighborhood took up arms at his order; the House of Burgesses and the councils of the governors beckoned him to labor. His wife, without public responsibilities, was burdened with the concerns of her children and household.

Nor did the patrician order of Virginia and Maryland devote itself entirely to money-making, politics, warfare, and nonintellectual pleasures, for the educational level in it was comparatively high and reading was a common pastime.[7] Its younger males and females were taught by older members of the family and also,

[4] The roads, safer than those of England, had their dangers. The Annapolis *Maryland Gazette,* December 20, 1764, reported that "Saturday evening last, a little after dark, as Mr. Hewitt of this town, was coming home from Prince-George's County, alone, at a little distance on this side South River, there suddenly rush'd out from the thicket of pines, two men, one from each side of the road, in order to seize him, crying out, Stop you son of a bitch, and one of them aim'd at his bridle, but miss'd his catch, which much frighten'd his horse, who sprung from them, and by pushing along the road, he got safe home."

[5] Johann David Schoepf, *Travels in the Confederation [1783–1784],* tr. and ed. by Alfred J. Morrison (Philadelphia, 1911), II, 94.

[6] The Landon Carter Diary displays the labors and worries of a planter.

[7] Louis B. Wright, *The First Gentlemen of Virginia; Intellectual Qualities of the Early Colonial Ruling Class* (San Marino, 1940), is a standard and instructive work.

especially the former, by tutors, use being made of the talents of local clergymen and of those of men specially imported for the purpose, such as Philip Fithian of Princeton, who was for some time a teacher at the Carters' Nomini Hall. Formal instruction for the girls ceased early, except for music and the fine arts; for the majority of the boys also, learning under the direction of more or less professional teachers soon ended, an elementary education with the rudiments of the classics and an introduction to literature being then usually thought sufficient even for the leaders of the two colonies. Some boys, like Thomas Jefferson, were offered opportunities toward a more generous learning at the College of William and Mary. Others, like the sons of Colonel Thomas Lee, Arthur and Richard Henry, were sent to Britain for public school, collegiate, and professional instruction. The scions of the house of Carroll of Carrollton, because of the Roman Catholicism of their race, sought intellectual advance in France. The Chesapeake society was adorned by the presence of men with a sound classical education, albeit slender knowledge of modern language other than their own, and less of the realm of science. There was no professor of science at William and Mary until 1773, when James Madison, kinsman of President Madison, began his lectures there.

The great planter of the Chesapeake was not usually the graduate of a college or of an English public school. William Byrd II, with his lifelong devotion to the classics and his literary abilities, the liberally learned Jefferson, and the James Madison who was both scholar and statesman were exceptional rather than representative. To be sure, Jefferson and Madison would have been remarkable in any American society, and inconspicuous in no European one. Nor was the great planter ordinarily merely a person of limited education whose chief interests were the bottle, the fox, the thoroughbred horse, the mulatto mistress, and the dueling pistol.[8] The typical patrician in terms of education is rather to be found in men like Edmund Pendleton, John Marshall,

[8] It may be significant that none of the men mentioned in this paragraph engaged in a duel. Of a different temper was John Churchill, who was attacked in a newspaper and threatened with legal action. Responded Churchill in an advertisement in the Williamsburg *Virginia Gazette* (Dixon and Hunter), July 10, 1778: "I shall only say that as long as I can wield a sword, or pull a trigger, the law shall be my last recourse."

and George Washington, who had little formal instruction, who acquired information by desultory reading, by the study of law, through their association with others in courtrooms, polite assemblies, and politics. The value of an education obtained by such means should not, of course, be despised. The reading of works upon statecraft, history, religion, the classics, and current poetry and fiction—and there was much of such reading in the mansions of the select—together with the inspiriting and refining influences of social and public intercourse produced well-informed and polished gentlemen, though not necessarily devoted scholars, and hardly pedants. The Chesapeake patrician, not unfamiliar with the world of books, was above all the man of the country, court, council, and camp.[9]

Decay frequently accompanies flowering, almost inevitably follows it. The great planters in the era of the Revolution were living on borrowed money, if not time. They were commonly in debt and approaching insolvency. They had been in debt for generations, chiefly because of reckless financial practices. When the proceeds of the tobacco they sold exceeded their obligations, they spent the surplus; when their revenues from tobacco were less than

[9] The genuine Virginia patricians were not like the planters whose conversation at Smithfield one evening in 1784 was reported by the amused and cynical Dr. Schoepf: "It was insisted that the noble Virginians are the 'most polished nation' on God's earth, the gentlemen of France perhaps alone excepted. . . . From the undeniable argument, that in fertility, size, navigable streams, &c. Virginia is superior to the other American states, a number of propositions followed to substantiate the claim that in every respect Virginia is in advance of all other states, all other parts of the world. Who in America would dare count himself the equal of the noble Virginian? The poor New Englander who gains his bread in the sweat of his brow? or the Pensylvanian, who drudges like a negro and takes butter and cheese to market? or the North Carolina pitch-boiler? or the South Carolinian with his everlasting rice? Above all these stands the Gentleman of Virginia, for he alone has the finest horses, the finest dogs, the most negroes, the most land, speaks the best English, makes the most elegant bow, has the easy grace of a man of the world, and is a baron on his estates, which yield him everything and could yield still more! What country, what nation in Europe can boast of such advantages as those of Virginia?—Spain, perhaps, superstitious and slavish? or tyrannical Great Britain? or groaning Italy, under yoke and ban? or the soul-selling Germany? The remaining barbaric northern nations, with their frigid lands, (as little known as these) were all passed in review and reckoned out of the account." Schoepf noted dryly "that the proud Indians, belittling all other nations, compared the whites, with no exception of the noble Virginians, to white dogs' dung." Schoepf, *Travels in the Confederation,* tr. and ed. by Morrison, II, 91-92, 93.

those obligations, English and Scottish merchants who supplied them with manufactures advanced the difference, at interest. Debts so contracted tended to endure and to increase, for credit was easy, and the great planter was apt to establish his standard of living in accordance with his income of years of large crops and high prices for them. There were years when the costs of production, freight, insurance, and handling were beyond the value of the tobacco crop. At the beginning of the Revolutionary crisis the great planter was in distress, hardly a coincidence. The years 1760–1765 were bad ones for tobacco. The year 1765, it is well known, was also one of crisis for the British empire. The wiser patricians sought to escape from their predicament by turning to the production of wheat, to lumbering, to mining, and to speculation in lands on and beyond the frontier.[10] Ultimately, however, few families escaped distress or disaster. Virginia estates of the nineteenth century were not what they were in the eighteenth. The glory of Mount Vernon and Monticello was then gone. Nor was the Virginia aristocrat of 1850, marked though his merits might be, the equal in public affairs of his colonial and Revolutionary predecessor.

Like the glory of the Chesapeake, the grandeur of the Low Country aristocracy also lingers only in monuments and memory. Dominating the coastal region of South Carolina, southern North Carolina, and northern Georgia, with Charleston as its capital, that aristocracy was also largely middle class in background, but newer and less in debt.[11] European titles were no more prevalent in that region than they were between the Susquehanna and the Dan rivers, although the rank of a landgrave deriving his status from the local Carolina nobility created in the seventeenth century

[10] Before 1765 some Virginia planters sought salvation in indigo, but lost rather than gained money. That year many turned to hemp, which was more profitable. William Allason to Alexander Walker, May 21, 1765, in *Richmond College Historical Papers* (Richmond), II (1917), 135.

[11] A Charleston merchant commented in 1775 that a planter recently deceased had left "a very visible estate behind him, but as is very common in this country, 'tis loaded with a heavy debt." Josiah Smith, Jr., to Messrs. Gunniss, October 19, 1775, Letterbook of Josiah Smith, Jr. (University of North Carolina Library, Chapel Hill). However, the planters of the Low Country were obviously less concerned about their debts than those of the Chesapeake.

was mentioned by his neighbors at the beginning of the Revolutionary crisis.

In the Low Country, too, there were men and women who could trace ancestry, often by way of seventeenth-century Barbados and Antigua, to English gentlemen and ladies. Some could claim conspicuous forebears in Scotland and France. On the whole, however, the Low Country patricians were of neither great nor remarkably humble origins, their wealth and social superiority being of comparatively recent coinage. Henry Laurens, son of a saddler risen in the world, and Jonathan Allston, owner of a fine estate in northern South Carolina, were self-made and very well-made men.[12] Their family trees resembled that of George Washington rather than the one of Lord Fairfax.

Nor did the Low Country aristocracy contemn commerce, if the person involved in it was engaged in large and far-flung operations rather than in retail selling in small quantity. Indeed, many of its prominent planters were, or recently had been, merchants. Henry Laurens traded extensively in slaves, rice, and indigo, and also owned vast quantities of land. Gabriel Manigault, probably the richest man in South Carolina, was engaged in the exchange of goods as well as in agriculture. The patrician class of the deep South was equally fluid with that of the Chesapeake, welcoming worthy recruits with wealth acquired from commerce, showing no obvious favor to those who had prospered on the land.[13] One of its conspicuous members, Christopher Gadsden, the son of a British naval officer, was in youth a purser, in maturity a merchant rather than a planter.

The immediate physical background against which the Low Country upper class appeared was less impressive than that of its

[12] Josiah Quincy, who was entertained by Jonathan Allston in 1773, described him as "a gentleman of immense income, all of his own acquisition." Quincy, *Memoir of the Life of Josiah Quincy, Jun.,* 113.

[13] In the New Bern *North-Carolina Gazette,* December 12, 1777, "A Carolina Planter" bitterly attacked merchants both as lovers of gain and Tories. He wanted to segregate them from good people. "Let no christian be a merchant," he said, "and if he will be so let him be cast out of the church." "A Carolina Planter" entertained an unusually strong prejudice, and was promptly assailed by other writers.

Virginia equivalent, for its newer homes were of wood rather than of brick and were somewhat less beautiful, though ideally suited to climate. Moreover, the great families commonly maintained two homes rather than one, for they spent a large part of each year in Charleston, the summer and fall, which were unhealthy periods on the plantation.[14] Not without charm, their country houses were comfortable rather than elegant. Their town houses were more attractive externally, and were often elegantly furnished, that of Miles Brewton being admittedly the finest mansion in any colonial city. Travelers noted that the wind blew dust up from Charleston's sandy streets and that buzzards flew about scavenging; they also observed, however, neat brick sidewalks, a city well kept and gay. Wrote a Yankee sailor who visited Charleston in 1778: "I believe there is a few who now & then go to church but by all the observation I have been able to make I find that horse racing, frolicking rioting gaming of all kinds open markets, and traffick, to be the chief business of their Sabbaths. I am far from supposing there is not a few righteous there but was it to have the chance which Soddom had, that if there were five righteous men it should save the city. I believe there would be only a Lot & family, & his wife I should be afraid would look back." [15] Pleasures and pieties were not quite the same in Charleston as they were in New England.

The Low Country patricians are said to have differed sharply in physique and temperament from those of the Potomac and the Rappahannock. The males may have been somewhat slighter and more agile. Their women are described as slender and of medium height, with and without bloom upon their cheeks. The men were quick in speech, passionate in temper, proud if not vain, courteous, fond of dress and display, generous in their thinking, and lavish with their substance. They were indeed addicted to horse racing, cockfighting, and gambling, but were also devoted to music, the theater, the dance, and the arts as a whole, evincing cul-

[14] They also traveled to the northward, especially to Newport, to escape disease and heat. See Bridenbaugh, *Myths and Realities,* 94–95, and articles by the same author cited there.

[15] Samuel W. Boardman (ed.), *Log-Book of Timothy Boardman* [1778] (Albany, 1885), 73–74.

tivated and genuine taste.[16] Ardent and sensitive, they were more inclined to appeal to sword and pistol to settle personal disputes than were the first men of the tobacco country.[17] Their faults were tempered by the affection, good sense, and stability of their women, who presided over happy households.

There may have been more idleness among the Low Country patricians than among those of Virginia and Maryland, for their slaves were proportionately more numerous, their climate less stimulating. In the realm of formal education, however, the Low Country leaders compared quite favorably. Elementary schools were not lacking; and instruction by able tutors was readily available to both sexes in all readily conceivable disciplines and arts. There was, it is true, no college to the southward of William and Mary, although one was often projected, notably in a message sent to the legislature of South Carolina in 1770 by Lieutenant Governor William Bull, who urged the establishment and public support of a College of South Carolina at Charleston and also the founding of several elementary schools in the interior of that colony. This scheme failed to pass into law, partly because a custom had developed among wealthy Carolinians of sending or taking their young men to Europe, especially to Britain, for advanced liberal and professional education. Among the numerous shining lights of the Low Country who studied abroad were John Rutledge, William Henry Drayton, Charles Cotesworth Pinckney, Arthur Middleton, and John Laurens.[18] There was among these

[16] Frederick P. Bowes, *The Culture of Early Charleston* (Chapel Hill, 1942).

[17] Thus the fatal duel of 1777 between Lachlan McIntosh and Button Gwinnett and a less unfortunate one between Isaac Huger and Charles Cotesworth Pinckney in 1785, in which each of the men fired three times, Pinckney being slightly wounded.

[18] It is sometimes contended that the Southern colonists were more frequently educated in England, that they had stronger ties with England, that they were more like the English than other Americans. Broad and unrefined opinions like these cannot be completely accepted, nor some advanced by Lord Adam Gordon, a Scottish army officer who toured New England in 1765 after traveling through the South. Gordon asserted that Boston was "more like an English Old Town than any in America,—the Language and manner of the people, very much resemble the old Country, and all the Neighbouring lands and Villages, carry with them the same Idea. . . . The Men here, resemble much the people of Old England. . . . The Women here, and at Rhode-Island, are Accounted the most beautiful of any, on the Continent, and I am apt to believe it is so." "Journal of an Officer

no Jefferson and no Madison, but they and their like were otherwise equals in intellect and education to their correspondents in the Chesapeake society, which nourished but one Madison and a single Jefferson.

It is doubtful that the Low Country upper class was less devoted to public service than its Chesapeake counterpart, although there may have been slightly less of statesmanship in the Commons House of Assembly of South Carolina than there was in the House of Burgesses. It would seem that the South Carolina patricians were less thoughtful of their own pecuniary interests, more altruistic in defending American liberty, than was the aristocracy of the upper South. They were also tolerant with respect to religion. The Anglican Church was established in South Carolina very much as it was in Virginia, and most of the rice-indigo aristocrats were Anglicans. Nevertheless, in Charleston and its environs other Protestant churches flourished unchecked and unhindered. There was a generosity of religious spirit, and doubtless an indifference toward religion, among the great planters. The prevailing attitude among them is symbolized in a poem which appeared in the *South Carolina Gazette* in 1732.

> *Since we see the long Surplice, and eke the short Cloak,*
> *Are effectual alike, in the conjugal Yoke;*
> *And that One can, as well ev'ry Jot as th' Other,*
> *Make the chaste blushing Maid, a virtuous Mother:*
> *Nay yet more, can induce the most gravely precise*
> *To believe, a brisk Girl 'tween the Sheets, is no Vice;*
> *And (provided he closely adheres to his Text)*
> *Lead as safe to the Bliss of this World, as the next,*
> *Let none of us doubt, in their guidance to Heaven,*
> *But (our Duty well done) their Virtues are even.*
> *And if we can do but contrive to lead honest Lives*
> *And be as kind as ever we can to our Wives,*
> *No doubt, the same Happiness still may attend us,*
> *To which ever of these we apply to befriend us.*[19]

[Lord Adam Gordon] Who Travelled in America and the West Indies in 1764 and 1765," in Newton D. Mereness (ed.), *Travels in the American Colonies* (New York, 1916), 449, 451.

[19] Cohen, *South Carolina Gazette*, 198.

It has been said that the culture of the South Carolina Low Country was still merely derivative immediately before the War of Independence, that its people were creative neither intellectually nor artistically.[20] Assuredly, no Carolina Laurence Sterne, after traveling from Charleston to Savannah, wrote an American *Sentimental Journey*, nor was any Charlestonian, ruminating about the melancholy destiny of man, inspired to compose an "Elegy Written in a Country Churchyard"; and it is also true that too much can easily be made of the achievements of scientists John Lining and Alexander Garden and of other worthy men of the Low Country. But that judgment must substantially be the same even for the old colonies on the Chesapeake and in New England. There was no Sir Joshua Reynolds in Boston, and no Sheridan writing *The School for Scandal* beside the James. Jonathan Edwards was not David Hume. Americans did not genuinely excel in the arts and literature before the appearance of Poe. Their genius in the eighteenth century was largely in the area of statecraft, where they performed superbly. There the Low Country aristocrats were not inferior; in political leadership they were second, with others, only to the extraordinarily able and far-sighted patricians of Virginia.

Because of the culture, the elegance, and especially the power of the Southern patricians, who numbered perhaps no more than 10,000 persons, they have received comparatively far more attention than the Southern middle class. Such emphasis is largely proper, since guiding forces always deserve the closer scrutiny. It is nevertheless true that prosperous but lesser planters owning but a few slaves and yeoman farmers who possessed one or two or no slaves, together with traders, storekeepers, professional folk, and artisans, gave substance and vitality to Southern society. Fundamentally, they differed in no way from their occupational counterparts in the Middle and Northern colonies. Finely or badly educated, they gave intellect as well as body to that society, many of them ultimately making their way, of course, into the aristocracy. Among them were Thomas Marshall, father of the chief

[20] Bridenbaugh, *Myths and Realities*, Chap. II, especially pp. 98–99; and by the same author, *Cities in Revolt; Urban Life in America, 1743–1776* (New York, 1955), particularly pp. 190–91, 395–96.

justice, farmer, land agent, soldier, and officeholder, a man of little more than local repute, but one of quality nevertheless; Peter Jefferson, father of the president, small planter, surveyor, map maker, also a sterling Virginian; Peter Timothy, able printer and publisher of the *South Carolina Gazette;* and Daniel Morgan, farmer, teamster, amateur pugilist, brilliant Revolutionary officer.[21]

This Southern middle class was largely rural in the Revolutionary time, although many inhabitants of the Southern towns must be classified within it. It did not flourish in the coastal regions devoted to tobacco, rice, and indigo. In those areas the grandees with their gangs of slaves occupied the best lands; in them the white man moved upward or downward, or he went elsewhere.[22] North Carolina, however, except for its southeastern corner and the region about Albemarle Sound, where there were some large tobacco plantations, was essentially middle class; and the Southern interior population generally must be similarly classified. It is perhaps needless to say that most Southern whites belonged to that stratum of society.

It is equally obvious that there were variations within this massive center of Southern society. Indeed, there were striking divergences between the lowest and highest layers of that group, between, for example, the landowning farmer with a few possessions and little education and the prosperous planter with much larger property and learning. Yet the latter hardly belonged to the genuine aristocracy, the former cannot be divorced from the middle stratum. Within that stratum there were dissimilarities not only in wealth and education but in occupation, and even in national background. While the Chesapeake aristocracy was almost exclusively of English descent and that of the Low Country of English and French stocks, in the middle class were the Scotch-Irish Presbyterian clergymen; the notoriously industrious German farmers of the Shenandoah and of Salem; the Scottish Highlanders engaged in trade with the Indians; the Jewish traders; the teachers,

---

[21] Daniel Morgan was, of course, not Southern-born.

[22] In the Low Country about Charleston Negroes outnumbered whites by six or seven to one.

of all breeds of the British Isles and northwestern Europe; and, easily forgotten because obvious, the numerous persons of English blood in all callings and occupations.

In religion, too, there was readily recognized variety in the middle class. The Scotch-Irish were commonly Presbyterian; the Baptists, New Lights and old ones, were numerous; German Lutherans and Pietists dominated certain areas of the Southern interior; there were Congregationalists; some of French ancestry remained Calvinist, although the French-Americans tended to become Anglican; and, there were, of course, the Anglicans. In that class there was greater piety and more "enthusiasm" than in the patrician order. In the Southern back country religious antics and frolics gave a fillip to a way of life frequently monotonous.[23] The Reverend Mr. Charles Woodmason, an Anglican to be sure, tells us that men traveled many miles to see country preachers baptize women clad only in thin shifts.[24]

There was also wide diversity of behavior in the middle class. People in its upper levels could not be easily distinguished from the aristocracy on the basis of manners, tastes, amusements, or conduct. Indeed, descendants of these people have classified them with the socially select and will continue to do so, not without some display of fact as well as fancy; if they commit a sympathetic fallacy, it is true that no arbitrary line can be drawn between the patricians and the more prosperous middle folk. There was no grand gulf between Richard Henry Lee, whose membership in the aristocratic order can hardly be questioned, and young Thomas Marshall, who spent some years of his life in a log cabin. That cabin was also occupied by a daughter of the house of Randolph, Marshall's wife. However, as the observer moves down the middle class, he sees not only a diminution in property but increasing inferiority in education, decorum, and taste. Manners become

[23] Intellectual oddities were not lacking in the South. In the Williamsburg *Virginia Gazette* (Dixon and Nicolson), September 13, 1780, Andrew Mann offered proof that he had squared the circle.

[24] Richard J. Hooker (ed.), *The Carolina Backcountry on the Eve of the Revolution; The Journal and Other Writings of Charles Woodmason, Anglican Itinerant* (Chapel Hill, 1953), especially pp. 95–113, offers much curious material regarding religion and morals in the South Carolina Upcountry.

plainer and then simple; wine is succeeded by whisky and beer; [25] the sword and pistol as means for settling personal disputes between males become fisticuffs, then fisticuffs accompanied by eye-gouging, biting, and even assaults upon sexual organs; [26] liberal learning is replaced by elementary education and that by illiteracy; clothing elegant even in England changes to sober dress and ultimately to homespun; the minuet alters to country dances and then to jigs. The bottom of the middle class was composed of folk humble in status, though hardly in spirit. There one finds many who were hardy but rough, courageous but uncouth, honest but narrow-minded. Such people were especially numerous in the interior and on the frontiers of settlement. Among these, more or less sophisticated travelers were not usually happy. Their defects in cleanliness, in courtesy, and in personal conduct generally have been sufficiently recorded by tired wayfarers who in the exasperations of difficult journeying made much of their not infrequent brutalities as basic qualities. The plain Southern farmer had his counterpart in Connecticut and Pennsylvania.

Too often the humbler contingents of the Southern middle class have been confused with the "poor white trash," who existed before the Revolution as well as after, and who formed the lowest echelon of Southern white society. Their shiftlessness, their immoralities, their ignorance, their squalor, their savage fighting are well enough known. The line between them and the middle class is no sharper than that between the latter and the aristocracy; it did, however, most decidedly exist. Southerners distinguished

[25] It was a North Carolina custom to have an eggnog or other alcoholic stimulant before breakfast.

[26] In 1787 the legislature of Georgia passed a law specifically prohibiting biting, gouging, and other mutilating practices, and providing for suitable punishment for offenders. A curious description of a quarrel at a North Carolina tavern is given in Lida T. Rodman (ed.), *Journal of a Tour to North Carolina by William Attmore, 1787*, in *James Sprunt Historical Publications* (Chapel Hill), XVII (1922), 43: "We arrived in the heighth of a quarrel there between two Men; the Landlady applied to me to part 'em, I told her, 'No, let them settle their own differences.'—They were going to fight out in the Road, when one of the company declared he wou'd massacre the Man who should attempt to Gouge, (that is, endeavors to run his thumbs into the eyes of the other, scoop out his eye balls) Womble, one of the disputants declared 'I cannot fight without a Gouge' One of the company supported his declaration saying 'Ay! A Gouge all weathers, by G—' the terms were not accepted; their passions cooled by degrees. . . ."

easily enough between the two, although they might have found it difficult to describe the criteria by which they made judgment. Indifference toward poverty, dirt, and disease was possibly the major mark of the "trash." These folk were to be found on sea-coast lands that had never been fertile or that had been ruined by vicious cultivation, and also upon the frontiers, to which many of them went to secure easy improvement in their lot, to evade payment of debts, to escape the sheriff, and for various and mingled reasons. The "trash" were not actually numerous. They and their poverty and their brutish way of life were less commonly encountered in the Middle and Northern colonies. Accordingly, they were more conspicuous in the Southern scene than they deserved to be.

One group of Southern whites cannot easily be placed on the social ladder, for their status was with few exceptions temporary. Bond servants were men and women who had contracted willingly or otherwise to work four or more years for a master, in return for payment of their passage to America, in lieu of punishment for crime in England,[27] and for diverse reasons. Released from service, they might with industry and good fortune rapidly climb the social ladder, but hardly to the very top, which, however, was not inaccessible to their descendants.

Below virtually all the Southern whites in status were virtually all the Negroes, even those who were legally free, these being scant in numbers, except in Virginia and Maryland. Although the first Negroes brought to Virginia had been looked upon as servants rather than slaves, slavery was recognized and perpetuated by Virginia law after the middle of the seventeenth century; and the example of the Old Dominion was followed by her neighbors with respect to the legal condition of the Negroes as it was in many matters. Any person born to a slave woman was by law a slave, except when manumitted, the color and legal standing of the father having no effect upon the status of his offspring. The Negro, while admittedly human, was considered by nearly all Southern whites to be a fundamentally inferior being, even when

[27] The Annapolis *Maryland Gazette* unhappily announced the arrival of larger batches of convicts on July 11, 18, 1765, June 19, July 17, 1766, June 25, July 9, 17, 1767.

he was a mulatto descended in part from proudest white stock. Dr. Schoepf, the Hessian physician who toured the United States immediately after the War of Independence, received a shock at Hanover Courthouse in Virginia. "On a very warm mid-day (18 Decemb.) we found here a fine circle of ladies, silk-clad and tastefully coiffured, sitting about a fire. This was not so extraordinary in itself, but it was something new to me that several pretty vigorous young blacks, quite in the natural state, should be tumbling about before the party without giving scandal." [28] The ladies were not disturbed because it did not enter their heads that they should be attracted by Negro boys.[29]

The Negroes were, of course, largely plantation hands, especially those recently from Africa. Working under the direction of a white overseer, sometimes under that of a Negro, and often under the supervision of their owner, the field laborers toiled lengthily, but not usually arduously. Plainly and scantily clad, they commonly were given one outfit of clothing each year; their food was equally simple, though generally adequate for the preservation of health and vigor; their cabins or huts offered protection enough except in winter, when they suffered more from cold than their masters. In the Revolutionary time in the upper South they were not employed in huge gangs, for the average master owned only eight or ten slaves. Only a handful of Chesapeake magnates possessed more than one hundred Negroes; and those magnates were likely to own several plantations, on at least some of which the number of slaves was a dozen or two rather than several scores.

Only in the Low Country about Charleston was the ownership of slaves heavily concentrated. There the average master possessed 25 or 30 Negroes. In the rural parts of Charleston district there were in 1790 no fewer than 79 persons who owned 100 or more slaves. William Blake had 695, Ralph Izard 594, Nathaniel Heyward 420, and William Washington 380 on plantations there;

---

[28] Schoepf, *Travels in the Confederation,* tr. and ed. by Morrison, II, 47.

[29] Boardman saw in Charleston in 1778 slave servants of both sexes dressed in "such dishabitable as to be obliged to display those parts which ought to be concealed," and was unable to suppress "a total grin." Boardman (ed.), *Log-Book of Timothy Boardman,* 75.

Izard, Heyward, and Washington maintained a few additional Negroes in Charleston itself. It is apparent that the storied great
plantation harboring large numbers of slaves did then exist in
the rice-indigo country, since Izard had only eight plantations for
his nearly 600 Negroes.[30]

The presence of the Negroes was felt everywhere, even the
Creek and Cherokee Indians keeping them as slaves. They were
not remarkably important because of African culture which they
brought with them, for that culture largely vanished, even among
themselves. They copied their masters, but could not, of course,
quickly identify themselves with the whites. Accordingly, they
were becoming virtually a new people, not African and hardly
American. They were customarily quiet in captivity. Although
they rose in occasional ferocious revolt, despair of successful struggle for freedom and their good-natured docility persuaded them
to accept their lot, usually in cheerful spirit.[31] The presence of
the Negro in large numbers worried meditative whites concerned
for their own future and that of their progeny. As yet, such whites
were little vexed by moral qualms arising from the ownership of
blacks. Some, however, were alarmed because of the continually
increasing Negro population and believed that the bringing in
of slaves in the past in large numbers had had unhealthy consequences, that it would be prudent to prevent further imports.

It was already too late, of course, so to solve the widening,
deepening problem of white-Negro relations, though it could be
diminished by such means. Natural increase among the blacks
was as certain as it was among the whites. The Negro had come
to stay. As yet, he was a hewer of wood and a drawer of water,
and inevitably inarticulate. He would remain so for several generations in the South, and for almost as long a time to the northward.

The Southern whites were by no means voiceless, nor were
they helplessly forced to accept domination by others. They had
long been conscious of their own rights as "Englishmen," and
had not been backward in asserting and defending those rights.

[30] Ulrich B. Phillips, *American Negro Slavery* (New York, 1918), 83-84, 95-96.

[31] A dramatic commentary upon slavery is contained in a story in the Charleston
Morning Post and Daily Advertiser, July 27, 1787. A slave sold at auction on the
day before gazed at his new master's face, was appalled by what he saw, and jumped
into water in a vain effort to kill himself.

With other colonials to the northward they were about to embark upon a fateful struggle with the British crown and Parliament in behalf of their own liberties and those of mankind. During the years 1763–1765 Britain entered upon a new colonial policy, one which provoked American disobedience, led to civil and international war, and at last to the creation of an independent American republic.

CHAPTER IV

MR. GRENVILLE'S PROGRAM

IN THE years immediately before the clash of arms in 1775 Americans contesting British authority often declared they desired a return to "the good old days" of 1763. Their wish was not merely nostalgic. The colonists, both Northern and Southern, were then and had long been a prospering people. Indeed, the half century before 1763 has been designated as "the Golden Age of the American merchant." Assured of shelter and sustenance, the colonists had long known only one serious external menace, that of the French, which was almost finally removed by the Peace of Paris. While the Indian remained to ravage their frontiers and to plague their councils, he could not imperil their existence; and the Spanish, expelled by the peace from Florida but given New Orleans and western Louisiana by France, were far too weak to be a grave danger. In that year the Americans felt themselves to be secure militarily as never before. Accordingly, they could hope that the demands of defense would in the immediate future do less injury to their purses. Even at the height of the long Anglo-French struggle, in the Seven Years' War, their taxes had been in no colony crushingly heavy, had been in some remarkably light. They were fortunate, too, in their political institutions, for they enjoyed greater freedom than any other European people in the Western world. Control over their domestic concerns was largely in American hands.

The Southern colonists, save for those too dependent upon tobacco culture, fully shared the happy outlook of their brethren to the northward. They gave forth taxes and fees to officeholders, but usually in sums far less than staggering; and frequently they avoided payment entirely. Now and then and here and there,

notoriously in North Carolina, they suffered because of incompetent, grasping, and dishonest officials, both those chosen locally
and those appointed in Britain. They knew, too, the evils of
favoritism, of large grants of land virtually donated to the influential at their colonial capitals and to the relatives and associates of ministers in London; of plural officeholders; and of
printers who pushed for the emission of more paper money because they would have the printing of it. The Virginians were
soon to be shocked by the revelation that John Robinson, their
respected public treasurer and speaker of the House of Burgesses,
had illegally lent about £100,000 in public money to his distressed friends in return for their personal paper, the latter being
only too often valueless.[1] In general, however, the Southerners
were not accustomed to the public corruption and the burdensome taxation of contemporary Britain and France. Certainly,
they were not resigned to those evils. The fruits of their labors
and of those of their slaves were commonly their own.

That such was the case must ultimately and chiefly be ascribed
to the fact that they dominated their domestic destinies. In all the
long-settled British colonies in America, even in Georgia, there
was a lower house of assembly which had thrust toward and had
attained power. To be sure, in the South in every provincial
capitol from Annapolis to Savannah a governor and an upper
house, or council, also served. Chosen in Maryland by Frederick,
Lord Baltimore, by virtue of proprietary and hereditary right,
and to the southward by the crown, these in British theory safeguarded British and proprietary authority, and the interests of
wealthy colonials as well, against the lower houses, the "popular"
branch of government. They were less potent than they appeared
to be. The strength of the governor, council, and other officers
chosen by the Calverts was waning before the assaults of the
representatives of the voters claiming control over taxation and
the spending of public money. Royal authority in Virginia and
the Carolinas had been defended even less effectively. Among
them the veto of the governor, his appointive rights, his leadership of the land and sea forces, the existence of an externally

[1] David J. Mays, *Edmund Pendleton, 1721–1803* (Cambridge, 1952), I, 174–223,
358–85.

chosen council, the right of disallowance of colonial laws by the British Privy Council, and the force generally of crown and Parliament had not thwarted a long-continued drive toward dominance by elected and aggressive assemblymen. These demanded for their house, in provincial affairs, the rights and privileges of the House of Commons in England, and they had substantially achieved their goal. They had successfully insisted upon the right of the lower house to initiate money bills; in South Carolina, indeed, the upper house was not even permitted to amend such measures. The public treasurer was their man. Through him, through allocation of funds, through control of auditing, they had much to say about expenditures. In South Carolina they elected several executive officers, in North Carolina some judges. In those colonies they even stipulated the time of election and the length of sessions of the Assembly. Although the lower house was less powerful in Georgia than it was to the northward, the trend was in the same direction. A little time and growth, and the "popular" branch in Georgia would seek and achieve similar powers and equal influence.

The governor in the South, as elsewhere, was not a mere figurehead. He was also no solid buttress of the British empire. In the event of serious dispute between Britain and the Thirteen Colonies, he would be especially weak, for in that case he could expect no sturdy support from the Americans who composed the council, no steadfast loyalty from the Americans who formed his militia. Indeed, he had no civil means of repressing a riot, should such a tumult occur in defense of American rights as against British authority. The sheriff, the justices of the peace, the town watch could hardly help him to quiet a mob, should they wish to do so; and he could not command the services of a mounted constabulary like the Royal Northwest Mounted Police, for, except in Georgia, there was none. In an Anglo-American struggle the royal governor was likely to be a frustrated and most unhappy person, and with him the other royal officeholders of his colony.

Suffering slightly in purse and in sentiment because of British governors and associated officials, the Southern colonists were not discontented in 1763 because of British authority asserted through laws passed by Parliament and decrees made by the crown. It was

47

irritating on occasion that appeals could be carried from colonial courts to Britain, and quite annoying sometimes that colonial laws could be set aside by His Majesty's Privy Council. But there was little, if any, displeasure because King and Cabinet conducted the foreign relations of the empire and decided whether the colonists were at war or in peace. Nor was there sorrow or anger in the South because Parliament had controlled the external commerce of the colonists, and their manufactures as well. The Acts of Navigation permanently placed on the statute books after 1660 required that the bulk of European goods destined for American ports be landed first in Britain, and that most important American exports, tobacco, furs, deerskins, indigo, and other products, similarly be sent to Britain, even when their ultimate destination was the European continent. In general, indeed, these laws demanded that traffic between the Thirteen Colonies and the British Isles and central and northern Europe pass through the hands of British merchants and British customs officers, so as to assure the mother country supplies of basic raw materials and markets for British finished goods, profits for her merchants, strength for her merchant marine, increased revenues from the duties collected in her ports. Parliament also had limited by law the size of colonial establishments making woolen goods and hats; such goods could not even be sent from one colony to another. By the famous Iron Act of 1750 it had limited colonial manufacture of steel or finished iron products; they could make bar iron and sell it to British manufacturers. But the limits and duties which had been placed upon their external trade, including the Molasses Act of 1733, did not empty the purses of the Southern colonists or prevent them from being filled.[2] In the absence of Parliamentary law their exports and imports would have followed much the same channels. Moreover, British bans upon American manufacturing were of very little interest to the colonists at that time, since they did not covet an opportunity to make and sell clothing or steel. Besides, Parliament had given them a virtual monopoly of the British tobacco

[2] The effects of British regulation of American commerce continue to be debated. Oliver M. Dickerson, in *The Navigation Acts and the American Revolution* (Philadelphia, 1951), contends that they were not seriously injurious, that "racketeering" by British customs men and others after 1763 did create colonial discontent.

GEORGE WASHINGTON by Charles Willson Peale. Courtesy of Colonial
Williamsburg, Inc.

market, had offered and was granting bounties to indigo growers and the tar-pitch-turpentine producers of North Carolina.

Before George Grenville became George III's chief minister, in the spring of 1763, the Southern colonists nearly as fully enjoyed private content and public weal as men may. When Marylanders sought during the Seven Years' War to be freed from the quitrents and fees exacted by their proprietor and his officials, their remedy was the establishment of a royal system of government such as their neighbors across the Potomac possessed, a change which would hardly have shaken the British empire. While there was no Utopia on the Pedee or Patuxent, and no Arcadia in the valley of the Shenandoah or the Savannah, government annoyed rather than seriously injured. Moreover, there was good reason to believe that time and continued colonial growth in numbers and wealth would bring further diminution of external authority and its abuses. But the Grenville ministry created new grievances far beyond the trifling and the transitory and soon impelled the Southern colonists, with Yankees and Yorkers, to revolt. It was Virginia, oldest of Britain's overseas progeny, that first strongly resisted and first challenged Parliament and King.

Seldom in the history of modern Europe has one nation occupied a pre-eminent position such as that enjoyed by Britain late in April of 1763 when Grenville became chief minister.[3] The Seven Years' War and the long struggle between Britain and France for European hegemony and colonial empire of which that war was the climax had just ended in overwhelming and astounding triumph for Britain. Devoting the bulk of her energies to warfare on the seas and in the colonial world, Britain had almost destroyed French sea power, had forced down the fleur-de-lis in Canada, captured French sugar islands in the Caribbean, Martinique, Guadeloupe, St. Lucia, and erased the French military strongholds in India. Charles III of Spain, belatedly joining his

[3] The title of this chapter is not intended to suggest that Grenville was exclusively responsible for the making of British colonial policy during the period 1763–1765. He was, however, its principal architect. Discussions of that policy have been offered by George Louis Beer, Claude H. Van Tyne, Clarence W. Alvord, John C. Miller, Edmund and Helen Morgan, and various others. The account of it given herein is conventional, save for the emphasis placed upon the decision to maintain an army in America.

49

forces to those of his Bourbon cousin in 1762, had also been grievously chastised. British troops and tars had taken Havana and Manila. In the Peace of Paris, concluded early in 1763, France had been restricted in India to small colonies and commerce, had made concessions to Britain in Africa and the Caribbean, had ceded to her Canada and all that part of Louisiana, except the island of New Orleans, lying east of the Mississippi. Spain had been forced to abandon to Britain her colony of Florida. So thoroughly beaten felt Louis XV and his ministers that during the bargaining at Paris they gave New Orleans and the western half of Louisiana to Spain, partly to compensate Spain for the loss of Florida, but also to dispose finally of an American continental empire that had brought France grief instead of strength. Thus a prospect of exploiting India, unhampered by a European rival, had opened before British politicians, and thus the eastern third of North America from the Arctic to the Gulf of Mexico and from the Atlantic to the Mississippi had become British. The outlook for Britain was ample, her defense and that of her colonies assured by a superb navy and a veteran if small army, her American mainland possessions burgeoning in people and wealth, her commerce certain to flourish, and her manufacturers already moving into the Industrial Revolution, well in advance of those of rival nations.

There were, however, reasons for concern as well as excuse for national conceit. Strangely, Britain, now feared and respected as never before in Europe, had no allies and no important friends beyond the Channel except for Hanover and Portugal, neither of which could offer major military assistance; and in the courts of the Bourbons at both Versailles and Madrid, however much respect there might be for the fighting qualities and quantities of the British, were many men who bitterly resented the rise and gall of the British empire and whose intellects burned with thoughts of and schemes for revenge. Already Étienne François, Duc de Choiseul, was rebuilding the French army and navy toward the day of reprisal. At Madrid Charles III and his advisers were engaged in an attempt to renovate the Spanish state and empire and to make Spain once more a great power. Should Britain become enmeshed in difficulties, both France and Spain were likely to strike at her. Moreover, it was probable that they would act in unison, for they were united by a "Family Compact" signed in 1733 and strengthened by a further agreement of 1761.

Britain was also threatened, and more immediately, by economic and financial strain. She suffered from a postwar depression, not likely long to endure, to be sure. The wars with France and Spain since the Glorious Revolution of 1688 had been extraordinarily expensive, by eighteenth-century measuring. Her national debt had climbed to £130,000,000. The figure to some British politicians seemed staggering; and the interest upon the debt, between £4,500,000 and £5,000,000, was no light burden. Taxes were far above the levels existing before the Seven Years' War—the tax on land had risen from two shillings per acre to four—and were likely to remain high. It was reasonable to expect that both trade and revenue would soon increase and that both the national debt and the higher taxes would be carried without excessive pain in the future. At the moment, however, British merchants were uneasy, and landowners were unhappy. Many of these were noblemen and country gentlemen, who were able to express their anguish both in the House of Lords and in the Commons.

Grenville had to listen to these people. He did so willingly, for they were of his kind, and he felt with them. Nevertheless, during the two years when he was chief minister, he did nothing remarkable toward lowering taxes. He might have done something by cutting civil expenditures, a policy which he did not seriously undertake. There was also the possibility of diminishing the costs of the armed services by reducing the size of the army. A decision had recently been taken to maintain a larger army than Britain had ever had before in time of peace; it might well have been reconsidered.

The British army swelled immensely in the Seven Years' War, the number of formal regiments in it reaching ninety-three in 1760 and two years later more than a hundred. It might have been expected, in view of past British policy, that the army be cut in half. In the spring of 1763 it was announced that seventy-five regiments were to be kept in service, on paper something like 40,000 troops. It was the Bute ministry, in which Grenville played an important role, that sponsored this rather astonishing measure. Undoubtedly, Grenville approved the step; he made no effort to alter the decision. As a result, the army had seventy-five regiments until 1770, when it was again reduced, slightly, to seventy. Of this force, sixteen were assigned to North America and a part of the British West Indies under the command of Sir Jeffrey Amherst. The redcoat regiments upon this American establishment remained approximately at that figure until 1775. Amherst and General Thomas Gage, who succeeded him in November, 1763, on paper thus controlled about 8,500 men. However, in time of peace regiments were usually at two-thirds strength, or less; and after the end of Pontiac's war in 1765, the British army under Gage numbered about 6,000 men. Although detachments were as far apart as bleak Newfoundland and the tropical island of Grenada, the bulk of it was stationed on the mainland of North America.

The increase in the British peacetime army is in large part explained by a momentous step, taken without sufficient foresight. Before the Seven Years' War there had never been as many as 1,000 redcoats in the Thirteen Colonies when Britain was at peace. Until 1754 Britain had relied principally upon her navy and the efforts of the colonists themselves to ward off attack on her North American colonies. She had sent two regiments of regulars at the beginning of the Seven Years' War, and then many. Now she would have what was for Britain and for that time a large standing army in North America. It was unnecessarily numerous, and correspondingly more expensive than it need have been. And since it was costly, inevitably men in London began to think of means to pay for it without digging into the pockets of British taxpayers, already unhappy.

A part of the new establishment was necessary. The 60,000 French Canadians who became British subjects in 1763 did not immediately become loyal to the House of Hanover; and the four regiments which were kept in the province of Quebec after that year constituted only a reasonable precaution. Since another Anglo-French war was a quite likely event, prudence demanded that the centers of French population in the St. Lawrence Valley, Montreal, Three Rivers, and especially the city of Quebec be safeguarded against internal revolt. That the remaining regiments were also requisite is less certain. Small detachments were placed in Newfoundland and the Bahamas to prevent sudden seizure, in the one case by France, in the other by Spain. Garrisons were maintained at St. Augustine, Pensacola, Mobile, and on the lower Mississippi, to ward off possible Spanish thrusts from Havana and New Orleans and also to provide advanced bases for an attack upon Louisiana, should Britain and Spain again engage in military conflict. Forts were occupied at Niagara, Detroit, and Michilimackinac to protect communications on the Great Lakes and to encourage and keep order in the civilian trade with the Indians. A small body of troops was sent to Fort Chartres on the upper Mississippi, as yet occupied by the French, to counter the Spanish across the river. These and the regulars on the Great Lakes would also serve to repress the French inhabitants of Detroit and of Kaskaskia and Cahokia in the Illinois country, and conceivably to deter uprisings of neighboring Indians, traditionally allies of the French and foes of the British. A garrison at Fort Pitt was to defend the Ohio River communication, to encourage trade with the Indians, and at the same time to serve as a protection against them. Various other posts were maintained as way stations, as centers of the Indian commerce, and as protection for the frontier settlements of the Thirteen Colonies, at Fort Prince George in upper South Carolina, Sandusky in Ohio, Albany, and other places. Crown Point and Ticonderoga were to be defenses for the communication between Montreal and New York.

It is patent that the British army was to be scattered all over the eastern third of the North American continent and adjacent islands, and that it was to be devoted to many and diverse tasks, some of them not worth undertaking. The Indian traders needed no encouragement to carry on their bartering in the villages of the savages. Cheating and abusing the Indians, they had in the past helped to arouse hatred of King George's children among their customers and so to create an Indian menace for the Thirteen Colonies. But redcoats would hardly be able to follow them through the forests, nor to witness and bring decency into their bargainings. Forts beyond the settlements in the Thirteen Colonies were of doubtful value as protections against attack by the savages, and indeed were in their isolation too vulnerable targets for the warriors of the woods. Even posts on or adjacent to the frontiers, though they possessed worth as centers for defense and for offense (which was the best defense against the red men), could easily be avoided by Indian raiders. It may even be questioned that forts on the Great Lakes waterway were immediately essential. Nor can it be effectively contended that the Spanish, taking over at New Orleans, would be so dangerous on the lower Mississippi and the shores of the Gulf of Mexico that strong places to check them were a compelling need.

When the problem of defense of the old and the new possessions in North America is carefully considered, one concludes that crown and Parliament tried to do too much with redcoats. When all is said, the French, the Spanish, and the Indians, even in combination—and it is inconceivable that all the Indians would have aided France and Spain—were not able to offer a challenge to the security of British North America unless the Bourbons balanced British sea power and sent large land forces across the Atlantic. After all, the British colonies in North America were far less exposed to attack than they had been in 1754. Then it had been sufficient for Britain to dispatch regulars after the conflict had begun.

It will be asked, Was not the new army intended also to warn the Americans that they must show greater respect in the future for British authority than they had in the past, that they must not think of independence? One unknown British writer of the time does say that the presence of a standing army in North America would encourage the Americans to remain loyal to the mother country, but no record has been found which indicates that King, Cabinet, or Parliament thought of that army as a force to repress them. In 1763, it may be added, no influential American, so far as is known, wanted independence; and the army was not at first stationed so as to threaten even by proximity the people who lived east of the Allegheny divide.

The new army, only partly necessary for effective defense, was actually a menace to British power in the Thirteen Colonies in several ways.

Had Britain quietly permitted the Americans to worry about

and to deal with the Indians, the colonists would have been more appreciative of their British connection, less disposed to push for their rights as British subjects. Actually, when the Indians of the Ohio Valley and the region of the Great Lakes, under the guidance of Pontiac, attacked both British posts in the wilderness and the American frontier settlements, Sir Jeffrey Amherst and General Gage made great efforts to crush those Indians; and redcoats with the aid of colonial troops forced Pontiac and his allies, soon short of ammunition and clothing, ultimately to sue for peace, though not before they had created havoc on the western borders of New York, Pennsylvania, Maryland, and Virginia. Moreover, the royal Indian superintendents, of whom more later, were used to prevent conflict between the colonists and the red men. After 1763 the British certainly did not follow, with reference to the colonists and the Indians, that familiar and frequently sound maxim, *divide et impera*.

The presence of a standing army in North America, to lessen the fears felt by the colonists toward the Indians and to offer them some assurance against possible attacks by the French and Spanish, aroused no great gratitude in the Thirteen Colonies, for it was assumed, correctly, by most Americans, that the new establishment was not vital for their protection. Moreover, the Americans were not consulted about it. And there came up inevitably the pregnant question: who was to pay for that army? To do British politicians justice, they did not create it without considering means for its support. On the contrary, they decided at the outset that the colonists must sooner or later supply the funds, something more than £200,000 per annum. They assumed that the redcoats were to be maintained for the protection of the colonists, a proposition arguable in 1763, dubious in 1765, very doubtful in 1768, and indefensible after 1770. The British taxpayer, they believed, was already overburdened with military charges, supporting as he did the imperial navy and the garrison forces in England, Wales, Scotland, and various parts of the empire. The colonists, who carried light tax loads and who had benefited greatly in the past from the exertions and sufferings of British tars and redcoats, could easily and should certainly bear the cost of the new establishment. The Grenville cabinet did not, however, attempt to place the entire cost of the new army in America upon the colonists. The Americans, when they learned of its intentions, objected so forcefully that the Grenville government chose to demand that they assume only part of it—hence eventually the famed stamp tax.

Hence also resulted the Quartering Act of April, 1765, actually a segment of the Mutiny Act of that year. Before 1765 the bulk of the redcoats in America were stationed outside the settled parts of the Thirteen Colonies. Some were more or less permanently kept in Albany and a few other places. Moreover, since the remainder were rotated in service, regiments and fractions of them frequently passed through colonial towns and villages and were sometimes posted in such places while transfer was arranged. It was an old practice in England to compel tavern-keepers, who profited from the proximity and the thirst of soldiers, to supply lodging and some supplies to British troops. With little thought in the matter, Parliament now required that the colonies undertake to furnish quarters for the redcoats located in the settlements, in barracks, taverns, empty houses, barns, or other outbuildings. They were also to supply certain kitchen utensils and supplies, firewood, candles, either cider or beer, and assistance in transportation. A routine bit of military business. But it was not so in the view of many colonials, who were to produce the money for it not by their own choice but as the result of a casually taken decision of politicians in London. In slightly different form the Quartering Act raised the same issue as the stamp tax. A struggle followed over provision for the troops, one which became increasingly serious as the redcoats more and more moved into cantonments within the occupied parts of the Thirteen Colonies.

The regulars trudged toward the seacoast from western wildernesses after 1765, in direct consequence of the British resolutions taken two years earlier to keep an army in America and to pay for its support with American money. When Cabinet and Parliament actually sought by law to extract funds from the colonists—in the Sugar, Stamp, and Quartering acts—the Americans rose in virtual revolt. Inevitably, that army was then considered as a means for buttressing British authority in the Thirteen Colonies. It was so used, increasingly; and the employment of the army, not sufficiently powerful to cow the colonists, led to the Boston Massacre, exacerbated American wounded feelings and contributed to the ultimate American determination to assert independence.

The Grenville ministry also vigorously and expensively sought to prevent Indian wars. Conflict with the Indians in the past had been chronic, harassing, and brutal. Suave French forest diplomacy, cheating by colonial traders, colonial encroachments upon Indian hunting grounds and towns, and English inferiority in the arts of persuasion had provoked savage attacks by this tribe and that upon this frontier farm and that border settlement. The departure of the French from Canada and the Mississippi Valley, to be sure, would lead to the withdrawal of French agents from the Indian villages and would also largely put an end to French trafficking with the red men. The warriors would become largely dependent upon British traders for their liquor, guns, ammunition, and clothing. On the other hand, many Indian tribes were certain to resent the going of the Gallics, an event depriving them of the benefits of an Anglo-French counterbalance and of hope for economic and military aid against the British. It was likely that relations with the Indians would be for some years troubled rather than improved. Indeed, given the ever-increasing numbers of the colonists and their lust for new lands, no permanent peace was possible until the warriors should be finally subjugated and forced to live and to toil where and how the white man dictated. It could not be reasonably hoped that the several colonies would do anything effective toward removing the grievances of the Indians. Competing in the Indian trade, for the lands of the red men, and for power as well, the colonies acting separately had compiled an uneven but generally dark and bloody record in Indian affairs. If there was to be improvement, it must be secured by imperial intervention.

One long step had already been taken by London officials. Alarmed because of the success of French machinations among the savages at the beginning of the French and Indian War, they had established two royal superintendents of Indian affairs, to seek to win friends and soften enemies among the red men. Sir William Johnson, commissioned to deal with the powerful Iroquois and their allies, was a veteran Indian trader, something of a linguist, and an expert in Indian psychology. He had been strikingly successful. His counterpart, Edmund Atkin, a South Carolina gentleman given the task of soothing the Southern tribes, was a mediocre man not gifted for his peculiar duties. Atkin, however, had died, and had been succeeded in 1762 by Captain John Stuart, a glamorous figure of the South Carolina frontier much cherished by the Cherokee. There was a good chance that he would do as well in the South as Johnson in the North. The two superintendents might, as wartime officials, have been looked upon as temporary and might have been discharged, particularly on the score of economy, for their salaries and their expenditures ran to several thousand pounds annually. Instead, the Grenville ministry chose to retain Johnson and Stuart and actually endowed them with greater authority and influence than they had possessed during the war.

Grenville and his associates also strove to protect the lands of the savages against colonial seizure. On October 7, 1763, a royal proclamation announced the creation of three new colonies, Quebec, East Florida, and West Florida, and the establishment of an Indian reservation in the American interior. There was to be, at least for the time being, no new white settlement west of the Allegheny divide. Moreover, the Indians were recognized as communal owners of the lands upon which they dwelt and hunted—a declaration which conceded Indian ownership of some regions east of the mountains as well as of all those lying to the west. It was further asserted that the red men could not sell land except at a public meeting presided over by a royal official, who would presumably not act save under orders from London. While some British politicians favored this measure as a more or less permanent one that would keep the colonists east of the Alleghenies—they fancied that the Americans would not engage in manufacturing on the coast until the trans-Allegheny area was occupied—the major motivation was a sincere desire to ward off Indian wars. Indeed, although royal restriction of colonial expansion had been considered for several years and plans for the proclamation had been drawn in June, 1763, the news of Pontiac's war and the sufferings of British soldiers and American settlers had impelled the Grenville ministry to early action. It would obviously not do to say that the proclamation proceeded from the decision of the cabinet to maintain an army of regulars in America. However, the losses of soldiers at the hands of the red men and the heavy expenses incurred in breaking down Indian resistance surely had their part in confirming and continuing the policy of restriction of white settlements.

Further to remove the grievances of the Indians, the Grenville ministry considered a scheme for imperial control of their trade. Military officers and Indian superintendents had tried to repress the traders during the war, and it had been believed in London for some years that conditions in the trade would remain vicious until royal action was taken. Collecting counsel from the superintendents and other sources, the Board of Trade, an advisory body which devoted itself to the gathering of information and to the making of recommendations with respect to the colonies, proposed in July, 1764, a "Plan for the Future Management of Indian Affairs." Designed to place control of the commerce with the red men largely in the hands of the superintendents, this plan, if carried out, would have brought the white traders to heel. After lengthy analysis, it was set aside, largely upon the score of expense. The superintendents, however, being instructed to do what they could to keep order in that trade, put into effect, with the support of General Gage, many of its provisions during the years 1764–1769. Accordingly, imperial authority was exerted in Indian villages east and west of the Alleghenies as never before in time of peace. Also in consequence, the budget for the army in America, which paid most of the bills of the Indian services, was swelled annually by some thousands of pounds.

Trying elaborately to meet the interrelated problems of defense and Indian affairs, King and Cabinet adopted measures certain to arouse serious colonial discontent. They also attempted to limit rigidly the overseas commerce of the Americans and to extract a revenue from them. It was these, with the measures discussed above, that provoked revolt.

In the spring of 1764, with powerful support from British West Indian planters, the Grenville ministry pushed through Parliament the Sugar Act, the passage of which marked a great turning point in British colonial policy. It called for, together with other duties, a threepence per gallon levy on molasses imported into North American harbors from foreign islands in the Caribbean. In part it was intended to replace the Molasses Act of 1733, which had put a prohibitive duty of sixpence upon molasses produced in the possessions of France, Spain, and other European nations. That law had been flagrantly violated by the Americans, for whom the principal constituent of rum was a most important item of commerce. The foreign planters could sell molasses cheaper than the British ones, and the Americans were determined to deal with the French and Spanish, the more so because the foreigners bought Negro slaves, lumber, flour, fish, and meat from the Americans and also because they paid for some of their purchases in hard money, much desired and needed on the mainland. American merchants accordingly had ignored and evaded the law. They had not ceased to deal with the foreigners even in the Seven Years' War, when the foodstuffs they carried to the Caribbean helped the French to hold on in that area against blockading and attacks by the British navy and army. It was hoped in London that the new law would be sternly enforced and that the British planters would profit. It was expected, however, that American merchants would often pay the tax rather than deal with those planters. In consequence substantial sums would be collected by customs officers in mainland ports. In this expectation appears the second goal of the act. Grenville intended not only to regulate trade but to raise a revenue. The double purpose of the Sugar Act was not denied, was in fact explicitly asserted in its preamble. Hitherto Parliament had often used taxes as a means of controlling trade. It had never before attempted to tax on the mainland in order to secure money. This striking and far-reaching change in policy must be linked to the decision to maintain a British army in America. Indeed, the proceeds of the tax were to be turned over to its deputy paymaster general to be used for the maintenance of that force.

The Sugar Act might have had relatively small effect except for accompanying measures to assure its enforcement. The British customs service in America, inadequate and corrupt, was given a thorough shake-up by Grenville. After 1764 it functioned with unwonted vigor. Moreover, the British naval squadron based at Halifax was ordered to do what it could to seize ships violating the Sugar Act and the older Navigation Acts, an order pleasing to naval officers and men alike, for they hoped to share in the moneys received from sales of merchant ships legally condemned because of the transgressions of their owners. They had special reasons to hope for such gains because of another Grenville decision, which called for the use of admiralty courts to try suspects. These courts operated without juries, and convictions would be much more easily secured than in the past, when a merchant's neighbors on a jury, men who did not think smuggling a crime and who perhaps remembered their own shortcomings, frequently found him innocent in the face of damning evidence.

After 1764 the British customs service in America not only earned its keep but produced annually a neat and unprecedented profit of several thousand pounds. Further, the enforcement of the Sugar Act limited until 1766 the supply of foreign currency reaching the mainland from the West Indies. The colonists were injured thereby, because of the tendency of cash to cross the Atlantic into the hands of British merchants. And the Grenville ministry narrowed the stream of currency in the colonies in another way. American assemblies had long put forth paper currency, and it had been very useful. Often, however, they had emitted unsupported paper and had even made it legal tender. Such bad practices had been disruptive in trade and had harassed creditors. Parliament by a law of 1751 had ordered the New England colonies to cease issuing or reissuing legal-tender paper. Now these restrictions were extended to all the colonies, at a time when the supply of foreign money was to be diminished—and at the moment when Parliament chose to try to obtain a large revenue from them.

The Pandora's Box of the Grenville ministry's new colonial measures had not been emptied. The most important of the Grenville laws, the Stamp Act, was passed in March, 1765. It was hardly a surprise, for the chief minister had announced a year earlier that such a tax or some equivalent bringing into the treasury an equal sum of money would be demanded. The money was to be used to support the army in America. Actually, Grenville had pretty well made up his mind by the summer of 1763 that there must be an American stamp tax, and he had spent some time planning it during several months before giving his official notice.

His suggestion that the colonials might be able to offer an equivalent, perhaps by stamp taxes levied by their assemblies, was merely an attempt to convince them that their good was dear to his heart and that he desired to make the assumption of an inevitable financial burden as easy as possible for them. Indeed, then and afterward, until the passage of the act, he did not tell the colonists what they must pay. In May, 1764, when he conferred in London with several of the agents of the colonies—each of them had one or more representatives in the imperial capital—Grenville claimed, with some justice, that there was no practicable way in which the many American assemblies acting separately could provide a sufficient and reliable revenue. He asked the agents that they give their approval to the proposed Parliamentary tax, to sanction a pig in a poke. They refused, and many of their constituents in America, being informed of the minister's scheme, vigorously condemned it as unfair and beyond the constitutional powers of Parliament. Petitions from America questioning Parliamentary authority to lay such a tax merely increased the determination of Grenville and of other British politicians to levy it. Early in February, 1765, still pretending solicitude for the feelings of the colonists, Grenville conferred with four of the American agents, representing their fellows. He would, he said, since the Americans had not offered and apparently could not present a suitable substitute, ask Parliament to approve the tax.

A few days later debate upon the proposal began in the House of Commons. Its wisdom was hotly questioned by Colonel Isaac Barré, an army officer who had served in America and who was acquainted with the Americans. He predicted those "Sons of Liberty" would resist. No one had the temerity to express doubt concerning the power of Parliament to tax them. The House approved the measure by a five-to-one majority, and the Lords promptly concurred. It became law on March 22 and was to go into effect on November 1.

The stamps, to be used upon bonds, newspapers, legal and commercial documents of various sorts, insurance policies, and playing cards, were to be sold by specially chosen collectors, and violators of the act were to be punished in the admiralty courts. As much as £10 in stamps was required upon a license to practice law. Most of the rates were low, lower than those of a stamp tax which had been in force in England for seventy years. The English tax had been quite easily and cheaply collected. It was expected that the Americans would grumble but pay, and that His Majesty's treasury would net £50,000 each year, possibly more. The money, spent upon the army in America, would pay one fifth or more of its cost. Had the colonists purchased stamps without serious complaint, the rates might have been raised and the list of items requiring them might have been expanded. It was not likely that the colonists, never fond of taxes, would cheerfully buy the stamps.

The Americans in the Thirteen Colonies would have none of the stamps. They saw a pattern of tyranny in the Grenville program—their occupation and exploitation of lands in the interior halted, their trade with the Indians injured, their maritime commerce interrupted, their currency difficulties increased, and their pockets emptied by novel taxes and quartering requirements. It may be said, and often has been said, that Grenville and his colleagues and supporters did not intend to establish a tyranny. It cannot be denied, however, that the Grenville measures offered a pattern of exertion of British authority in America as never before. Had Grenville had his way, he would have turned back the colonial clock, and that without consulting the Americans. He was not permitted to move the hour hand. Finding grievances everywhere in his program, the Americans denounced large parts of it, especially the Stamp Act, as "unconstitutional," and resisted.

The Grenville program was not entirely abandoned by British politicians until 1778, two years after the Declaration of Independence. Its continuance, in part, to the mid-point of the Revolution constantly exasperated. During a decade of troubled relations with the mother country, the colonists steadily, though with varying vigor, insisted upon its abandonment, asking for a return to "the good old days" of 1763, to that time when a permanent British army in America and Parliamentary taxation for revenue did not exist. Then, as the War of Independence approached, they enlarged their definitions of American liberties within the British empire; and not long afterward, in the crucible of that conflict, they resolved to seek freedom without that empire.

CHALLENGE FROM THE CHESAPEAKE

ANDREW BURNABY, a British traveler in the Old Dominion in 1759, reported that the Virginians were "haughty and jealous of their liberties, impatient of restraint, and can scarcely bear the thought of being controlled by any superior power." He asserted that "Many of them consider the colonies as independent states, not connected with Great Britain, otherwise than by having the same common king, and being bound to her by natural affection."[1] Burnaby's "many" must be translated as "relatively few." Virginians generally neither despised nor displayed such sublime contempt for Parliament until years of Anglo-American conflict had passed. Nevertheless, in 1764 her planters and farmers vigorously condemned the Sugar Act and the proposed stamp tax, and her House of Burgesses made it evident that year that Virginia would not meekly follow Grenville in his "new course."

Officially, Virginia and her sister colonies did not complain against the maintenance of a British army devoted to the defense of both the old and the new British possessions—even though they were not consulted—so long as it cost them nothing and did not threaten them. Indeed, they were doubtless pleased that the British regulars bore the brunt of the fighting and the British treasury the bulk of the expense in Pontiac's war, which began late in the spring of 1763 and dragged on to an uneasy end toward the close of 1765. Nor was there serious and early protest from the capital of Virginia against the proclamation of 1763, in spite of the fact that the Virginians were the people peculiarly interested in speculation concerning, and settlement of lands beyond

[1] [Andrew] *Burnaby's Travels Through North America,* ed. by Rufus R. Wilson (New York, 1904), 55–56.

the Allegheny divide. Again, Pontiac's war explains temporary acquiescence at Williamsburg, for schemes to secure wealth and homes over the mountains seemed dubious as long as that conflict continued in the Ohio Valley. It was likewise with the British decision to retain the royal Indian superintendents in office and with attempts on their part to control the Indian trade. For the time being Virginia kept silence about Sir William Johnson, John Stuart, General Thomas Gage, and their efforts to protect the Indians against exploitation.

Nor did the burgesses inveigh against the Currency Act of 1764, although it was aimed specially at them, for they had declared Virginia paper money legal tender and had made it possible for planters in the toils of the law on account of their debts to pay British creditors in such currency and also to cut down their obligations in terms of British money. In fact, the Committee of Correspondence of the Virginia house, writing in July, 1764, to the agent for the Old Dominion in London, said that the act aroused no rage in Virginia. Perhaps burgesses who had borrowed the Virginia paper from John Robinson, and Robinson himself, were not eager at that time to stimulate discussion about that kind of money. But the Virginians objected vigorously and specifically to the Sugar Act, because it raised the duty on Madeira wine, a beverage of which the planters were more than commonly fond, and to Parliamentary taxation in terms which positively applied to the proposed stamp tax and possibly also to the sugar law in so far as it was a revenue measure. The Committee of Correspondence declared that "no man or body of men, however invested with power, have a right to do anything that is contrary to reason & justice, or that can tend to the destruction of the [British] constitution." [2] The house itself later protested in three separate petitions addressed to the King, the Lords, and the Commons. According to that constitution, they asserted, "the people are not subject to any taxes but such as are laid on them by their own consent, or by those who are legally appointed to represent them." Were it otherwise, they would be "slaves." [3]

[2] *Virginia Magazine of History and Biography* (Richmond), XII (1904), 8–14.
[3] John P. Kennedy (ed.), *Journals of the House of Burgesses of Virginia, 1761–1765* (Richmond, 1907), 302–304.

More than half of the assemblies of the Thirteen Colonies similarly protested that taxation without representation was a denial of the rights of British citizens, and those of New York and North Carolina precisely pronounced both the Sugar Act and the stamp tax to be Parliamentary usurpations. But the colonists did not present a solid front, the Yankees lagging behind. Connecticut and Rhode Island were far from forthright in denouncing even the Stamp Act, and Massachusetts presented only economic arguments against it.[4] Briefly debating that measure, the House of Commons refused even to peruse such documents from America, since a standing rule of that body precluded petitions against money bills.

Neither the Grenville ministry nor the House of Commons was alarmed by the challenges to Parliamentary power to tax received from America; and Americans in London, including Benjamin Franklin, supposed that their people at home would puff but pay. Richard Henry Lee, scion of the great house of Stratford, was of the same opinion. Those who would supply the stamps to a reluctant public, the so-called stamp collectors, would have light labors and solid reward. He pushed for an appointment as collector in Virginia, then prudently ceased pressing when it became evident to him that if successful he was more likely to gather trouble for himself than taxes for the crown. George Mercer, a fellow Virginian who was in London and who could not assess sentiment in Norfolk and the Northern Neck, persevered in his efforts to secure the plum, obtained it, and found it bitter fruit.

Richard Henry Lee's aborted attempt to win for himself the office of stamp distributor is explained in part, no doubt, by a division of opinion among his relatives and friends concerning the shape of things to come. Certainly there was strong feeling among the Virginia planters in the late spring of 1765 against offering further defiance to Parliament. When reports came to Williamsburg that their petitions and the others from America denouncing the new levy had been ignored and that it had been sanctioned by Commons, Lords, and King, the burgesses were

[4] Edmund S. Morgan and Helen M. Morgan, *The Stamp Act Crisis; Prologue to Revolution* (Chapel Hill, 1953), 33–39.

in session and occupied with small business. They continued with their minor affairs until the session was about to close, in part, perhaps, because they lacked for some time positive assurance that the reports were true. There can hardly have been, however, a burning desire among the whole body to express officially either their anguish or their anger, much less a resolute determination to resist, for a majority of the house, including the renowned Edmund Pendleton, went home when it was but too apparent that the bad news was true.[5] Only 39 members of 116 were present on May 29, when Patrick Henry, admitted to the house on May 20, became a nine-day wonder, introducing and securing the passage in committee of the whole of five resolutions denouncing the behavior of the British government.

To Lord Byron, Henry was "the forest-born Demosthenes." Jefferson, for whom Henry was frequently a trial, once said of him that he was "all tongue without either head or heart." [6] Edmund Pendleton, a veteran and able observer of men and things, did not admire his learning or his intellect, but was impressed by Henry's remarkable ability to sense and to use the arguments having most appeal to his listeners. Said George Mason, "Your passions are no longer your own when he addresses them." [7] Henry was an orator rather than a statesman—but what an orator! He had already won local fame as a lawyer in the celebrated Parson's Cause, which arose from diminished affection among the Virginians for their Anglican clergymen. The Anglican Church was established by law in Virginia after 1609. Its clergy, supported by the public, whether Church of England, Presbyterian, or agnostic, was long paid in fixed amounts of tobacco. In the 1750's, however, when the price of tobacco was high, the burgesses made it possible to compensate the official gentlemen of the cloth in

[5] William Allason, merchant of Falmouth, declared in May that talk about the Stamp Act had "subsided much." Allason to Alexander Walker, May 21, 1765, in *Richmond College Historical Papers*, II (1917), 136. An extract of a letter dated New York, July 11, 1765, in Annapolis *Maryland Gazette*, July 25, 1765, asserts that many members left early for home because they were uncertain what stand to take.

[6] Julian P. Boyd *et al.* (eds.), *The Papers of Thomas Jefferson* (Princeton, 1950—), VI, 205.

[7] *Virginia Historical Register* (Richmond), III (1850), 28.

cash of less value. The Churchmen suffered from the new arrangement, and secured from the crown in 1759 the disallowance of the legislation which so offended them. Not content with this victory, which protected him for the future, the Reverend Mr. James Maury of Hanover County in 1763 sued the public for the losses he had incurred in the past. The Hanover county court conceded the legality of his claim. There remained only the matter of setting the amount Mr. Maury was to receive, when Henry appeared in the case. The sum, alas for the clergyman, was determined by a jury, not by the gentlemen planters who formed the county court. The planters were almost invariably Anglicans, though commonly not warm in their faith; on the jury were some Presbyterians and plain folk. In a long, heated, and inflammatory address to the jury, Henry peremptorily denied the right of the crown to set aside laws passed by the burgesses, whatever British and Virginia judges might say, and inveighed against the rapacity of the Anglican clerics. He astutely appealed to local political prejudice, to the love of money among the Anglicans on the jury, and to both the love of money and the hearty dislike for the official church among the Presbyterians sitting with them. Hastily the jury awarded Mr. Maury one penny. Mr. Maury and the county court were hardly moved to ecstasy by Henry's performance—they must have called it pettifoggery—or by the response of the twelve good men and true, but the almost perfect pleader had made his mark.

The five resolutions introduced by Henry on May 29, 1765, were all bitterly opposed by an "Old Guard" both in committee of the whole and in formal session, in spite of the fact that most of them said precisely what petitions of the burgesses of the preceding fall said. John Robinson, Peyton Randolph, Robert Carter Nicholas, Richard Bland, and George Wythe are reported to have fought against their adoption or, at least, to have sought softening amendments. Were, then, the traditional leaders of the burgesses, having made their protest, inclined to avoid further dispute, to accept taxation via stamps, rather than to struggle? Some of them, just possibly. Were they disposed to keep quiet until feeling in Virginia and other colonies could be found out? Here was an important factor, perhaps. They may also have wished to take no action when only one third of the house was present. Very likely, they resisted against the resolutions simply because they were offered by an upstart who had been a member only for a few days, one whom they did not know well or trust, a too-forward man. The Tidewater aristocrats who controlled the burgesses could not fail to see in Henry and his resolutions a threat to their dominance.

Certainly, John Robinson, leader of the "Old Guard," and his associates discovered that the Hanover County lawyer could appeal forcefully to burgesses as well as to plain farmers. On May 30 Henry delivered in support of his resolutions the memorable speech which was afterward reconstructed—and constructed—by William Wirt, his biographer, also a potent spellbinding courtroom pleader. Wirt's version, long a favorite for declamation among American teachers and schoolboys, was hardly precise. The only strictly contemporary description of the scene in the burgesses that afternoon was written by a French agent touring the colonies to discover whether there was antagonism between Britain and the Americans sufficient to bring advantage to France.

"May the 30th. Set out early from half-way house in the chair and broke fast at York, arrived at Williamsburg at 12, where I saw three negroes hanging at the galous for haveing robed Mr. Waltho of 300 pounds. I went immediately to the Assembly which was seting, where I was entertained with very strong debates concerning duties that the Parlement wants to lay on the American colonys, which they call or stile stamp dutys. Shortly after I came in, one of the members stood up and said he had read that in former times Tarquin and Julus had their Brutus, Charles had his Cromwell, and he did not doubt but some good American would stand up in favour of his country; but (says he) in a more moderate manner, and was going to continue, then the speaker of the House rose and, said he, the last that stood up had spoke traison, and was sorey to see that not one of the members of the House was loyal enough to stop him before he had gone so far."

Thus far, the Frenchman's narrative does not vary seriously from the Wirt version. However, it continues: "Upon which the same member stood up again (his name is Henery) and said that if he had afronted the Speaker or the House, he was ready to ask

69

pardon, and he would shew his loyalty to His Majesty King George the third at the expence of the last drop of his blood; but what he had said must be attributed to the interest of his country's dying liberty which he had at heart, and the heat of passion might have lead him to have said something more than he intended; but, again, if he said any thing wrong, he beged the Speaker and the House's pardon. Some other members stood up and backed him, on which that afaire was droped." [8]

If Henry was not quite so defiant as he was once thought to have been, he was vigorous enough. The burgesses, apparently by votes of twenty-two to seventeen,

"*Resolved,* that the first adventurers and settlers of this his Majesty's colony and dominion of *Virginia* brought with them, and transmitted to their posterity, and all other his Majesty's subjects since inhabiting in this his Majesty's said colony, all the liberties, privileges, franchises, and immunities, that have at any time been held, enjoyed, and possessed, by the people of *Great Britain.*

"*Resolved,* that by two royal charters, granted by King *James* the First, the colonists aforesaid are declared entitled to all liberties, privileges, and immunities of denizens and natural subjects, to all intents and purposes, as if they had been abiding and born within the realm of *England.*

"*Resolved,* that the taxation of the people by themselves, or by persons chosen by themselves to represent them, who can only know what taxes the people are able to bear, or the easiest method of raising them, and must themselves be affected by every tax laid on the people, is the only security against a burthensome taxation, and the distinguishing characteristick of *British* freedom, without which the ancient constitution cannot exist.

"*Resolved,* that his Majesty's liege people of this his most ancient and loyal colony have without interruption enjoyed the inestimable right of being governed by such laws, respecting their internal polity and taxation, as are derived from their own consent, with the approbation of their Sovereign, or his substitute; and that

[8] The anonymous Frenchman's account is readily available in Samuel E. Morison (ed.), *Sources and Documents illustrating the American Revolution and the formation of the Federal Constitution* (2d ed., London, 1929), 15.

the same hath never been forfeited or yielded up, but hath been constantly recognized by the Kings and people of *Great Britain.*" [9]

That day the burgesses also passed, after heated debate and only by a vote of twenty to nineteen, Henry's fifth declaration, which apparently asserted "that the General Assembly of this colony have the only and sole exclusive right and power to lay taxes and impositions upon the inhabitants of this colony and that every attempt to vest such power in any other person or persons whatsoever other than the General Assembly aforesaid has a manifest tendency to destroy British as well as American freedom." [10] And Henry and persons supporting him asked the house, either that day or the following one, to approve two additional resolutions, in substance:

"That his Majesty's liege people, inhabitants of this colony, are not bound to yield obedience to any law or ordinance whatsoever, designed to impose any taxation upon them, other than the laws or ordinances of the General Assembly as aforesaid.

"That any person who shall, by speaking, or writing, assert or maintain, that any person or persons, other than the General Assembly of this colony, with such consent as aforesaid, have any right or authority to lay or impose any tax whatever on the inhabitants thereof, shall be deemed, an enemy to His Majesty's colony." [11]

But these assertions, urging civil disobedience and outlawing individuals who should contend for the constitutionality of the stamp tax, were too much for the house. Forty years later, Jefferson, who as a young man was a fascinated spectator, recalled that Henry went home in the evening of May 30. Henry's departure would have assured their defeat. In any case, whether the orator was on the floor or riding through green fields to Hanover, the burgesses on May 31 refused to accept his sixth and seventh resolutions and even voted to withdraw their approval of the fifth one.[12] The following day the house was dissolved by the lieu-

[9] Kennedy (ed.), *Journals of the House of Burgesses of Virginia, 1761–1765,* p. 360.
[10] *Ibid.,* frontispiece.   [11] Annapolis *Maryland Gazette,* July 4, 1765.
[12] The evidence concerning Patrick Henry's speech, his resolutions, and the behavior of the burgesses is scanty and conflicting. The most helpful analysis is to be found in Morgan and Morgan, *Stamp Act Crisis,* 89–98.

tenant governor, Francis Fauquier, a cultured gentleman who had watched its proceedings in alarm and who had doubtless quietly done all he could to persuade it into a moderate course.

One may be tempted to reduce too sharply the role played by Henry at Williamsburg during those May days, to assess too slightly the significance of what was done by the burgesses, because of what he and they did not do. They did, indeed, fail to counsel resistance; they would not, to their credit, it might be said, brand a defender of the stamp tax as an enemy of Virginia; and they kept silence about the Sugar Act. Nevertheless, the burgesses, speaking for the oldest, the largest, the most populous, and one of the least commercial of the British colonies, had precisely and decisively, *after* the enactment of the Stamp Act, denounced it as beyond the powers of Parliament; and if they had not demanded disobedience, neither had they called for tame acquiescence. It was evident that those who had opposed Henry did not defend the legality of the tax; and it went without saying that many thousands of Virginians were ready to support the official words of the burgesses with their deeds.

The peremptory challenge to Parliamentary power from Virginia was the signal for action in the other American colonies, a signal that was the more impressive because reports circulated concerning the stand taken by the burgesses made it appear even more defiant than it was. Joseph Royle, publisher at Williamsburg of the *Virginia Gazette,* was upset because the house had gone as far as it did, and did not print its resolutions. Dependent for information about them from other sources, newspapers outside Virginia one way and another secured copies of them, perhaps originating from Henry's drafts, which indicated that the burgesses had approved the substance of his fifth, sixth, and even his seventh propositions. The result was extraordinary. In no fewer than eight colonies the lower house aligned itself with the burgesses and solemnly condemned the Stamp Act as *ultra vires,* adopting on occasion even their language. The Massachusetts and Connecticut assemblies now came out sturdily to denounce it as a violation of the rights of their people; and that of Rhode Island, in erroneous emulation of Virginia, went still further, urging its citizens and officials to disobedience. The lower house of Massachusetts, on June 8, also issued an invitation to all the assemblies in British North America asking that they send delegates to a gathering at New York in October to prepare a general protest and demand for redress. The result was the Stamp Act Congress.

Virginia was not physically represented in the Congress, because Fauquier refused to convene the burgesses and so prevented them from accepting the invitation. Nine of the Thirteen Colonies, however, sent more or less official spokesmen. The Congress prepared and sent across the ocean a declaration of American rights, petitions to the King and the House of Commons, and a memorial to the Lords which specifically condemned the stamp tax and portions of the Sugar Act that extended the jurisdiction of admiralty courts (these not employing juries) as beyond the authority of Parliament. Their repeal was demanded. Indeed, the delegates insisted that the Sugar Act be entirely withdrawn, the chief argument against it being the distress it inflicted upon American business. It has been cogently argued that the phrases used by the Congress also describe the Sugar Act in its entirety as an infringement upon their rights.[13] Certainly the delegates did not make their opinion on that point clear. They left no doubt whatever concerning their sentiments with respect to the stamp tax. They said about it for America what the burgesses had said for Virginia.

There could be no answer in England to the outpouring of American sentiment after May until Parliament should meet again, late in the year. The Stamp Act was to go into effect on November 1, however, and it was necessary for the colonists to decide whether they would obey it or disobey. They were overwhelmingly opposed to the tax, but would they refuse to purchase and use the stamps, as Parliament had required them to do? If the royal collectors made available the stamps, necessary for the conduct of legal business and also for the clearance of ships from American ports, some persons almost certainly would buy them; and if a few did, many others would very likely follow their example. Were the Americans to use the stamps, Parliament would probably consider their deeds to be more expressive of

[13] *Ibid.*, 114–15, and references there cited.

73

their sentiments than their words. Ardent souls in Boston determined to prevent the execution of the act, and they supplied an effective method toward that end. On August 14 a mob ransacked the house of Andrew Oliver, who was reported, correctly, to have been appointed stamp distributor for Massachusetts, forced him to flee for his life, and secured a promise from him that he would not try to do the duties of the office. Lieutenant Governor Thomas Hutchinson sought to protect Oliver's property and restore order, and his house was pillaged and gutted by another mob two weeks later.

The helplessness of British civil officials in the face of united American opposition was promptly and nakedly exposed. The sheriff of Suffolk County did not dare to interfere; it was useless to think of calling out the militia; and Governor Francis Bernard retired to Castle William, located on an island in Boston Harbor, where he was safe from physical insult. Nor was he able to secure the assistance of the redcoats to stop further outbreaks. Soldiers could be used by magistrates, under British law, to suppress rioting. But under his instructions from his superiors in London a governor could not call in troops for that purpose without the consent of his council, and Bernard's advisers refused to consent to the sending of an appeal for aid to General Gage at New York. There was a final and even more drastic remedy. Gage could act upon his own initiative, on the ground that revolt existed in Massachusetts. Bernard tried to persuade him to do so, but Gage declared that Boston was afflicted by rioting rather than attempted revolution and would send no troops except upon official request from the governor. He had, in any case, very few troops in locations from which they could promptly be sent to Boston or any other city or town on the seacoast of the Thirteen Colonies. No redcoats appeared on Boston Common. November 1 came and went, but neither Andrew Oliver nor any other person tried to sell stamps in Massachusetts. Moreover, Bernard and other royal officials were forced to permit civil cases to continue, ships to sail, and newspapers to print without them in open violation of the Stamp Act.

Massachusetts had supplied a pattern for successful resistance, and it was copied, though not in detail, in every one of the Thirteen Colonies—an informal alliance of Virginia and Massachusetts in defense of American rights had made its first appearance. In the late summer and fall of 1765 stamp officers and other royal and proprietary personages were menaced by mobs throughout the Thirteen Colonies, and everywhere the result was ultimately the same. The stamp men were unable to sell their papers, the great majority of them being forced to resign by violence and threats of violence. The stamps were either destroyed or secluded so that they could not be used. Newspapers appeared without them; without them upon their clearances ships sailed from Annapolis to Antigua, from Georgetown in South Carolina for Genoa. Here and there the civil courts, because of the opposition of officials, of lawyers who feared to proceed without stamps, and of debtors who enjoyed a respite, ceased to move. The tendency, however, was to open or reopen them, since their failure to function was indirect evidence that the colonists conceded the validity of the Stamp Act.

In Virginia George Mercer, like his fellow stamp officers, suffered, although he escaped some of the agonies which the less fortunate and more obstinate ones underwent. He was burnt in effigy at Dumfries early in September, and again at Williamsburg on September 24.[14] He reached Williamsburg from England on October 30, just two days before the stamps were scheduled to be sold. Because of legal proceedings the town was jammed with visitors. The news of his arrival spread rapidly, and a large crowd of well-known planters and merchants, among whom Richard Henry Lee was conspicuous, confronted him in the street and demanded his resignation. He requested time to consider, and walked on to the coffee house, trailed by an angry if élite mob. There he was received in friendly fashion by Fauquier and other officials sitting on the porch. When the planters and merchants moved to lay hands upon him, Fauquier, courageous as well as courteous, took him by the arm and led him through the crowd, none of which dared to act, to the governor's palace. There Fauquier, who believed that the Virginians would eventually bow to Parliamentary authority and even hoped that the burgesses would retract the resolutions passed in May, told Mercer that

[14] Annapolis *Maryland Gazette*, September 12, October 17 (Supplement), 1765.

"his honor and his interest" required him to cling to his office. The lieutenant governor admitted, however, that Mercer's father and brother, lawyers who were in town, were alarmed for his safety. Should Mercer wish to resign because he feared for his life, Fauquier would not try to dissuade him. That night Mercer left the palace undecided. The following morning, presumably after some discussion with his relatives, he resigned.[15]

The shipping in Virginia's harbors was not hindered for more than a few days at most. Mercer, who had brought a quantity of stamps from England, said he had none assigned to the customs officials. He thus offered an easy escape from an awkward situation to Peter Randolph, Surveyor General of the Customs, who was not only one of *the* Randolphs but also the well-paid clerk of the House of Burgesses. Randolph ordered his customs men to approve clearance papers without the stamps, since they were not available. Fauquier gracefully made the best of things and worked together with Randolph. He soon began to issue to shippers documents certifying that the required stamps were not to be had. The Virginia civil courts were, however, mostly closed after November 1, in the main because the Virginians preferred to strive for the repeal of the Stamp Act rather than constitutional consistency. They were not overly concerned because the idle courts tended to concede the validity of the act. Those inactive courts barred efforts by British creditors to collect the large sums owed them by their planter clients. And, as George Washington predicted, "if a stop be put to our judicial proceedings, I fancy the Merchants of G. Britain trading to the Colonies will not be among the last to wish for a Repeal of it." [16] The Virginians also sought to bring pressure upon those merchants, and through them upon British manufacturers and the British government, by boycott. They, like many colonists, followed the example of the New York City merchants, who collectively undertook to buy no goods from Britain until the tax was rescinded. Importations from the

[15] The Mercers were furious against Richard Henry Lee, and were doubtless responsible for a bitter attack upon him by "An Enemy to Hypocrisy" which appeared in the Williamsburg *Virginia Gazette* (Rind), July 18, 1766. Lee was referred to as a "rogue" who solicited the collectorship and assailed another man for accepting it.
[16] John C. Fitzpatrick (ed.), *The Writings of George Washington* (Washington, 1931–1944), II, 426.

mother country were already falling, because of economic distress. They fell, of course, even further as the result of the boycott; Britain sent goods to Maryland and Virginia worth more than £500,000 in 1764, but valued at less than £400,000 in 1765.[17] The exporters of London, Glasgow, and Bristol suffered from these economic blows and were impelled to do what the colonists desired.

Less injured immediately by the new British policy than were the New Englanders and Pennsylvanians, the Virginians, thanks in large part to Patrick Henry, nevertheless led in defying Britain in the Stamp Act crisis. And there was a sharp hint from the Old Dominion during that crisis that the Virginians might be in the future even more aggressive, should Parliament fail to withdraw the act and otherwise accede to colonial demands. Richard Bland, mulling over events and arguments, wrote and published at Williamsburg in 1766 a remarkable essay, *An Inquiry into the Rights of the British Colonies*. Although he had opposed Henry's famous resolutions, Bland in his *Inquiry* went well beyond them in defining American rights. These were, he said, based upon those of Englishmen and of human beings. He laid greater emphasis upon the rights of mankind, as opposed to the narrower rights of Englishmen, than any earlier writer defending American freedom, save for the erratic and irresponsible James Otis. One of the rights of mankind was government only by the consent of the governed. Bland's argument, shorn of its references to merely English liberties, appealed to Benjamin Franklin and profoundly to Thomas Jefferson and was adopted within nine years by the majority of American leaders.

[17] Arthur M. Schlesinger, *The Colonial Merchants and the American Revolution, 1763–1776* (New York, 1918), 82–83.

CHAPTER VI

THE SOUTH FOLLOWS MR. HENRY

MARYLAND, the creation of the Calverts, was the scene of almost continuous political strife between proprietor and people until the extensive rights of the Baltimore family under their charter of 1632 were at last destroyed in the Revolution. The Calverts tried to raise a feudal régime in Maryland, with themselves as hereditary overlords, and not without result; they also sought to extract revenue from Maryland, and successfully. Their powers and privileges under the charter were increasingly limited in the seventeenth and eighteenth centuries by royal mandate and especially by the encroachments of the lower house of the Maryland Assembly, which claimed and secured for itself as a body representative of the people ever larger authority at the expense of the proprietor, his lieutenant governor, his council, and other officials appointed by him. The lower house was, however, not uniformly successful in its campaigns against proprietary prerogative, not only because the legal position of the Calverts was strong, but also because many Marylanders gave allegiance to them from principle and for pelf. The many offices in the colony at the disposal of the proprietor enabled him to win the support of influential Marylanders and to nourish a "court party." So effective was patronage as a means of maintaining proprietary right and privilege that Cecilius Calvert, who as the secretary of Frederick, Lord Baltimore, managed for him his Maryland affairs, drew up toward the close of the Seven Years' War a scheme to purchase a decisive majority of the lower house. He believed that fifty-six posts of profit and prestige well distributed would win a majority in a body of fifty-eight members.[1] But

[1] Lady Edgar, *A Colonial Governor in Maryland; Horatio Sharpe and His Times, 1753–1773* (London, 1912), 198–200.

this proposal, "on no account designed toward corrupt views," as Calvert blandly described it, was not carried into execution. Accordingly, the "court party" remained a minority in the lower house, which continued to expand its authority, seeking for itself standing equivalent to that of the House of Commons in London. The proprietary edifice was slowly crumbling under its attacks as the Stamp Act crisis approached.[2]

So determined was the "country party"—those opposed to the proprietor and his allies—that it preferred that Maryland do far less than its proper share toward waging the Seven Years' War rather than give up attempts to secure control over expenditures and to tax the lands of the proprietor. Accordingly, while Britain and some of the Thirteen Colonies were straining to wrestle down the Bourbons and their Indian allies in America, Maryland raised few troops and little money, even though the red men ravaged her own frontiers. So bitter was the "country party" that some of its members sought to escape from the clutches of the proprietor through royalization of the colony.[3] Such an extraordinary remedy for the public ills of Maryland could then have brought only a shift from a proprietary pot to a royal pan; and when the news of the Grenville program reached Annapolis and Frederick Town, all thought of finding surcease from proprietary woes in the loving arms of the King vanished. Viscount Baltimore continued until his death to draw a handsome revenue from taxes collected and lands sold above the Potomac. He dissipated it in the dissolute pleasures of an eighteenth-century British rake, and willed his Maryland rights and properties to his illegitimate son Henry Harford.

The people of Maryland were long unable to voice loudly and collectively their sentiments regarding the new British policy, because the Assembly was not in session between November, 1763, and September, 1765.[4] They had not yet learned to declare

[2] Charles A. Barker, *The Background of the Revolution in Maryland* (New Haven, 1940), Chaps. VII–VIII.

[3] The same cure for similar conditions was popular in Pennsylvania in the later years of the Seven Years' War. It will be recalled that Franklin was sent to London in 1757 in part to work for the royalization of Maryland's northern neighbor.

[4] There is an excellent account of the Stamp Act crisis in Barker, *Background of the Revolution in Maryland*, 290–312.

their opinions through means other than the lower house, and Lieutenant Governor Horatio Sharpe preferred that it should not meet, an added reason for not convening it being an outbreak of the dreaded smallpox in the spring of 1765. In consequence there was no formal protest from Maryland against the Grenville program until after it had been substantially adopted. However, the *Maryland Gazette* gave much information about the stamp tax in the spring of 1765, referred to it as "tremendous" on May 2, declared on May 30 that "we were . . . THUNDER-STRUCK" by the news of its passage, and reminded its readers a week later that November 1, the date when the duties would become effective, was the tenth anniversary of the Lisbon earth-quake.[5]

Zachariah Hood of Annapolis was, like George Mercer, in England when the Grenville ministry chose its stamp officers; and he sought and obtained the post of distributor for Maryland. He reached Annapolis toward the end of August and became immediately the object of unwanted attention, for the news of his appointment had preceded him, and Marylanders were no more disposed to permit him to sell stamps than were the Virginians to allow Mercer. By that time, indeed, it was evident that the colonists generally were disposed to take vigorous countermeasures. Hood was met at the dock and forcibly prevented from landing; and when he later managed to slip ashore, he was both shunned and insulted. At Annapolis and elsewhere his effigy was whipped, placed in the pillory, hanged, and burnt. On September 2 a mob of several hundred pulled down a house in which he was preparing to place a cargo of goods, and the *Maryland Gazette* almost simultaneously suggested that "sycophants" and "court cringing politicians" could expect harsh treatment in Maryland. Shortly afterward a British naval officer, Lieutenant Mowbray, appeared in the harbor of Annapolis with the tender of *H.M.S. Hornet.* It was suspected that the vessel carried stamps; and when Mowbray and civilian friends ventured ashore, both he and they were roughly handled by an armed mob. Hood be-

[5] In the Annapolis *Maryland Gazette*, September 5, 1765, Benjamin Welsh announced "That I will pay no tax whatever, but what is laid upon me by my representatives."

THE GOVERNOR'S PALACE (RECONSTRUCTED), WIL-
LIAMSBURG. Courtesy of Colonial Williamsburg, Inc.

came alarmed for his own safety and began to meditate resignation of his post. Being "very uneasy & much terrified," he asked
the advice of Sharpe, who gave him no more helpful counsel than
Fauquier had offered to Mercer. Hood thereupon sailed off to
New York to evade further losses and indignities.[6] There he for
some time hoped to return to Annapolis and to sell stamps from
a British warship. On November 26, however, a New York mob
undertook to complete the work begun at Annapolis. He could
not again escape, and he resigned his post.[7]

Meanwhile, heavy pressure was brought upon Sharpe to compel
him to convene the Assembly, so that protest against the Stamp
Act could be sent to England and that Maryland might be represented in the Stamp Act Congress. Sentiment against the tax was
high throughout the province. Fearing that the members of the
lower house would meet and act upon their own authority, Sharpe
chose to make the best of an awkward situation and issued the
call. The house gathered on September 23.

Meanwhile, Sharpe had informed General Gage that he could
not prevent a mob from burning a shipment of stamps en route
to Maryland "unless Your Excellency can order a Detachment
of the Kings Troops hither to guard it, & to assist in suppressing
any Insurrection which might happen." Gage promptly sent an
order to the governor authorizing him to bring in a hundred Royal
Highlanders from Pittsburgh but suggested that stamps might
be safer on board a British warship than ashore. Sharpe received
Gage's authorization the very day the Assembly met, but he
feared to use it, since a hundred men were hardly enough to compel quiet when Maryland was wholeheartedly and heatedly hostile.[8] He prudently made no attempt to use the authority given
him by Gage. Moreover, when consignments of stamps intended
for Maryland appeared in Chesapeake Bay, he accepted the suggestion of the lower house that they be placed in the care of British

[6] *Ibid.*, August 29, September 5, 1765; William H. Browne (ed.), *Correspondence
of Governor Horatio Sharpe*, III, in *Archives of Maryland* (Baltimore), XIV (1895),
220–26.

[7] Morgan and Morgan, *Stamp Act Crisis*, 154.

[8] Browne (ed.), *Correspondence of Governor Horatio Sharpe*, III, in *Archives of
Maryland*, XIV (1895), 222, 228–29; John R. Alden, *General Gage in America*
(Baton Rouge, 1948), 116.

naval officers cruising off the coast. The house bluntly declared that the stamps must not be landed.

Scolding Sharpe because he—and the smallpox—had so long deprived it of an opportunity to denounce the stamp tax, the lower house quickly and unanimously resolved to send three delegates to the Stamp Act Congress; and the council, though composed of Calvert appointees, consented to the supply of the necessary funds. William Murdock, Edward Tilghman, and Thomas Ringgold were sent to New York to join in asking for "relief from the Burthens and Restraints lately laid on . . . Trade and Commerce, and especially from the . . . Stamp Duties." [9]

On September 28, in a series of forthright resolutions, the lower house formally and unanimously castigated the Stamp Act as a violation of the rights of Englishmen and also of the charter of Maryland, declared that "Taxes and internal Polity" were beyond the authority of Parliament, and roundly asserted that "the . . . imposing levying or Collecting any Tax on or from the Inhabitants of Maryland," except by its Assembly, were "Unconstitutional." In passing, the members also took a fling at the doctrine of "virtual" representation advanced in England to justify the stamp tax. The people of Maryland were not represented in Parliament, they flatly asserted.[10]

Temporarily, most of the Maryland courts closed rather than proceed without the stamps, and the *Maryland Gazette*, the only newspaper in the province, was not published for some weeks. The Frederick County court continued to function, however, without stamps, and several other lower tribunals soon resumed business. The *Gazette* made its reappearance in January, 1766, and in the following month the "Sons of Liberty" organized in Baltimore, Anne Arundel, and Kent counties. These demanded that all offices and the Superior Court at Annapolis reopen. At the beginning of April, overawed, the judges of the Superior Court and other officials complied.[11] Although some of the lower tribunals had not then reopened, it was evident that they would soon have done so,

[9] J. Hall Pleasants (ed.), *Proceedings and Acts of the General Assembly of Maryland, 1764–1765*, in *Archives of Maryland*, LIX (1942), 23.
[10] *Ibid.*, 30–32.
[11] Barker, *Background of the Revolution in Maryland*, 308–11.

when the news of the repeal of the hated tax reached the Chesapeake. In sum, Maryland had utterly refused to obey.

Maryland not only flatly flouted the authority of Parliament but produced the most persuasive polemicist in the defense of American rights in the first great Anglo-American crisis, Daniel Dulany. Able and wealthy, superbly educated at Eton, Cambridge, and the Middle Temple, Dulany was no passionate revolutionary, was content in his comfortable way of life at Annapolis. Privately prosperous and publicly honored with office, he ultimately found it impossible to share the dangers and destinies of the patriots and became a cautious loyalist. But he, like almost all Americans, found the Stamp Act to be most offensive; and it was he that most effectively argued against the constitutional power of Parliament to levy the tax. His *Considerations on the Propriety of imposing Taxes in the British Colonies, for the purpose of raising a Revenue, by Act of Parliament,* a pamphlet which first appeared at Annapolis in the autumn of 1765, was extraordinarily popular among the colonists, molding their views and also, to a degree, those of William Pitt, whose influence was to make possible the repeal of the detested tax.

Dulany was peculiarly successful in demolishing the contention that the Americans were "virtually" represented in Parliament and that the Stamp Act was therefore unquestionably within the powers of that body. American protests against the act when it was first proposed had asserted that taxation without representation violated the rights of Englishmen. Grenville and others supporting him thought it easy to dispose of the argument offered by the untutored colonists, on the ground " 'that the colonies were all virtually represented in Parliament, in the same manner as those of the subjects in Great Britain, who did not vote for representatives.' " [12] The Grenvilleites thus incautiously admitted the doctrine that representation was inseparable from taxation. If the theory of "virtual" representation could be demolished, the Grenville position would collapse; and Dulany made it clear that "virtual" representation was preposterous with respect to the stamp duties. He conceded that the many unenfranchised in England might be "virtually" represented, since there were men

[12] Morgan and Morgan, *Stamp Act Crisis,* 76–77.

in the Commons who had been elected by their neighbors, whose interests could conceivably be described to be their own. He then pointed out in a devastating argument that no American voted for a member of the Commons nor had a neighbor who did, and that there was accordingly no one in that body to speak for the Americans or to defend their interests.

Unlike Richard Bland and lesser figures among the colonists who were tempted to question totally the powers of Parliament in America, Dulany freely admitted that Parliament was sovereign in the British empire, save in the field of taxation. And, while he asserted that the colonists "ought with spirit, and vigour, and alacrity, to bid defiance to tyranny," he counseled a moderate measure to secure the repeal of the act, that the Americans make their own clothing, so that by ceasing to buy British manufactures they could bring economic pressure upon London politicians.[13]

Virginia's neighbor to the southward was far more outspoken in its denunciations of the Grenville measures than was Maryland, and at least equally determined in its defiance of Parliament and crown. Once a part of the magnificent domain of Carolina given by King Charles II to eight speculative gentlemen and courtiers, North Carolina had become a royal and separate colony by 1729 and had by that time largely escaped from the clutches of the proprietors. Its people had fought against the original proprietors and their successors; and they continued to struggle with royal governors and other defenders of British prerogative. In no royal colony had the lower house striven more heartily and more vigorously to expand its powers at the expense of His Majesty's officials. By 1763 it was well on the road toward establishing itself as a local House of Commons, for it had kept full pace with its counterparts of Virginia and South Carolina in their common effort to limit the power of the crown. It had substantially seized control of finances; it had secured the right to regulate the length of its sessions; and it had even won authority to choose the asso-

[13] Aubrey C. Land, *The Dulanys of Maryland* (Baltimore, 1955), offers a recent scholarly study of Daniel Dulany and of his father, Daniel Dulany the elder. By 1770 Dulany was critical of William Pitt and Lord Camden, heroes of the colonials, and had turned away from the American cause. Landon Carter Diary, May 5, 1770.

ciate justices of the superior courts of the colony. That North Carolina should be in the forefront in the contest with Parliament and crown in the fateful years 1764–1766 is not, therefore, astonishing, despite the facts that the North Carolinians were little injured by British trade restrictions, and that they received bounties from Britain for the production of naval stores.

Yet it is rather surprising that the lower house of North Carolina was one of only two such bodies, the other being that of New York, to attack both the Sugar Act and the stamp duties as unconstitutional before the latter became law. When other colonies, save for New York, were describing the Sugar Act as hurtful but avoiding direct denunciation of it as beyond the powers of Parliament—perhaps because it had already been enacted and because they doubted the wisdom of trying to prevent its execution—the representatives of North Carolina spoke out boldly and precisely, even though the economic interests of the North Carolinians were far less grievously injured by the Sugar Act than were those of the inhabitants of the New England and other commercial colonies. In a formal address to Governor Arthur Dobbs on October 31, 1764, they declared that "it is with the utmost concern we observe our commerce circumscribed in its most beneficial branches diverted from its natural channel and burthened with new taxes and impositions laid on us without our privity and consent, and against what we esteem our inherent right, and exclusive privilege of imposing our own taxes." [14] When word came to North Carolina that the Stamp Act had been enacted, the Assembly was not in session, nor was it convened until long after the Stamp Act crisis had ended. As a result there was no way in 1765 by which the people of North Carolina could officially express themselves, nor were they able to send delegates to the Stamp Act Congress.

William Tryon, a military man and a respectable one, succeeded Dobbs at the end of March, 1765. He managed to avoid serious controversy during the long, hot summer that followed, fortunately for him, since he was suffering from malaria. At length, however, he, too, became enmeshed in difficulties. The North

[14] William L. Saunders (ed.), *The Colonial Records of North Carolina* (Raleigh, 1886–1890), VI, 1261.

Carolinians, disturbed by a general failure of crops, became restive as the time approached when the Stamp Act was to become effective; there were meetings of citizens in the summer and early fall at Cross Creek, Edenton, New Bern, and Wilmington at which the participants pledged themselves not to use the stamps; and on October 19 a Wilmington mob of "near five hundred people" assembled, hanged and burned an effigy of a gentleman who had counseled obedience, and drank a toast to "Liberty, Property, and No Stamp-Duty." Twelve days later, on Halloween, another huge crowd there gathered to bury an effigy of Liberty, but happily discovered she was still "alive" just as she was about to be interred.[15]

In mid-November the North Carolinians disposed of their stamp distributor, Dr. William Houston of Duplin County, a man unfortunate in his friendships. He had not sought the office, but had been given it at the instance of Henry McCulloh, who had refused it for himself.[16] When a letter addressed to him from the Stamp Office in London reached Wilmington, it was handed about, as letters so often were at that time; and interested persons in Wilmington did not need to open it to discover its purport. When Dr. Houston came to town on November 16, to receive his mail, he was given time to read it and was then visited by three or four hundred men, who vigorously suggested that he would do well to avoid contact with the stamps. He indicated that he was impressed by their arguments, was paraded in his armchair about town, and was given three cheers. The same crowd persuaded Andrew Steuart, publisher of the *North-Carolina Gazette*, that it was quite proper to print and circulate his newspaper without using stamps, and it merrily celebrated two victories for "LIBERTY" with toasts and "several sorts of liquors." [17]

Tryon made a determined and rather shrewd attempt to soften the North Carolinians. He invited fifty of the most prominent men of Brunswick, New Hanover, and Bladen counties to wine and dine with him at his home near Brunswick on November 18, harangued them with sweet words, and offered generous inducements to dissuade them—and their fellow citizens of North Carolina—from opposing the collection of the new duties. He

[15] *Ibid.*, VII, 123–24. [16] Morgan and Morgan, *Stamp Act Crisis*, 156.
[17] Saunders (ed.), *Colonial Records of North Carolina*, VII, 124–25.

conceded that there was not enough cash in the colony to purchase the stamps for more than one year, and promised to use his influence in London to secure at least part exemption from the duties for North Carolina—if her people peacefully used the stamps until the act was repealed or modified in their favor. He held out another seductive bait, remarking that North Carolinians obeying Parliament might gather in lucrative trade abandoned by the people of other colonies defying it. Still further, he offered to pay out of his own pocket for the stamps required upon official documents emanating from his office. It was all in vain, for his guests refused to bite at any of his lures. The following morning, in a formal address, they informed him that "submission to any part of so oppressive and (as we think) so unconstitutional" a measure would open "a direct inlet for slavery, which all mankind will endeavor to avoid." Said they, "An admission of part, would put it out of our power to refuse with any propriety, a submission to the whole." While they would do their utmost to prevent insult and injury to officers of the crown, they felt that they could not protect stamp men against the "resentment of the country." [18]

Firm though they were in refraining from taking Tryon's hand, the men of the Cape Fear region must have been tempted; and they were punished for their independence. The governor, the customs men, and judges brought business to a standstill, preventing the movement of ships and the operations of the courts. The distress which bad harvests had inflicted upon the North Carolinians was increased, although the ports outside of the Cape Fear district soon resumed their activities, and without using stamps. In view of sentiments of the North Carolinians and the fact that no distributor was available, Tryon prudently chose not to try to land a consignment of stamps which reached the mouth of the Cape Fear in *H.M.S. Diligence* on November 28. Instead he requested Captain Constantine Phipps of the *Diligence* to keep them on board, and that officer agreed to do so.[19] Phipps remained on the coast for more than two months, but kept almost as cool as he afterward did in his famous exploration of the Arctic, and avoided stirring up trouble. Captain Jacob Lobb of *H.M.S. Viper,* who also came to the Cape Fear, was less prudent

[18] *Ibid.,* 127–30, 143. [19] *Ibid.,* 143–44.

and stung the inhabitants of the southeastern part of the colony into armed resistance. Captain Lobb chose to assert the authority of Britain by seizing three merchant vessels which entered the Cape Fear River with unstamped clearance papers; and the King's attorney, Robert Jones, with even greater temerity, asserted the seizures to be legal and recommended to William Dry, the collector at Brunswick, that steps be taken to condemn the ships. "Philanthropos," in a letter which appeared in the *North-Carolina Gazette* of February 12, 1766, proposed a remedy consistent with his pseudonym, demanding the arrest of the offending officers and the immediate opening of all closed ports. "Wilmingtonians, Brunswickers, and New-Hanoverians," he cried, " 'tis Liberty calls you, dear Liberty." [20]

The vehement urging of "Philanthropos" was doubtless quite unnecessary. On February 18 once more a huge crowd gathered in Wilmington, formally pledged faith and honor, "at any risque whatever" to prevent "entirely" the execution of the act. Choosing leaders, the Wilmingtonians proceeded to Brunswick on the following day, being joined by hundreds of men as they went. More than a thousand, many of them armed, appeared at Brunswick, where they offered protection to Tryon and the threat of violence to other naval and civil officers, unless the three ships were promptly released and the port of Brunswick immediately opened to traffic. Among their leaders were John Ashe, speaker of the lower house of Assembly, Moses John DeRosset, mayor of Wilmington, Cornelius Harnett, Hugh Waddell, Thomas Lloyd, Alexander Lillington, and others conspicuous in the colony. Tryon scoffed at the offer of protection, asked Captains Lobb and Phipps to defend Fort Johnston in case of need, and begged Lobb not to yield to the insurgents. But the captain, after indicating to the governor that he would continue to keep possession of at least one of the ships, bent before their demands. He had already been denied supplies from the shore, and he did not like the look of things. Rather than try to use the guns at Fort Johnson, he had them spiked to prevent their use by the aroused citizens, the insurgents occupying the fort as well as the town of Brunswick. On February 20 Lobb, after conferring with some of their leaders,

[20] *Ibid.*, 168a, 168b.

released the three ships and substantially gave in to their demands. Within a few hours every customs man in the vicinity, and other officials as well, solemnly promised to make no further attempt to execute the Stamp Act. The following day the armed citizens triumphantly marched off and joyously sailed away to their homes.

Tryon was infuriated by his own helplessness and by the failure of Lobb to resist. However, the Stamp Act had become a dead letter in North Carolina. Departing for England, Constantine Phipps turned over the stamps in his possession to Lobb, who placed them in Fort Johnston, where they did no more injury than its guns had done. On April 15 Houston, who had earlier managed to save his commission, was forced to abandon it to Mayor DeRosset. Otherwise North Carolina was calm from the latter part of February until June, when it became known that Parliament had repealed the Stamp Act. The quiet was then broken by celebrations of various sorts, in which Tryon himself participated. He had escaped public censure, even though he had removed from his office as assistant judge for Salisbury district Maurice Moore, because Moore had both written and marched against British authority. He might have done well not to touch Moore, for he placed in his room Edmund Fanning of notorious memory.[21]

Were it true that things economic dictate the feelings and actions of mankind, there should have been no serious protest from South Carolina against the British "new course." At the close of the Seven Years' War that colony was prosperous and had long been so. In no other of His Majesty's possessions in North America was there, at least for those born free and in families not destitute, greater opportunity to secure wealth. Moreover, South Carolina suffered little from the British Navigation Acts and received more liberal largess from Britain, in the form of a bounty upon indigo, than any other American colony. While her plantation economy ultimately could not match in the production

[21] Most of the available relevant documents upon the later stages of the Stamp Act crisis in North Carolina are printed *ibid.*, 168b–223. It should be added that two later accounts of the crisis in that colony, in Samuel A. Ashe, *History of North Carolina* (Greensboro, 1908–1925), I, 312–25, and Hugh T. Lefler and Albert R. Newsome, *North Carolina; The History of a Southern State* (Chapel Hill, 1954), 179–84, have been very useful.

of riches others in which commerce and industry were major elements, an observer in the year 1763 wandering through Charleston and the adjacent Low Country might well fail to see the fundamental inferiority of the South Carolinian economy and would instead probably consider himself to be in one of the most promising areas in the Thirteen Colonies. The only obvious evidence pointing toward a darker future was the fact that the white population of South Carolina was far smaller than that of her neighbors to the north, while her slaves were becoming ever more numerous both because of propagation and because of heavy importations.

While it is true that the British acts of trade channeled to the benefit of the mother country the principal exports of South Carolina, rice, indigo, and deerskins, in the main Parliament directed these products into economic paths which they would in any case have followed. Moreover, British limiting of manufacturing in America had little meaning in the colony, where there was trifling interest in processing and fashioning of raw materials. The planters of South Carolina were pleased to buy clothing, furniture, and ironware from their British makers. And they could afford such luxuries. They did not find growing rice and indigo to be so unprofitable that they sought to turn to other products; rather they wished to devote more land and more Negroes to producing more rice and more indigo. They were not submerged in debt as were the tobacco planters of Virginia. While it has been contended that economic distress among the tobacco planters drove the Virginia aristocracy into revolt against Britain, it has never been argued that the rice and indigo magnates of South Carolina who struggled in defense of American rights were similarly motivated.

Certainly the planters of South Carolina were not without means of expressing themselves, for they easily dominated the Commons House, the body of elected representatives in the colony, in 1763 and for many years thereafter. The Piedmont, beginning to fill with settlers, especially from the northward, sent no members as yet to the Commons House; the mechanics and artisans of Charleston could not control the elections of members from that city; and its merchants, themselves planters and would-be planters, could not and would not long stand against the wishes of the landed aristocracy. A few dozen families, including the Pinckneys, Rutledges, Manigaults, Middletons, and Lowndeses, directed the Commons House and through it spoke for South Carolina. They also composed the upper house, or council, until after the Seven Years' War, when natives of Britain and British officeholders increasingly found their way into that body.

The Commons House of South Carolina had sturdily defended local right and privilege against proprietary and royal prerogative. In 1719 the proprietors were deprived of their authority in the colony at the instance of the settlers; and thereafter the Commons House devoted itself to diminishing the powers of the crown, with success. The very name of the body indicates its claim to be the equivalent of the House of Commons in England, an assertion which was largely translated into fact. The Commons House secured almost complete domination of finances and ultimately even chose several of the most important officials in the colony. In 1756 one of its champions even went so far as to question the right of the royal council to sit as the upper house of the Assembly.[22] It is not, therefore, surprising that Governor Thomas Boone became involved in a bitter struggle with the house in 1762 when he took it upon himself to deny that Christopher Gadsden was entitled to a seat in it on the ground that the church wardens supervising the election had been guilty of technical violations of law. The Commons House furiously insisted that it had the right to judge of the qualifications of its own members, and that no law and no governor could ever deprive it of that right. Boone obstinately refused to abandon his ill-founded stand, and on December 16, 1762, the house formally resolved to engage in no further business with him until he did so. Accordingly, the Assembly did not function again until the spring of 1764, after Boone had left for England.[23] Soon after this hard-fought con-

[22] Jack P. Greene, "The Quest for Power of the Lower Houses of Assembly in the Southern Royal Colonies" (Ph.D. dissertation, Duke University, 1956), 167–68

[23] There are good descriptions of this celebrated struggle in Edward McCrady, *The History of South Carolina under the Royal Government, 1719–1776* (New York, 1899), 353–66; W. Roy Smith, *South Carolina As a Royal Province, 1719–1776* (New York, 1903), 340–47; and David D. Wallace, *The History of South Carolina* (New York, 1934), II, 38–40. Wallace's *History* offers in Volume II the best brief account

troversy came to a close, the news reached Charleston that the Sugar Act had been passed and that the stamp tax was under consideration in London. The Commons House in general, and Christopher Gadsden in particular, readily transferred their hostility from Boone to the stamp duties.

Yet South Carolina was at first very moderate in expressing disapproval of the stamp duties. Early in the fall of 1764 Charles Garth, agent for the colony in London, was urged by the Committee of Correspondence of the lower house to join agents for other colonies in the imperial capital in a campaign to persuade the Grenville ministry to drop the proposed tax. And, while Garth was informed that it was inconsistent with "the inherent right of every British subject, not to be taxed but by his own consent," he was also told that "we shall submit most dutifully at all times to acts of Parliament." Even Gadsden, soon to be so conspicuous in opposition to British measures, subscribed to the latter statement.[24] After all, the Sugar Act did little injury to the interests of South Carolina; the stamp tax was not yet a reality; and payment of the stamp duties would not greatly affect the planters.

After the enactment of the duties, however, there was a decided shift in sentiment in South Carolina. William Bull II, lieutenant governor, who became temporarily the chief executive in the colony after the departure of Boone, determined to do his duty and his best to enforce the act. Himself a Carolinian, a planter, a man of character, and one well educated, he was much respected and had influence. Moreover, William Wragg and Henry Laurens, two men of wealth and standing, though condemning the duties, counseled obedience while repeal was sought. But word that the colonies to the northward were preparing to do all that might be done to prevent the execution of the act stirred other South Carolinians to action; and the Commons House no longer advised obedience. Rather it arranged to send

---

of South Carolina in the Revolutionary period. Elsewhere, the work of McCrady is frequently cited, because it is more detailed and because it is generally sound. It is well, however, to consult Wallace upon important and disputed points.

[24] R. W. Gibbes (ed.), *Documentary History of the American Revolution . . . 1764-1782* (New York, 1853-1857), I, 1-6.

Christopher Gadsden, Thomas Lynch, and John Rutledge to speak for South Carolina in the Stamp Act Congress and itself vigorously stigmatized the duties as unconstitutional.

At New York Gadsden and Lynch were among the most forward in asserting American rights, even suggesting that the Congress petition only the crown for repeal, on the ground that the Americans properly had nought to do with Parliament; [25] and at Charleston in October force was added to words. On October 18 the *Planter's Adventure*, carrying a consignment of stamps, cast anchor in the harbor under the guns of Fort Johnson; and the papers were unloaded in the lightly garrisoned post. In the city it was correctly suspected that the ship carried either stamps or a stamp distributor; and the following morning an effigy of a stamp collector upon a gallows bearing the words "Liberty and no Stamp Act" was found in the central part of the city. Crowds gathered about it, and in the evening a huge mob, ignorant of the location of the stamps, paraded through the streets with the effigy and sought to find them. The mob went first to the home of George Saxby, who had been appointed stamp inspector for the Carolinas and Bermuda, and who was then en route from England. Captain William Coats, Saxby's tenant, could not prevent a search of the house, which the crowd vainly ransacked, causing much damage. The mob then went in search of Caleb Lloyd, commandant of Fort Johnson, who had been chosen distributor for South Carolina, but failed to find him. The following day Lloyd sought to ward off unwanted attention by announcing that he had not been commissioned, that he did not know he had been appointed, that he had no stamps. On October 20 Bull tried to put a stop to further mob action by offering a reward to anyone who would furnish information regarding those who had invaded Saxby's house, but to no avail. Three days later a wild rumor spread that the stamps had been surreptitiously deposited in Laurens' house; and at midnight a mob heated with liquor, some of its members carrying cutlasses, forced its way into the house and spent more than an hour exchanging remarks and profanity with Laurens and vainly searching his premises. Laurens was furious and considered that he had been persecuted at the

[25] *Ibid.,* 9.

instance of Gadsden, a "malicious villain." [26] The same mob also visited Chief Justice Charles Shinner, who soothed by inviting the men to search his house and supplying them with punch. It is even said that he drank a favorite toast with them, "Damnation to the Stamp Act." [27] There might have been more visits to persons suspected of harboring the stamps had Bull not announced that they were in Fort Johnson.

Thus far, mob action seemed to have achieved nothing, but results were soon manifest. By October 27 both Saxby and Lloyd, now definitely known to have been appointed stamp officers, were in Fort Johnson. There they announced they would not try to sell stamps until the British government had had an opportunity to consider American protests; and on the following day they made a similar declaration before a huge crowd in the city. Shipping ceased to move outward and the courts closed on November 1, but public opinion persuaded Bull to arrange for ships to depart without stamped papers in February. The Court of Common Pleas in Charleston failed to resume its activities until news came of the repeal of the Stamp Act, because of the opposition of Chief Justice Shinner and Dougal Campbell, its clerk. Ultimately Campbell was forced to express regret that he had acted so offensively; and Shinner, who had secured his post through a powerful friend in England rather than through his merits, was suspended at the request of both the Commons House and the council. While resistance to the Stamp Act was not unanimous in South Carolina, it was nevertheless successful.[28]

The principal moving spirit in organizing that resistance was Christopher Gadsden, whose activities after his return from the Stamp Act Congress included a major role in securing the punishment of Shinner. In 1765 and thereafter Gadsden was steadily in the forefront among South Carolinians in the assertion of American rights. His many writings in defense of those rights were tedious and verbose. He was, however, tireless as well as tiresome

[20] David D. Wallace, *The Life of Henry Laurens* (New York, 1915), 118–19.

[27] John Drayton, *Memoirs of the American Revolution* (Charleston, 1821), 48.

[28] Enlightening reports on the crisis are contained in letters from Bull to the Board of Trade, November 3, 1765, February 6, May 8, and May 20, 1766, in Sainsbury Transcripts.

in argument; and his sober, steady determination to oppose British "tyranny" has led historians—properly, it would seem—to couple his name with that of Samuel Adams, the most potent fomenter of popular discontent in the northern colonies, who may appropriately be called "the Christopher Gadsden of Massachusetts."

Georgia had no Gadsden, and it had less reason to complain of the Stamp Act than any of the other Thirteen Colonies. The newest of the Thirteen Colonies, Georgia was subsidized from its beginning by Parliament; four fifths of its finances were supplied from London during the first twenty years of its existence, and thereafter, until 1775, about £4,000 yearly.[29] In consequence, it could not reasonably be argued in Georgia that the tax was unjust, though it might be contended that it was burdensome. Despite the gifts which steadily came from London, the Commons House of that colony from its appearance in 1754 had steadily claimed for itself all the rights of its counterpart across the Savannah,[30] and not without success. On the other hand, Georgia's royal governors Henry Ellis and James Wright had ably defended the prerogative of the crown. Both were wealthy, worthy, and respected; and Wright, an American born, who served from 1760 to 1775, and again from 1779 to 1782, retained throughout his stays in Georgia a certain popularity, in spite of his steady loyalty to Britain.

The first official reaction in Georgia to the new British program was an instruction sent in April, 1765, to William Knox, agent for the colony in London, asking him to work against the passage of the Stamp Act but to stress its flattening effect upon Georgia purses rather than to deny its constitutionality, although doubt was expressed concerning the right of Parliament to levy the duties.[31] The general belief in Georgia, as in her sister colonies to the northward, was that they were beyond the powers of Parlia-

[29] Albert B. Saye, *New Viewpoints in Georgia History* (Athens, 1943), 134–35.

[30] William Wright Abbot, III, "Georgia under the Royal Governors, 1754–1775" (Ph.D. dissertation, Duke University, 1953), 15. The account of the Stamp Act crisis in Georgia given in the text is substantially based upon Chapter V of this dissertation, which deals with the subject in detail. An older brief description is offered in Charles C. Jones, Jr., *History of Georgia* (Boston, 1883), II, 56–72.

[31] *Collections of the Georgia Historical Society* (Savannah), VI (1904), 32.

ment. The lower house was unable officially to send emissaries to the Stamp Act Congress because Wright refused to call it into session, but sixteen of its members gathered at the call of Alexander Wylly, its speaker, and indicated their approval of the Congress. As word came to Georgia of the rebellious behavior of the older British colonies, many Georgians mulled over schemes to deal with stamps and a stamp distributor, should either appear at Savannah. The usual crowd destroyed the customary effigy of the stamp agent on October 25; and three days later a gathering of "Sons of Liberty" at Machenry's Tavern in the capital agreed that the distributor for the colony must be forced to resign.

Governor Wright, though he apparently did not approve of the Stamp Act, resolved to enforce it; and he was loyally supported by his royal council, especially by James Habersham, its president and his close friend, who considered the duties unconstitutional but insisted upon obedience coupled with request for repeal. On October 30 five gentlemen received letters "from the inhabitants of Savannah" accusing them of stamp agency or possession of the papers and demanding that they clear themselves. Three of them protested their innocence, one sailed for England, and the fifth, Habersham, refused to answer. Wright and the legislature offered a reward for knowledge concerning the authors of the letters; and the governor forbade all "riots, routs, and tumultuous assemblies." On November 1 he saw to it that all official business requiring the use of stamps was promptly stopped. The sole exception to this enforcement was that vessels were permitted to leave Savannah; and when copies of the act became available early in December, he and the customs officials also closed the port. To preserve order in Savannah he called in to the town sixty-four rangers, mounted troops in royal pay who had been raised to protect the frontiers of the colony. To avoid unnecessary trouble, however, he prudently permitted the legislature to discharge William Knox, who had pamphleteered in defense of the act.

Meanwhile, a shipment of stamps had arrived and had been placed in a warehouse, without disturbance. Wright and his council decided that they must be sold, with or without the services of George Angus, the distributor, who had not yet appeared in the colony; and they were supported by many merchants of Savannah, principally Scottish-born, who asked the governor to put the papers on sale so that they could send cargoes to sea in numerous vessels idly anchored in their harbor. On January 2, 1766, Wright cowed a mob of two hundred men in the port, personally leading a detachment of rangers who removed the stamps to their guardhouse. Angus having arrived at Tybee Island, the governor had him quietly brought to his own house three days later. Wright reopened the ports of Savannah and Sunbury on January 7, and Angus supplied stamps for dozens of sets of clearance papers. Angus soon fled from Georgia, but Wright faced down the "Liberty Boys" of Savannah, and many vessels set sail to sea, although he found it prudent to promise to issue stamps only when keeping a ship in port caused hardship. He had yet to deal with the country people, who gathered by hundreds and approached the capital with arms toward the end of January. It was said that they intended to shoot him unless use of the stamps ceased immediately. He sent the remainder of the papers which Angus had left in his hands to Fort George on Cockspur Island for safekeeping and thence to *H.M.S. Speedwell,* which appeared in the Savannah River when he most needed help. Captain Fanshawe of the *Speedwell* not only received the stamps but sent twenty armed sailors into Savannah to support Wright. With these, the rangers, and a few merchants who came to his assistance, he defied the country people, three hundred of whom finally entered the town on February 4. They dared do nothing and, after a few hours in which open fighting seemed very likely, dispersed, saying they would return in greater force. They did not reappear. Public opinion in Georgia swung to the side of "law and order." Wright had won his struggle, and the Stamp Act was not successfully defied in Georgia.

There was far less disposition in the infant British colonies of the Floridas to challenge Britain than there was in Georgia. The civilian population of East Florida was very scanty; there was as yet no legislature through which popular protest might be made; and St. Augustine, the capital, was garrisoned by British troops. Governor James Grant, a soldier by profession, saw to it that the infection of rebellion did not spread southward from Savannah.

In West Florida, where civilians were more numerous, there were murmurs. Again, however, no engine for organizing opposition existed. The settlers were in part French- and British-born, and inclined to respect Parliamentary authority; and the presence of garrisons of redcoats at Pensacola and Mobile suggested the futility of resistance. Governor George Johnstone informed his superiors in London that he had lost popularity by enforcing the act, but enforce it he had.[32]

Although the Stamp Act was executed in Georgia, the Floridas, Nova Scotia, and Quebec, it was flouted everywhere between the Kennebec and Savannah rivers. Among the Thirteen Colonies only in Georgia was resistance unsuccessful; and it is to be believed that Wright must eventually have given in to the "Sons of Liberty," had not the duties been repealed in the spring of 1766. The Southern colonies, with fewer economic grievances against Britain, were as ardent in the defense of American rights as were the New Englanders. Tryon, Bull, and Wright asserted that the Carolinas and Georgia were inspired to resist by the example of appeals from the north. It was, however, Virginia which had taken the first long step toward rebellion; and Carolinians and Georgians needed little prodding to push them into the common struggle of the people of the older British colonies against the Stamp Act.

[32] Wilfred B. Kerr, "The Stamp Act in the Floridas, 1765–1766," in *Mississippi Valley Historical Review* (Cedar Rapids), XXI (1934–1935), 463–70.

CHAPTER VII

THE TOWNSHEND CRISIS

T HE resolution, the passion, and the virtual unanimity
displayed by the colonists in their struggle against the
execution of the Stamp Act thoroughly frustrated all attempts to compel obedience in the Thirteen Colonies by the
use of civil authority. It profited nothing for a governor to pro-
claim the illegality of rioting, and calls upon constables, town
watches, sheriffs, and militia—these being American—to repress
tumult could bring only derision and laughter. Repression was
possible only through the use of troops and tars in British pay;
and these were not available in sufficient numbers in the later
months of 1765, save in Georgia. There were several governors
who considered calling upon General Gage for armed support
but did not do so because of prudence and the fact that they
could not secure the consent of their councils. One or two of
these would have been pleased to have the general send troops
to their assistance upon his own responsibility. Gage, however,
would not act to suppress disorder except at the request and
under the direction of civil officers. He would himself intervene
only to counter armed rebellion. Indeed, he had few troops who
could be employed even for that purpose and but some dozens
of men near the scenes of greatest disorder. The army was scattered between Mackinac Island and Mobile, St. Augustine and
Fort Chartres on the upper Mississippi. Gage collected a small
force in New York City to protect his arms depot and moved
detachments from interior posts to Albany and Lancaster, whence
they could be brought to New York City or Philadelphia in case
of need. He would do no more,[1] and the question whether or not

[1] Alden, *General Gage in America*, 113–25.

the redcoats should be used had to be answered by his superiors in London. British politicians chose not to coerce in 1766, and British politicians, particularly Charles Townshend, created a second Anglo-American crisis in 1767. Again Parliamentary power to tax in America was sharply challenged, again the British empire was threatened with dismemberment.

Had George Grenville had his way, the refusal of the colonists to pay the stamp duties and their harsh treatment of British officials in America would have been countered by the exertion of force, for Grenville contemptuously rejected both the constitutional arguments and pleas of hardship offered by the Americans. Further, he thought it wise, as did Gage, to deal sternly with disobedience before it should flower into revolution. But Grenville was no longer at the head of the cabinet when information concerning American resistance poured into London. George III had been temporarily insane, and Grenville had sought to provide a regency for future emergencies, one without the King's mother. Enraged, the King had dismissed him, and the Marquis of Rockingham had replaced him. While the new chief minister was no more impressed by American constitutional arguments than was Grenville, he preferred to try to soothe rather than to try to crush the Americans. Diminishing trade with America at a time when Britain had not yet recovered from postwar depression also led him to seek repeal of the obnoxious measure. British merchants and manufacturers had been injured by an American boycott of British goods which threatened them with ruin, and the merchants also had felt the effects of nonpayment of debts by their American customers; both groups accordingly supported Rockingham by petitioning for repeal. William Pitt, who found the colonial argument against the constitutionality of the duties completely convincing, lent his powerful support to the ministry. Benjamin Franklin, too, gave a helping hand, appearing as a witness at the bar of the House of Commons and offering a description of the Americans as a loyal and dutiful people who firmly believed the levies to be contrary to their rights as Englishmen and regretfully found it necessary to oppose their collection. George III informed his many followers in Parliament that they were free to vote as they wished; and in

March, 1766, the repealer was carried, despite bitter opposition offered by Grenville and many others, both in the Lords and Commons.

So numerous and so vehement were those denouncing the repealer that Rockingham, in order to secure its passage, was forced to couple with it the Declaratory Act, which asserted that Parliament had "full power and authority to make laws and statutes of sufficient force and authority to bind the colonies and people of America, subjects of the crown of Great Britain, in all cases whatsoever." This remarkable pronunciamento, which displeased only Pitt and his scanty following in Parliament, and which was approved by heavy majorities in both houses, in the phrase "in all cases whatsoever" peremptorily denied the validity of all American arguments against taxation by Parliament.[2] With few exceptions British politicians fancied that the powers of Parliament and crown were limited in America only as they might be in Britain.

British politicians not only rejected American constitutional arguments; they misunderstood them. Rockingham and his followers preferred to believe that the colonists distinguished sharply between internal taxes, such as the stamp duties, and external levies, those collected at the ports; that they had no constitutional objections to external taxation, whether to regulate trade or to secure revenue. In fact, however, the Sugar Act had been condemned by many Americans as beyond the powers of Parliament, in that it was intended to provide revenue as well as protection. Trying to please the colonists, the Rockingham ministry in the spring of 1766 repealed the threepence per gallon duty on foreign molasses and replaced it with a tax of one penny per gallon on all molasses imported into the mainland ports. So doing, it levied a duty which could in no way be described as regulative of trade but was purely directed toward securing cash. Were this measure acceptable to the colonists, they could hardly in logic object to other taxes collected in their ports to extract a far larger revenue. They failed to denounce it, because they did not consider the

---

[2] William T. Laprade, "The Stamp Act in British Politics," in *American Historical Review* (New York), XXXV (1929–1930), 735–57; Morgan and Morgan, *Stamp Act Crisis*, Chap. XV.

new duty to be burdensome, and because they were so pleased to have gained the victory with respect to the Stamp Act. Nor did they sharply condemn the Declaratory Act, because it was not in itself injurious. Had they made it clear that they would oppose substantial levies collected in their ports for revenue, they might have prevented the passage of the Townshend duties of 1767, which quickly caused the second Anglo-American crisis.

As it happened, many members of Parliament believed the Americans objected only to internal taxes, and many were disposed to tax them regardless of their constitutional objections. There was resentment in London because the repeal of the Stamp Act had been extorted. That resentment was increased by the refusal of New York to comply with the Quartering Act in connection with troops stationed at Albany and also by the tardy and grudging responses of some of the colonial assemblies to a British demand that they compensate those who had lost property in the Stamp Act riots. Meanwhile, British taxes on land remained at the high level they had reached during the Seven Years' War, and the cost of the army in America continued to fall upon the British treasury. Early in 1767 there was tinder available for a conflagration, and "Champagne Charley" Townshend thoughtlessly applied the match.

It is unlikely that the Rockingham ministry would have done anything to provoke uproar in America, but the Rockingham people were driven from office in August, 1766, by George III and William Pitt, who proceeded to form a "broad-bottom" government of "All the Talents," the talents actually being found among the personal followings of its two creators. Nor is it probable that this new and novel ministry would have caused anguish in America, had it been dominated by Pitt, as might have been expected. But Pitt temporarily lost prestige with the British people by simultaneously seeking and obtaining the Earldom of Chatham, and removed to the Lords. What was more important, the gout soon drove him to the waters of Bath and away from public business. Even so, had the Duke of Grafton, his follower, who was technically head of the cabinet, determinedly followed in his master's steps, an American explosion might have been prevented. Grafton, however, was neither gifted nor experienced nor resolute and was devoted to private pleasures, particularly a beautiful mistress, rather than public perplexities; and Charles Townshend, chancellor of the exchequer, came to the fore to play his great role. The talents which he contributed to the new ministry were largely in the area of mimicry, in which he was an adept. He was popular in the House of Commons because he frequently amused the members by his clever portrayals of both his foes and his friends. It was Townshend who offered a new scheme to tax the Americans, to a house unhappy because of high taxes in Britain and sore because it had been driven into yielding to colonials.

When, early in 1767, despite ministerial opposition, the Commons, pushed on by Grenville, voted to reduce land taxes from four shillings per acre to three, Townshend and his colleagues might well have resigned. Instead, he strove to placate the house, informing it that he had a plan whereby the colonists could be compelled to pay at least part of the expense of the army in America. They had offered constitutional objections, he said, only to internal levies for revenue. Since they had distinguished between internal and external levies—he blandly informed the Commons that he himself could not do so—it would be appropriate to draw money from their pockets by taxing goods imported by them from England. He was applauded, and late in the session the levies which he proposed were enacted. Before passage, however, Townshend again moved irresponsibly. He modified his scheme, so that the bulk of the expected revenue would be used to pay salaries of royal officials in America rather than to defray the cost of the army. Parliament, nevertheless, quite readily gave its approval to his project and accordingly imposed duties upon red and white lead, painters' colors, glass, paper, and tea imported into America. It was expected that something like £35,000 or £40,000 would be realized. At the same time, toward collecting these duties and others, Parliament created an American Board of Customs, to serve at Boston and to bring all the customs officers in America under close direction. In the following year Parliament, for similar purposes, strengthened the system of admiralty courts in America, a step for which Townshend was not largely responsible, since after September, 1767, he was rendering accounts to a Heavenly Master rather than to earthly ones.

So it was that Britain embarked upon a second major attempt to draw revenue from America, a most unwise venture. The sums which British politicians hoped to obtain could bring no help to the British taxpayer, especially since they were not to be spent, except in trifling amount, for imperial defense. Moreover, the constitutional scruples of the colonists were carelessly disregarded; and they were required to pay, not toward the cost of protection by the army, but largely for the salaries of royal officials who had hitherto been dependent upon colonial good will for at least a part of their income. It was evident that the Townshend Acts were intended not only to produce a revenue but to flout American views about taxation and at the same time to strengthen the hands of servants of the crown in America.[3]

Nor have all the liquors which the ministry of "All the Talents" mingled for the American cup been mentioned. It peremptorily demanded that the legislature of New York comply with the Quartering Act in its entirety, the penalty for defiance being deprivation of its "privilege" of meeting, a step hopelessly at variance with American views of the rights of their legislatures. Further, in the spring of 1768, after a reorganization of the ministry which weakened Chatham's following and enlarged that of the King, new measures hardly calculated to please the colonists were adopted with respect to the West and the army. Control over the Indian trade, expensive to the crown, was returned to the colonial régimes but was coupled with a renewed attempt to establish a boundary line between whites and reds. More important, a far-reaching decision was taken to evacuate many interior posts and to move the army toward the Atlantic coast. Thereafter, there were continuously at least three regiments in the settled parts of the middle colonies and other contingents at St. Augustine, Halifax, and Quebec—in stations not far distant in space or time from the inhabited places of the older English

[3] Had it been merely a matter of securing money, Parliament might easily have evaded American scruples by substituting export taxes on the goods as they left England for the import duties collected in America.

colonies. The motives for this change were mixed, but observant colonists could not fail to see that the new concentration placed portions of the army where they could more readily attack the colonists than defend them.[4] Suspicion thus aroused in America was confirmed in the fall of 1768 when redcoats were sent to Boston to preserve order there. It would then have been absurd for British politicians to contend, as they had earlier, that Parliamentary levies to secure an American revenue were benevolently intended to provide for colonial defense.

Hailing the repeal of the Stamp Act in triumphant joy, with copious libations and an abundance of expressions of loyalty to Britain and His Majesty George III, the colonists had resumed their normal occupations, ordered large quantities of goods from Britain, and prepared to be as happy and prosperous as they might be. With few exceptions they wished no further quarreling, ignored the challenges of the Declaratory Act and the molasses duty. Merchants and propertied folk were especially eager to avoid further struggle, for they had been alarmed by the increasing assertiveness of the artisans, mechanics, and other hitherto humble people in the later stages of the Stamp Act crisis. They no more desired to be ruled by the lower orders of Americans than by British aristocrats. But the Townshend measures drove them again toward disobedience. Considering the blows prepared for them by "Champagne Charley," they began to think of the wrong inflicted upon them by the molasses duty and recalled also that new levies upon wines imposed by the Sugar Act were onerous, if not unconstitutional. They gave more attention to the Declaratory Act and found its doctrine unpalatable. They discovered that neither Parliament nor crown had power to prevent the legislature of New York from meeting and functioning, although this matter was not so serious as it might have been, since the New York Assembly had complied with the Quartering Act before receiving the British ultimatum. Well aware that the Townshend duties could be passed on to the consumer, they saw that their trade was likely to be restricted as never before and that their political influence was likely to suffer, should they not resist. Fearing that their fellow Americans of less property and inferior

[4] Alden, *General Gage in America*, 142-44.

status might again strive to seize power, they re-entered the lists reluctantly and slowly; and many of them preferred to do no more than ask for redress.

The mercantile classes in the South, particularly in Virginia and North Carolina, where merchants were commonly British-born and factors of British firms rather than independent operators, were less disposed to resist than their counterparts in the Middle and Northern colonies. They also exerted less influence among their neighbors. Since the planters and plain folk upon the land in the South suffered little economically from the Townshend Acts, they, too, were slow to react. Nor were Southern people on the land, more affected by British efforts to limit westward expansion than other colonists, lashed into fury on that account, for the British restrictions were vexing rather than maddening. Temper accordingly rose less rapidly in the South, but Southerners were as interested in political wrongs and constitutional rights as other colonists, and it did rise.

Confronted by the Townshend duties, the colonists quickly removed all doubt concerning their constitutional views with respect to external taxation for revenue. Like Townshend, they found no difference between such levies and internal taxes; but they found both to be beyond the powers of Parliament. The doctrine of "no taxation without representation" applied to duties upon imported goods when intended to secure a revenue. And some Americans now found the tax on molasses to be as much a violation of their rights as the Townshend levies. Most, however, principally attacked the latter and followed the leadership of John Dickinson, whose "Letters from a Farmer in Pennsylvania," published in the colonial newspapers in the winter of 1767–1768, were generally thought to offer the truth and the way. Dickinson, an English-trained lawyer, preferred to found his arguments upon the rights of Englishmen rather than the larger—and vaguer—ones of mankind. Wealthy and moderate-minded, he conceded the right of Parliament to use taxation as a means of channeling and even destroying trade and manufacturing; it could not be employed, however, merely or chiefly, to obtain funds. Dickinson called upon the colonists to form a common front in defense of this position, and they very generally responded.

The first American assembly to speak out against the Town-shend duties was that of Massachusetts. It was logical that a commercial colony should act early, especially that one where the new Board of Customs sat; and Samuel Adams was available to fan the flames of discontent. On February 11 the House of Representatives of that province voted to send forth its famous Circular Letter, which denounced the constitutionality of the Townshend duties, payment of royal appointees from its proceeds, and the peremptory treatment accorded the New York Assembly, and called for a concerted colonial defense of American rights. It proved impossible for the colonists to collect in an American congress and so to voice the general anguish, even to the degree that they had in 1765, largely because the Earl of Hillsborough, the British colonial secretary, instructed the American governors to prevent the meetings of the legislators necessary for the choice of delegates.

There were, however, other means of separately asserting American rights, and protests poured into London from the colonies. The Southern provinces were as forward in protest as those to the northward, though not for precisely the same reasons. The Virginia planters sent communications to King, Lords, and Commons which should have received the most careful reading. Approved by the burgesses, the council, and the governor—the last being at the moment John Blair, himself a Virginian—these were sponsored not by Patrick Henry but by such men as Edmund Pendleton, Richard Bland, and Archibald Cary. They condemned the Townshend duties as unconstitutional and softly threatened a boycott of British goods. What was even more significant, the Virginians considered the highhanded treatment given the New York legislature a grievance greater than the Townshend taxes. To them the right of an American legislature to function was of more importance than pence and pounds unconstitutionally exacted. Protesting vigorously for themselves, they called upon all other Americans to speak forth.[5] The lower house of Maryland, its members officially told by Horatio Sharpe in consequence of orders from Lord Hillsborough that they would be sent home if

[5] John P. Kennedy (ed.), *Journals of the House of Burgesses, 1766-1769* (Richmond, 1906), 166-68, 172, 173, 175, 177; Saunders (ed.), *Colonial Records of North Carolina*, VII, 746-49; Mays, *Edmund Pendleton*, I, 249.

they attempted to express sentiments similar to those of the Circular Letter, indignantly denounced the duties in a petition to the King.[6] After sending to London an early request for their repeal, the Commons House of South Carolina was silent for many months, because it was not called into session. When a new house was elected in October, 1768, the part to be played by the colony in the crisis was an important issue, especially in Charleston. Men such as William Henry Drayton and William Wragg, disposed to yield to Parliament rather than struggle, were elected. They had, however, lost the solid support of Laurens, whose business had recently been much injured by the persecution of royal officials; and the majority, led by Christopher Gadsden, John Rutledge, and others, insisted that South Carolina must stand firm with her sister colonies. Before the governor, Lord Charles Montagu, could put an end to its proceedings, the Commons House took as firm a stand as those of Massachusetts and Virginia.[7] The story was much the same in Georgia, where the defenders of American liberty were stronger than they had earlier been; the lower house similarly issued its defiance before James Wright could dissolve it.[8] North Carolina, torn by the troubles of the Regulation, which brought its interior settlers into harassing conflict with its people of the coastal plain and with Tryon, did not react so vigorously. Perhaps members of the lower house from its lowlands were so closely allied with Tryon with respect to the Regulators that they hesitated to quarrel with him on other grounds. Nevertheless, on December 2, 1768, the house formally resolved to protest against the Townshend duties as unconstitutional.[9] With Virginia taking the lead, the older Southern colonies uniformly and officially again questioned Parliamentary power to tax in America for revenue.

Memorials, addresses, and petitions, however handsomely phrased, could not be expected greatly to alter minds and hearts in England, and the colonists had to find other means to con-

---

[6] Barker, *Background of the Revolution in Maryland*, 316–18.
[7] Wallace, *Life of Henry Laurens*, 137–56.
[8] Allen D. Candler (ed.), *The Colonial Records of the State of Georgia* (Atlanta, 1904–1916), XIV, 643–45, 655; Abbot, "Georgia under the Royal Governors," 218–24.
[9] Saunders (ed.), *Colonial Records of North Carolina*, VII, 973.

vince crown and Parliament that they should again bow to American scruples and wishes. There was renewed resort to smuggling, in order to evade all duties, and the Townshend ones in particular, but the invigorated customs service made smuggling more risky than it had been; and it could not in any case persuade British politicians to withdraw the Townshend taxes, the prime American desideratum. There was violence directed against the customs men, especially in Massachusetts, but they were not usually American-born and could not be so easily coerced as had been the stamp men; and where they were most threatened, in Boston, they were ultimately protected by troops and warships. The colonists therefore placed their chief reliance upon boycotting British goods, so effective in the first Anglo-American crisis. They hoped that British merchants and manufacturers would urge the rescinding of the Townshend duties as they had the repeal of the Stamp Act, and with equal force. Boston led the way, in the fall of 1767, forming an association to limit importations of British goods and to stimulate American manufacturing. Boycotting of British goods rapidly spread through New England. Many merchants, fearing financial loss and social upheaval, held back, but an association was formed at New York in 1768, and another in Philadelphia in March, 1769.[10] The movement then gained strength in the Southern colonies.

And again Virginia led the way in the South. In May, 1769, Lord Botetourt, a gracious, amiable, and bankrupt nobleman of the Berkeley family so long connected with Virginia, recently chosen governor, called the burgesses into session. He was sedulous to please; he gave spirited support to Virginian aspirations to western wealth and empire; and he acquired a personal popularity in Virginia which he never quite lost. Soon after the Assembly met, however, news came to Williamsburg of certain actions of Parliament which provoked bitter feelings among the burgesses. In order to protect the Customs Board in Boston, the cabinet had arranged to put four regiments of troops in that city in and after the fall of 1768. In the winter following, both the Lords and Commons, despite vigorous minority opposition, gave their

[10] Schlesinger, *Colonial Merchants and the American Revolution*, 105-34.

blessing to the employment of military force, described the Massachusetts Circular Letter as "subversive of the constitution," accused Massachusetts men of plotting to organize government "independent of the crown of Great Britain," and urged the ministry to seize and transport their leaders to England for trial under an old statute of Henry VIII providing means to deal with persons committing treason outside England. The burgesses promptly and unanimously, on May 17, passed resolutions prepared by George Mason and introduced by Washington declaring once more that taxation without representation was unconstitutional, that the Massachusetts House of Representatives was within its rights in calling upon the several American assemblies to join in the defense of common American liberties, and that Virginians accused of treason had a right to be tried in their own colony. In an address to the crown adopted on the following day they condemned trials of Americans under the statute of Henry VIII as "unconstitutional and illegal." When they were dissolved by Botetourt, they repaired to a private home and as private persons resolved upon a nonimportation program and an association to enforce it.[11] Provoked into boycotting by a desire to assist their fellow Americans and the reckless and contemptuous Parliamentary proposals to deal with American "traitors," the burgesses, and the Virginia planters in general, were not adepts in economic warfare. They were careless in enforcing the boycott; and the Scottish and English mercantile people in the Old Dominion disliked it. Nonimportation was not too successful in Virginia. But Virginia had taken its stand; and what was far more important, the planters had made it clear enough that they would fight rather than bend the knee to what they thought to be British tyranny.[12] Moreover, they called upon the representatives of the people in neighboring colonies to emulate their example.

The behavior of the burgesses, legal and extralegal, was observed from the northern side of the Potomac. A boycott had already been agreed upon in Baltimore and in Anne Arundel County,

[11] This dramatic episode is well described in Claude H. Van Tyne, *The Causes of the War of Independence* (Boston, 1922), 300–305.

[12] Washington had already indicated that he was prepared, if necessary, to take up arms. Fitzpatrick (ed.), *Writings of George Washington*, II, 501.

which included Annapolis. In June a majority of the lower house of Maryland, with other persons, arranged for colony-wide enforcement which proved to be rather effective, since it was possible to watch and compel the merchants of Baltimore and Annapolis to live up to the terms of association.[13]

South Carolina soon followed the example of the Chesapeake colonies, and even improved upon it. The merchants of Charleston were long opposed to any attempt toward economic coercion of the mother country.[14] However, the mechanics of that city, led by Christopher Gadsden and Peter Timothy, publisher of the South-Carolina Gazette, for whom Boston was the "north star" [15] in politics, were eager for action, as were many of the planters. On June 22 Gadsden, through Timothy's paper, urged these groups to form an association and to impose it upon the merchants. On July 4 the mechanics, with some planters, 230 persons in all, subscribed to a boycott. The merchants would have none of that agreement, condemning it as "an unjust attempt of one part of the community . . . to throw a burden on the rest," and prepared their own, one far less stringent in its provisions. Two weeks later, however, a compromise was reached and a new agreement was announced under Liberty Tree. With many other provisions it contained a lengthy list of British goods not to be imported, and stipulated that Negroes were not to be brought into the colony during the year 1770. It was to remain in force until all the Townshend measures should be repealed. A committee of 39 members composed equally of planters, merchants, and mechanics was entrusted with the execution of this thoroughgoing compact. It was rigidly enforced.[16]

The Commons House, unlike its counterparts in Virginia and Maryland, indulged in no extralegal activities and was not responsible for the South Carolina Association. That body did, however, formally and unanimously give its support to the resolutions of the burgesses of May 17, in mid-August, despite the fact that it was then known in Charleston that the British cabinet had

[13] Barker, Background of the Revolution in Maryland, 318–25.
[14] Bull to Hillsborough, October 18, 1768, in Sainsbury Transcripts.
[15] Bull to Hillsborough, July 16, 1770, ibid.
[16] Bull to Hillsborough, March 6, 1770, ibid.

decided to seek the repeal of the Townshend duties save for that on tea. As long as the duty on tea continued, the constitutional question endured. Almost simultaneously the house defied British authority in another connection, flatly refusing to provide barracks and certain supplies for British troops temporarily stationed in Charleston. As early as 1757 the Carolinians had denied the right to quarter British troops in private dwellings in the colony without the consent of the owner and had specifically refused to supply quarters for the officers of a British contingent sent to assist in the defense of the colony.[17] Those redcoats who came in 1769 were to be placed in Charleston only because there were at the moment inadequate facilities for them in St. Augustine. When Lord Charles Montagu, at the request of General Gage, asked the house to arrange for housing them and to vote the supplies, in accordance with the Quartering Act, a committee chosen to consider the matter, in which Gadsden and Thomas Lynch were conspicuous, asked pointedly whether the troops were sent to defend the frontiers of the colony. Receiving a reply in the negative, the committee and the house then rejected the request, offering several reasons for so doing, one, that the British could pay for the needs of the troops from the proceeds of the Townshend duties.[18] Thus the South Carolinians gave support in spirit to the people of Massachusetts, who had declined to make similar provision for the troops stationed in Boston.

Nor were the South Carolinians content to defend only the rights of British citizens in America. John Wilkes, the famous English radical, who was persecuted by George III and the King's Friends, even being denied a seat in the House of Commons to which he was twice properly elected, was a hero under the palmettos as well as in London coffeehouses. A "Society of the Supporters of the Bill of Rights" formed in London to defend Wilkes and to struggle for the reform of Parliament needed funds to carry on its work. The Commons House, consulting neither governor nor council, in December, 1769, sent £1,500 to the society "for

[17] William Henry Lyttelton to Board of Trade, December 22, 1757, December 2, 1758, Colonial Office 5/376, Public Record Office. Dr. Jack P. Greene kindly supplied copies of these documents.

[18] McCrady, *South Carolina under the Royal Government*, 617–20.

the defense of British and American liberty." [19] Thereby it not only offered offense to the crown but began a far-reaching controversy with the South Carolina council, which conceived that its constitutional powers in connection with the spending of money had been arrogantly ignored.

Not every South Carolinian supported nonimportation and John Wilkes. William Henry Drayton objected to both. Backed by William Wragg, he waged a newspaper war with Gadsden and John Mackenzie in which he scored repeatedly at the expense of "Kitt," especially with the argument that "Kitt" and his associates sought to deprive Drayton of *his* rights as an Englishman. Drayton was, however, pompous, referring to the Charleston mechanics as the *profanum vulgus* and correcting the grammatical errors of his opponents; he thus exposed himself to ridicule and reduced his appeal. Gadsden struck vigorously at "Master Billy" in rebuttal, returning abuse for insult. Defending economic pressure as a suitable means of compelling Britain to redress American grievances, he insisted that they must be removed. Should Britain continue to attack the liberties of the Americans, they could exercise ultimately the right of revolution. Gadsden was wordy and diffuse; he was also forthright.[20] After a vain appeal to the Commons House for protection of his rights as a citizen and an importer, Drayton abandoned the contest early in 1771, sailing for England.

Georgia followed closely in the wake of South Carolina. In September, 1769, the "Amicable Society" of Savannah, a group of Georgians forward in the defense of American liberties who stressed friendship among themselves rather than cordial relations with Britain, undertook to establish boycott and association in the colony. Led by Jonathan Bryan, who played the role of Gadsden, they compelled the merchants, reluctant, like those of Charleston, to agree to a compact less drastic than that of South Carolina, though sufficiently so to suggest in London that many Georgians desired the duty on tea to be set aside with the other Townshend taxes. Nor was the lower house of Georgia backward in asserting American rights, for it formally aligned itself in November with the House of Burgesses. There was, however, less zeal for the

[19] Wallace, *Life of Henry Laurens*, 159–66.
[20] William Henry Drayton, *The Letters of Freeman, &c.* (London, 1771), *passim*.

boycott on the right bank of the Savannah than on its left; and it seems that merchants continued to import British goods, even those Townshend-taxed. In June, 1770, a meeting of the inhabitants of Charleston indignantly resolved that the Georgians ought "to be amputated from the rest of their brethren, as a rotten part that might spread a dangerous infection" and demanded that all commercial intercourse with Georgia be ended. Again Georgia, because of its peculiar relationship with Britain, was less vigorously opposed to British "tyranny" than most of her sister colonies. Moreover, Bryan suffered for his aggressiveness; he was deprived of his seat in the provincial council.[21]

North Carolina was the last of the older Southern colonies to adopt nonimportation. The merchants of Wilmington were as loath to embark upon economic warfare as were those of Savannah. After the end of September, however, the "Sons of Liberty" of that town and of Brunswick, led by Cornelius Harnett, demanded that the merchants do their share toward securing a reversal in British policy. Thereafter, the pattern of events in North Carolina was precisely like that in Virginia nearly six months earlier. Tryon urged the lower house, which met late in October, to be calm, since Parliament would soon repeal the Townshend levies, except for that on tea;[22] the house responded by adopting for itself George Mason's resolutions and was promptly dissolved by Tryon; the members failed to disperse, but gathered in the courthouse at New Bern on November 7 and proclaimed the adherence of North Carolina to nonimportation. The terms of the agreement there prepared were almost precisely those adopted by the burgesses in May. Observed Tryon despondently, "This province appears to be in a stricter union with Virginia than any other colony, and I believe will steadily pursue the public conduct of that colony."[23] Tryon's prediction proved to be accurate, in the months and in the years which followed. It would seem, however, that the North Carolinians waged economic warfare against the mother country somewhat more effectively than the Virginians,

[21] Schlesinger, *Colonial Merchants and the American Revolution*, 147–48, 207–208; Abbot, "Georgia under the Royal Governors," 226–28.

[22] Saunders (ed.), *Colonial Records of North Carolina*, VIII, 122–24.

[23] *Ibid.*, 152.

who often carelessly ordered proscribed goods. The South Carolinians were far more zealous than either. They boycotted British
goods so effectively that their imports from Britain into the Carolinas in 1770 were worth only half of those of the preceding year.
The Marylanders compiled a similar record.[24]

The American boycott against British goods did less injury to
their makers and conveyors than was hoped. While American
imports sank sharply during the years 1768–1770, especially in
the Middle and Northern colonies, the British economy had recovered from postwar depression; and business other than the
Americans' was so profitable that the curtailment in their orders
was not a major blow in London and Liverpool. Nevertheless,
the boycott was not entirely without result. If the colonists themselves suffered in consequence, so did the British, who would
have preferred even greater prosperity than they actually enjoyed.
Requests for repeal of the Townshend duties were submitted in
London, and they were not entirely ignored. They doubtless
encouraged members of the Grafton ministry who had been fond
neither of Charles Townshend nor of his American measures to
seek to do away with his taxes. Frederick, Lord North, who succeeded Townshend at the exchequer, though a follower of George
III rather than Pitt, was then, as he was later, more moderate in
his attitude toward the Americans than were most of the politicians who gave their loyalty to the King. North contended that
the enactment of the duties had been a mistake, because they
were hurtful to British trade. On that ground they should all be
withdrawn. However, since the Americans had raised constitutional argument against them, he urged that the duty on tea be
retained in order to deny by specific example the American claim.
To insist upon the tea tax, he said, was to demand a grain of
pepper in acknowledgment of right. North's view ultimately prevailed as a compromise in a ministry badly divided. An announcement was made in May, 1769, it will be recalled, informing the
colonists that Parliament would be asked to pass appropriate
measures. At the same time, Francis Bernard, unpopular governor
of Massachusetts, was recalled and made a baronet; and General
Gage was authorized to remove the troops from Boston.

[24] Schlesinger, *Colonial Merchants and the American Revolution*, 197–202, 206–209.

The new British program consisted of half measures, and was inefficiently executed. Some of the redcoats remained in Boston, because Thomas Hutchinson, Bernard's successor, believed they were necessary to preserve order. Their presence actually provoked tumults which brought death to a Boston boy in February, 1770, and led to the famous "Massacre" on March 5. The troops then departed from the town. Not until the very day of the "Massacre," ten months after the announcement that most of the cabinet would ask Parliament to repeal the Townshend duties, did North ask the Commons to act. The repealer was then promptly approved.

Widely circulated reports of the "Massacre" prepared by Massachusetts defenders of American liberties portrayed those slain in the affray as martyrs, and their fate aroused indignation throughout the colonies. At the same time the bloodshed in Boston alarmed and sobered thoughtful persons. The news that most of the Townshend duties had actually been withdrawn persuaded many Americans that they had substantially won their battle. The merchants, never heartily united in support of the boycott and now distressed by the cessation of business, were commonly eager to cease struggling. Some colonists called for an end to nonimportation; a second group urged that the boycott be continued only with respect to tea and other taxed goods; and a third demanded that it be maintained in full force until Britain had completely abandoned her efforts to secure a revenue. Jealousy among the merchants in the several ports, each group afraid that another or others might secure advantage by an early resumption of importation, weakened the common front. The result was a general decision in the later months of 1770 to continue the boycott only upon tea.

The Southern colonists, the last to adopt nonimportation, were also slowest to drop it. Their programs were hardly settled when they learned that those who had been among the first to boycott were threatening to drop it, partly or entirely. They followed the example of the colonists to the northward. The nonimportation movement collapsed almost without a quiver in Georgia, North Carolina, and Virginia. In Maryland planters and politicians strove to preserve the boycott, but were successfully defied by the merchants of Baltimore and Annapolis, who agreed not to purchase British tea but otherwise insisted upon conducting their business as they would. Only in South Carolina was there a real fight. The planters and the Charleston mechanics were reluctant to give up the program they had so recently imposed upon the merchants. They were furious with the Northerners because of their defection from the cause, and talked of boycotting *them*. But ultimately they could not control even the Charleston merchants, who preferred to follow the example of their Northern brethren rather than to struggle with them. In a great public meeting held at Charleston on December 13 Thomas Lynch "exerted all his eloquence and even the trope of rhetorical tears for the expiring liberty of his dear country," which the merchants would sell like any other merchandise.[25] The meeting nevertheless voted to boycott in the future only tea and other goods British-taxed.[26] The planters and mechanics who agreed with Lynch—and Gadsden—were routed. Their defeat was even more decisive in practice than it was on paper, for the South Carolinians, like the colonists elsewhere, afterward failed to observe even the boycott upon British tea.

The Townshend crisis so ended, the colonists winning less than decisive victory. Three years of colonial prosperity followed, years in which Anglo-American tensions eased. During that period serious discontent with Britain continued only in Massachusetts and South Carolina; and even in those colonies many were disposed to let dormant dogs lie.

[25] Bull to Hillsborough, December 13, 1770, in Sainsbury Transcripts.
[26] Schlesinger, *Colonial Merchants and the American Revolution*, 233–36.

CHAPTER VIII

ADVANCE INTO THE
OLD SOUTHWEST

THE American Revolution was not confined to the eastern coast of northern America, nor was Anglo-American struggle limited to disputes over taxation, overseas trade, currency, quartering of troops in colonial towns and villages, and other issues of great moment to people of Tidewater and Piedmont. British policy concerning the occupation of unsettled lands to the west, especially those beyond the Allegheny divide, also created unrest, particularly among American pioneers and land speculators. In at least minor degree the clash of arms at Lexington and Concord proceeded from quarrel over colonial advance in Pennsylvania, Kentucky, Tennessee, and Upper South Carolina after 1763. Some of the seeds of warfare were sown in the Old Southwest. Southern settlements spread to and over the mountains between the Ohio and the Gulf of Mexico; the foundations of a greater South began to appear before 1775.[1]

Britain, triumphantly acquiring not only the eastern part of Louisiana but Spanish Florida, in 1763 seemed firmly in control of all the territories east of the Mississippi save for New Orleans, and the heiress apparent of the remainder of Louisiana as well, for it seemed obvious that the Spanish could not long defend it against British aggression. Indeed, the Spanish themselves looked upon their new acquisition as cover for their older colonies rather than as a permanent addition to their American dominions. Thereafter, the British, anticipating future conflict with the Spanish crown, looked upon possession of New Orleans as a first goal in such a struggle. Ironically, when the long-expected war came,

[1] This chapter is largely based upon John R. Alden, *John Stuart and the Southern Colonial Frontier . . . 1754–1775* (Ann Arbor, 1944).

because Britain was heavily involved in the American rebellion, it was Spain that took the offensive, conquering all the northern shore of the Gulf of Mexico east of New Orleans and regaining also the peninsula of Florida in the treaties ending that war. The resurgence of the power of the dons was, to be sure, only temporary, for they could no more stand unaided against the Americans than they could alone have held off the British.

The Spanish made no attempt to occupy their new territories until 1766, the French régime continuing because of the failure of Spain to move. When the first Spanish governor, Don Juan Antonio de Ulloa, finally appeared, the French inhabitants, refusing to accept Spanish rule, revolted and drove him to sea, in 1768. Not until August of the following year, when General Alexander O'Reilly came up the Mississippi with an army from Havana, did the Frenchmen submit. Even after 1769 the Spanish grip upon New Orleans remained uncertain and largely dependent upon the good will of the French settlers, for the Spanish made no serious attempt to bring in their own people. Had the inhabitants of Louisiana been unitedly loyal under Spanish rule, they were not numerous or powerful enough in themselves to threaten seriously the British on the Mississippi before the American rebellion. Louisiana contained only about six thousand whites, and New Orleans was its sole major town. Except for the capital, there were few settlements, and they were principally hamlets strung along the Mississippi, the chief of them strategically, St. Louis, founded in 1764. The colony was almost stagnant. The French inhabitants, with the aid of Negro slaves, produced indigo, naval stores, a little tobacco, and some inferior sugar. They also raised cattle of no better quality than their sugar. Louisiana's most lucrative resource was commerce carried on with the Indians. That trade, largely limited to the western half of the Mississippi Valley after 1763 because the British resented the competitive intrusions of Spanish subjects upon British soil, was less valuable than it had earlier been, but remained profitable. Even so, revenues derived from the colony did not match the cost of government and defense. The burden thus placed upon the Spanish crown was more than counterbalanced, however, by the defensive usefulness of Louisiana as a barrier province.

The British sent garrisons as soon as possible after the peace to St. Augustine, St. Mark's (Appalachie), Pensacola, and Mobile, thus securing by February, 1764, effective control of the coasts

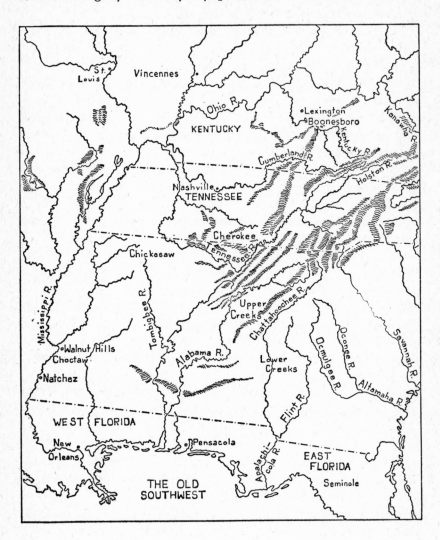

of the Floridas. Meanwhile, the Proclamation of October 7, 1763, announced the establishment of two new royal colonies in the far South. Georgia was extended to the St. Mary's River, and the region to the south and west as far as the Apalachicola River was designated East Florida. The strip of land between the Gulf of Mexico and the thirtieth parallel, the Apalachicola on the east, and the Iberville and Mississippi on the west, became West Florida —the northern boundary of that colony being altered in 1764 to take in all the lands below a line drawn eastward from the mouth of the Yazoo to the Chattahoochee.

The Floridas did not flourish, despite favor they steadily received from London. In both, the expenses of government were borne by Britain; and British ministries did what they could to encourage immigration. However, heat, disease, Indian troubles, lack of capital, the poverty of lands along the coasts, more attractive regions to the north, and other circumstances prevented rapid growth.[2] So long as British rule in the Floridas continued they were valuable chiefly for military purposes.

West Florida grew more rapidly than her sister colony, because of the attraction of the fertile lowlands on the east bank of the lower Mississippi. It was claimed in 1774 that they were occupied by 2,500 whites, together with 600 Negro slaves.[3] Many of the new settlers came down the great river from the older colonies. The British garrisons stimulated economic activity, and trade with the Creeks, Choctaw, and Chickasaw tended to fall into the hands of Pensacola and Mobile merchants. On the whole, despite great hopes, the colony developed slowly in wealth as well as numbers. West Florida was, however, not badly governed. British officials, including a governor, councilors, and judges, appeared in 1764, and an Assembly functioned after 1766. West Florida thus soon became in form a typical royal colony. The first governor, George Johnstone, a Scottish naval officer, was pompous, quarrelsome, and cunning; his bickerings with military officers and civilians kept the colony in turmoil until he left Pensacola in 1767. His successors behaved themselves better; and the settlers profited from a relatively beneficent colonial régime. The foundations for a

[2] Annapolis *Maryland Gazette*, July 3, 1766, commented dryly that West Florida was certainly a fertile country, since an unmarried woman of seventy had become pregnant three months after settling in the colony.

[3] Cecil Johnson, *British West Florida, 1763–1783* (New Haven, 1943), 149.

prosperous colony were laid. They were torn down in the War of Independence.[4]

East Florida was more fortunate in management than her sister province. So few British civilians settled in the colony, these concentrating about St. Augustine, that it did not seem worth while to form a house of representatives until 1781. Almost as long as East Florida endured, civil government therefore remained under the control of the governor, assisted by his council. The first chief executive, Colonel James Grant, a Scottish army officer, was sensible, able, industrious, relatively good-humored, and hospitable. He invested money of his own in his colony, and he encouraged the ventures of others. Those who followed him in office after 1771 were less impressive, but no worse than the average British colonial governor.

Nevertheless, East Florida could not promptly prosper. The scanty Spanish population removed at the peace, and was replaced by another which was impressive only by comparison with its predecessor. Large grants of land were made to favored persons in Britain and America. These were seldom peopled. Planters from South Carolina and Georgia moved into the northern part of the province. Denys Rolle strove to establish a large settlement at Mount Pleasant on the east bank of the St. John's River; and Dr. Andrew Turnbull undertook a similar venture on Mosquito (later Ponce de Leon) Inlet. Rollestown, into which its owner imported English beggars and debtors and Negro slaves, did not thrive; and Turnbull encountered even less success with his "New Smyrna," to which he brought Minorcans, Italians, and Greeks in the hope of raising semitropical products. His Mediterranean people died by hundreds, and his scheme ultimately collapsed in almost total failure. The province acquired and long labored under a reputation of being a forbidding land of swamps, pine barrens, mosquitoes, and mortal fevers. Its governor was not much more than a "Commissioner of the mildew." [5]

There were other disappointments and vexations for the Brit-

[4] See *ibid.* for a well-told brief history of West Florida. Clinton N. Howard, *British Development of West Florida, 1763–1769* (Berkeley and Los Angeles, 1947), possesses value.

[5] Charles L. Mowat, *East Florida As a British Province, 1763–1784* (Berkeley and Los Angeles, 1943), is the standard work on the colony.

ish in the Floridas. An alluring scheme to clean out the Iberville River, so that British shipping might pass between the Mississippi and the Gulf of Mexico without traversing Spanish waters, proved at last to be unworkable. Troubles came from the presence of the Spanish and their French subjects in Louisiana. The French who had traded with the Choctaw and other Indian tribes on the lower Mississippi continued as of yore to do so after the Peace of Paris. Their activities were intensely resented, especially because they mingled anti-British propaganda with trade talk. In 1766 British garrisons were established in Fort Bute at the source of the Iberville and Fort Panmure at Natchez to bar the path of the Frenchmen. They continued, however, to slip across the Mississippi and the Iberville. Moreover, Spanish officials seem to have tampered casually with the Choctaw after Don Luis de Unzaga y Amezaga became governor of Louisiana in 1770. Visits of Spanish fishermen from Havana to the west coast of the Florida peninsula and of Lower Creeks to Cuba also caused concern. The Creeks as a whole had little love for the Spanish, but one of their chiefs, Escotchabie, became decidedly pro-Spanish and visited Havana in 1775. On the other hand, the British were embarrassed by the activities of Lieutenant John Thomas, one of Indian superintendent John Stuart's agents stationed on the lower Mississippi after 1771. Thomas meddled with the Arkansas tribe on Spanish soil and even laid plans for an attack by Indians upon New Orleans. He was disavowed by Stuart, but Spanish suspicions were roused, and the West Florida–Louisiana frontier remained uneasy.

Fostering without much fruit the mainland colonies beside the Gulf of Mexico, British politicians were commonly cool toward the westward expansion of Virginia, the Carolinas, and Georgia, as they were also toward that of the Northern colonies. In the main, they were opposed to rapid burgeoning to the westward because of Indian wars almost certain to follow. Some would have preferred that the interior of British North America remain more or less permanently an Indian country, believing that settlement of that region would persuade the inhabitants of the old colonies to engage in manufacturing, presumably to the detriment of the makers and marketers of British goods. A few favored the prompt peopling of the lands east and west of the Alleghenies occupied only by the red men. Accordingly, British policy altered with shifting political tides in Britain; it was also affected by colonial pressures and by the views and behavior of General Gage and the Indian superintendents, Sir William Johnson and John Stuart.[6] The restrictions upon settlement in the Proclamation of 1763 were therefore not permanent. However, what might be called the moderate view generally prevailed in London. Expansion was not banned, but uncontrolled and swift settlement likely to cause Indian resentment and onslaught was commonly discouraged.

Commissioned to soothe chiefs and to please warriors for Britain among the red men south of the Ohio, John Stuart was principally responsible for the execution of British policy concerning the settlement of the Old Southwest. Stuart was a remarkable man and a worthy and loyal servant of the crown. Born in Scotland and descended from the royal Stuarts, the son of a merchant of Jacobite sympathies, he was one of the fortunate survivors of Admiral George Anson's expedition around the world, which brought him a small fortune in prize money. Turning from the sea, he established himself as a merchant in Charleston. He failed, and entered upon a career of arms. As a captain of South Carolina militia he became the hero of the Anglo-Cherokee war. Made prisoner by the Cherokee at the fall of Fort Loudoun, he was saved from the stake by Attakullakulla, also known as Little Carpenter, one of the principal chiefs of the tribe. Returning to his own people, Stuart was rewarded both with public esteem and with office. His knowledge of the Cherokee and his friendships among them, particularly with Attakullakulla, together with his quality and his experience, secured him the Southern Indian superintendency in 1762. From headquarters in Charleston, and after 1775 in St. Augustine and Pensacola, Stuart did all that he could to prevent and abate the horrors of warfare between reds and whites. In later life a Charleston aristocrat [7] speculating

<hr />

[6] The pioneer work of Clarence W. Alvord, *The Mississippi Valley in British Politics* (Cleveland, 1917), and Thomas P. Abernethy's close study of *Western Lands and the American Revolution* (New York, 1937), deal in detail with British policy. George O. Virtue, *British Land Policy and the American Revolution . . .* (Lincoln, 1955), thoughtful and well written, is useful, but is largely based on Alvord.

[7] A Charleston tradition that Stuart married into the wealthy Fenwick family is,

in land, he was nevertheless opposed to immoderate westward expansion.

Toward preserving peace between red men and white on the frontiers of the Southern colonies during the period 1763–1775 Stuart assiduously employed all the arts of diplomacy among his charges. Persuasion and presents had their effect. Moreover, since the Indians could not be entirely prevented from engaging in battle—a red male was not a warrior until he had acquired a scalp—he permitted and even fomented feuds between the Cherokee and the Six Nations, the Cherokee and the Creeks, the Creeks and the Choctaw. It was preferable that his clients attack each other in traditional Indian style rather than assail their white neighbors. He also strove to mollify the Southern tribes by securing the punishment of whites who slew Indians, demanding in return the execution of braves who murdered palefaces. Thus he tried to prevent the creation of feuds between the two races.

To secure peace between the two peoples Stuart also sought to compel good behavior on the part of the whites who traded with his charges. The men who engaged in commerce with the Indians, exchanging clothing, guns, ammunition, tomahawks, knives, trinkets, and rum for pelts of the beaver and the deer, caused contention. The traders, visiting the Indian towns and sometimes residing in them for long periods, were not as a group distinguished for high character. All too often they were rapacious rascals who took advantage of their unsophisticated clients. The trader's most effective approach was to "marry" an Indian girl and through her influence obtain the patronage of her male relatives and their associates. The forest traffickers, because of their familial connections, and more because of need for their wares, were welcomed. But they were not trusted. Even when they dealt fairly and offered useful merchandise rather than rum—a curse to the Indians, and recognized as such by the wiser ones—the attitude of the red men toward them was ambivalent. When they cheated—a complaint by one Southern Indian that they skimped even on loincloths has been recorded—they aroused antagonism

however, incorrect. Alden, *John Stuart and the Southern Colonial Frontier*, 162–63; Alexander Wedderburn, *The Wedderburn Book* (n.p., 1898), I, 229–30.

not only against themselves but against men of their color. What could be done to prevent the traders from cheating their clients and debauching them with rum, to force them to abandon their various iniquitous practices? The Southern colonies, like those to the northward, had failed to find a solution, had not resolutely tried to discover one. They had enacted laws regulating the trade, but these had been frequently violated, usually with impunity. South Carolina and Virginia had attempted to secure order by establishing public companies to compete with private barterers, and even public monopolies. Such devices had also been unsuccessful, partly because the several colonies interested failed to make a common effort. Moreover, the Proclamation of 1763 specifically required that private persons be permitted to engage in the commerce with the red men. Had the "Plan for the Future Management of Indian Affairs" of 1764 [8] received royal assent, Stuart would have had authority to act, although the colonists were certain to find that he had violated their constitutional rights. But the plan, which contained many clauses concocted by Stuart and Sir William Johnson, never was sanctioned in London. In 1765 Stuart hit upon a similar scheme. He proposed to the several Southern governors, who had the power to license the traders, that they give permits only to men who obeyed rules prepared by Stuart. The rules forbade, among other things, cheating and the sale of rum and rifles to the Indians. Stuart was sending deputies and commissaries to the several tribes to defend English interests. These would watch the traders and report the delinquent ones to him and to the governors for suitable punishment.

Stuart's plan had Gage's support, but the Southern governors were reluctant to cede authority to him. In fact, he became involved in debates with one or two of them and also in a quarrel with the Assembly of Virginia, because of a Virginia law of 1765 setting up a public trading company to deal with the Cherokee. His scheme could not be executed if the Virginians proceeded with their own. He asked that the Virginia act be disallowed in London, and it was, to the displeasure of the House of Burgesses. Unable to carry on without the general support of the governors, he dropped his plan. He revived it early in 1767 when he received

[8] See p. 59.

orders from Lord Shelburne to do everything possible to make the traders behave, until the home government should develop a program for dealing with the Indians. Shelburne wrote in a similar vein to Gage and the Southern governors. Again Stuart sought the support of the governors and received it from them, except for Francis Fauquier and James Grant. During the years 1767–1768 he and his aides, helped by traders who themselves sought order, materially improved conditions in the trade. However, in the spring of 1768, the British cabinet ordered him to cease his efforts and to discharge most of his aides. Thereafter, the burden of maintaining order in the Indian commerce was placed once more upon the several Southern colonies. They quite generally refused to assume it, and the familiar troubles reappeared in pristine vigor.

A major menace to peace between whites and reds was not the trader, but the settler. The trader was useful to the Indians, and he came and went. The arrival of the settler threatened their independence and even their existence, and they were well aware that he did. When he planted corn and potatoes upon their hunting ranges most remote from their towns, they worried and protested; when his cultivated fields and his cattle approached their towns, they took up arms in defense of their freedom. In 1769 a Shawnee chief, Captain Will, warned Daniel Boone and some companions to keep away. " 'Now, brothers . . . go home and stay there. Don't come here any more, for this is the Indians' hunting ground, and all the animals, skins and furs are ours; and if you are so foolish as to venture here again you may be sure the wasps and yellow-jackets will sting you severely.' " [9] Boone did not "go home and stay there," nor did his fellow pioneers. The Southern backwoodsmen, like their fellows to the northward, did not seek eagerly and persistently to please the red men even as neighbors, and they would hardly have succeeded. To most of them the ideal Indian was one who pursued the deer and the bear in the Happy Hunting Ground. Even before the Seven Years' War pioneers had crossed the mountain divide in Virginia. Driven back during that conflict, they returned as soon

[9] Quoted in Randolph C. Downes, "Dunmore's War: An Interpretation," in *Mississippi Valley Historical Review*, XXI (1934–1935), 312.

as the end of hostilities permitted; and they were followed by others. By 1768 settlers were swarming into the valley of the Kanawha River, and into those of the Holston River and adjoining streams in what is now eastern Tennessee. Six years later they were throwing up cabins and planting crops beside the Kentucky River. Meanwhile, to the southward, they were pressing across the Piedmont in the Carolinas and Georgia, and even pushing inland in the Floridas.

Closely linked with the pioneer, and also imperiling Anglo-Indian peace, was the land speculator. Almost from the founding of Virginia shrewd men had profited in the South by acquiring land in advance of white settlement, paying little for it, then advantageously selling or renting it when the region in which it lay was occupied. Occasionally they themselves moved westward to new homes upon such land. This road to prosperity was open only to those who were able to wait long for returns and who had influence in a colonial capital or in London. The large land grants necessary for such a gamble had to be secured from the governor and his council or, possibly, from His Majesty's Privy Council. It was therefore principally the planters who were among the governor's advisers, who had relatives among them, who were liked or feared by the governor, that embarked upon such ventures. The fortunate ones secured great tracts in return for putting a few settlers upon them and paying certain fees—and officials did not always insist upon either receiving the cash or seeing the settlers.

Speculation in lands over the mountains began in Virginia a decade before the Seven Years' War, and continued on a vaster scale than ever before through the War of Independence. Between 1745 and 1754 Virginia issued papers to more than twenty individuals and companies giving them rights to areas ranging from 20,000 to 800,000 acres in the Ohio Valley. The names of the venturers upon those papers were commonly those of proudest Virginia patricians. Most famous of these combinations was the Ohio Company, in which Thomas Lee, president of the Virginia council and father of Richard Henry Lee, Dr. Arthur Lee, and other Lees conspicuous in the period of the Revolution, and Lawrence Washington, older brother of George Washington, were early leaders. This company, however, formed to trade with the Indians and to build a fort against the French as well as to fill the pockets of its members, neither arrested the progress of the fleur-de-lis nor successfully traded nor managed to secure the 500,000 acres its investors sought to acquire. The Loyal Company, granted 800,000 acres at Williamsburg in 1749, had ultimately a somewhat happier history, thanks to the energy of its guiding spirit, Dr. Thomas Walker. Most effective immediately of the Virginia combinations was one headed by James Patton, which was given 100,000 acres on and beyond the Kanawha River in 1746 and which was largely responsible for the settlements along that stream created before the French and Indian War. That conflict temporarily interrupted both the occupation of and speculation in the western lands, but was not ended, so far as the Indians were concerned, when a new and grandiose combination, the Mississippi Company, made its appearance. This organization, containing a sprinkling of Marylanders and many Virginians, including four Lees, two Fitzhughs, and two Washingtons, in the fall of 1763 asked from the crown 2,500,000 acres north and south of the lower Ohio, each of fifty members to receive 50,000 acres. Its remarkable request could hardly be acceptable at a time when Pontiac and his allies were scourging the region of the Great Lakes and the upper Ohio Valley, nor was the company more successful when it transferred its wishes to the latter region in 1768.

Most successful of all the Virginia speculators was George Washington, who received no dividends as a shareholder in the Ohio and Mississippi companies, but who eventually secured Western estates through his service as a colonel of Virginia militia in the Seven Years' War. In 1754, eagerly seeking recruits to protect the frontier, Lieutenant Governor Robert Dinwiddie of Virginia had promised reward in land; and Dinwiddie's pledge was finally recognized by officials in England. As a colonel and as a purchaser of claims of his officers and men after 1767 Washington became entitled to a large quantity of land across the mountains. When, in December, 1769, Lord Botetourt and his council authorized him to locate 200,000 acres for himself and his men, Washington promptly arranged for surveying on the Kanawha and tried to have corn planted on areas set apart for himself.

Difficulties and delays developed, and he received little revenue from his efforts and his investments until after the War of Independence. Then, however, they brought him handsome amounts of cash and enabled him in his will to dispose of more than 40,000 acres beyond the divide.

Land speculation in the South was not, of course, confined to Virginians, or even to Southern colonists. Carolinians and Georgians also gambled for easy wealth beyond the frontier, but in fewer numbers and on a smaller scale until after the Revolution. However, Judge Richard Henderson of North Carolina was one of the boldest and most successful of all the speculators. Marylanders, Pennsylvanians, and British merchants and noblemen likewise participated in the scramble for easy wealth, casting covetous eyes upon the valley of the Ohio.

To preserve peace on the frontier, Stuart believed that pioneers and speculators had to be restrained. He was not utterly opposed to white expansion but desired that it be confined as much as possible to areas remote from Indian towns, where it was less likely to arouse the resentment of the red men. As a faithful servant of the crown, he tried to enforce the Proclamation of 1763 and other British restrictions upon settlement in the Old Southwest. When it was possible to lower those barriers and to please pioneers and speculators without angering the Indians, he urged his superiors in London to do so.

During the years 1763–1768 Stuart sought eagerly to avoid conflict with the Southern Indians by establishing and marking a boundary between them and their white neighbors. In a series of treaties he secured the agreement of reds and whites to a boundary running behind colonial settlements from the northern limits of North Carolina to the Florida peninsula and thence westward to the Mississippi. Much of this line was actually surveyed and designated by natural and artificial markings. Soon, however, pioneers and speculators sought to break through that limit; and Virginia fought vigorously against the establishment of a similar ban to her westward progress.

Until 1754 the Old Dominion remained unconfined upon the west, except for the national rights of the French in the Mississippi Valley and of the Spanish beyond it, the Indians being more or less recognized as private owners of the lands upon which they lived and hunted, but not as sovereign possessors. When France abandoned to Britain the vast territory between the Appalachian Mountains and the Mississippi, it was promptly assumed at Williamsburg and elsewhere in Virginia that her western verge was now at the great river. Moreover, the Virginians conveniently read "west and northwest" in their charter of 1609 to mean that their southern boundary, the line of 36' 30", ran due west and that their northern limit proceeded northwest beyond Maryland, an interpretation which brought the present states of West Virginia, Kentucky, Ohio, Indiana, Illinois, Michigan, Wisconsin, and parts of the states of Minnesota and Pennsylvania, including Pittsburgh, under their control. They arrogated to themselves a lordly empire.

The Proclamation of 1763, it has been remarked above, was not a final statement of British policy regarding the West. It was, in fact, for the Virginians only one royal order among many affecting their advance over the divide. As early as 1754 the governor of the colony was instructed from London, because Indian claims to the south bank of the Ohio had not been extinguished, to prevent further grants of more than 1,000 acres to a person. This order pleased Francis Fauquier, who preferred the pioneer to the entrepreneur. In 1759 he declared all the great grants beyond the mountains, except for one to James Patton, lapsed, because their possessors had not developed them as required. The board, however, tried to restrict settlers as well as speculators. Early in 1761 Fauquier was ordered to make no new tramontane grants whatever unless Indian claims had been erased and its own sanction secured; and before the end of that year he and all the colonial governors were told that they would be removed from office, should they sign papers yielding lands owned by the red men. At the same time London officials forbade the purchase of lands by private persons without royal consent and commanded the governors to put forth proclamations ordering persons illegally settled upon them to remove. The Proclamation of 1763, more solemn in form, was hardly more drastic in essence.

Fauquier vainly attempted to defend to his superiors the rights of the Patton grantees and of others who had legally taken root in the Kanawha Valley. Sympathizing with the Kanawha residents, many of whom had fled eastward during the conflict with the French and Indians but had turned back as soon as it seemed safe, he made no effort to drive them from their homes. Nor would he force out Virginians and others who were by 1765 throwing up cabins on the branches of the Monongahela in territory claimed by both Virginia and Pennsylvania. These pioneers defied both civil and military authority. The commanding officer at Fort Pitt, under orders from General Gage, burned their cabins and herded them eastward. They boldly returned. Executing the Proclamation by using troops was risky, especially in the year of the Stamp Act; and Gage chose not to accept their challenge. Fauquier satisfied his official conscience by telling them to vacate.[10] He could hardly have been surprised when they ignored his command. He was cautious also in dealing with requests from Stuart that he join in the making of a boundary line between Virginia and the Cherokee, who expansively claimed that the region between the Appalachians and the Kentucky River was part of their hunting grounds. Fauquier sought to avoid negotiations, certain to cause discontent in Virginia. On December 13, 1766, the House of Burgesses expressed its opinion of the claims of the Cherokee and also of British Western policy in an address to the crown which demanded that the rights of the Kanawha Valley settlers under Virginia law be recognized and urged that the region between Pennsylvania on the north, the Ohio on the west, and North Carolina on the south, merely used for hunting by only a few Indians, be opened to occupation.

Meanwhile, London officials took action. On November 14 Lord Shelburne, British secretary of state for the southern department, ordered Fauquier to join Stuart and the Cherokee in running a boundary from John Chiswell's lead mine on the Kanawha behind the Virginia settlements to "that point from whence [the Indian boundary of] the northern provinces sets out." Soon afterward Sir William Johnson, who had been trying to secure permission to buy claims to the south bank of the Ohio as far west as the mouth of the Tennessee River from the Six Nations, was told that the Cherokee owned the region west of the Kanawha. Johnson could purchase from the Iroquois territory to

[10] Alden, *General Gage in America*, 140–41.

the eastward of that river. Shelburne chose to define the rights of the Cherokee in very generous fashion. They feared Virginia advance to the southwest rather than to the west. They wanted particularly protection on the upper Kanawha. He gave it to them as at least part owners of a region extending indefinitely to the west of the Kanawha, perhaps as far as the mouth of the Tennessee. Undoubtedly he relied upon Stuart's advice; but he gave more to the Cherokee than Stuart asked for them. The Earl of Hillsborough as colonial secretary and the cabinet also accepted Shelburne's view, as did the Board of Trade, in a famous report of March 7, 1768. The British government was willing to let the early settlers west of the Kanawha remain and to permit others to move to its right bank and slightly beyond its upper reaches in Virginia. When Stuart suggested that it was unnecessary to be so generous to his Indian charges and that they would accept a line drawn from Chiswell's Mine to the mouth of the Kentucky River, a proposal which must have been pleasing in Virginia, Hillsborough refused to listen.

In a great congress at Hard Labor, North Carolina, in October, 1768, the Cherokee happily agreed to the boundary demanded by the ministry. But the Old Dominion refused to accept it. Virginians Dr. Thomas Walker and Andrew Lewis, the one the head of the Loyal Company, the other the leading spirit in a Greenbrier Company, had been appointed as representatives of the colony in the preceding June to work with both Johnson and Stuart in drawing the Indian boundary. In the fall, at Fort Stanwix, the Six Nations "insisted," undoubtedly at the instigation of Johnson, Walker, and Lewis, upon selling to the crown the south bank of the Ohio as far west as the mouth of the Tennessee. As soon as this sale was arranged, Lewis hurried south, hoping that Stuart would be as understanding as Johnson and the Cherokee as liberal as the Six Nations. He was too late for the Hard Labor Congress. He and Walker convinced Virginia's new governor, Lord Botetourt, who had just arrived from England, that Virginia had been wronged. Botetourt urged Stuart to delay the marking of the Hard Labor line and to ask the Cherokee to cede their claims between the Kanawha and the mouth of the Tennessee, and he sent Walker and Lewis to see Stuart in South Carolina.

En route they encountered two prominent Cherokee chiefs, Saluy and Usteneka, and brought them to Charleston. The two whites talked persuasively to the two red men about injury done to a few Virginians whose homes had inadvertently been left outside the Hard Labor line. Wouldn't the Cherokee make a change in the boundary to help those distressed people? The Indians would. Then Stuart asked the two speculators to put their wishes on paper. They wanted the Cherokee to abandon all territory north of the line 36' 30". Their performance angered Stuart, long irritated by the refusal of Virginia officials to co-operate with him and even to answer his letters. He agreed to put their proposal before Hillsborough and did, but now recommended only a moderate change, by which the Cherokee would abandon all territory northeast of a line running westward along the southern boundary of Virginia to the Holston and thence directly to the mouth of the Kanawha. The rights of the settlers earlier neglected would thus be protected.

The British cabinet, ratifying the treaty of Fort Stanwix, approved Stuart's proposal and authorized new settlements as far west as the Hard Labor line, thus definitely abandoning for Virginia the policy of restricting the pioneers to the eastern side of the Appalachian divide. Botetourt and the burgesses were not satisfied and protested bitterly, to no avail. The governor became convinced that he had been the tool of Virginia expansionists and he abandoned the struggle. In June, 1770, the burgesses also bent to the will of the cabinet, for a different reason. It had become apparent that the recently formed Grand Ohio Company, composed principally of Pennsylvanians and British merchants and officials, was laboring mightily to obtain a huge proprietary grant stretching from Pennsylvania to Cumberland Gap and including most of the Kanawha Valley. Should it succeed, Virginian speculators would suffer, and Virginia herself would be virtually cut off from the West. It was important in Williamsburg to secure a grip as firm as possible on the West; the burgesses accordingly voted £2,900 for expenses toward executing Stuart's proposal.

The Cherokee braves agreed to it, although there was much unrest among them. Proclamations and agreements notwithstanding, Virginians and North Carolinians had pushed southward down the valleys of the Watauga, Holston, and Nolichucky rivers in 1768 and into that of the Powell in 1769. They had established the first settlements in Tennessee. Squatters on the Watauga had neatly evaded the rule against private purchases from Indians. They persuaded some of the Cherokee to sign a perpetual lease; and they defied the efforts of the Cherokee nation and Alexander Cameron, one of Stuart's deputies, to remove them.

At Lochaber, South Carolina, in October, 1770, the Cherokee ceded what had been asked, except for the Long Island in the Holston River, which they earnestly desired to be recognized as their property. Once again, they indicated they were not overly concerned about lands adjacent to the Ohio and offered to abandon their claim to all, or most, of northeastern Kentucky in exchange for the little island. Once again Stuart indicated he opposed Virginian advance southward, but not westward. He suggested that Virginia push this bargain with the ministry. Hillsborough would have none of it. It was nevertheless substantially made. In the following year Cameron, John Donelson as representative of Virginia, and a party of Cherokee headed by Attakullakulla, set out to mark the Lochaber line. Instead, they agreed to run it from the Holston northwestward across the Cumberlands to the Kentucky River and thence to its mouth, and they did so. The Cherokee nation gave its consent. John Murray, Earl of Dunmore, soon after assuming office as governor of Virginia, deceitfully informed Hillsborough that the change made was a small one and asked that it be approved. The minister was not hoodwinked, but he left office in August, 1772. His successor, the Earl of Dartmouth, gave his sanction, but hardly to please Virginia. In 1773, with his blessing, the proprietary colony of Vandalia proposed by the Grand Ohio Company was formally sanctioned by the Privy Council, which, however, forbade it to grant lands beyond the Lochaber boundary.

But Virginia was not beaten, nor were her speculators. The Vandalia project was sharply opposed not only in Williamsburg but also in New York and London, by General Gage. Worsening relations between Britain and America after the Boston Tea Party doubtless encouraged British officials to delay final action. It languished, and died in the War of Independence. Lord Dunmore actually secured advantage for Virginia from the seeming success of the Grand Ohioans. If they were in the future to be allowed to grant lands within the Lochaber line, why shouldn't Virginia —and immediately? Himself interested in acquiring a western estate, the Scottish lord found pretext after excuse after reason to justify him in making grants to the Lochaber boundary, then to the Donelson line. By 1774 surveyors under his direction were toiling on *both* sides of the Kentucky River. Injunctions and protests from Dartmouth he circumvented or ignored.

By different means Dunmore dealt quite successfully with another obstacle to Virginian expansion, the Shawnee, who also claimed for themselves the south bank of the Ohio. In the latter part of 1773 and the early months of 1774 murderous affrays on the upper Ohio brought on open warfare between their braves and Virginia. Dunmore collected about 3,000 militiamen, and they marched in two divisions toward the Shawnee capital on the Scioto River in the summer of 1774. One of these, led by Andrew Lewis, was attacked by the Shawnee at Point Pleasant on October 10. The fighting was desperate, the result a drawn battle. The Virginians lost more than fifty men, and the Indians many. The Shawnee had no stomach for further hostilities at the moment. When the two contingents joined in their towns, the Indians sued for peace. Thereafter they raided, but did not claim as their own, territory south of the Ohio.

Neither Dunmore, nor Stuart, nor Governor Josiah Martin of North Carolina, nor all three together, could prevent colonization of Kentucky by the astute and resolute North Carolinian Richard Henderson. After 1768 it became evident that individuals among the Cherokee, and even a majority of them, would sell or lease lands to private persons well supplied with sweet words, abundant goods, and strong rum. Henderson, a judge, was aware of this fact and also of a British legal opinion by Lord Camden and Charles Yorke supporting the validity of private purchases of land from princes in India. He therefore concluded that he could lawfully secure possession of a vast territory in Kentucky and the Tennessee country, notwithstanding the Proclamation of 1763, a statute of North Carolina forbidding private purchases from the red men without the consent of the governor and his council, and the authority of Virginia above the line 36′ 30″.[11] He formed in August, 1774, at Hillsboro, the Louisa Company, which became five months later the Transylvania Company, containing nine members. Stuart tried to persuade the Cherokee not to deal with Henderson; Martin ordered him to desist; but the Transylvania Company purchased from the Cherokee in a great congress at Sycamore Shoals on the Watauga River in March, 1775, a magnificent domain stretching from the Ohio and the Kentucky rivers to the southern edge of the Cumberland River watershed, and in addition a corridor between the Watauga and the Cumberland range, so that pioneers emigrating from North Carolina could make use of Cumberland Gap without intruding upon Cherokee territory. One should avoid excessive pity for the Cherokee. They had tried vainly to sell to Henderson the region east of the Kentucky which they had previously ceded to Virginia—Virginia had not paid them the full price. Moreover, it was very doubtful that all the territory they actually sold was their hunting land. Stuart berated the Cherokee, and Dunmore denounced the Sycamore Shoals deal as illegal. Henderson, however, was soon selling land in quantity and sending settlers in numbers into Kentucky. With his fellow North Carolinian Daniel Boone, he helped in laying solid groundworks of the Commonwealth of Kentucky. Pioneers who relied upon his titles soon discovered that they were not so firmly founded.

Richard Henderson posed no profound threat to Virginia's control over Kentucky. Accordingly, by 1775, since Vandalia was slowly vanishing, the Old Dominion was effectively establishing her claim to empire south of the Ohio. It was otherwise to the north of the great river. Her charter of 1609, by the interpretation given to it by her people, permitted Virginia to extend to Lake Superior, and even beyond. Other colonies, however—Massachusetts and Connecticut, on the basis of their sea-to-sea charters —could assert right to parts of that vast region afterward known as the Old Northwest; more important, there were many Americans who would concede lands south of the Great Lakes to no particular colony of the thirteen, with or without charter. Im-

[11] It has also been asserted, by Archibald Henderson, that the judge was fortified by a legal opinion prepared by Lord Mansfield.

mediately after the Peace of Paris Pennsylvanians and Yorkers as well as Virginians began to dream dreams of wealth secured through the acquisition and sale of Indiana and Illinois prairies. In 1774 all the Americans personally or politically interested in the Old Northwest were sharply shocked by the passage of the Quebec Act, which pushed the boundaries of Quebec southwestward to the Ohio and the Mississippi, except "that nothing herein shall in any wise affect the boundaries of any other colony." [12] Although it cannot be said that the act cut off Virginia at the Ohio, it raised for her a potential rival for power beyond the river; and if the rich lands above the Ohio were distributed by officials on the St. Lawrence rather than those of Williamsburg, Virginians would certainly have smaller opportunity to secure and settle upon them. For these reasons and for others which alarmed the Americans generally, the Quebec Act was heartily condemned in Virginia, even though actual occupation of the Old Northwest was not yet possible.

And the year 1774 brought more bad news from London for Virginians and other Americans interested in dealing in and settling upon the lands beyond the mountains. In February Lord Dunmore was instructed to sell public land only at auction, to multiply the existing minimum price by five, and to double the quitrent rate. He was also to reserve to the crown not the traditional fifth of mines of gold, silver, and precious stones, but all of these valuables. Similar orders went to the other royal governors.[13] Here was a severe blow to the Virginians, accustomed to low sale prices and special personal arrangements, and never eager to pay quitrents.

Trans-Appalachia before 1775 was unquestionably of the greatest importance to the Virginians in terms of both political pride and personal opportunity. When Dunmore, on the day of Lexington and Concord, in order to punish Washington for too ardently defending American rights, declared that Washington's Kanawha lands had not been properly surveyed and thus put his

---

[12] American writers have often failed to give consideration to this "saving clause."
[13] St. George L. Sioussat, "The Breakdown of the Royal Management of Lands in the Southern Provinces, 1773–1775," in *Agricultural History* (Chicago, Baltimore, Evansville, Wis.), III (1929), 67–98.

lands in jeopardy, the canny governor aimed at a vulnerable spot. Were earlier British measures and actions by British officials in connection with the West so offensive to Virginians upon public grounds, so injurious to their personal fortunes, that they impelled planter and pioneer to take up arms in 1775? Certainly they looked upon the Quebec Act with profound suspicion; and Jefferson protested in 1774 against both it and Vandalia as machines to curtail Virginia's just claim to the West. He also denounced the increase in land prices and quitrents—indeed, denied the legality of quitrents.[14] But Jefferson was then defining American rights in language more liberal than most of his fellow planters employed.

Evidence exists in abundance that the Proclamation of 1763 and other British measures threatening and hindering the westward advance of the Old Dominion caused vexation in Virginia. Accordingly, they contributed to a rising feeling of antagonism toward the mother country. It should be remembered, however, that the royal governors of Virginia commonly defended her interests beyond the mountains; that settlement was legal, even by British law, beyond the Kanawha by 1769; that pioneers venturing beyond the Indian boundaries, even across the Kentucky, were not seriously molested by British officials; that not every Virginia planter was a speculator in Western lands; and that many of those who were, invested little in money, time, or thought. It would appear that British policy regarding Western lands seriously irritated both plain and potent people in Virginia. It was not the reason above all why the Virginians took up arms, nor even a major force impelling them to take the field.[15]

The westward advance of the pioneers of the Carolinas and Georgia inevitably caused clash with the Cherokee and Creeks, in the same fashion and for the same reasons that the expansion of Virginia brought conflict on the Kanawha and the Kentucky between the frontiersmen and the Cherokee and Shawnee. Moreover, land speculators of South Carolina and Georgia, although

[14] In Thomas Jefferson, *A Summary View of the Rights of British America* (Williamsburg, [1774]).
[15] This conclusion is substantially the same as that expressed by Thomas P. Abernethy, *Western Lands and the American Revolution* (New York, 1937).

their projects were less grandiose than those of the Grand Ohio and Transylvania companies, created Indian troubles. The Indian boundary stretching across the Carolinas and Georgia established after 1763 was soon threatened and then violated, partly because the Cherokee could not resist suasion coupled with rum. Cherokee gave a lease to the pioneers who settled in eastern Tennessee, and other Cherokee tried to give a tract in the valley of the Saluda River above their boundary with South Carolina to an Indian son of Stuart's deputy, Alexander Cameron, arguing that they loved Cameron and that a donation of land to his son, an Indian, did not violate the Proclamation of 1763. Stuart easily quashed that deal, since Cameron was under his control. But Richard Pearis, a trader, saw possibilities for himself. He, too, had a half-breed son among the Cherokee; they owed him trade debts; and he had no job in the Indian department to lose. The Cherokee gave to his son a second tract, in the same region, and he canceled their debts to him. Stuart was able to interrupt Pearis' scheme by invoking a South Carolina law of 1739 which forbade private purchase of Indian lands. Pearis was actually fined for breaking it, but he profited ultimately, securing compensation for the tract from the British government as a loyalist, after the end of the War of Independence. Inspired by Pearis' example, Edward Wilkinson, another trader, sought a third piece of land in exchange for debts the Cherokee owed to him. Perhaps he had no son among them, since the district was to go directly to him. Stuart prevented Wilkinson from securing title, and the Indian boundary of South Carolina was not seriously violated before the War of Independence, although even a small reservation set aside for the Catawbas in 1764 was threatened.[16]

However, the schemes of Pearis and Wilkinson inspired another, which led to a cession of Indian lands to Georgia. By 1770 the Cherokee generally owed their traders, because of their own improvidence and poor hunting; and the traders owed the mer-

[16] In 1772 Stuart had to deal with a curious proposal from William Henry Drayton, who asked South Carolina to lease the Catawba reservation to him for a period of twenty-one years. Drayton would pay each Catawba warrior goods worth a guinea per annum and guarantee to the tribe free use of their villages and free hunting. Ostensibly, Drayton sought to protect the Indians. Stuart advised against the lease as illegal and unwise, and it was denied.

chants who supplied them with goods. Both traders and merchants began to hope to recoup by securing soil, or cash from the sale of it, in return for canceling debts. They secured the support of Governor Wright, who was eager to promote the growth of Georgia, and Wright arranged a bargain early in 1771 whereby the Cherokee ceded to them a large area on the south bank of the Savannah River, receiving in exchange clean slates with the traders and all the goods which the latter had on hand. Then Wright sought to complete the transaction by arranging for the transfer of the district to the colony of Georgia, the traders to be compensated either in land or in cash derived from it.

Stuart fought against the Cherokee traders and against Wright. Even if the deal were sanctioned in London, as Wright hoped, trouble must come, for the lands sold by the Cherokee, who were wiser than they seemed, included territory claimed by the Creeks. However, Wright brushed aside all difficulties. With his blessing merchants and traders dealing with the Creeks, led by George Galphin and Lachlan McGillivray, agreed to cancel the debts of the Creeks in return for a cession on their part; and Wright personally sought and obtained royal consent in London for a formal purchase of the rights of the two Indian nations. Further difficulty arose because the Creeks offered territory belonging to the Cherokee as well as some of their own. However, in a great congress at Augusta in June, 1773, Georgia secured from the two tribes more than two million acres of land between the Savannah and Ogeechee rivers, the so-called "New Purchase."

Bad conditions in their trade and especially the designs and intrusions of whites upon their hunting grounds gravely disturbed the Cherokee and Creeks after 1763. The Cherokee, seriously injured by their defeat in the Anglo-Cherokee war of 1760–1761 and menaced both from the north and from the east, engaged in a number of frays with frontiersmen during the years 1763–1775 in which both sides committed aggressions and suffered casualties. When the War of Independence came, the Cherokee almost inevitably became allies of the crown. Indeed, Stuart could not prevent them from taking the warpath against the Southern colonists. The Creeks, resenting in 1763 the loss of a very favorable bargaining position which had permitted them to play the British, French, and Spanish against each other, displayed greater hostility toward the Southern colonists than did the Cherokee during the twelve years that followed. In the winter of 1763–1764 and again in that of 1773–1774 they murdered several frontier folk. Stuart was able in the end to restrain them by building among the Upper Creeks a pro-British faction headed by his friend, the chief Emistisiguo, and by stimulating a feud between the Creeks and Choctaw. He was bitterly opposed by The Mortar, rival of Emistisiguo and violent foe to the Southern colonists. Stuart's efforts were crowned with success in the fall of 1774 when The Mortar fell in battle at the hands of the Choctaw. It was extremely doubtful, however, that the Creeks would remain neutral in the War of Independence, certain that they would not assist the Americans. Some of them, with the Cherokee and Shawnee, forced the Americans to fight on a southwestern front. In 1775 the prospect was disturbing for the new settlers east and west of the Southern Appalachians, and it long remained so.

CHAPTER IX

SECTIONAL CLASH

ARLY in the War of Independence, when the patriots began to form an American union, a sectional conflict between South and North commenced; it has continued. Even earlier there had been East-West clash, which never grew into a great civil war but which also endures. The struggle in Virginia in 1676 between the forces led by Nathaniel Bacon and Governor Sir William Berkeley was largely one of West against East, and there was East-West antagonism in the Southern colonies immediately before 1775. One may therefore be tempted to think of Hermon Husband and Rednap Howell, leaders of the famous North Carolina Regulators, as later Bacons and to make too much of collision at that period between Piedmont and Tidewater in North Carolina and also in the other Southern colonies. Once it was even contended that the North Carolina Regulators supported the crown in the War of Independence because their old enemies were principally patriots. The contest between Tidewater and Piedmont in the Carolinas in the 1760's and 1770's, sharp enough, was less severe than has been commonly believed; and there was then little of such strife in Maryland, Virginia, and Georgia.

It was at one time fashionable among historians to describe the young Patrick Henry as a champion of the sturdy yeoman farmers of the Virginia Piedmont, a manful fighter against the entrenched and privileged plantation aristocracy of the seaboard. Such a figure was and is appealing. That Henry in youth was no ardent champion of the established Anglican Church is doubtless true, and also that he had a following among back-country folk, especially Presbyterians, because of his role in the Parson's Cause.

However, Henry embarked upon no campaign against the Established Church, stronger on Tidewater than in the interior of Virginia; during the War of Independence he wished to have all the orthodox Christian churches supported by tax money rather than to effect separation of church and state. Nor is there any evidence that he strove either to modify the existing political system (save with respect to Britain) or to escort the yeoman into the seats of power, whether at the county capitals or at Williamsburg. He may have declaimed against the county courts, the centers of local authority, because they were dominated by gentlemen who had pleased other gentlemen, who were not required to win elections; it is not known that he did. He may have delivered philippics against an unrepresentative House of Burgesses to which the Tidewater planters sent more members than their numbers justified; no record of such an oration has been found. Nor has it been shown that he objected to the governor's council as an exclusive club of Tidewater aristocrats. Essentially, Henry —and Richard Henry Lee, who also rose to fame after 1765— was moved by a desire to push his way into the small circle of those who exercised authority in Virginia. His personal ambition was a conventional one; his methods of achieving it were unorthodox, for he did not seek the support of those already in power. Both Henry and Lee profited politically by independently and very ardently opposing the Stamp Act; and both ultimately achieved their ambition, though they incurred the hostility of the "Old Guard," John Robinson, Robert Carter Nicholas, Edmund Pendleton, and their like.

It is doubtful, in fact, that there was any cause for Henry to lead, since substantial evidence of political discontent in the Piedmont—and in the Shenandoah—before the War of Independence has not been brought forward. It would seem, rather, that the newer Virginia was not then unhappy because of the dominance of the older, that the colony did not divide at the fall line. It is true that the western districts were insufficiently represented, especially if white population were the criterion.[1] They

[1] Jamestown was apparently a "pocket borough" belonging to Champion Travers, its representative in the burgesses immediately before the War of Independence. Smyth, *Tour in the United States of America*, I, 9.

were, however, not without voices in the House of Burgesses, for new counties, each of which sent members of that body, were steadily established in Virginia as the tide of settlement advanced toward and over the mountains. Moreover, the Tidewater aristocracy encouraged the development of the West, speculated in its lands, sent its younger sons and clients into it. As yet, it would appear, there was insufficient economic and social cleavage to cause the West to challenge the established leadership of the eastern planters.[2]

Nor is there any clear indication of East-West contest in Maryland before the War of Independence;[3] and it is likely that there was no more regional conflict north of the Potomac than south. All of which is not to deny the existence of jarring elements in the colonies bordering upon the Chesapeake from which sectional clash might have sprung. The back country in both contained large non-English populations as opposed to the English on Tidewater, Germans especially in Maryland's Frederick County, Scotch-Irish remarkably in Virginia's Shenandoah. There were also religious contrarieties, the seacoast being Anglican, the inland parts Presbyterian, Lutheran, Baptist, and otherwise. Economic variations existed; and it is well known that Negro slavery was less prevalent in the West than in the East. These divergences were perhaps not yet acute enough to excite political passions; possibly the rise of such passions had been prevented by the relatively just and sensible conduct of the people in power at Annapolis and Williamsburg.

Georgia also did not suffer before 1775 from East-West bitterness, because Georgia had as yet no considerable West, but South Carolina was riven by controversy, by strife almost as sharp as that

[2] Carl Bridenbaugh, *Seat of Empire; The Political Role of Eighteenth-Century Williamsburg* (Williamsburg, 1950), 48–71. See also Bridenbaugh, *Myths and Realities,* 156–57. That cleavage and sectional contest later developed in Virginia is not to be doubted. Charles H. Ambler, *Sectionalism in Virginia from 1776 to 1861* (Chicago, 1910). However, Jackson T. Main, "Sections and Politics in Virginia, 1781–1787," in *William and Mary Quarterly* (Williamsburg), 3d ser., XII (1955), 96–112, contends that the major opposing forces in the state in the 1780's were the Northern Neck and the South Side, each possessing allies in the Shenandoah, the basis for division being largely economic.

[3] Barker, *Background of the Revolution in Maryland,* 23–26, 32–33.

in North Carolina. South Carolina, like her sister colony, had a Regulation movement.

Low Country and Upcountry were far more distinctly opposed in South Carolina than were Tidewater and Piedmont in the Chesapeake region. The Low Country was a stronghold of aristocracy and Anglicanism; a region in which Negro slaves outnumbered whites, in some parts by as many as six to one; a congeries of rice and indigo plantations scattered about commercial Charleston; a home of English people, together with fusing French Calvinists and Scots and others; and a center, particularly in Charleston, of refinement and culture. The Upcountry, in contrast, was heterogeneous in religion and humble in social status; peopled by Scotch-Irish and Germans, with English, French, and Scots; inhabited by small farmers and cattlemen with few slaves; and lacking in education and elegance. Even so, regional dispute need not have become acute. It became so because the needs and wishes of the back country were neglected by Low Country politicians and royal officials.

Long before the Seven Years' War it was evident that the inhabitants of the Upcountry entertained two grievances which deserved remedy: They were inadequately represented in the Commons House, and they suffered from a lack of convenient courts and law-enforcing officers. The local units of government in the colony, the parishes, had been established on the seacoast. However, instead of creating new ones as the Upcountry began to fill with settlers, the Assembly merely extended inland those existing. Theoretically, every settler in South Carolina was thus included in a parish and, if otherwise qualified, could vote for members of the Commons House. However, the boundaries of the parishes had not been run far into the interior, and it was difficult for an Upcountry man to discover in which he resided. Moreover, the voting place was likely to be distant from his home and perhaps could be reached only at serious cost in time, money, and physical effort. In effect, many backsettlers were disfranchised; and the votes of those who managed to find the polling places counted little as against those of Low Country folk. A word from the strand was worth two or more from the bush. Accordingly, there were no spokesmen for the Upcountry people in the Commons House until the later 1760's and then but a few as the result of a great effort on their part. The second grievance arose from the fact that legal machinery was concentrated, except for justices of the peace, in Charleston. There was neither a sheriff nor a county or circuit court outside the city, for a system unequal to Low Country needs and obviously unfitted for those of the Upcountry endured despite sporadic efforts toward change. It was almost impossible as a result to deal with lawbreakers in the interior; and at the same time well-behaved citizens of that region were required to make arduous and expensive journeys to Charleston to assert their legal rights and to defend themselves in courts.

These grievances became ever larger as the Upcountry settlements grew in numbers and spread farther and farther inland, especially after the Seven Years' War. They also expanded because of a rapid and alarming increase among them of the criminal element. The South Carolina frontier, like any American frontier, was a refuge for outlaws, rascals, and ne'er-do-wells as well as a land of opportunity for the honest and industrious. Checked neither by courts nor by sheriffs, criminals became ever more numerous and their offenses more atrocious. The influx of Scotch-Irish and others from the north further stimulated social sin, for these had learned in their earlier homes in American hinterlands to live without law or order. A lack of schools and disciplined clergymen had its customary bad effects.

The Reverend Charles Woodmason, an Anglican missionary, has bequeathed to us a lurid description of society in the Upcountry in the later 1760's. He tells of drunkenness, fornication, profanity, robbery, rape, sacrilege, and murder; groups of naked men and women bathing together; horse thieves; religious orgies; and varied brutalities committed by individuals and gangs of outlaws. The region was crowded with "Banditti, profligates, Reprobates, and the lowest vilest Scum of Mankind." [4] Woodmason was fond of colorful invective, and his vision was doubtless clouded by the hardships he endured and by the hostile reception Presbyterians, Baptists, and unchurched sinners gave him. Quite surely

[4] Hooker (ed.), *Carolina Backcountry on the Eve of the Revolution*, 25. Professor Hooker's account of the Regulation in South Carolina, pp. 165–89, is the principal basis for that given in the text.

he made too much of vileness there. Nevertheless, the social scene in the back country was shocking, and decent people there were profoundly disturbed. They determined to establish order with or without the assistance of authorities in Charleston.

After 1752 petitions from the Upcountry asking for representation, courts, and help in establishing schools were frequently sent to Charleston. Grand juries in the capital almost as frequently denounced lawless acts in the interior and urged action to establish order there. Governor James Glen asked the Assembly to provide additional courts as early as 1754, and Lieutenant Governor Bull made similar requests in 1765. Chief Justice Charles Shinner also championed the cause of the Upcountry settlers in the years immediately following the Seven Years' War. Shinner had little influence in South Carolina, being an Irishman who had secured his post because of friends in London rather than through merit; he had even less after the Stamp Act crisis, in which he played the part of a loyal British officeholder. Bull was Carolina-born, able, and respected. Yet his pleas, despite the obvious good sense contained in them, went unheeded. The provost marshal of the colony, after 1764 Richard Cumberland, who was responsible for law enforcement throughout the province, had a lucrative office, and he was not disposed to abandon part of an easy revenue. Residing in England, he performed his duties by a deputy, Roger Pinckney. He wanted no sheriffs who would collect fees that had been and were his. Lawyers were opposed to the change, for they preferred to carry on their profession comfortably and economically in Charleston. Those who profited from the nonlegal business which came to Charleston as the result of the concentration of the judiciary in the city also objected to Bull's proposal. Others in the Low Country were simply indifferent to the needs of the backsettlers. Upcountry soliciting for representation in the Assembly was given even less attention than prayers for judges and sheriffs; it was apparently ignored. The Low Country aristocrats preferred to maintain the Commons House as an exclusive club for themselves. They did not care to give political power to men who paid little in taxes. Bull himself did not urge that its doors be thrown open to men from the backlands, possibly because he knew it was useless to try to persuade his fellow planters.

Desperate, the better people of the Upcountry took the law into their own hands in the spring of 1767. Forming local associations, they attacked some of the outlaw bands which infested their country and dispensed crude justice. When fall came, they were also meditating a march upon Charleston to demand remedies for their grievances. The governor, Lord Charles Montagu, responded by issuing a proclamation that ordered them, as "Regulators," to disperse and asking the Assembly to pass laws to restrain them; and the criminal court in Charleston impartially punished some of them with conventional evildoers.

But Montagu and the Assembly were soon forced to give heed to the wishes of the Upcountry. On November 7 Benjamin Hart, John Scott, Moses Kirkland, and Thomas Woodward presented in Charleston a formidable "Remonstrance," [5] written by Woodmason in behalf of four thousand settlers, it was claimed. Their grievances were described in detail, at length, and in passionate language. They had no access to a superior court except "in a nook by the seaside," and they were taxed without representation. They peremptorily demanded action. Discomfited, Montagu and the Assembly promised to provide additional and convenient courts, and to give temporary relief they sent out two companies of militia to round up criminals in the Upcountry. The militia performed useful service, but were unable to seize all their prey.

Unfortunately, the coming of judges and sheriffs to the backlands was long delayed. It was necessary to make arrangements to pay off Richard Cumberland and two other officials who would lose financially by the establishment of the new courts, especially Cumberland, who was strongly entrenched in office, had influence in London, and would lose his post as provost marshal. His price for abandoning it was £5,000 sterling, and he got it. An act providing for six circuit courts, together with judges, sheriffs, clerks, and jails, was not passed until the following April. Moreover, the law was put in such form that it could not receive the approval of the British Privy Council, for it gave to the prospective judges tenure during good behavior rather than at the pleasure of the crown. It was disallowed in London, and a second bill to the same effect was vetoed by the governor in July, 1769. The Commons

[5] *Ibid.*, 213-33.

House then finally gave in to the wishes of the crown and passed a law which received approval. There was still further postponement. The act stipulated that the new courts were not to function until courtrooms and jails had been completed. The judges did not take their seats until 1773.[6]

Well aware that the act of 1768 would be set aside in England, Thomas Bell, William Calhoun, Patrick Calhoun, and Andrew Williamson, for themselves and other Upcountry settlers, presented in July, 1768, a second major protest to the Assembly, condemning it for the useless enactment of a law which would certainly be annulled in London and insisting that additional parishes sending members to the Commons House be organized. Another memorial to the same effect was sent in to Charleston at the same time. A committee headed by Joseph Kershaw of Camden, who was one of the first Upcountry men to sit in the Commons House, promptly recommended that new parishes be established and urged that provision be made for some schools in them at public expense. Before it could consider the report, the Commons House was sent home by the governor because of its anti-British zeal; and a similar plan pushed by Kershaw in April, 1770, died for the same reason.[7] Attempts by Bull to revive the measure during the following year bore no fruit.

Deep discontent with the behavior of the Low Country aristocracy continued in the backlands until 1770. In 1769, informed that John Rutledge had referred to the Upcountry folk as "a pack of beggars," Woodmason wrote to him in bitter protest.

"Pray, are We not all Subjects of the same King? Fellow Protestants? Fellow Xtians? Fellow Britons? Of the same Blood and Origin? Are any of Your Descents, Greater, Nobler, ancienter, more reputable than ours? Many of You (tho' You abound in Riches) far ignobler; Have You more Virtue, more Religion More Goodness than Us?—Many, far less; Indeed You may be said to have more Learning, Politeness, Wealth, Slaves, and Lands but We speak of Intrinsic Worth— All we wish is, that You had better Hearts than we can boast; But what hinders that We be not your

[6] McCrady, *South Carolina under the Royal Government*, 625-39, 642-43.
[7] *Ibid.*, 639-41.

Equals in ev'ry Respect? Nothing but Your Pride Vanity, Selfishness, and Meanspiritedness— Had You any Seeds of Honour, Love
of your Country, or Value for Mankind, You would strive, use
Your utmost Endeavours, exert Your whole strength strain evry
Nerve, to render all others around You, equally Easy Happy, Independent, Affluent, and genteel as Yourselves." Woodmason continued with irreverent and pungent phrases concerning Low
Country claims to permanent superiority.

"You call us a Pack of Beggars—Pray Sir look back to Your own
Origin? Draw the Curtain up but for one twenty Years only, and
View Persons as then, and now; It is a strange Succession of
Fortuitous Causes that has lifted up many of Your Heads— Not
Your own Wisdom or Virtue: Quite the reverse— But step back
only to the beginning of this Century— What then was Carolina?
What Charlestown? What the then Settlers (Your Ancestors)—
Even such as We now are.

"Will you pronounce that in 50 Years, our Posterity may not
ride in their Chariots, while Yours walk on foot? Or do you fear
it? It seems so by Your Conduct toward Us—" [8]

The Regulators, promptly achieving neither of their major
goals, continued for many months to deal roughly with lawbreakers, and perhaps with others. Some were arrested and con-
victed of crime in Charleston in 1768. As a result, in June of that
year, a mass meeting at the Congarees composed of delegates from
various parts of the Upcountry declared that writs and warrants
emanating from the capital were not to be served without the
consent of the Regulators. During the summer attempts to do so
were resisted; fracases resulted; in one on the Pee Dee River, some
members of a constable's posse, it was reported, were killed.

The challenge of the back country to governmental authority
persuaded Lord Charles Montagu, and even Bull, that force must
be exerted. Roger Pinckney, deputy provost marshal, went with
militia to the Pee Dee to arrest Regulator leaders. Faced by overwhelming opposition, he was compelled to withdraw without completing his mission. In February, 1769, Joseph Coffell set out from
Charleston with troops to seize twenty-five active Regulators. He

[8] Hooker (ed.), *Carolina Backcountry on the Eve of the Revolution*, 272–73.

did not confine himself to legal activities, and he was confronted on the Saluda River by a body of armed men. Hostilities were barely averted by the arrival of news that Coffell had been disowned by Charleston authorities. In the spring of that year the Regulators despairingly decided to petition the King for redress and to send Woodmason and a Mr. Cary to London for the purpose. Woodmason refused to go, and the project collapsed. Perhaps word of it, together with the threat of warfare in the Upcountry, persuaded Low Country leaders to abandon efforts to use force. Thereafter, Bull carried through a policy of conciliation. He pardoned Regulators and embarked upon a successful campaign to establish order in the Upcountry, completing the work of the Regulators. Tension waned, and the backsettlements were quiet as the War of Independence approached.

In that war the sentiments and behavior of the Upcountry people were diverse, with many neutral and many giving their support to Britain in strong language and vigorous deeds. There can be no doubt that some residents of the interior refused to give allegiance to the patriot camp primarily because Low Country men were conspicuous in it.[9] That grudges remaining from the sectional conflict drove the bulk of the former Regulators into Toryism must remain doubtful. Tories and neutrals also appeared conspicuously among Charleston merchants and rice-indigo planters. In the end it was the Upcountry that offered determined, desperate resistance to British arms.

It will have been observed that geographical, economic, and social cleavage between Low Country and Upcountry did not compel bloody conflict, that the tumult on the South Carolina Piedmont quieted as soon as some of the grievances of the backsettlers were removed. Nor did similar cleavage in North Carolina produce clash so bitter that Piedmont and Tidewater could not have lived together in peace. North Carolina also had her Regulator movement. It was ended by force and in bloodshed, but the slain were few. It was not necessary that any should have been killed. Moreover, the struggle between the Regulators and their enemies in North Carolina was not exclusively or even basically one between Piedmont and Tidewater.

[9] *Ibid.*, 187–89.

East-West divergence in North Carolina at that period is evident. Tidewater and Piedmont were physically separated by barren and almost unoccupied lands. Below them were plantations and their wealthy owners, together with their numerous slaves; a dominant English aristocracy; and a favored Anglican Church. Above them was a country of small farms; few slaves; fewer aristocrats; Scotch-Irish, Germans, Welsh, and English; Presbyterians, Baptists, Moravians, and Dunkards. The Piedmont people came from the north as well as the east, and their commerce was with Charleston, Petersburg, and even Baltimore rather than with Wilmington and Brunswick. Even so, had the needs and wishes of the Western folk received sympathetic attention from the Tidewater aristocracy and the royal governor, all might have gone reasonably well. Squabbling between the two sections, to be sure, could hardly have been averted—it continues, although not for precisely the same reasons.

But the North Carolina Tidewater aristocracy, less imposing than that of South Carolina, almost equaled it in indifference toward the back countrymen. In the 1750's and 1760's, while the Assembly of South Carolina was refusing to organize new parishes in the Upcountry and so depriving her new settlers of decent representation, that of North Carolina established counties on the Piedmont and accorded to their inhabitants the right to elect members of the lower house. These counties, however, were not set up with remarkable rapidity. Besides, their creation was frequently accompanied by the making of new ones on Tidewater; and five of the Tidewater counties were allowed to send five— rather than the usual two—members of the Assembly. In 1776 Orange County in the Piedmont contained a larger white population than all of those five together and had two spokesmen and votes in the Assembly to their twenty-five. Almost without representation in South Carolina, the backsettlers were startlingly under-represented in North Carolina.

In both colonies, of course, offices at the capital were almost exclusively held by men of the Tidewater and the British Isles, a minor grievance. A far more serious one in North Carolina, and the chief cause of the Regulation in that colony, arose from a pernicious system of local government and abuses committed by county officials in the Piedmont.[10] While the Regulators of South Carolina fought to secure judges and sheriffs, those of her sister province struggled against such officials. The system of county government in North Carolina, like that of Virginia, was strikingly undemocratic. The governor, assisted by his council, filled all the offices save one, with or without nomination or recommendation of the local dignitaries; the county clerk was named by a provincial clerk of the pleas, himself a British or American placeman. The result in North Carolina, as in Virginia, was a concentration of power in a few persons responsible only to each other and an often distant governor. While the great powers they exercised are not known to have corrupted the county magnates in Virginia, it is certain that the local "big-wigs" of the North Carolina Piedmont, if not thievish, used all their opportunities to secure lucre and kudos. It was notorious that the sheriffs, who were responsible for remitting tax money to the provincial capital, kept part or all of it, temporarily or permanently. Plural officeholding was common, and fees—men in county posts were not paid salaries—were frequent and at least occasionally exorbitant. The "sheriff and his bums" formed a vicious "courthouse ring" in the Piedmont. He and his associates were hated the more because they were often of English blood and Tidewater or British birth and because the new settlers from the North had learned to dislike and disobey law in their earlier homes.

Especially odious in the Piedmont was Edmund Fanning, a native of New York's Long Island, a graduate of Yale, and a client of Governor William Tryon. It has been said that Fanning's "crime seems to have been only that he was Tryon's friend," [11] and it is true that his enemies could bring forward no evidence proving him to be the thorough scoundrel they said he was. Moreover, he enjoyed a long and, except in North Carolina, successful career. Fan-

[10] Hugh T. Lefler and Paul Wager (eds.), *Orange County—1752–1952* (Chapel Hill, 1953), 26. Chapter IV of this volume, written by Professor Lefler, offers the most recent study of the North Carolina Regulation. His interpretation seems the most acceptable. A full description of it is given in John S. Bassett, "The Regulators of North Carolina (1765–1771)," in American Historical Association, *Annual Report*, 1894 (Washington, 1895), 141–212. See also Archibald Henderson (ed.), "The Origin of the Regulation in North Carolina," in *American Historical Review*, XXI (1915–1916), 320–32; Lefler and Newsome, *North Carolina*, 164–78.

[11] Bridenbaugh, *Myths and Realities*, 162.

ning was, however, register of deeds, judge, colonel of militia, member of the Assembly from Orange County, and the leader of the "ring" in that county. Favorite of the governor and a "foreigner," he extracted from his offices all possible revenue. He was a grasping young man "on the make," and may be described as an "honest grafter." Associated with him was Virginia's Francis Nash, court clerk, justice of the peace, member of the county court, militia captain, and assemblyman. Nash was also detested, and with him the three Frohocks, Thomas, John, and William, all of them public officers, though not in Orange County, which had enough to bear. Regulator verses, probably written by Rednap Howell, who was a schoolmaster, harshly describe Fanning.

> *When Fanning first to Orange came*
> *He looked both pale and wan,*
> *An old patched coat upon his back*
> *An old mare he rode on*
>
> *Both man and mare wa'nt worth five pounds*
> *As I've been often told*
> *But by his civil robberies*
> *He's laced his coat with gold.*

Nor did all the Frohocks escape Regulator balladry.

> *Says Frohock to Fanning, "To tell the plain truth,*
> *When I came to this country, I was but a youth.*
> *My father sent for me, I want worth a cross;*
> *And then my first study was to cheat for a hoss.*
>
> *"I quickly got credit and straight ran away*
> *And haven't paid for him to this very day."*
> *Says Fanning to Frohock, "'Tis a folly to lie;*
> *I rode an old mare that was blind in one eye.*
>
> *"Five shillings in money I had in my purse,*
> *My coat it was patched but not much the worse.*
> *But now we've got rich and it's very well known*
> *That we'll do well enough if they'll let us alone."* [12]

[12] Arthur P. Hudson, "Songs of the North Carolina Regulators," in *William and Mary Quarterly,* 3d ser., IV (1947), 470–85.

Fanning and Frohock had no bards to compose songs in their favor, and they lost the literary battle.

Various other circumstances contributed to create upheaval on the Piedmont. In 1766–1767 the Assembly voted £15,000 to build a "Governor's Palace," a capitol, at New Bern.[13] It was to be paid for by a poll tax, which the backsettlers were reluctant to pay, partly because they fancied that the new and expensive building meant nothing to them, partly because they believed that the tax was unjust. They thought it unfair that the poor farmer in the Piedmont pay as much toward it as the wealthy Tidewater planter —they ignored the fact that it was levied upon slave and free alike. A scarcity of currency enhanced all their discontents. The Earl of Granville, who owned the northern half of the colony, also added to them. He did not bother for seven years after 1766 to keep open an office where people might purchase from him. Moreover, his exactions were greater than those of the crown in the southern half of the province. Still further cause for exasperation came from troubles between landlord speculators on the one side and settlers, some of them squatters, on the other. There were "rent wars" in the Piedmont during the years immediately before the Regulation movement began.

Too much may be made, and has been, of the mistreatment given the backsettlers by Tidewater and local officials. In part the sufferings of the Piedmont people arose from poverty, from conditions beyond the control of governor, Assembly, and sheriff alike. Moreover, it is quite certain that the Regulation in North Carolina had its roots to a degree in a confirmed distaste for law and civil order and in ignorance; it is significant that the local Presbyterian and Baptist clergy did what it could to discourage the movement. Too much may also be said, and has been, about the Regulators as champions of democracy, since their chief goal was honest and inexpensive local government, which might have been attained by mere changes in management and personnel.

If the complaints of the Regulators were not always justified, they were certainly put forward frequently and at length. In June, 1765, in *An Address to the People of Granville County,* George

[13] Alonzo T. Dill, *Governor Tryon and His Palace* (Chapel Hill, 1955), is a history of the "Palace" and of the time in which it was a center of North Carolina life.

Sims, schoolmaster of Nutbush, denounced high taxes, rents, and fees, and the "malpractices" of county officers.[14] In August of the following year far more serious protest came when a mass meeting at Sandy Creek in Orange County asked its officials to appear before a public committee and justify their behavior. The request drawn up for the gathering has been called "Regulator Advertisement Number 1," although the word "Regulation" was not used by the discontented of the North Carolina Piedmont until 1768, when it was imported from South Carolina. The officers of Orange, led by Fanning, refused to answer to an extralegal body; and Fanning assailed the Sandy Creek gathering as insurrectionary. Further protests were similarly ignored in Anson, Granville, Halifax, and other counties, and the Piedmont was seething by 1768. Moderate men who had taken the lead in voicing the unhappiness and demands for reform of the backsettlers, such as Hermon Husband, who had been a Quaker and was opposed to violence, were set aside. More vigorous ones, like James Hunter and William Butler, took their places.

Early in 1768 the Regulators proceeded further. In Orange and other counties they announced that public fees must be changed to their satisfaction and that they would pay no taxes until their demands were met. On April 8, 70 of them, armed, rode into Hillsboro, freed a horse which had been seized because its owner had not paid taxes, and fired a few shots into the roof of Fanning's home. Fanning summoned the local militia to suppress "rioting and rebellion" and called upon Governor Tryon for aid. In May he arrested Butler and Husband, but "the Mob" of Regulators, 700 of them, set out to release them from the Hillsboro jail, and Fanning prudently released the two men. Meanwhile, Tryon asked the discontented to submit their complaints to him, promised to consider them, sponsored some legal reforms, and announced his determination to preserve order. During the summer he paraded with militia through the restless districts to prevent interference with the courts. In September he appeared at Hillsboro with more than 1,400 men, many of them collected on the Piedmont, to see to it that the county court there was not molested.

[14] William K. Boyd (ed.), *Some Eighteenth Century Tracts concerning North Carolina* (Raleigh, 1927), 182–92.

A body of 3,700 Regulators gathered nearby, but was awed by his display of strength and melted away. Husband and Butler, with other Regulation leaders, were tried on several charges, Husband going free and Butler being sentenced to pay a fine and to serve six months in jail. In the same courtroom Fanning, who was accused of extorting illegal fees, was found to be only technically guilty and was compelled to pay nominal fines. Government provincial and local had triumphed, and Tryon left behind him a subdued people when he returned to New Bern.

But Tryon had done little to remove abuses, and disorder flared up after his departure. The sheriff of Orange County, John Lea, was severely beaten in the spring of 1769 when he tried to serve papers on Ninian Hamilton and other Regulators. However, most of the unhappy backsettlers turned to peaceful means to secure redress. The Regulators of Anson, Orange, and Rowan counties petitioned the Assembly, asking for taxation by property rather than by person and for salaried judges and clerks, restrictions on legal fees, secret ballot in the election of representatives, and many other reforms. To back up their demands they put up candidates for the legislature in 1769, several of them victorious. Hermon Husband was elected in Orange County. Fanning was defeated but was soon returned by the borough of Hillsboro, created at the instigation of Tryon in order to give him a seat. The Regulators now had spokesmen in the Assembly, to no avail, for that body did nothing to soothe the Piedmont until late in 1770.

Just as the Assembly was about to act, violence flared once more in Orange. On September 24 a Regulation mob of 150 men, headed by Hunter, Butler, Husband, and Rednap Howell, invaded the courtroom at Hillsboro and engaged in a quarrel with Richard Henderson, who was the only judge present. They received no satisfaction from him. When John Williams, a lawyer, appeared, they turned furiously upon him and thrashed him. They then found Fanning in the courthouse, dragged him into the street, and whipped him. Other officials and lawyers suffered the same brutality, Thomas Hart, Michael Holt, and Alexander Martin among them. Judge Henderson was also threatened, but finally escaped town on a fast horse. The following day the mob permitted Fanning to leave town on condition that he run until he was out of their sight. It then destroyed his fine house, built, as they believed, with the money he had extorted.[15] On November 12 Henderson's barn and stables in Granville were burned down, doubtless by Regulators. The news of these events, together with reports that the Piedmont men were marching toward Tidewater, caused panic and fury at New Bern.

At last Tryon and the Assembly, alarmed, not only conceded the justice of many of the demands of the Regulators but did something substantial to meet them. Four new counties were set up in the Piedmont, thus increasing the representation of the West in the Assembly, and various measures to improve the courts and to limit fees were quickly enacted. These changes proceeded, however, in part from fear and were accompanied by repression. The lower house expelled Husband, who was promptly arrested on several charges and held in jail for six weeks, being released in February, 1771, because a grand jury could find no evidence of crime on his part. The Assembly gave the attorney general power to bring a charge of rioting against any person in any superior court in the colony, declared outlaws all those who failed to appear to answer to such charges within sixty days, and authorized Tryon to use the provincial militia to compel obedience. This measure made it possible to try men on Tidewater for offenses committed in the Piedmont. It also exposed to sudden death those who refused to come to court to face rioting charges, for any person could kill an outlaw with impunity.

The reforms made by the Assembly, coupled with the threat of the punitive act, would in all probability have brought the Regulation to a peaceful end. It will be recalled that the South Carolina Regulators became quiet as soon as part of their wishes was granted. Tryon lacked the prudence of William Bull. He was an army officer, and preferred force to persuasion. He had excuse for using the militia, and the first response of the discontented in the Piedmont to the news of Husband's arrest and the passage of the riot act gave him further reason. The Regulators continued to gather and to utter threats of marching upon New Bern, and the local militia in their region was unable to disperse them. They

[15] Richard Henderson's account of the rioting is in Saunders (ed.), *Colonial Records of North Carolina*, VIII, 241–44.

talked, however, of arbitration, a sign that they would bend before authority. Tryon did not give them time to cool.

In April, 1771, Tryon took the field with a body of militia, moving forward from New Bern toward Hillsboro and gathering men as he went. Meanwhile, General Hugh Waddell led a second column into Salisbury. The two forces were to meet at Hillsboro. Confronted by large numbers of Regulators, Waddell chose to temporize and to fall back to Salisbury rather than to try to reach the rendezvous. Tryon pushed on into Hillsboro, meeting no opposition. There he learned that his lieutenant was in trouble. On May 11 he set out from that place to go to Waddell's assistance. On May 14 he arrived at the Alamance River, with fewer than a thousand men. There he learned that two thousand Regulators were camped only five miles beyond that stream.

The Regulators confronting Tryon had superior numbers, but were inferior in strength. It is said that only half of them were armed. They had no artillery, and Tryon did. Besides, they had no recognized leader. Hermon Husband, who was with them, would not fight. They were badly divided among themselves, some hoping merely to make a show of resistance and so gain concessions from Tryon, others prepared to shoot it out. That they were engaged in a lost cause was indicated by the fact that the militia under the governor included many backsettlers. Their principal men, aware of the ultimate impossibility of resistance, if not of their immediate peril, opened negotiations with Tryon through an intermediary, a prominent Presbyterian clergyman, David Caldwell. Meanwhile, some of their followers, capturing Captain John Walker and Lieutenant John Ashe, scouts for Tryon, tied them to trees and flogged them. The governor was not disposed to bargain in any case; and the treatment given Walker and Ashe confirmed his resolution to insist upon unconditional submission. On May 16 he ordered his men forward, placed them in two battle lines within a half mile of the encampment of the Regulators, and demanded that they give up their leaders to him, lay down their arms, and accept whatever punishment the law required. They refused, and formed crudely and loosely for defense. Disconsolate, Hermon Husband fled, making his way to Maryland and thence to western Pennsylvania, where he again became involved in insurrection, in the Whisky Rebellion, and again escaped death.[16] Rednap Howell also vanished to the northward. Tryon ordered his artillery to fire, sent forward his infantry. The Regulators resisted, even momentarily seized Tryon's cannon. Some departed, however, at the first fire, and the remainder were driven into protecting woods. There they found shelter behind trees, continued the struggle for more than an hour, and then fled in wild disorder, pursued by the victors. Nine of the Regulators were slain, and many were wounded and captured. Tryon's "signal and glorious victory," as he called it, was not won without cost. Nine of his men were killed, and sixty-one wounded.

On the following day, as an example, Tryon hanged James Few, one of his prisoners, on the ground that Few was an outlaw, because he had failed to appear in court to answer a charge under the riot act. He then moved on with his prisoners to Reedy Creek, where he was joined by Waddell, to Wachovia, and then to Salem. He destroyed homes and buildings of notorious Regulators as he went. His march was not resisted. Instead, hundreds and then thousands accepted an offer of pardon from him, in exchange taking a special oath of allegiance by which they promised henceforth to obey law and to pay their taxes.

Tryon did not extend forgiveness to all the Regulators. His prisoners and several of their leaders who had escaped him, including Husband, Howell, James Hunter, William Butler, and Thomas Person, were excepted. In June he had a batch of his prisoners brought to trial at Hillsboro, and twelve of them were found guilty of treason and sentenced to death. The governor reprieved six, who were eventually pardoned; the others were hanged in the presence of his remaining prisoners and his army on June 19. One Thomas Donaldson earned £30 in North Carolina money by serving as executioner. Order had been restored, gruesomely.[17]

All of the principals in the Regulation managed to elude pursuit, and all of them, save for Husband, eventually received for-

[16] He died after being released from prison. The only detailed study of Husband is that by Mary E. Lazenby, *Herman Husband, A Story of His Life* (Washington, 1940).

[17] The Williamsburg *Virginia Gazette* (Rind), January 5, 1769, contains a poem praising Tryon for his wisdom, mildness, and generosity, and comparing him with the emperor Titus.

giveness. Tryon, having been appointed governor of New York, departed from the province soon after the executions at Hillsboro.[18] He was followed by Fanning, who became his secretary. After service in the British army during the War of Independence, Tryon returned to England. He died there and was buried in the yard outside Twickenham parish church. By a most remarkable coincidence the remains of Sir William Berkeley and Sir William Howe were placed within the church, the three men who played principal parts for England in three American rebellions being buried within a few yards of each other. The church is a shrine for Americans, but not because the building and its grounds shelter whatever may endure of Berkeley, Howe, and the victor of the Alamance. A great poet, Alexander Pope, was buried in the same church.

Like Tryon, many of the North Carolina Regulators afterward fought in the War of Independence, some of them on the same side with him. Indeed, it was once believed that the Regulators were prevailingly Tory, and it was contended that they became so largely because of the enmity they harbored against their enemies, the Tidewater men, who were commonly patriots. However, information regarding their later views and behavior is scanty. Of 883 known Regulators, 289 were patriots, 34 were Tories, and 560 cannot be classified.[19] Governor Josiah Martin, who found merit in the complaints of the Regulators, treated them graciously and hoped to secure valuable military assistance from them in the early months of the war. He was disappointed. One of their leaders, Thomas Person, became a patriot; another, James Hunter, took up arms for the crown, was captured, and later adhered to the American cause. Many backsettlers supported Britain in the war, but they had many reasons for doing so. Among some of them resentment against Tidewater tyranny was certainly a moving force. The Tidewater people, it should be remembered, also had their Tories.

The struggles of Regulation in the Carolinas were not pre-

[18] Marshall D. Haywood, *Governor William Tryon and His Administration in the Province of North Carolina* (Raleigh, 1903), offers a friendly analysis of Tryon's career in North Carolina. A more thorough study of Tryon is needed.
[19] Lefler and Newsome, *North Carolina*, 178.

liminary phases of the War of Independence. They were, however, the first stages of East-West conflict which continued in those states long after that war had ended. The same conflict, with local variations, later arose in Georgia and Virginia, if not in Maryland.

CHAPTER X

TEA AND TRUMPETS

FREDERICK, Lord North, was a good-humored, witty, and likeable man. He was George III's first minister for twelve years, from 1770 to 1782. He was not assertive, and he avoided rather than courted trouble. It is rather odd that America revolted during his ministry, and all the more surprising in that the Earl of Dartmouth, North's stepbrother, who was both peaceable and pious, was in charge of the American department of the ministry when the colonists grasped arms. But these good men were not strong men. Dartmouth tried to understand the colonists, but failed; and North hardly made an effort. Moreover, North was weak of will and poor in goods, with a large family to shepherd into the fashionable and expensive world of the British aristocracy. He became, therefore, the tool of George III, who lacked North's intelligence but possessed both will and the power to reward with cash and dignities. North became a kept man, and after 1775 an ever more unhappy one. Ultimately, he broke from the royal grip and became again a free man. By that time the older American colonies had cut themselves off from the British empire.

From the fall of 1770 to that of 1773 the American colonists were generally content and avoided controversy with the mother country. There were clashes between customs men and the British navy on the one side and American merchants and sailors on the other, these reaching a mild climax in the burning of the revenue cutter *Gaspée* off Providence in the summer of 1772; there was squabble in Massachusetts because judges in that colony were placed on a royal payroll; and there was the persistent and irritating quarrel in South Carolina between the Commons House and the council. These affairs caused few fevers among colonists not directly concerned. Nor did the Townshend duty on tea exacerbate. Dutch tea smuggled into American ports was sold much cheaper than the British product and made up nine tenths of the colonists' consumption. The British tea sold so badly in America that it did not seem important to many colonists whether or not duty was paid on it. Washington, who was not backward in defense of American liberties, purchased Townshend-taxed tea during this period. Samuel Adams, to be sure, continued everywhere to find evidence of British tyranny, and in the fall of 1772 he laid the foundations for a system of committees of correspondence in the towns of Massachusetts which would keep each other informed of British iniquities and arrange for common resistance. In the following spring the Virginia House of Burgesses arranged to set up a permanent committee to correspond with and to consult with similar bodies in other colonies toward a more effective defense of American rights, the occasion for this step being the unsuccessful efforts of British officials to find and punish the burners of the *Gaspée*. The Commons House of South Carolina and its counterparts of New England promptly established similar committees at the suggestion of the burgesses, that of Massachusetts blandly asserting that "great and good Effects . . . may reasonably be expected to flow . . . not only to the Colonies but the Parent State." [1] But neither Adams nor any other American could find an issue to put the new political machinery in motion. Lord North carelessly supplied it.

Tea, that comforting beverage, was the means of rearousing American discontent. In the spring of 1773 the British East India Company was in distress. It had one asset which might serve to relieve its embarrassment, seventeen million pounds of tea leaves which lay unsold in its warehouses. The fortunes of the company were of the first importance to Britain; and when its officials asked Lord North for assistance in disposing of its unsold tea, he listened. Hitherto the British had been unable to compete with Dutch smugglers for the American market because British tea was taxed on arrival in England at twelvepence per pound and Townshend-taxed at threepence per pound on reaching America, and because the company had been forced by law to unload and sell its

[1] *Archives of Maryland*, LXIV (1947), 423–31.

tea to British merchants. The company asked that it be relieved, in effect, of both duties, and that it be permitted to sell its tea in America. Freed of both duties and handled without "middlemen," its tea could be sold cheaper in America than the Dutch. North approved of the scheme. However, he calculated, correctly, that the company could pay the Townshend duty and still undersell the Dutch tea. He also believed that the colonists would buy the cheaper tea, even though it was Townshend-taxed. Certainly, they would not be able to persuade the East India Company to enter into nonimportation compacts. At his request Parliament, in May, passed the legislation necessary to carry out the scheme as he had revised it.

The colonists, not overly concerned about the Townshend tea duty so long as little British tea was sold in America, now became alarmed. Should they buy the taxed tea in quantity, they could hardly continue to contend against taxation without representation; and if they failed to struggle, other exactions might follow. The merchants were given additional reason for discontent, for the company arranged to dispose of its tea in America through a few favored men in each colony (only five men were to have the business in Massachusetts, including two sons and a nephew of Thomas Hutchinson). The pulses of constitutional principle rose among the merchants who were ignored by the company, who saw favorites monopolizing then the business in tea and engrossing later trade in other commodities. Many of them returned to the political arena which they had so long avoided. A general determination sprang up in the colonies to prevent the sale of the company's tea and so to assert once more the indissoluble tie between taxation and representation.

The colonists were put to the test late in 1773, when tea ships approached four American ports, Boston, New York, Philadelphia, and Charleston. At Boston, because Thomas Hutchinson was obstinate, three shipments were tossed into the harbor to prevent their being landed and sold by the customs service; a captain reaching Philadelphia prudently sailed off without unloading; another did likewise in New York (one who later appeared there had his tea thrown into the water). The procedure at Charleston was less vigorous but equally effective. Captain Alexander Curling brought his vessel, the *London,* over the bar and into the harbor on December 2. He had on board consignments of tea belonging to the East India Company.

When Captain Curling put in to shore, political feeling was running high in South Carolina. Ever since the Wilkes fund affair, the Commons House and the council, the latter supported by the governor, had been engaged in furious controversy. The council, a majority of which was composed of British-born officials, questioned the right of the Commons to disburse money to support an English enemy of the crown and to do so without the approval of either council or governor. The Commons met the challenge squarely, not only continuing to claim for itself control over public expenditures but also denying that the council, representative of the wishes of the crown rather than of the people of South Carolina, was actually a legislative body. For that house the issue was clearly one between American rights and British tyranny. In 1771 the Commons put in jail Henry Peronneau and Benjamin Dart, the public treasurers, who fancied they should not disburse money without the consent of the council. In reprisal William Bull and Lord Charles Montagu several times sent home the delegates, several times forced new elections. Montagu also compelled the Assembly to meet at Beaufort rather than at Charleston, in a fruitless attempt to soften the lower house. The elections merely brought back the same members, including Rawlins Lowndes, the speaker after 1772, who firmly championed the cause of his house. In August, 1773, William Henry Drayton, who had been appointed to the council for his services to the crown [2] and who had hitherto fought against the Commons House, broke with his colleagues; [3] and his father, John Drayton, also a member, joined him in publishing a protest against its behavior. When Thomas

[2] William Henry Drayton to the Earl of Dartmouth, August 30, 1774, in Sainsbury Transcripts.

[3] Described by Bull in December, 1770, as attached to the crown and "free from constitutional prejudices," Drayton was then recommended by his uncle for a post as assistant judge, an important appointment. In the following year Bull pushed his nephew for the office of deputy postmaster general in the Southern district. Drayton secured neither position. It is possible that he felt his services were not appreciated, and that the shift in his political views is thereby partly explained. Bull to Hillsborough, December 5, 1770, August 19, 1771, *ibid.*

Powell printed their protest in his *South-Carolina Gazette*, the council highhandedly sent him to jail for breach of privilege and contempt. Edward Rutledge, as counsel for Powell, early and easily won fame by asking and securing a writ of *habeas corpus* for him from Rawlins Lowndes and George Gabriel Powell, who were judges as well as legislators. Rutledge had opportunity to inveigh against arbitrary imprisonment by a pretended legislative body, and he did not fail to seize it; and Lowndes and George Gabriel Powell as judges held the same opinions they had voiced as members of the Commons House. Infuriated, the majority of the council urged the lower chamber to punish the legislators-judges, a foolish action. Instead, the Commons House formally asked the crown, in the fall of 1773, for the removal of the offending members of the upper house. Its petition was later, in effect, rejected.[4]

The South Carolina planters, exasperated with "placemen" and a British régime that tried to vest legislative powers in them, were not inclined to let the East India Company dispose of any of its tea in South Carolina; and the mechanics of Charleston were, of course, of like mind. On December 3 a huge mass meeting in the exchange secured promises from the merchants to whom the company's tea was consigned that they would refuse to receive it, and demanded that Curling take it back to England. The merchants, however, objected to a boycott upon all duted teas adopted at the meeting, partly because certain men who handled smuggled tea would profit from it. They organized a Chamber of Commerce on December 9 to defend their interests. In a second mass meeting presided over by Powell on December 17 they prevented the establishment of a boycott upon all British taxed goods, and secured one against all tea, duted or otherwise. Meanwhile, Curling's ship remained in the harbor, because he could not legally take his cargo back to England. On December 22 customs officials entered his vessel, seized the company's tea for nonpayment of duty, and quietly unloaded it in a public warehouse. They were not molested, nor was the tea destroyed.[5] But neither they nor any other

[4] Bull to Dartmouth, December 24, 1773, *ibid.*

[5] There is an excellent account of this struggle in McCrady, *South Carolina under the Royal Government*, 683–723.

British officials dared to try to sell it, and eventually it was sold for the benefit of patriot South Carolina.

There was thus no Tea Party at Charleston at that time. Threats of violence were offered, but none was executed. It was nevertheless evident that the planters and mechanics were prepared to go far in defense of American rights. In March the Commons House gave further and remarkable testimony of its intransigent spirit. Because of the conflict between the two houses of assembly, no tax bill had been passed since 1769, and the creditors of the colony had not been paid during the same period. To pay these the Commons House of its own authority issued to them certificates which could be used as paper currency, of which there was at the time great need. The certificates, countersigned only by some members of the Commons, and sanctioned only by that body, were accepted as sound currency, even by some councilmen.[6] So the Commons House successfully circumvented council and governor and exercised exclusively a sovereign power.

Although the East India Company's tea was "drowned" and otherwise prevented from being sold in the colonies, the violent means by which victory was achieved at Boston and New York aroused concern in many colonial quarters. The use of force was distasteful, and the employment of it against private property was even less liked. Benjamin Franklin condemned the destruction of the tea at Boston; many Americans who were devoted to the defense of their liberties admitted that a great wrong had been committed against the company; and not a few believed that it should somehow be compensated for its financial losses. American opinion shifted, however, when Britain at last resolved to coerce rather than to bow once again before colonial resistance.

The news of Boston's tea frolic and of less dramatic opposition elsewhere to North's enterprise created a storm in London. The King's ministers had become increasingly suspicious that the Americans, and particularly the people of Massachusetts, entertained thoughts of denying utterly Parliamentary power and even

[6] Josiah Smith, Jr., to John Ray, Jr., April 22, 1774, Letterbook of Josiah Smith, Jr. Bull reported to the Earl of Dartmouth that the scheme could not work, but that it did. Bull to Dartmouth, May 3, 1774, in Sainsbury Transcripts.

of asserting independence. Immediately before news of the Tea Party reached London, Alexander Wedderburn, solicitor general, appearing before the Privy Council, had castigated Franklin and those in Massachusetts who employed him as agent in the imperial capital as conspirators seeking to create a free American republic; and Franklin had been deprived of his valued appointment as deputy postmaster general in America. There was little doubt among ministerial minds or among Parliamentary politicians that coercive action was required. Accordingly, it was resolved to beat Boston into submission and to alter the system of government in Massachusetts so as to increase and buttress British authority within that colony; other cities and provinces might learn by example. The port of Boston was closed until such time as her people should offer due respect to Britain; the seat of government was temporarily removed to Salem; town meetings were restricted; the House of Representatives was deprived of its power, exercised since 1691, to participate in the choice of members of the council; jury panels were thenceforth to be selected by sheriffs rather than through town meetings. General Gage, on leave of absence in England, was sent back to America as both commander in chief of the army in America and governor of Massachusetts. He was authorized to bring as many troops into Massachusetts as necessary to compel obedience. A new Quartering Act was passed to make sure that Massachusetts gave part subsistence to those troops. Still further, Parliament strove to protect British civil and military officers by providing for a change of venue to another colony or to England, should one of these be accused of crime as the result of attempts to enforce the "Coercive Acts" described above. That same spring of 1774 Parliament enacted the Quebec Act, which was not intended, so far as is known, to be a punitive measure, but which threatened the authority of colonies claiming lands north of the Ohio, including Virginia, and also the interests of their people.

The method of coercion was ill-chosen; the response to what many in Britain thought to be moderate measures was entirely different from what had been hoped. Boston did not break, and Massachusetts did not bend. Instead, a Boston town meeting on May 13 called upon the colonists generally to ban all imports from

Britain and all exports to Britain and her West Indian possessions until Boston port should be reopened; and the Massachusetts House of Representatives one month later hurried off messages urging all the colonies to send delegates to a Continental Congress at Philadelphia. In the fall, amidst commotion and rioting, General Gage abandoned hope of asserting British civil authority outside Boston, concentrated troops in that town, and built entrenchments across Boston Neck. Meanwhile, the House of Representatives assumed governmental power elsewhere in the colony and began to prepare for armed conflict. And America from the district of Maine to the confines of the St. Mary's made common cause with Boston and Worcester.

Throughout the Thirteen Colonies the coercive laws, coupled with the Quebec Act and called "Intolerable," aroused deep resentment. If one American city could be ruined by Parliamentary fiat, others might be; if the system of government in one colony could be so materially and unconstitutionally altered by British law, others might similarly suffer; if troops browbeat on Boston Common, they might also insolently parade in the streets of Trenton and Charleston. Colonists everywhere called for the election of a Continental Congress to speak for America and for stopping of trade with Britain and the British West Indies. Many merchants, and some others, to be sure, held aloof or opposed these measures, because of economic distress certain to follow, because of fear of turmoil, bloodshed, and social upheaval. These, however, were unable to prevent either the meeting of the Congress or the boycott.

British governors, of course, did what they could to prevent meetings of the assemblies, attempting thus to ward off semiofficial American action. The result was the creation in colony after colony of more or less formally elected extralegal conventions which in many cases a year or two later seized all local governmental authority. In the closing weeks of 1773 and the early months of 1774 committees of correspondence, town, city, county, and colony, sprang up everywhere like mushrooms after a heavy rain, and they served as engines to procure the election of the conventions. These, in turn, often consisting in large part of men who were also members of the colonial legislatures, which blossomed ultimately into American state assemblies, also sent delegates to the First Continental Congress, the seed of American national government.

The response of the Southern colonists to Massachusetts' appeals for help and a common front differed in no way from that given in New England and the Middle colonies. More than two hundred barrels of rice were sent from Charleston and Georgia to Boston before the end of June to help feed those who were unemployed and needy because of the closing of her port, and further generous contributions of rice and cash followed from South Carolina.[7] Ill feeling which had been aroused in South Carolina against the Northern colonists because they had precipitately dropped the nonimportation agreements in 1770 was set aside. Some in the Southern provinces continued to believe that the violence of the Boston Tea Party was unnecessary. Others, however, were inspired to follow Boston's example and to improve upon it. In October, 1774, an Annapolis gathering not only refused to permit the landing of duated tea on board the ship *Peggy Stewart* but insisted that the vessel which carried it be destroyed, a curious application of the principle of "guilt by association." The *Peggy Stewart* was burnt; Annapolis outdid Boston.

Again the Virginia planters supplied leadership and inspiration, for the Southern colonists and for all America. In the spring of 1774 many Virginians were already prepared, if necessary, to fight. "R" in the *Virginia Gazette*[8] warned George III and North that they would "dye th' Atlantick's verge with noble gore" rather than submit to force of arms; and a toast given at a celebration of Saint Tammany at Norfolk predicted that in the event of an appeal to arms America would successfully resist

And shine sole empress of the WESTERN WORLD.[9]

On May 24 the burgesses, spurred on by Patrick Henry, Richard Henry Lee, and Thomas Jefferson, declared that June 1, the day

[7] McCrady, *South Carolina under the Royal Government*, 742–44, asserts that South Carolina donated more generously to the relief of Boston than any other colony, including Massachusetts.

[8] Williamsburg *Virginia Gazette* (Purdie and Dixon), April 28, 1774.

[9] *Ibid.*, May 19, 1774.

when the Boston Port Bill went into effect, should be a day of fasting and prayer. Lord Dunmore then quickly dissolved the house. Most of the members promptly gathered at Williamsburg's Raleigh Tavern, where they demanded a boycott of the East India Company and urged the calling of a Continental Congress —indeed, annual meetings of such a body. Some of the members later arranged for the election of a convention, which met on August 1. Before that assemblage convened, Thomson Mason, in a series of newspaper letters, urged not only sending delegates to Philadelphia but instructing them to propose disobedience to all Parliamentary laws and to push for armed resistance and separation from the British empire, unless Parliamentary attempts to tax and to tyrannize were entirely abandoned. The convention would not go so far, but it chose delegates to the Congress and put in operation in Virginia a thoroughgoing plan to coerce Britain by economic means, one later substantially adopted in Philadelphia for all America. Importation and use of any kind of tea were immediately forbidden; no British goods except medicines and no Negroes were to be brought in after November 1. Should redress not be offered by August 10, 1775, there was to be a complete embargo upon exports to Britain. An association was formed to enforce these arrangements and to measure out social and economic punishment to the recalcitrant. The Old Dominion had spoken vigorously and almost unanimously and had proposed practical and specific steps.

That the Virginians were determined and that they were neither to be cajoled nor tricked is indicated by sentiments expressed by the cool Washington that August. "For my own part, I shall not undertake to say where the line between Great Britain and the colonies should be drawn; but I am clearly of opinion, that one ought to be drawn, and our rights clearly ascertained. I could wish, I own, that the dispute had been left to posterity to determine, but the crisis is arrived when we must assert our rights, or submit to every imposition, that can be heaped upon us, till custom and use shall make us as tame and abject slaves, as the blacks we rule over with such arbitrary sway." [10] Here was no mouthing of a rabble-rouser, no unconsidered rhetoric.

[10] Fitzpatrick (ed.), *Writings of George Washington*, III, 242.

Even before the Virginians, Marylanders in committees and convention agreed to the appointment of delegates to the Philadelphia conclave, and also to wage economic warfare as that body might direct. The North Carolinians, defying Governor Josiah Martin, who issued a proclamation forbidding "illegal meetings," held their convention late in August, and followed closely in the footsteps of the Virginians. In South Carolina, however, the Chamber of Commerce strongly opposed suspension of trade, and even the planters were alarmed lest the exportation of rice be interdicted. Nevertheless, Gadsden, Peter Timothy, and others in favor of vigorous action managed to secure a "General Meeting" of the people of South Carolina at Charleston on July 6; that gathering chose men to attend the Congress and agreed to support whatever decisions were reached at Philadelphia; and the Commons House, being convened by William Bull early in August, met early one morning and voted to pay the expenses of the delegates, before Bull could put a stop to their proceedings. The story was otherwise at Savannah, where "radicals" strove to array Georgia with her sister colonies. The Georgia frontier was in uproar in the summer of 1774, however, and warfare with the Creek Indians gravely threatened. As a result people in the back-settlements were more interested in obtaining the aid of British soldiers than in defying British tyranny. Those in Georgia who had long opposed anti-British measures were accordingly stronger than they had earlier been. Governor Wright, recently knighted, remained popular. There were gatherings at Savannah and others of a local nature in which the "radicals" demanded that delegates be chosen and that Georgia go on record in favor of economic warfare. But in a "General Meeting" on August 10 at Savannah "conservatives" were in control. Although a "General Committee" to defend American rights made its appearance, Georgia was not represented at Philadelphia.[11]

Early in September the First Continental Congress, composed of fifty-four delegates from twelve colonies, began its work in Carpenters' Hall in Philadelphia. Much has been said about the remarkably high level of ability and character in that assemblage,

[11] A good brief account of Southern reaction to the "Intolerable Acts" is given in Schlesinger, *Colonial Merchants and the American Revolution*, 362–92.

and justly, even though the members would hardly have recognized themselves as they were afterward described in American panegyrical prose. The twenty delegates from the Southern colonies raised rather than lowered the average in both talent and moral courage. No other colony sent to Philadelphia a galaxy of eminent men like that which came from Virginia, Washington, Henry, Edmund Pendleton, Richard Henry Lee, Peyton Randolph, Richard Bland, Benjamin Harrison; and the delegation from South Carolina, consisting of John and Edward Rutledge, Christopher Gadsden, Thomas Lynch, and Henry Middleton, was also impressive. John Adams, meeting these gentlemen, put down in his diary with an honest, harsh, and sometimes misguided pen his estimates of several of them. He thought Lynch was "a solid, firm, judicious man." [12] His early impression of John Rutledge was anything but favorable. "There is no keenness in his eye, no depth in his countenance; nothing of the profound, sagacious, brilliant, or sparkling, in his first appearance." Nor was that impression soon altered, for he later recorded that Rutledge maintained an "air of reserve, design, and cunning," and that he "don't exceed in learning or oratory, though he is a rapid speaker." Edward Rutledge, wrote Adams, "is young, sprightly, but not deep; he has the most indistinct, inarticulate way of speaking; speaks through his nose; a wretched speaker in conversation. How he will shine in public, I don't yet know. He seems good-natured, though conceited." He was to Adams at one time, "young and zealous, a little unsteady and injudicious," and afterward, "a perfect Bob-o-Lincoln,—a swallow, a sparrow, a peacock; excessively vain, excessively weak, and excessively variable and unsteady; jejune, inane, and puerile." The Massachusetts man conceded that the South Carolina brothers were good lawyers. [13] He saw in Richard Henry Lee, on the other hand, "a masterly man," a "sensible and deep" thinker. [14] Adams was never a fine judge of men. Had he been so, he might have observed that John Rutledge was a remarkably steady and trustworthy person, for the South Carolinian, like Washington and Edmund Pendleton, was entirely reliable. Indeed, it might be contended that these three were

[12] Charles Francis Adams (ed.), *The Works of John Adams* (Boston, 1856), II, 360.
[13] *Ibid.,* 361, 364, 396, 401.   [14] *Ibid.,* 362.

in the last analysis the ablest and most potent figures in the Congress from the Southern colonies, albeit they did not shine as orators with Patrick Henry and Richard Henry Lee, nor as polemicists with Richard Bland and Gadsden.

The vinegary comments which Adams inserted in his diary should not be construed as evidence of animosity between Northern and Southern delegates, or even of serious ill-feeling between the men of Massachusetts and those of South Carolina. There was dispute in the Congress, and tempers at times rose high. The quarrels, however, were principally between those who wished to take stronger measures against Britain and those who favored a more moderate course; and divisions, save for one, were not sectional. There can be no doubt that Patrick Henry voiced the general sentiment when he proclaimed that he was more an American than a Virginian.

The Congress, because of the informal manner in which its members were chosen, was possibly more determined to assert American rights than were the colonists in general, but many delegates, including Joseph Galloway of Pennsylvania, James Duane of New York, and Edward Rutledge, wished to avoid extreme measures. Nevertheless, the Congress unhesitatingly, and with only Galloway and Duane dissenting, gave its support to the people of Massachusetts, counseling them to avoid conflict with Gage's troops, but assuring them that all America would come to their aid if the redcoats marched out of Boston to attack them.[15] It also resolved that any attempt on the part of the British to seize and carry any American "beyond the sea" for trial "ought to meet with resistance and reprisal."[16] Clearly, the Congress would not tamely permit Gage to send Samuel Adams, John Hancock, or Dr. Joseph Warren to England to face a charge of treason there. Galloway's famous plan for an American federation, though it would have prevented Parliamentary taxation in the future without the consent of an American council, was defeated by a vote of six colonies to five, with one divided; and, what was even more significant in terms of assessing the sentiments of the members, all

[15] Worthington C. Ford *et al.* (eds.), *Journals of the Continental Congress, 1774–1789* (Washington, 1904–1937), I, 58, 61–62.
[16] *Ibid.*, 102.

direct reference to it was expunged from the Congress's journal. It is not known precisely which delegations supported and which opposed the scheme. Among the Southerners Edward Rutledge, and possibly his older brother, favored it; strongly against it were Richard Henry Lee and Patrick Henry.[17]

Demanding redress from Britain, the Congress sent to London a Declaration of Rights, a petition to the King, and an address to the British people which condemned all Parliamentary efforts to tax in America, the "Intolerable Acts," and several other British laws and measures adopted after 1763, these being specifically described. Harmony could be restored, asserted the Congress, only by a general rescinding of the obnoxious and unconstitutional measures put into effect after the close of the Seven Years' War. Many delegates, including Gadsden and Thomas Lynch, would have gone further, would have denied to Parliament even the power to regulate American trade. They were not quite numerous enough to carry their point, five colonies favoring the proposal, five opposing, and two, Massachusetts and Connecticut, being divided.[18] The colonists were not yet disposed to assert that their only tie with Britain was that of a common crown, but they were moving toward that position. Besides, they were thinking more and more in terms of "the rights of mankind" rather than of the narrower and derivative "rights of Englishmen." In their address to the British people the delegates declared that they as well as the colonists were threatened with "slavery," and urged them to resist.

"But if you are determined that your Ministers shall wantonly sport with the rights of Mankind—If neither the voice of justice, the dictates of law, the principles of the constitution, or the suggestions of humanity can restrain your hands from shedding human blood in such an impious cause, we must then tell you, that we will never submit to be hewers of wood or drawers of water for any ministry or nation in the world." [19] Since the colonists could hope to establish their "natural rights" only by

[17] Julian P. Boyd, *Anglo-American Union; Joseph Galloway's Plans to Preserve the British Empire, 1774–1788* (Philadelphia, 1941), 29–38.
[18] Adams (ed.), *Works of John Adams*, II, 379, 393–94, 397.
[19] *Journals of the Continental Congress*, I, 89.

collective action, they tended increasingly, of course, to consider themselves Americans rather than Rhode Islanders, Jerseymen, or Carolinians.

To compel Parliament and King to yield to their wishes, the Congress bound "ourselves and our constituents" to import after December 1 neither British goods nor slaves, called for nonconsumption of British goods imported after that date, and imposed an embargo upon shipments, except for rice, to Britain or the British islands in the West Indies after September 10, 1775, unless grievances had been earlier redressed. The "provincial conventions" and "the committees" in the several colonies were to execute these measures. The singular exception of rice was the result of protest from the South Carolina delegation, which, except for Gadsden, asked that both indigo and rice be freed from the general embargo. Its request caused hot controversy, and the Carolinians accepted freedom to export only rice as a compromise. That they sought special treatment for rice and indigo does not mean that they demanded special advantage, nor that they were lukewarm in the common cause. They asked rather that they should not be required to make an unique sacrifice. Unlike the other colonists, they could not grow profitable crops for export other than rice and indigo; and these by British law had to be sold largely in Britain. Hence a general embargo would have injured the Carolinians, with their neighbors on the seacoasts of North Carolina and Georgia, more than the Northern colonists, who sent their fish, meat, flour, and wheat to ports outside the British Isles; and they felt that they should not be required to suffer beyond colonists to the northward.[20] That Gadsden, whose fortune was largely invested in a wharf and warehouses at Charleston, was willing to make a greater contribution to the common cause than the colonists to the northward and to ask his neighbors to do likewise, is striking testimony of his devotion to that cause.[21]

[20] *Correspondence of Mr. Ralph Izard, of South Carolina, from the Year 1774 to 1804* (New York, 1844), 23–25. Edward Rutledge was willing to accept absolute stoppage of both exports and imports. The Northern delegates would not listen to his proposal, one which would have injured American commerce unnecessarily.

[21] Schlesinger, *Colonial Merchants and the American Revolution*, 373 n., 421–22. Franklin thought it reasonable that the Chesapeake colonies and North Carolina claim exceptions for tobacco and naval stores on the same ground. However, Mary-

After calling for a second Congress to meet at Philadelphia in the following May, to act in the light of the response of Britain to these measures, the delegates returned home. Before the Second Continental Congress convened there was fighting at Concord and Lexington. During the intervening months committee and convention executed the program of economic bludgeoning, with extraordinary precision, and began to prepare for armed conflict, with far less success. Many merchants continued to oppose boycotting; and among these, and among men of all occupations, there appeared a large minority without zeal for American rights secured by warfare with and separation from the British empire. That minority contained men, particularly royal officials and recent emigrants, who had all along preferred British authority to American liberty; it also included men who had been opposed to the stamp and Townshend duties, but who chose to submit, if necessary, rather than to grasp gun and bayonet. As it became ever more likely that Britain would use military force rather than yield to the demands of the colonists, these loyalists, as they called themselves—they were Tories to their American neighbors—became alarmed and often active, to no avail. The Continental "association" was put into effect throughout the Thirteen Colonies, except in Georgia; and those who sought to oppose it or flout its provisions suffered for their rashness. Town, county, and colony committees to enforce it sprang up in profusion; conventions endorsed and sanctified it. The committees dealt harshly with recalcitrant merchants and others who dared to defy them. Economic reprisals, social ostracism, and the ugly practice of tar and feathering humiliated and temporarily crushed the loyalists. Emerging patriot régimes exercised power with a vigor and success envied by royal governors; and by the spring of 1775 there was an almost total stoppage of imports from Britain, except, of course, into Georgia.

In the older Southern colonies the nonimportation and nonconsumption agreements were vigorously enforced. The planters, the "Sultans of the South," compelled the English and Scottish

---

landers and Virginians could grow wheat instead of tobacco and export it to European countries; and the continued export of naval stores was not vital to the North Carolinians.

merchants and factors, and balky American-born merchants as well, to comply; and when they were threatened with legal procedures on the score of their debts, they prevented their creditors and their agents from securing legal counsel and access to the courts. Enforcing committees were as zealous between the Savannah and the Mason-Dixon line as they were in Massachusetts and New Jersey. Charleston at length emulated Boston by staging a salt-water tea party, most of its population and the consignees participating. Gambling and horse racing were abandoned as frivolities unsuitable in a crisis. A convention held at Annapolis in November called upon all Marylanders to support the program of the Continental Congress. Others later met at Charleston, Williamsburg, and New Bern, and did likewise. These conventions chose delegates to the Second Continental Congress. Composed largely of men who were members of the lower house of Assembly, the conventions supplied both leadership for the present and the nucleus for independent government to come.

The Maryland convention was remarkably vigorous, especially in making arrangements for armed resistance. That Britain would very likely resort to military force rather than bow to colonial demands was evident enough to its members; promising aid to any colony attacked, they undertook to prepare Maryland for war. A "well-regulated Militia" being "the natural strength and only stable security of a free Government," they "recommended" that all Marylanders between the ages of sixteen and fifty form themselves into companies, elect officers, and furnish themselves with weapons and ammunition. Funds to support the citizen soldiers were to be raised in each county by subscription or "other voluntary manner." [22] In December, in consequence, Governor Martin, once himself a British army man, was shocked to see at Annapolis militia drilling under the eye of General Charles Lee, a British officer who had cast his lot with the Americans.

In January, 1775, with George Washington serving in the chair, the "committee" of Fairfax County, Virginia, copied the example and the words of the Maryland convention, calling upon its free-

---

[22] Peter Force (comp.), *American Archives* . . . (Washington), 4th ser. (1837–1846), I, 1032.

holders to enroll and do their duty.[23] There was already in Virginia a military stir; it was increased by the action of Washington and his colleagues. Other committees in other counties followed suit, and Washington, as an experienced soldier and officer, was tendered the command of no fewer than six separate companies. When the Virginia convention met in March, Patrick Henry demanded that it adopt the Maryland program for Virginia as a whole, and offered a resolution that "this Colony be immediately put into a posture of defence." [24] Edmund Pendleton and others offered vigorous opposition, contending that it was unwise for the convention to go on record and so to aggravate a troubled situation, especially since the county committees were already raising and training men, buying and collecting supplies. But Henry, as he did in his speech against the Stamp Act, carried all before him in a magnificent oration that overwhelmed his opponents. Perhaps he did not say in so many words:

". . . Gentlemen may cry, peace, peace,—but there is no peace. The war is actually begun! The next gale that sweeps from the north will bring to our ears the clash of resounding arms! Our brethren are already in the field! Why stand we here idle?

". . . Is life so dear, or peace so sweet, as to be purchased at the price of chains and slavery? Forbid it, Almighty God! I know not what course others may take; but as for me, give me liberty, or give me death." But his language was to the same effect, and profoundly moved his listeners. His resolutions were carried. Having proven again his declamatory genius, Henry urged the convention to raise two regiments for the defense of the colony. These, even with the militia gathering in the counties, would hardly suffice for the purpose; and Robert Carter Nicholas, perhaps convinced by Henry that the convention must act but certainly unimpressed by the means of protection proposed by him, demanded that ten thousand, even twenty thousand, men be raised. The delegates decided merely to call forth as many men as were needed and appointed Pendleton, Nicholas, and Benjamin Harrison to a com-

[23] *Ibid.*, 1145–46.
[24] Compare Patrick Henry's resolutions, *ibid.*, II, 168–69, with those of Maryland, cited above.

mittee of defense to oversee military preparations. They recommended only increased activity in the counties, these being called upon to raise and train both horse and foot to meet any emergency.[25]

The North Carolina convention, urged by that of Virginia to take similar action, declined to do so,[26] and undertook no military measures until news came that America must either fight or submit. Perhaps its members chose not to push the issue for fear of stimulating to action many persons in the province more disposed to fight for Britain than against her, especially Scottish Highlanders who had settled after the '45 in the Cross Creek country and quondam Regulators in its western regions. Early in 1775 hundreds of men of Rowan, Surry, Guilford, and Anson counties signed addresses pledging loyalty to Britain and sent them to Governor Martin.[27] As late as March, Martin fancied that with the assistance of these elements and others in the colony, he could dominate North Carolina. At that time he urged Gage to send him arms and ammunition to equip the loyalists.[28] Martin saw more roses in his garden than were there, as he sadly discovered when he tried to gather them. He was insufficiently impressed by the aggressiveness of the convention, which functioned despite his denunciation of it as illegal; and he did not give due weight to the activities of local committees on the seaboard, which did not hesitate to raise and drill militia. Colonel John Ashe began to put New Hanover County men through maneuvers, and Colonel Robert Howe did likewise with patriots at Brunswick.[29] When some citizens of Wilmington displayed reluctance to engage in economic reprisal against Britain, Ashe convinced them of its wisdom by appearing in the town at the head of five hundred armed men.[30] And if, as Martin reported, the seaboard patriots considered an attack on Fort Johnson, but forbore,[31] there was

---

[25] In Mays, *Edmund Pendleton*, II, 1–12, Henry's behavior is made to appear somewhat more precipitate than it was, and Henry's estimate of the number of men to be collected by order of the convention is properly criticized. Henry has been a tempting target for critical twentieth-century historians.

[26] Saunders (ed.), *Colonial Records of North Carolina*, IX, 1214.

[27] *Ibid.*, 1160–64.   [28] *Ibid.*, 1164.   [29] *Ibid.*, 1157.   [30] *Ibid.*, X, 48.

[31] *Ibid.*, IX, 1167.

no assurance that they would remain quiet, no good reason to believe that he could handle them.

The convention of South Carolina similarly failed to provide for putting its militia in trim until it became evident that hostilities could not be avoided; otherwise it acted with remarkable vigor. Meeting in January, 1775, it promptly assumed the title of "Provincial Congress." There was sharp dissension among its members, but only upon the issue of expanding the nonexportation agreement adopted by the Continental Congress. Many felt that for the sake of the common American cause rice should not be excepted, and some believed it was unfair to favor rice-growers as against indigo men and others. A motion to make nonexportation total was lost by the narrow margin of 87 to 75. It was agreed that one third of the rice crop should be used to assist the producers of other products.[32] As the vote regarding rice indicates, patriot sentiment was rising high in the colony. A secret committee of five men was ordered, in veiled language, to seek supplies of arms and ammunition. Symptomatic of the trend was the behavior of William Henry Drayton. That winter "Freeman," four years earlier so vigorous an opponent of boycott and mob rule, reappeared in the newspapers as a challenger of Parliamentary power over America. By spring Drayton was hot on the heels of Gadsden as a defender of American liberties. William Bull, at the solicitation of placemen on his council, felt forced to suspend his nephew as a member of it. Drayton was hardly injured by his uncle's action; and he was a very important addition to the ranks of those who would stop at little in the approaching struggle. He was one of the secret committee appointed to gather weapons.

Georgia continued to lag behind her sisters. Only five parishes of twelve sent delegates to a convention which gathered at Savannah in January, and that body adopted a watered-down version of the Continental Association. It chose delegates to the Second Continental Congress, but these refused to attend it, because so many Georgians did not wish them to go to Philadelphia. When "Liberty Boys" sought to use the provincial Assembly as a means

[32] For an interesting discussion of this controversy, see McCrady, *South Carolina under the Royal Government*, 764–70.

of securing more drastic and more effective action, Sir James Wright swiftly dissolved it. Except in Savannah, and in St. John's parish, where settlers of New England background demanded that Georgia take common ground with the colonies to the northward, the Georgians seemed uninterested. Merchants traded as usual, seized business abandoned by Charleston rivals, and profited. Nor were they made desperate when the "General Committee" of South Carolina forbade all commercial intercourse with Georgia. Wright, like Josiah Martin, conceived that he could beat down the patriots, if necessary, with only a little military assistance. He no longer had rangers at his call, for the British government had disbanded them in 1767. He hoped to secure a few troops from Gage and the help of British warships. Actually, Wright's position was weak, and the future lay with his political enemies. What was to come was indicated by an incident which took place at Savannah on February 16. The day before, the collector of customs there seized a shipment of smuggled molasses and sugar and placed it on board the schooner *St. Johns* in the care of three of his employees. A face-blacked mob of twenty or thirty men boarded the vessel about midnight, tarred and feathered one of his men, and threw the smuggled goods and the other two into the water. The mob prevented one man from coming to shore, and he was apparently drowned.[33]

By mid-April, through letters arriving from England, it was known throughout the colonies that Britain had refused to consider seriously the papers sent across the water by the First Continental Congress and that British policy called for coercion rather than generous concession. Armed clash, at least in Massachusetts, was accordingly to be expected. Stores of ammunition therefore became objects of the greatest interest both to British officials in America and to the patriots, all the more so to the latter because their importation, except for use of Gage's army, had earlier been forbidden by the cabinet. Lord Dunmore, always forthright and bold, believing that twenty kegs of powder in the provincial magazine at Williamsburg would probably be used and conceiving that it should be ignited in defense of British authority rather than in patriot guns, had it seized in the night of April 20 by the

[33] Abbot, "Georgia under the Royal Governors," 245–55.

commander of the British *Magdalen*. Uproar followed, and hostilities were barely averted. When Williamsburg people demanded that the powder be given up, Dunmore refused; and only the calming influence of Edmund Pendleton and Robert Carter Nicholas prevented them from using force. Hundreds of riflemen hastily assembled at Fredericksburg, issued a similar demand, and received the same answer. When they threatened to march upon Williamsburg, Dunmore put his family on board *H.M.S. Fovey* for protection, called upon all men loyal to Britain to rally to him, returned threat for menace, asserting that he would arm and lead his own slaves and declare free all others who would come to his aid. Again leaders among the patriots, Washington, Richard Henry Lee, Pendleton, and Peyton Randolph, intervened, persuading the enraged militia not to march. The news of Lexington and Concord arrived immediately after the riflemen dispersed. Had it come a day or two earlier, an immediate outbreak of hostilities in Virginia might well have resulted.[34]

About twenty-four hours after Dunmore seized Virginia's supply of powder, both weapons and powder were taken from the magazines and armory of South Carolina. The raiders were not, however, British, but American. The secret committee of the South Carolina Provincial Congress, headed by Drayton, staged the raid in the night—so as not to embarrass William Bull, it was said—and carried away guns and cutlasses with powder and flints. There was little that Bull could do about it. He reported the affair to the Commons House, then sitting. Several of its members had participated in the seizure, but the house nevertheless informed Bull that it was unable to obtain "certain intelligence," that there was "reason to suppose, that some of the inhabitants of this colony, may have been induced to take so extraordinary and uncommon a step, in consequence of the late alarming accounts from Great Britain."[35] Soon afterward word of Lexington and Concord reached Charleston.

[34] Mays, *Edmund Pendleton*, II, 13–15.
[35] Drayton, *Memoirs of the American Revolution*, I, 221–26.

CHAPTER XI

EARLY AMERICAN VICTORIES

IN THE winter of 1774–1775 innumerable papers in diverse hands describing events in America in the preceding summer and fall and urging various responses poured into London; and King, cabinet, and Parliament had to decide what to do. Many British merchants and manufacturers, concerned because of imminent loss of business and probable failure of colonials to pay their debts, counseled a policy of conciliation toward America. William Pitt and Edmund Burke, among other politicians, called for understanding and moderation in the Commons and the Lords. Many British, believing that George III and his followers sought to establish tyranny at home as well as in the colonies, looked upon the Americans as allies in a common struggle and defended their conduct. There never was much doubt, however, that King and cabinet would favor coercion; and there never was any possibility that Parliament would object to the use of force.

The news from America was, to be sure, ominous, and remarkably so were the reports of General Gage, whose opinions should have received the most thorough analysis. Penned up in Boston, Gage carefully avoided conflict and urged his superiors to weigh their decision. They might, he said, give in to the colonials; compel them to obedience by naval blockade; or order the army, with the assistance of the fleet, to destroy all opposition. Should it be decided so to employ the redcoats, he advised the ministry to negotiate with the Massachusetts patriots to gain time and to prepare for a hard struggle. The New Englanders would fight and fight well, and much larger forces than he had and a year or two would be needed merely to subdue them. To deal with the colonists generally, since the other Americans would probably come to the aid of the Yankees, he urged that the ministry estimate the number of men and the sums of money needed, and then double their figures.

Ministers, however, discounted the warnings of Gage and various British officials and the strong language used by the First Continental Congress and other American gatherings. They preferred to believe that many colonials would support Britain, that the remainder could not offer serious combat. In any case, they, and the King, only too well aware that the sovereignty of Parliament, not merely its power to tax, was at stake, were determined to assert that sovereignty. Like most Europeans, they could not conceive colonials to be their equals; nor could they envision a British empire with ultimate power to rule distributed between Britain and America. Even Lord North and the Earl of Dartmouth, more moderate than the King and their colleagues, found it impossible to reconcile rightful British power with bowing to the demands of the Congress. Negotiating quietly with Benjamin Franklin, they found a gulf between him and them.

Unwilling to proceed to violence without making a gesture toward accommodation, North procured, with difficulty, the passage through Parliament of his Conciliatory Resolution. This extraordinary measure offered freedom from British taxation to any colony in which the Assembly voted appropriate sums for the support of its royal officials and imperial defense in America. Addressed to the colonies separately rather than to the Congress, it was clearly intended to give an impression of British generosity and at the same time to cause division among the colonists. Further, it made a mockery of their claims against taxation without representation. Even so, it was subjected to severe criticism in Parliament on the ground that it gave too much to the Americans. On the other hand, ministerial measures for coercion were approved by heavy majorities. An address to the throne declared Massachusetts to be in a state of rebellion; additional funds for increasing the army were promised; the New Englanders were barred from the Newfoundland fisheries; and their commerce overseas was confined to Britain and the British West Indies.

These steps were coupled with secret orders sent out to Gage, which reached Boston in mid-April and spurred him to action.

He was told that he should quell patriot "riots," enlist loyalist militia, and arrest Massachusetts patriot leaders, even though hostilities resulted; that the cabinet preferred early resort to arms, while the colonists were still unprepared, to a later struggle with organized Americans. In effect, in military parlance, he was ordered to "do something." He obeyed, sending out troops to Concord to destroy arms and equipment stored there by the Massachusetts patriots. There followed shooting at Lexington, more of it at Concord, a running fight between redcoats and militia which ended only at nightfall of April 19, when the remainder of the British contingent, together with troops sent to succor them, found refuge on Charlestown peninsula. All New England flew to arms, and Boston was soon invested, the British army within it penned up until March, 1776, when it finally sailed off to Halifax.

A report of the bloodshed of April 19, coupled with assertions that the British troops were brutal aggressors, was hastily prepared by Massachusetts patriots and was rapidly relayed as far southward as Savannah. It was not likely that hostilities, once begun, would soon cease, nor that they would or could be confined to Massachusetts. There was no thought among the patriots outside Massachusetts of abandoning her to her fate; and serious fighting was delayed for some months in the Southern colonies only because the British had no troops between Boston and St. Augustine, and but a small garrison in the latter place. Before the British were able to make a major effort in the South, royal régimes in that region entirely collapsed; and patriots, assuming firm control of government, prepared as best they might for the day of battle in their own region. Meanwhile, Southern delegates in the Second Continental Congress gave loyal support to the common American cause, and four companies of Southern riflemen served in the army investing Boston and some in the force which Benedict Arnold led through the wilderness of Maine against Quebec.

The Second Continental Congress, its composition much the same as that of the first, but without Galloway and with Franklin, convened three weeks after Lexington and Concord and labored into the heat of August. With little hesitation the delegates "adopted" the Yankee troops about Boston, made it clear that the colonies outside New England were in the war, and assumed general direction of the patriot war effort and governmental powers of one sort and another. Feeling ran very high against Britain, and in the first flush of anger many delegates were prepared to take extreme measures. John Adams urged that the colonists immediately declare independence, then negotiate with Britain regarding reunion; and if his later recollections are to be relied upon, half of the delegations agreed with him. According to him, the South Carolina men held the balance, and they at first strongly supported his view, except for Arthur Middleton, who had taken his father's seat. As Adams recalled, the Rutledge brothers and Thomas Lynch drew back because of influence exerted by Pennsylvania reluctants, leaving only Gadsden in favor of independence.[1] Doubtless, the men in the Pennsylvania Statehouse generally took a more moderate course upon second and third thoughts.

Adams indulged in warm debate with Middleton, and also with John Dickinson, who devoted all his efforts against a premature declaration of independence. A letter in which Adams imprudently described the Pennsylvanian as a "piddling genius" fell into the hands of the British, and was published by them. Dickinson and Adams were never friendly thereafter. No letter of the easily irritated Massachusetts lawyer making personal attacks on the South Carolina men appeared in print, but his relations with them, except for Gadsden, became and remained a bit uneasy. They were too proud, too aristocratic to suit his taste. On the other hand, there had been for some time suspicion in South Carolina and elsewhere that Massachusetts men were deliberately provoking conflict with Britain; and Middleton and the Rutledges now had reason to indulge in distrust of their colleague. There was, however, no serious break, and Adams helped to forge a steel chain around Yankees and Southerners by pushing for the appointment of Washington as American commander in chief. Washington, openly opposed only by members of the Virginia delegation, including Pendleton, who contended that New England generals doing well enough ought not to be superseded,[2] was eventually chosen unanimously. With Washington in the supreme command

[1] Adams (ed.), *Works of John Adams*, II, 408–409. [2] *Ibid.*, 416–18.

Virginia was firmly committed to Massachusetts,[3] and the Southern colonists almost so to the Northern, for the planters of the Carolinas could not but be flattered and pleased by the selection of a man of their kind and country.

To be sure, the appointment of Washington did not remove all causes for controversy between North and South. Nor were Southerners who were coming more and more into close contact with Northerners always pleased with their new acquaintances. In the early years of the war, enmity appeared in Washington's army between Pennsylvanians and Delaware men on the one hand and New Englanders on the other,[4] and Southerners also found the "easterners" strange creatures. Commented one of them, "The inhabitants hereabouts are all yankees. I mean not to reflect *nationally;* but their manners are, to me, abhorrent. I long to leave and get clear of their oddities. They are, for the most part, a *damned* generation." [5] Eventually, however, Southerners perceived the finer qualities of the New Englanders, not so readily evident then or later to the stranger as their defects. In the fall of 1775, Governor Martin observed in them a "lust for domination" and asserted that they hoped "to give law" to the Southerners.[6] In 1776 James Anderson, a Britisher, predicted that American independence would be followed by a bitter contest between North and South because of incompatible economies; that the more numerous Northerners would have their way in any general government formed; that the Southerners would resort to arms in order to defend their interests; that they, fewer in numbers and enervated by the climate in which they lived, would be quickly crushed and reduced to exploited subjects.[7] Perhaps Anderson saw what he wished to see. In any case, the majority of the South-

[3] It is probable that Pendleton opposed Washington in order to prevent this union of interests. Mays, *Edmund Pendleton,* II, 24–25.

[4] Men of Pennsylvania and Delaware were then designated "Southerners." See Christopher Ward, *War of the Revolution,* ed. by John R. Alden (New York, 1952), II, 934–36.

[5] James Fallon to Thomas Burke, April 1, 1779, Thomas Burke Papers (University of North Carolina Library).

[6] Saunders (ed.), *Colonial Records of North Carolina,* X, 268.

[7] [James Anderson], *Free Thoughts on the American Contest* (Edinburgh, 1776). Dr. Fred J. Ericson graciously brought this pamphlet to the writer's attention.

erners long refused to believe that union with the Northerners must bring about their own destruction.

In September, 1775, when the Congress resumed activity after a brief vacation, delegates from Georgia took their seats. Thereafter the Southern colonists were as fully represented as the others. During the ensuing fall and winter Congress was plagued and perplexed with many problems, one of these hinting of the serious troubles between North and South to come. On September 26 Edward Rutledge moved that all Negroes, whether slave or free, be discharged from the Continental army under Washington. He was "strongly supported by many of the Southern delegates but so powerfully opposed that he lost the Point." [8] However, one argument which Rutledge and his supporters apparently used, that Negroes could not be expected to fight as well as whites who had more at stake in the war, was an appealing one; and in January, 1776, in accordance with a recommendation from Washington, the Congress reversed itself in principle, resolving to permit enlistment only of Negroes who had earlier served.[9] There can be little doubt that the recruiting of slaves by Lord Dunmore also contributed to this decision, and that Rutledge was bitterly opposed to a policy which might have led to the arming of the numerous Negroes of his own South Carolina Low Country.

If Northern delegates were not eager to humor the men from the far South with respect to the employment of Negro soldiers, they were nevertheless ready to offer assistance in defending the Southern colonies. The Congress undertook to maintain three regiments in South Carolina and one in Georgia for the protection of those provinces against British attack. In February, 1776, in response to urging from Virginia, those colonies, with Virginia and North Carolina, were placed in a Southern military district, and Continental officers were supplied for it on March 1. It was then rumored in Philadelphia, correctly, that the British would soon send troops against the Southern colonies as well as the Northern. For the command in that district Edward Rutledge and others from the Southern colonies sought the services of Gen-

[8] Edmund C. Burnett (ed.), *Letters of Members of the Continental Congress* (Washington, 1921–1936), I, 207.
[9] *Ibid.*, 217–18; *Journals of the Continental Congress*, IV, 60.

eral Charles Lee, who was thought to be by many in Congress the ablest among the Continental officers. Lee had already been appointed to succeed General Richard Montgomery as head of the American army in Canada, where his knowledge of French would be very useful in a critical situation. But Lee suffered from "rheumatism" and gout, and was quite willing to serve in a warmer climate; and the Congress reversed itself in compliance with the wishes of the Southern men and ordered Lee southward. Even before his appointment serious fighting was underway in Virginia and North Carolina.

The news of Lexington and Concord impelled the Southern patriots into frantic activity, and nowhere were its results more striking than in Georgia, so long reluctant to partake in what many Georgians had not thought to be a common cause. The bloodshed on the country roads outside Boston and the certainty that the colonists generally would take up arms now persuaded some Georgians who had not felt themselves to be the victims of tyranny that they could no longer stand aloof, that Georgia must align herself with her sister colonies. The "Liberty Boys" of Savannah both took advantage of this shift in opinion and stimulated it. On May 2 Sir James Wright was hopeful that violence would not spread to Georgia. Nine days later the "Liberty Boys" seized five hundred pounds of powder from a provincial magazine. On June 2, when a British armed schooner appeared in the Savannah River, a mob expressed its contempt for the British navy by spiking a battery in Savannah town. Three days later, while Wright and others decorously celebrated George III's birthday, the patriots erected a liberty pole in Savannah, the first in the colony, paraded with bayonets fixed, and fired cannon. They had now found an able leader, young Joseph Habersham, and they frightened neutrals and friends of Britain into quiet. On June 13 they issued a call for a Provincial Congress on July 4. Before that day they joined South Carolinians in fruitless pursuit of Indian Superintendent John Stuart, who was accused of plotting to instigate a Cherokee attack upon the frontiers. Stuart escaped to St. Augustine. They also seized six tons of powder from a ship at Tybee Bar. Toward the end of the month Wright despairingly wrote to General Gage and to Admiral Samuel Graves, who commanded the British ships in American waters, asking for armed assistance. They had little to give, being much occupied at Boston. On July 4 the Provincial Congress met and assumed control of the colony.[10]

Wright lingered in Savannah for more than six months, and was long personally unmolested. Meanwhile, the Provincial Congress sent delegates to Philadelphia; took over the Georgia militia and the courts; seized a shipload of powder and goods sent out from England for distribution among the Indians; chose a Council of Safety, which exercised executive powers; and began to raise a Continental regiment. At length, in January, 1776, the military support so long sought by Wright appeared at the mouth of the Savannah, two warships and a transport carrying redcoats. It was, in the familiar phrase, too little and too late. The Council of Safety promptly resolved to seize the persons of Wright and other royal officials, to prevent them from rallying the Georgia loyalists; and Habersham arrested the governor in the very presence of his council. Wright, held incommunicado for a month, finally made his escape to a British warship. But neither before his flight nor for three years afterward was it possible for him to rally the supporters of Britain in Georgia; and plans for strong measures against Georgia had to be abandoned. The day would come when the Georgia loyalists had an opportunity to strike, and they seized it, to their later sorrow. For the moment most of them carefully kept quiet, remembering the treatment given Thomas Browne, one of their kind, who had not cautiously maintained silence and who had been tarred and feathered at Augusta.

Sir Robert Eden, last colonial governor of Maryland, departed in more dignified style than Wright. He was both popular and prudent. Not strong enough to interfere with the Maryland patriots after the news of Lexington and Concord reached Maryland, he gracefully refrained from taking steps offensive to them. They quietly seized the provincial military stores, raised troops, and transferred all authority from Eden and the colonial Assembly to their convention and Councils of Safety. Eden was not molested until April, 1776, when Samuel Purviance, a warm patriot of Baltimore, instigated by General Lee, sought to arrest him. Pur-

[10] Abbot, "Georgia under the Royal Governors," 256–66.

viance was rebuked for his impudence by the Annapolis Council of Safety. In the following month, however, with the day of independence rapidly approaching, the Convention suggested to Eden that his presence was embarrassing and that he should leave. Accordingly, in June, he went on board a British warship and peacefully departed for England.[11]

Lord Dunmore did not leave in such amicable fashion, but rather sought desperately to do what he thought to be his duty. The fighting in Massachusetts stirred him to action. After paying for the powder he had taken, he went hastily on board *H.M.S. Fovey*. From the *Fovey* he tried to instigate an Indian attack upon the Virginia frontier, in vain. But other British warships came to the Chesapeake and some redcoats from St. Augustine; and a few loyalists and Negro slaves took up arms under his banner. Hovering off the coast, he occupied at one time and another Gosport, Portsmouth, and Norfolk, intercepted Virginia shipping, raided plantations along the shore, and pushed away small forces of patriots which sought to interfere with him. On November 7 he proclaimed all able-bodied white men who failed to join him to be traitors and offered freedom to all slaves who would serve under him. Thereby this lord who had been respected and liked in Virginia and who had humorously referred to himself as "lieutenant governor of Gosport," acquired an enduring reputation for infamy in the Old Dominion, for he who called for servile warfare was utterly beyond the pale.

While Dunmore harried the coasts with his motley forces of redcoats, "Scotch," and "Sables," the Virginia convention deliberated, chose the usual Council of Safety, and prepared for war. In December, 1775, Colonel William Woodford, under orders from the Council, led more than a thousand patriot militia into position at one end of the Great Bridge, ten miles from Norfolk. The Great Bridge was actually a small one over the Elizabeth River

---

[11] In the Annapolis *Maryland Gazette*, August 3, 1769, Eden had been poetically welcomed to Maryland:

> Long as, or grass shall grow, or rivers run,
> Or blow the winds, or shine yon glowing sun,
> May EDEN, and his sons, here deign to stay,
> Themselves as happy as the realms they sway.

connecting two parts of a long causeway through swamp lands. Dunmore came out of Norfolk and occupied the opposite end of the causeway. North Carolinians were en route to join Woodford, and the earl therefore chose to attack, with two hundred regulars, some sailors and marines, a few Tories, and his "Loyal Ethiopians." He was unfortunate. He was able to replace planks of the bridge prudently removed by the patriots, but his plans for a flanking move went awry, and his attack, made on December 9, was confined to a frontal assault along the causeway. The result, on a small scale, was worse for the British than their charges at Bunker Hill. Patriot musket and rifle fire completely smashed the redcoats as they came forward six men abreast; within thirty minutes Dunmore's "army" had suffered sixty casualties, and its backbone had been broken. One patriot was wounded. Dunmore fell back to Norfolk, disbanded his Negro troops, which had been useless to him, and evacuated the port. On January 1 he celebrated the New Year by bombarding it from the water and sending out parties to burn houses in the town. Patriot militia took part in the festivities, destroying even more houses than did the British, presumably to punish Tories and to deprive Dunmore of a possible base. Making the best of a bad business, the Council of Safety then ordered the town razed, so that it was of no use either to him or to the patriots.

In February, 1776, the Virginians were alarmed by the appearance of additional British ships and marines in the Chesapeake. These, however, were on their way southward; and Dunmore's force lost rather than gained strength. His ships became fouled, his supplies ran low, his men became disgruntled. He made a few more raids. Finally, in the summer, he led the remains of his heterogeneous "army" and "navy" off to New York. Meanwhile, the Virginia convention, stung to action, raised more troops, printed paper money, adopted a constitution, and urged the Continental Congress to declare American independence. It also arranged to send troops southward to the assistance of the patriots of the Carolinas, where a major British attack impended.

Governor Josiah Martin was a soldier, but a sensible one. Reports of Lexington and Concord, followed by rumors of Tory and Negro uprisings, caused wild excitement in North Carolina.

Without supporters or protection in New Bern, he watched militia form there, sent his family to New York, and fled to Fort Johnston on the Cape Fear on May 31, 1775. Had he not departed so hastily, he must soon have become a prisoner of the patriots. That same day a gathering of Mecklenburg County patriots at Charlotte resolved that all Parliamentary laws respecting America were "annulled and vacated," asserted that "no other legislative or executive power does or can exist at this time in any of these colonies" except that wielded by Congresses provincial and Continental, declared all commissions from the crown "null and void," denounced any man who should accept one as "an enemy to his country," and urged the people of Mecklenburg to elect military officers "independent of Great Britain." [12] Other patriots of North Carolina were less forward in their views; and there were many loyalists within her boundaries. Nevertheless, at the moment Martin could not hope, as he had earlier, easily to maintain royal authority. He dared not, indeed, remain even at Fort Johnston, for Robert Howe, John Ashe, and Cornelius Harnett led militia into it on July 18 in search of him. He escaped to the British *Cruizer* offshore, his rapid departure illuminated by the burning fort. Thereafter, from the *Cruizer* and later *H.M.S. Scorpion*, he strove to mobilize forces to restore British control.

While Martin bounced about at sea, the North Carolina patriots, organizing their Provincial Congress and Committee of Safety, raised troops, appointed officers, printed money, levied taxes, and otherwise made ready for war. They were more energetic than they might otherwise have been, because Tories and neutrals were so numerous in the colony. Royal officials, many merchants, some of the wealthy Tidewater planters, Scottish Highlanders in the Cross Creek country, and some of the quondam Regulators on the Piedmont were vigorously pro-British; and other old Regulators, Quakers, and Germans of the Piedmont sought to remain aloof. Perhaps no more than half the Tarheel

---

[12] Saunders (ed.), *Colonial Records of North Carolina*, IX, 1282–85. The body of literature concerning the "Mecklenburg Declaration of Independence" of May 20 continues to grow; no contemporary copy of it has been found; professional historians continue to look upon it as mythical.

population was firmly patriot.[18] The Provincial Congress vainly sought to win over the Highlanders and had no remarkable success in an attempt to secure the adherence of the old Regulators. However, since the Tarheel Tories failed to move for several months, the patriots were able to send help from North Carolina to Virginia and South Carolina in the closing weeks of 1775 and were ready to act when their own loyalists took up arms.

Happily for the patriots, Martin miscalculated the strength of the North Carolina Tories and called them into the field too soon. In June, 1775, he fancied that no fewer than twenty thousand of them would bear arms for Britain and that he could call into service nine thousand men early in 1776. He told his superiors in London and General Gage in Boston that these, with a British naval squadron and a redcoat contingent, would be strong enough to suppress the patriots in his colony. The British cabinet, receiving other optimistic reports from royal officials in the South, let Martin know that ships and troops would leave Ireland for the Southern colonies by December 1. Martin made preparations accordingly. On January 10, 1776, he called upon all faithful subjects of George III to rally to the royal standard and to help him put down a "most daring, horrid and unnatural rebellion," and authorized Donald McDonald, whom he had commissioned brigadier general, Donald McLeod, named by him as colonel, and others to enlist men. The Tories were to rendezvous at Brunswick on February 15. The Highlanders, especially very recent emigrants among them, responded to the call. By February 18 about fifteen hundred Tories, chiefly Scots, were assembled four miles below Cross Creek (now Fayetteville). Neither the British squadron nor the promised redcoats were on the coast. They nevertheless set out for Brunswick, which none reached, except as prisoners. Meanwhile, James Moore, colonel of the first North Carolina regiment, had gathered patriot troops and militia in a camp three miles away, between the Tories and Brunswick. Moore ordered Colonels

[18] Lefler and Newsome, *North Carolina*, 195–98. As usual in civil strife, even families divided. A patriot in British hands in 1782 asked Nathanael Greene to arrange to exchange him for his loyalist brother, an American prisoner. Thomas Mayers to Greene, July 10, 1782, in *South Carolina Historical and Genealogical Magazine* (Charleston), XVI (1915), 145.

Alexander Lillington, John Ashe, and Richard Caswell to dig in at and hold Moore's Creek Bridge, which the Highlanders had to use to cross Moore's Creek en route to the coast. Moore himself set out to assail the Scots from their rear. His flanking movement was not successful. The Tories, led by McLeod, pushed forward to the bridge. There McLeod committed the same mistake that Dunmore had made at the Great Bridge. A thousand patriots under Caswell held the east bank of the stream; and they had removed the flooring of the bridge and had greased the supporting beams. Arriving at the creek at dawn of February 27 after an all-night march, McLeod immediately led the Highlanders forward and into the trap prepared for them. As they struggled across the bridge, they were met by a heavy fire which they could not return; in three minutes they lost McLeod, and fifty men had been killed or wounded. They fled, but more than half of them, together with General McDonald, weapons, and gold, were captured by Caswell and Moore, who came up in time to push the pursuit. The patriots had one man slain and one wounded. Which of their leaders was most responsible for the victory is disputed. Lillington was, claimed many, hence:

> Moore's Creek field, the bloody story,
> Where Lillington fought for Caswell's glory.[14]

Doubtless Caswell also deserved praise, and certainly Moore. Whatever lights among the patriots shone, the battle brought only gloom to Martin and the Tories. Martin at length departed on a British warship. Most of the North Carolina Tories stayed at home quietly for four years.

When the promised British ships and troops began to appear in force, in March, they were not welcomed. The Provincial Congress responded by authorizing the North Carolina men in the Continental Congress to vote for an American declaration of independence; and the British chose to assail South Carolina.

Reports of Lexington and Concord led to convulsions also in South Carolina, where they "caused the boiling of much blood." [15] The colonial Assembly, lingering on through the summer, gradu-

[14] Lefler and Newsome, *North Carolina*, 199–201.
[15] Josiah Smith, Jr., to James Poyas, May 18, 1775, Letterbook of Josiah Smith, Jr.

ally disappeared, and the Provincial Congress, in session after June 1, seized all authority. A Council of Safety composed of its leading lights was entrusted with executive powers. The patriots raised three regiments of troops, seized Forts Johnson and Charlotte, and voted large sums for the defense of the colony, especially of Charleston, an obvious target for British attack. They even sent out an armed vessel under Captain Clement Lemprière to seize gunpowder in the Bahamas. Such drastic steps were opposed in the Congress by a large minority which continued to hope that hostilities could be avoided or mitigated; and Charles Pinckney, hitherto prominent in public affairs, withdrew to private life and loyalism. But William Henry Drayton, leading the majority, drove it with passionate energy toward ever more drastic measures. Rumors of British plots for a slave insurrection and for an attack upon the frontier settlements by the Cherokee filled the air, arousing public sentiment. That summer Jerry, a slave, was executed because he had said he would pilot British warships over Charleston bar. John Stuart, his influence over the Cherokee too great not to cause alarm, was accused of conspiring to persuade them to take the warpath, and fled precipitately to East Florida to escape Captains Joyner and Barnwell, sent out by Drayton to apprehend and question him. Two loyalists who too publicly swore in Charleston that they would give aid to Britain, Laughlin Martin and James Dealy, were tarred and feathered there, not by an irresponsible mob but by the order of patriot leaders.

Although the Rutledge brothers and other patriots were reluctant to take extreme measures, there was cause for alarm, and there were reasons for aggressive action. Slave Jerry was not in himself a menace, but the numerous Negroes of the Low Country, if armed and employed by the British, formed one. Stuart was not urging the Cherokee to seize gun and tomahawk, but he was telling them that the British rather than the Americans were their friends. Serious as were the possibilities of Negro insurrection and Indian attacks, there was even greater cause for concern in the attitude of many South Carolina whites. Among the Low Country merchants and planters were hundreds of loyalists and thousands who gave firm allegiance neither to the patriot cause nor to Britain; and neutrals and Tories were numerous in the

Upcountry. German settlers in Saxe-Gotha, the Orangeburg district, and between the Broad and Saluda rivers were indifferent or hostile; Highlanders who had ventured across the ocean after the '45 were likely to be as firmly pro-British as they had recently been Jacobite. Most disturbing of all was the fact that many of the Scotch-Irish, who were a dominant group in several parts of the Upcountry, seemed hostile to the patriots. The Council of Safety sent Drayton and the Reverend William Tennent inland in August to stir up patriot sentiment, organize patriot militia, win over neutrals, and stamp out loyalism. Drayton and Tennent were energetic and persuasive, but by no means entirely successful in their mission. Colonel Thomas Fletchall, Moses Kirkland, Robert Cunningham, Patrick Cunningham, and Thomas Browne, the last smarting then and long afterward from the abuse he had suffered at Augusta, intrigued against them, collected armed Tories, and took the field. Drayton gathered 1,000 patriot militiamen; Fletchall confronted him with an even larger force near Ninety-Six in September. Avoiding combat, Drayton shrewdly persuaded Fletchall and most of his men to declare that they were not enemies to American freedom and to disperse. He secured, however, only an uneasy peace. Efforts by Drayton to soothe the Cherokee were even less successful. They accepted a consignment of goods sent forward by him and offered fair words in return. It was clear, however, that they were not likely to remain quiet.

In November hostilities broke out both in the Upcountry and at Charleston. The Upcountry loyalists, doubtless encouraged because Drayton had not been able to bring large forces against them, took the field once more. About the middle of the month a body of more than 1,800 of them gathered near Ninety-Six, and on November 19 attacked the fort there, garrisoned by one third their number of patriots led by Major Andrew Williamson. After two days' fighting, and some bloodshed, the opponents agreed to an armistice and separated. In the meantime, however, the Council of Safety resolved to crush all opposition in the interior of the colony and sent Colonel Richard Richardson out to do it. He collected patriot militia as he went, both South and North Carolinians joining him by hundreds. By December he had more than 4,000 men. Resistance collapsed before him as he moved through the Tory stronghold between the Broad and Saluda rivers, and he captured Fletchall and other Tory leaders. Only one Tory detachment refused to disband, and it was easily routed by a part of Richardson's force on November 22 at Reedy River. Richardson not only disarmed hundreds of loyalists but compelled many of them to pledge themselves to pacific behavior in the future. With their leaders in patriot hands they were thoroughly discomfited, and did not dare again to appear in the field in numbers until British troops captured Charleston in 1780. Even then, remembering, perhaps, Richardson's expedition, they were hardly so active as they might have been.

The shooting actually began at Charleston a week earlier. Lord William Campbell, the last royal governor, who had arrived at his post during the summer, fled to the British warship *Tamar* in the harbor on September 15. From it he did what he could for Britain. It was suspected, doubtless correctly, that he encouraged the Up-country Tories, and also that the *Tamar* and other British vessels would be used against the patriots. Accordingly, patriot efforts to prepare defenses for the city were increased. A party trying to close a channel in the harbor so as to prevent British entrance was fired upon by the *Tamar* on November 12, the patriot schooner *Defense* was cannonaded both by the *Tamar* and by *H.M.S. Cherokee,* and the guns of Fort Johnson were discharged against the British ships, all without casualties. Shortly afterward *H.M.S. Scorpion* under Captain Tollemache, carrying Josiah Martin, appeared in the harbor, and Tollemache proposed a plan to seize control of the harbor. He had not force enough, however, to attempt it. He and his fellow naval officers and the two governors, indeed, could not remain in the harbor and were forced to take to sea. It was likely, however, that the British would soon return in force. In March, 1776, as British attack became ever more certain, the Provincial Congress adopted a temporary constitution for South Carolina; the embryo state was growing.[16]

Had Lord George Germain, Sir Peter Parker, and General Henry Clinton had their wish, South Carolina would quickly

[16] A detailed history of the early months of the war in South Carolina, with many documents, is offered in Drayton, *Memoirs of the American Revolution,* I, Chaps. VII–IX; II, Chaps. X–XV.

have reverted to colonial status. News of Lexington and Concord, Bunker Hill, the American invasion of Canada, the refusal of the colonists to consider Lord North's Conciliatory Resolution as a means of accommodation, the formation of the Continental army, and the appearance of American Revolutionary governments did not persuade Britain to draw back before the embattled Americans. Instead, King, cabinet, and Parliament, despite minority protest, resolved to send forces as large as possible across the Atlantic to crush the rebels. By the Prohibitory Act of November, 1775, the Thirteen Colonies were deprived of the protection of the crown and declared to be under naval blockade. Troops from the British Isles, with thousands of German mercenaries, the so-called Hessians, were sent off to America, and naval reinforcements as well. About ten thousand men were ordered to join General Guy Carleton in Canada, to drive the patriots from the province, and to assist, if possible, General William Howe in overrunning New York and New England. Howe, replacing Gage as commander in chief in the Thirteen Colonies, was supplied with reinforcements increasing his army to more than thirty thousand men. His older brother Richard, Admiral Viscount Howe, was placed over the British fleet in American waters to assist him; and the two Howes were authorized as commissioners to restore the King's peace and also to pardon rebels. In the belief that much might be accomplished in the Southern colonies before summer, at which time the Howes were to begin their campaign by attacking New York City, arrangements were also made to send a part of the forces destined to serve under them to the coasts of the Carolinas for a swift stroke. It was hoped that a British naval squadron together with a small army would stir the Southern loyalists, believed in London to be numerous and eager to act, to rise, and that a short campaign in that region might produce great benefit to Britain. The too-sanguine opinions of Josiah Martin, James Wright, and other royal officials in the South concerning sentiment there were undoubtedly largely responsible for this venture. Commodore Sir Peter Parker was sent out from home waters with the naval squadron and transports carrying troops under Charles, Lord Cornwallis; and General Henry Clinton, who was to command the land forces, sailed southward from Boston with another small redcoat contingent.

Fortunately for the Southern patriots, Parker departed late from British waters and arrived tardily in American ones. Both Parker and Clinton failed to reach the rendezvous at Cape Fear in February, 1776, when Martin expected them. Hence the premature rising of the Highlanders. Clinton arrived on March 12, but the first ship of Parker's fleet did not appear until April 18. Parker himself came in on May 3, and the last of his ships did not strike the coast of the Carolinas until May 31. The general and the commodore, learning that the loyalists in both Carolinas had been routed, were disconcerted. They agreed they must do something with the fleet and the three thousand men at their disposal. Clinton rather favored the establishment of twin posts near the lower Chesapeake and Albemarle to serve as bases for future operations, but Parker, learning that the defenses of Charleston, especially a fort on Sullivan's Island, were not finished, urged instead that they turn southward. Clinton acquiesced, and they sailed for Charleston. Securing possession of Sullivan's Island as a base for subsequent operations was the major purpose. Charleston itself was not to be attacked "without a moral certainty of rapid success." What good might come from seizing an island that could hardly be held by small British garrison forces neither Parker nor Clinton ever explained.[17]

Early in June Charleston patriots learned that Parker's fleet was cruising off the bar at the entrance to their harbor. Fearing an attack, not merely upon the fort on Sullivan's Island and other defensive works but on the city itself, they were alarmed. "For God's sake," wrote John Rutledge, who had become president and chief executive of South Carolina, to Charles Lee, en route to the city, "lose not a moment." Rutledge and the South Carolina patriots had reason to be apprehensive, for they were confronted by a triple menace, British assault, loyalists' uprising, and Indian attack as well, since the Cherokee were about to assail the frontier settlements. Moreover, the defenses of Charleston, although Rut-

[17] William B. Wilcox (ed.), *The American Rebellion; Sir Henry Clinton's Narrative of His Campaigns, 1775–1782* (New Haven, 1954), 27–29.

ledge had made every effort to prepare them, were incomplete. Old Fort Johnson and adjacent installations covering the harbor were in good shape and well manned; but the fort on Sullivan's Island, commanded by William Moultrie, was unfinished, and no attempt had been made to throw up defensive works on the mainland. Rutledge had collected more than 4,500 men, more than a hundred cannons, and plenty of small arms and powder, but had been unable to secure more than a meager supply of cannon shot. Had Clinton and Parker been able to push immediately into the harbor, they could hardly have failed to seize Sullivan's, and even the city itself. They had to wait until the last of their warships arrived, and their passage across the bar was delayed by weather. Troops under Clinton landed on Long Island, north of and adjacent to Sullivan's, as early as June 8 and the remainder of the redcoats later, and Parker's fleet crossed the bar into the bay, but there was no fighting until June 28.

Meanwhile, Lee hurried into Charleston, which was being fortified, with hundreds of Virginia and North Carolina troops; when the British finally made their attack, they were confronted by more than 5,000 patriots. Rutledge ordered the South Carolina men to obey Lee's orders; and Lee assumed command of all the American forces. Observing that the British would in all likelihood assail Sullivan's Island, he proposed to abandon its fort, finished only on the south and east and open to naval bombardment from the southwest, and to concentrate the bulk of his men on the mainland. But Colonel Moultrie insisted that Fort Sullivan could be held, and was supported by Rutledge. Compelled for the sake of unity to let them have their way, although he thought the fort to be a potential "slaughter-pen," Lee with frantic energy sought to strengthen its works, without much success. The fort did have twenty-six guns available, though only twenty-eight rounds of shot for them, on June 28. On the northern tip of the island were 780 riflemen under Colonel William Thompson, to hold off Clinton. To make the retreat of the garrison and Thompson's men possible, Lee constructed a floating bridge between Sullivan's and the mainland, but the bridge was too slight for its purpose. Otherwise the patriots were well prepared, and Charleston itself, one may believe, could hardly have been taken.

Fort Johnson, under Gadsden, seemed safe enough, since the British forces were rather obviously directed toward the northern side of the harbor, and Haddrell's Point on the mainland opposite Sullivan's was guarded by a patriot detachment.

When Clinton landed on Long Island, his plan and that of the British commodore called for a joint attack upon Sullivan's, the warships bombarding the fort and landing marines and seamen from the bay and Clinton's men advancing through shallow water across the channel between Long Island and the northern tip of Sullivan's. To his sorrow, however, Clinton discovered that the channel was deeper than reported; he could not reach Sullivan's except in boats. Faced by American batteries and Thompson's men, the British general realized that the plan could not be executed. He suggested an attack upon Haddrell's Point rather than upon the island. Parker, confident that he could silence the guns of the fort and put ashore landing parties, was determined to proceed. Clinton was able to assist him only by threatening a diversion, which he could not actually undertake until Parker's venture was well on the road to success. The commodore failed.

In the morning of June 28 Parker's fleet of nine war vessels, including two ships of fifty guns and six frigates, sailed up the channel. Three of his frigates, *Syren*, *Sphinx*, and *Actaeon*, were to pass the fort, and to bombard it from the southwest, where there were no entrenchments to cover its defenders. Meanwhile, the other ships were to throw shot and shell from the southeast. But, alas for Parker, the three frigates ran upon a shoal and could not execute their mission. Parker then had to rely upon frontal bombardment of the patriot works. Surprisingly, the palmetto log fortifications withstood his fire. Moreover, Moultrie, firing slowly so as to make the best use of his scanty ammunition, did heavy damage to the frigates caught upon the shoal and also to Parker's other ships. His untrained men stuck to their guns, even when ammunition ran low. Having received new supplies from Lee, who also reinforced Thompson when it became apparent that Moultrie was doing very well against Parker, the garrison kept the British ships at a distance until night. Then, his squadron rather badly battered—*Actaeon* had to be abandoned—the commodore ceased firing and withdrew. The patriot casualties were fewer than fifty. Parker's ran to scores, and his fleet was unfit for further combat. Lingering on into July, Parker and Clinton at length disappointedly gave up their venture and sailed off to New York.[18]

While the South Carolinians were still in the first flush of rejoicing because of the removal of the menace from the sea, came menace from the mountains. The repulse of Parker and Clinton persuaded the loyalists, though restless, to remain quiet, but the Cherokee took the warpath at the beginning of July, ravaging the Southern frontier from Virginia to Georgia. The Indians were soon beaten back, however, and during the summer and fall following, the Carolinas and Virginia sent out expeditions into the country of the Cherokee which severely punished them.[19] Before the end of 1776, although the Tories of the Carolinas were still troublesome in isolated spots, the four Southern states (for so they had become) represented in the Continental Congress were completely and easily under patriot control. The Floridas were still in British hands; a projected patriot expedition against St. Augustine had been abandoned because of lack of ships and supplies. The British in the Floridas were not, however, dangerous, either in themselves or with their Indian allies, until powerful British forces again appeared on the south Atlantic coast.

[18] For a later description of British tactics written by Clinton, see *ibid.*, 30–38.
[19] A fuller account of the conflict with the Cherokee is offered in Chapter XV.

CHAPTER XII

SEPARATION AND UNION

IT IS evident now, as it was manifest to shrewd observers of the Revolutionary time like John Adams and Benjamin Franklin, that the Americans would sooner or later decide for themselves what their relations with Britain should be—that if they insisted upon independence, they must ultimately obtain it. The time, the manner, the circumstances in which they should secure their freedom from colonial and inferior status were not, of course, predetermined. They depended largely upon the growth of colonial wealth and population, the rise of Anglo-American clash, the development of a community of sentiment among the Americans, and the policies and powers of Britain's European rivals. The colonists early sought and obtained independence because they were relatively numerous and rich, because they felt themselves to be much injured by Britain, because they believed themselves to be and acted as one people, because France and Spain gave them assistance.

At the beginning of the War of Independence, and later, there were men on both sides of the Atlantic who conceived that the colonists were so diverse in interest and viewpoint that they could neither think nor act in unison, despite impressive evidence to the contrary during the period 1763–1775. The variety among the colonists in terms of geographical, racial, national, linguistic, and cultural backgrounds impressed such men; and they made much of the lack of commerce on the grand scale between the colonies, of cultural as well as economic isolation. They noted that the colonists had retained loyalty to Britain and had developed local attachments, that their economy was similarly local and oceanic rather than continental. They saw among the colonists, in part doubtless because they wished to, clash rather than concord.

Actually the inhabitants of the Thirteen Colonies were both like each other and variant from the British. They were not so dissimilar in background as might appear. Their European origins were largely in the British Isles and the west central part of the continent adjacent, the British—English, Welsh, Scottish, Scotch-Irish—forming the bulk of the European element and a substantial majority of the whole. They were overwhelmingly Protestant and differed little in physique, ancestral wealth, and social status. Moreover, the English element, itself altering in the American environment, both set a pattern for the other groups and intermarried with them. In 1775 there were still enclaves of Dutch at Albany, of Germans in Pennsylvania, of Germans and Scotch-Irish in the Carolinas, and these minority peoples and others elsewhere. Such communities, however, tended to dwindle. Save for these enclaves, the English language was almost universally used, and English culture was a common heritage. So effective was the cultural melting pot that William Livingston, an intelligent and perceptive patriot, three parts Dutch and one part Scottish, referred to himself as an "Anglo-Saxon"; so prevalent was physical intermingling that an American ancestral tree of that time might have branches from four or five European nations or regions. The American environment tended to produce similar rather than disparate persons in physique, speech, ways of thought, and modes of behavior. If economic contact was limited, it is also true that economic clash was not yet remarkable. Moreover, the existence of common enemies, the Indians, the French and the Spanish, had driven the colonists toward union of sentiment. When Britain also became their foe, another powerful cementing force appeared. Before 1775 the colonist was conscious, though not fully, that he was one of a new people, that ever since the founding of Jamestown he had walked in one path and the Englishman across the Atlantic in another. It is a striking fact that some years earlier the colonist had adopted for himself the name "American." While this term was used even before 1700 to designate British people in North America, it was not a commonplace term until after 1750. That it became so as the Revolution approached, even though increasing use of it must be explained in part because of its convenience, testifies clearly both to community of sentiment and to awareness of it. Patrick Henry, not profound intellectually, had a gift for plumbing, sharing, and expressing human emotions. When he announced in the First Continental Congress that he was an American rather than a Virginian, he spoke for scores of thousands.

Every day of warfare after Lexington and Concord swept the patriots on toward a declaration of independence and American union. Separation from Britain was inextricably linked with American political association, for independence could neither be achieved nor maintained without such coalescence. Both would be advanced, of course, by the entrance into the war of foreign allies, especially France. As it became apparent in America in the closing months of 1775 and the early ones of 1776 that Britain would exert as much force as she could command, that she would employ foreign mercenaries, that she would make use of Tory troops and Negro and Indian auxiliaries, the patriots moved step by step toward declaring independence. Before the end of 1775 Washington, Nathanael Greene, and other high officers in the American army investing Boston moved to the side of Gadsden, the Adamses, and Franklin, who were already convinced that separation must be sought. In January of the new year appeared Thomas Paine's *Common Sense,* which eloquently battered the principle of royalty in general and British royalty in particular. Paine both brought the question of dependence versus independence out into the open and contributed powerfully to the final decision to attempt separation.

Many patriots continued to hold back. Sentimental ties, awareness of the value of the imperial connection, concern for personal and family safety, preference for monarchical institutions rather than republican (an American crown was almost unthinkable), alarm lest the struggle lead to social upheaval and anarchy rather than to political freedom, fear that British misrule might be replaced by French domination, and other factors counseled caution. Wishing to believe that the Howe brothers would bring an offer of accommodation, the reluctants did so believe, though they had no good reason for their faith. They managed to stave off a declaration of independence until the early summer of 1776, but the tide rose steadily against them and finally overwhelmed them. They were unable to prevent the Continental Congress from authorizing American privateering against British merchant vessels on March 19. Less than three weeks later that body set aside the British Acts of Trade and Navigation, opening the ports of the Thirteen Colonies to foreigners. On May 10 the Congress urged the several colonies in which no satisfactory government then existed to "adopt such . . . as shall, in the opinion of the representatives of the people, best conduce to the happiness and safety of their constituents in particular, and America in general." Five days later it declared that "authority under the . . . crown should be totally suppressed, and all the powers of government exerted, under the authority of the people of the colonies." It was clear then that the Congress, which, it was generally agreed, should speak for all the colonies, would before long assert independence.

The prolonged debate in Congress between the reluctant and the forward patriots was essentially one between delegates from colonies in which hostilities had occurred or were seriously threatened and those colonies in which the impact of the fighting was not yet severely felt. It was largely the patriots between the Hudson and the Potomac who held back, and principally those to the eastward and southward who insisted upon a declaration. There were, to be sure, men everywhere who urged against undue haste, and with them in all places those who clamored for decisive action. One of the arguments for delay, that continental union and assurance of foreign aid should precede a declaration, appealed to Edward Rutledge and other South Carolinians, to Carter Braxton, member of the Continental Congress from Virginia, and even to Patrick Henry, along with John Dickinson, John Jay, and other men from Northern regions.

North Carolina ultimately both led the way and supplied the formula for common action. On April 12, with the forces of Clinton and Parker gathering off Cape Fear, her Provincial Congress unanimously took the plunge: "And whereas the moderation hitherto manifested by the united colonies and their sincere desire to be reconciled to the mother country on constitutional principles, have procured no mitigation of the aforesaid wrongs and usurpations, and no hopes remain of obtaining redress by those means alone which have been hitherto tried. . . .

"Resolved, that the delegates of this colony in the continental congress be impowered to concur with the delegates of the other colonies in declaring independency, and forming foreign alliances, reserving to this colony the sole and exclusive right of forming a constitution and laws for this colony, and of appointing delegates from time to time (under the direction of a general representation thereof), to meet the delegates of the other colonies for such purposes as shall hereafter be pointed out."[1] The Provincial Congresses of South Carolina and Georgia, acting even earlier, were less precise in their instructions to their representatives in Philadelphia. That of South Carolina on March 23 instructed its delegates "to concert, agree to, and execute, every measure which they or he, together with a majority of the Continental Congress, shall judge necessary, for the defence, security, interest, or welfare of this colony in particular, and of America in general." The South Carolinians in Philadelphia were thus permitted to vote for a declaration of independence, should they think it desirable. However, their principals at Charleston asserted on April 1 that "we still earnestly desire" an accommodation with Britain.[2] The Georgia Congress, on April 5, also hesitating, similarly empowered its emissaries in general terms to use their discretion.

The Southern colonies were more forward in authorizing their representatives to take the great plunge than others, and North Carolina was the first to give specific authority. Virginia also dis-

[1] Saunders (ed.), *Colonial Records of North Carolina*, X, 512.

[2] For William Henry Drayton such accommodation meant only that the Americans might remain within the empire on their own terms. As Chief Justice of South Carolina he delivered a charge to a grand jury in which he asserted that the British King should have "such a limited dominion over us, as may tend, *bona fide,* to promote our true commercial interests, and to secure our freedom and safety—the only just ends of any dominion." He demanded that British troops and ships be withdrawn from America, that the Acts of Navigation be modified to please the colonists. He declared that "True reconcilement never can exist between Britain and America—the latter being in subjection to the former. The Almighty created America to be independent of Britain." Henry Laurens' thought at that time seems to have been much the same. Gibbes (ed.), *Documentary History of the American Revolution*, I, 276–89. After the engagement at Sullivan's Island, if not before, Drayton wished total independence. *Ibid.,* II, 29.

tinguished herself by decisive behavior and gave powerful impetus to the movement toward a declaration of independence. The Virginia convention did not meet until after the beginning of May. When it convened, it was flooded with letters from all parts of the colony, and members received others from Richard Henry Lee and Thomas Jefferson, delegates in Philadelphia, urging that the Old Dominion throw her impressive weight upon the scales in behalf of separation. Patrick Henry momentarily hesitated, and Robert Carter Nicholas heartily opposed action, but Edmund Pendleton, its president, succeeded in securing unanimous and vigorous action. The convention on May 15 instructed the Virginians in Philadelphia to push for a declaration, urged that they and their colleagues seek foreign alliances, also that they form an American confederation with powers beyond "internal concerns," these to be reserved to the local legislatures.[3] The Continental Congress and other patriot conclaves throughout the colonies were informed and were, in effect, asked to join in carrying out the program. On June 29 the convention went further. It promulgated a constitution for Virginia and with it a preamble prepared by Jefferson which announced that "the government of this country, as formerly exercised under the crown of Great Britain, is totally dissolved," thus virtually asserting the independence of Virginia three days before the Continental Congress proclaimed it for the "United Colonies."

It was Richard Henry Lee who had the honor, on June 7, of introducing at Philadelphia three fateful resolutions embodying the Virginia program. They called for a declaration of independence, attempts to secure foreign alliances, and confederation, a plan toward that end to be prepared by the Congress and to be submitted to the several colony-states for approval. Hot debate followed upon the first resolution, the delegations of Virginia, North Carolina, Georgia, and New England for it, those of South Carolina, Maryland, Pennsylvania, Delaware, New Jersey, and New York opposing, because of conviction that it was premature or preventing instructions from their principals. Decision was postponed until July 1. However, on June 11, so as to be prepared to announce the great event, should it come, a committee

[3] Mays, *Edmund Pendleton*, II, 106–11.

was appointed to prepare a proper proclamation. Others were chosen to do something toward obtaining foreign help and domestic union, these parts of the Virginia program being sanctioned by all. Before July 1 Maryland moved into the camp of the majority, and eight delegations then voted for separation. Before the end of that day the South Carolina men announced that they would no longer oppose the will of that majority. On July 2, with the New Yorkers abstaining only because of their instructions, and with twelve colonies voting aye, the Congress resolved "That these United Colonies are, and of right ought to be, free and independent states." A week later New York officially announced her consent. The last step had been taken.

The men of Virginia and the deeper South, joining the New Englanders in pushing on those of Maryland and the middle colonies to complete separation, also gave their warm approval to the famous document of July 4 which informed a candid world why the Congress had done what it had done. The Declaration of Independence, prepared by the committee assigned for the purpose three weeks earlier, was, of course, largely the work of Thomas Jefferson. Only one important part of Jefferson's magnificent manifesto was deleted by the Congress. Making his list of the tyrannous acts of George III as complete as possible, the Virginian asserted that "he has waged cruel war against human nature itself, violating its most sacred rights of life and liberty in the persons of a distant people who never offended him, captivating and carrying them into slavery in another hemisphere, or to incur miserable death in their transportation thither. This piratical warfare, the opprobrium of *infidel* powers, is the warfare of the *Christian* king of Great Britain *determined* to keep open a market where *Men* should be bought and sold he has prostituted his negative for suppressing every legislative attempt to prohibit or to restrain this execrable commerce . . . he is now exciting those very people to rise in arms among us, and to purchase that liberty of which *he* has deprived them by murdering the people upon whom *he* also obtruded them. . . ." According to Jefferson's recollection, doubtless accurate, this stirring and rhetorical passage was set aside because it was offensive to delegates from both the far South and New England, Charleston and Newport merchants having been major transporters of slaves. This does not mean that either the Rhode Islanders or the Carolinians were heartily disposed to defend the oceanic slave trade, but that they could hardly condemn the crown for fostering a traffic—by disallowing colonial legislation against it—in which their own people had freely engaged.

In view of later and continuing debate over the meaning of Jefferson's immortal propositions that "all men are created equal, that they are endowed by their Creator with certain unalienable rights, that among these are life, liberty, and the pursuit of happiness," it may be asked: why was there not objection to them on the ground that, by implication at least, they denounced Negro slavery? It may be conceived that delegates did not necessarily observe the implication, that they did not think Negro slaves to be included in the word "men," that they were not then inclined to quibble and quarrel seriously about definitions, that many of them, whether from New England or the South, if aware of the implication, would have considered it acceptable. Certainly, sentiment against both the slave trade and slavery itself was increasing, not only in Virginia but far to the southward.

Two other propositions were denied by no one in Congress, that an American union was nearly indispensable toward securing independence and that one was certainly requisite for the maintenance of American freedom. Indeed, many members, fancying that foreign allies could not be secured unless there existed in America a stable central government, believed that constitutional union must precede the attainment of freedom. Happily for the patriots, these were mistaken, and Louis XVI and his ministers agreed to sign an alliance endorsed on the patriot side only by a Congress possessing dubious authority. There could be no doubt, however, that thirteen states, if they became separately independent, were unlikely to remain so. Successful defense in the future required permanent junction. Moreover, the flame of American nationalism, already burning brightly, was fusing discordant elements. Accordingly, the Congress strove mightily to form a union upon a constitutional basis.

The committee chosen by the Congress to prepare a constitution was at first under the leadership of John Dickinson. It brought in a draft within a month, on July 12. Such remarkable speed could not be maintained. The plan brought in, in which the influence of Dickinson was evident, called for a strong central government; and on that account alone it encountered heavy opposition. Besides, there were jarring interests and emotional clashes which made difficult the achievement of any sort of agreement. Delay was therefore inevitable; and the many other duties of Congress, the exigencies of warfare, and the appearance of British troops in New Jersey and Pennsylvania further retarded progress. Working gradually and sporadically, the delegates rewrote the Dickinson document. The product, the Articles of Confederation, was not submitted to the several state assemblies for ratification until November, 1777.

The Articles sent to the state capitals called for a perpetual union but proposed a weak central government consisting basically of a one-house Congress with power to make war, declare peace, and negotiate treaties and alliances; conduct diplomatic negotiations; maintain an army and navy; coin money; regulate Indian affairs; and set up a postal service. Authority to regulate commerce, whether interstate or foreign, was withheld, as was the power to tax, the Congress being authorized merely to send requisitions to the states, which were to contribute in proportion to the value of privately held lands, plus improvements upon them, within their borders. Although the Articles were to be "inviolably observed by every state," no means to coerce a state were provided, nor was the central government given authority effectively to compel obedience of individuals. The states were to possess "sovereignty, freedom and independence," and voting in the Congress was to be by states, the legislature of each electing from two to seven members. In sum, the proposed central government was to have powers roughly equal to those formerly exercised by the crown and Parliament and a form much like that of the existing central revolutionary régime. One special provision, that the inhabitants of every state were "entitled to all the privileges and immunities of free citizens in the several states," deserves mention, for it aroused antagonism in the South.

The reduction by the Continental Congress of the large central authority envisaged in the Dickinson plan was not the work of any one person, or delegation, or group of delegations but was almost a matter of general agreement. Fear of tyranny, dislike of taxation, solicitude for local interests, the necessity of securing the approval of the state régimes, inexperience—all these and other factors persuaded men from all parts of the thirteen states to adopt this unworkable system.

The men who spoke for the Southern states in the Continental Congress were probably as eager as any to prevent the creation of a dominant central government. Even before the Dickinson document was brought to the floor, before, indeed, the Declaration of Independence, Edward Rutledge asserted that "The idea of destroying all provincial distinctions and making everything of the most minute kind bend to what they call the good of the whole, is in other terms to say that these [Southern] colonies must be subject to the government of the eastern provinces," [4] also that "we have made such a Devil of it [the Articles] already that the Colonies can never agree to it." [5] It was Thomas Burke of North Carolina who moved the inclusion of the pregnant statement that "Each state retains its sovereignty, freedom, and independence, and every power, jurisdiction and right, which is not by this confederation expressly delegated to the United States in Congress assembled," and it was the South Carolina deputies who seconded his motion. On the same issue, however, Virginia stood out against particularism, her men offering the only vote against Burke's amendment.[6]

Sharing in the quite general fear of a central tyranny, the men from the Southern states were seriously at odds with their colleagues from the Northern ones on another important issue. In July, 1775, Congress, facing the problem of making good its paper currency, had stipulated that the colonies should be responsible for it in proportion to their population, including Negroes.[7] Making use of this scheme, the Dickinson draft similarly called for the states to donate to the common treasury on the basis of numbers, excluding only Indians not taxed. This arrangement was the cause of a hot sectional debate toward the end of July,

[4] That is, New England.
[5] Burnett (ed.), *Letters of Members of the Continental Congress*, I, 517-18; II, 56.
[6] *Ibid.*, II, 345-46.   [7] *Ibid.*, 221-22.

1776, even before the signing of the Declaration of Independence. Samuel Chase of Maryland thought it highly improper, because Negroes, in his opinion, should be classed as property, like cattle, rather than as persons. He moved that the basis be changed so as to omit Negroes. John Adams, replying to Chase, contended that slaves produced as much wealth as white laborers, and hence should be included. He was supported by James Wilson of Pennsylvania, who asserted that Chase's proposal would permit the Southerners to reap all the economic benefits of slavery and Northerners to bear the burden of it. It was obvious enough, however, that to count slaves as if they created wealth equally with whites was unjust to the Southerners, as Benjamin Harrison of Virginia pointed out. He suggested that two Negroes should be considered as the equivalent of one white. His fractional solution was acceptable to the Southerners, but not to the Northerners, according to a later report. Nor did the scheme of using the value of private lands and improvements, offered by John Witherspoon of New Jersey, who saw that there was merit in the Southern viewpoint, please all Northerners. Men from the South rallied behind Chase, and the debate became bitter. Thomas Lynch of South Carolina declared it vain to talk further about union if Northerners denied slaves to be property. They were so in South Carolina and were taxed as such, asserted Lynch and Edward Rutledge. Rutledge would not defend slavery, indicated his disapproval of the institution, but declared it unfair to tax property in Negroes when profits from merchant shipping, certain to come to the New Englanders, would be untouched. William Hooper of North Carolina offered sound criticism of the use of population as a formula, reminding his associates that North Carolina's numbers were large, her riches proportionately small. The Northerners, however, would not give way, or consider compromise. Put to a vote, Chase's amendment was defeated by a solid sectional vote, Pennsylvania, New Jersey, New York, and the New England states opposing it, Maryland, Delaware, Virginia, and the Carolinas supporting it, with Georgia divided.

But that vote was not final. Chase and others from Maryland declared that their state would never ratify the Articles unless the provision was altered, and some delegates from the far South surely felt as strongly as they. The question of contributions was brought up again a year later. It was then suggested that all property be used as a criterion and that the value of land be employed as a measuring device. The New Englanders vigorously campaigned against the worth of land as a yardstick, because the farms in their region, though small, were improved and proportionately more valuable. They continued to feel that Negroes should not be omitted from any formula for donations, all the more so because the states were asked to supply troops for the Continental army on the basis of white inhabitants only. By that time, however, sentiment had swung against them. When Witherspoon's solution was finally moved, it was carried by the unanimous votes of five states, Maryland, Virginia, the Carolinas, and New Jersey, with the New England states as solidly opposed, and Pennsylvania and New York split.[8]

This sectional issue was thus settled by Congress, but it was revived and others appeared when the Articles were studied by the state assemblies. That of Connecticut offered an amendment calling for a return to numbers, including Negroes, as the basis for donations.[9] Those of New Jersey and Pennsylvania raised a new but related question. Observing that the Articles permitted Congress to set state quotas for the American army according to white numbers, they asked that both whites and blacks be counted. Otherwise, claimed the Jerseymen, the Southerners would greatly profit from the labors of their slaves during the war period and others would not.[10] Maryland raised a third issue involving the Negro, and Georgia a fourth. From Maryland came a proposal that "one state shall not be burdened with the maintenance of the poor" migrating into it from others—in effect, that Maryland should not be loaded with the task of caring for impoverished free Negroes, who tended to settle about the Chesapeake.[11] The legislature of Georgia, desiring neither free Negroes nor traitors nor pacifists within her bounds, urged that all these be denied rights under the "privileges and immunities" provision.[12]

---

[8] This sectional struggle is well described in Merrill Jensen, *The Articles of Confederation* (Madison, 1940), 145–50.

[9] *Journals of the Continental Congress*, XI, 640.   [10] *Ibid.*, 651–52.

[11] *Ibid.*, 671.   [12] *Ibid.*

It was South Carolina, however, that voiced the sharpest sectional fears and offered the most far-reaching amendments, largely, doubtless, because of the efforts of William Henry Drayton. He found innumerable faults in the Articles and offered to the legislature of his state his own version of a satisfactory constitution. He believed that the Articles granted too much authority to the Congress and that it would be exercised against the South, unless safeguards were established. He would not give to Congress "any power, that can with propriety, be exercised by several states— or any power, but what is clearly defined beyond a doubt." He was not satisfied with the requirement in the Articles that all major actions of the Congress required the consent of nine delegations: "When I reflect, that from the nature of the climate, soil and produce of the several states, a northern and southern interest in many particulars naturally and unavoidably arise; I cannot but be displeased with the prospect, that the most important transactions in congress, may be done contrary to the united opposition of Virginia, the two Carolinas and Georgia; states possessing more than one half of the whole territory of the confederacy; and forming, as I may say, the body of the southern interest . . . the honor, interest and sovereignty of the south, are in effect delivered up to the care of the north. Do we intend to make such a surrender?" Denying fear that "the north would abuse the confidence of the south," he nevertheless insisted that all important business done by Congress require the approval of eleven delegations. Thus the consent of at least two deputations from *his* South would have to be secured before the Congress could declare war, make peace, ratify a treaty, or do anything of great moment.[13]

Anticipating regional clash and supplying a protection for the South that would have pleased the mature John Calhoun, Drayton seems to have voiced sentiments which appealed strongly to South Carolinians in January, 1778. The legislature set aside his personal constitution but approved of much of it in substance. It offered many amendments to the Articles based upon his suggestions, urging that Negroes be excluded from the "privileges

[13] Hezekiah Niles (ed.), *Principles and Acts of the Revolution in America* (New York, 1876), 357–75.

and immunities" [14] and that eleven votes be required for important Congressional business.[15]

In view of later events one may be tempted to lay too much stress upon the forebodings of, and measures proposed by, Drayton and his fellow Carolinians in the early weeks of 1778. South Carolina did not insist upon changes in the Articles as a price for ratifying them; and when the Congress refused to adopt them, the state gave its approval without further debate. Certainly, if there was for a moment grave distrust of the Northern people in South Carolina, there was less feeling somewhat later in that state and relatively little in the other Southern states. Georgia, asking for change with respect to "privileges and immunities," told her men to sign the Constitution whether her amendment was or was not accepted. Maryland did not insist that she be relieved from caring for her neighbors' free Negroes; and Virginia and North Carolina sought no alteration whatever. The amendments offered by South Carolina were swiftly rejected in Congress, only two delegations voting for them, doubtless those of South Carolina and Georgia; [16] and the changes urged by Connecticut, Pennsylvania, and New Jersey were similarly speedily and overwhelmingly rejected. While it is evident that the Congress pushed aside all amendments in the hope of putting the Articles promptly into operation, it is also clear that the legislatures and delegates of the other Southern states did not share the concern at least momentarily felt in South Carolina. Except for Maryland, they did not long delay their entrance into the first American constitutional union.

In Maryland there was intense dislike of the Articles, not because Marylanders saw in them a menace from the North but rather because they were jealous of Virginia and Virginians. In part they harbored ill will toward their neighbors because the people of all the smaller states feared domination by those of the larger ones, Massachusetts, Virginia, and Pennsylvania. Of far

[14] Drayton had rhetorically inquired: "Would the people of Massachusetts have the free negroes of Carolina eligible to their general court?" *Ibid.*, 359.

[15] *Journals of the Continental Congress*, XI, 652–55. Drayton and South Carolina also recommended that future amendments to the Articles be permitted after approval by eleven states rather than thirteen.

[16] *Ibid.*, 655.

more importance, however, in creating among them hostility toward Virginia, and the Articles, was the fact that the constitution did not limit the territories of the several states on the west. Early in the war the Maryland convention proclaimed that the region between the Appalachians and the Mississippi, if it became a part of the United States, should be the common property of all Americans. It was contended, on the whole justly, that this vast region should belong to all because it must be won, if it were won, by the sacrifice of all. Marylanders steadily clung to this position. Accordingly they demanded that the sea-to-sea claims of Virginia and other states be canceled by the Articles. Thus Maryland state pride would be assuaged, for the disparity in size and numbers between Maryland and Virginia would not be increased; further, the Marylanders would have equal opportunity with Virginians to acquire private holdings beyond the mountains, since they would not be forced to compete with Virginians at the capital or county seats of Virginia. Some Marylanders, however, were motivated not so much by desire for justice and state jealousy as by personal economic advantage. Thomas Johnson, Charles Carroll of Carrollton, and Samuel Chase, among others, were investors in land companies which hoped to acquire and exploit vast tracts over the mountains in regions claimed by Virginia. Those companies, the Indiana, the Illinois, and the Wabash, were striving to perfect titles on the basis of purchase from the Indians and by any other means possible. Their operations had been greatly hampered because Virginia denounced them as completely illegal.

The demand of Maryland, supported by the delegations of other states possessing no claims beyond the mountains, these also containing speculators opposed by Virginia, was strenuously denounced by the men from the "landed states," which were Massachusetts, Connecticut, New York, the Carolinas, Georgia, and, above all, Virginia. The Virginians, well aware of the special personal interests behind the demand of Maryland and not unmoved by state pride and the economic interests of their own people, countered with claims to authority over the south bank of the Ohio and the "Old Northwest" on the basis of their royal charter of 1609. Maryland and the "landless states" won the first round, for the Dickinson draft in substance met their wishes. However, the "landed states" succeeded in forcing revisions, and the Articles as submitted to the states offered little comfort to their opponents. Despite their defeat, the "landless" sisters, except for Maryland, did not long delay giving their consent to the Articles. They did so reluctantly, however, and Maryland positively refused, unless trans-Appalachia were put under the control of the central government with a specific proviso which would protect the claims of her speculators. Virginia, declaring void those claims in *her* domain, then proposed, in the spring of 1779, a union without Maryland. But such a union could not and did not appeal to thoughtful men, although the Connecticut men in Congress indicated that their state would accept it. As time passed, sentiment in Congress veered toward the views of the "landless" states; and ultimately their endowed neighbors were asked to make concessions to them. In February, 1780, New York, which had claim to empire beyond the divide only because of a dubious suzerainty over the Six Nations and their equally dubious suzerainty over other western tribes, announced she would abandon for the common good at least a part of her pretensions. In the fall of 1780 the Congress asked all the "landed" states to do likewise. Virginia particularly was thus put to the test. Her response had the most far-reaching effects.

The Virginians were loath to surrender any part of the vast domain which they claimed for their state, even though the region beyond the Ohio was largely in British and Indian hands rather than in their own. Nevertheless, Richard Henry Lee had suggested as early as November, 1778, that a Virginia stretching to the Great Lakes would be too vast to govern in a republican manner and that his state should cede to the central government all its claims beyond the Ohio River for the welfare of Virginia and the general good; and the Virginia legislature had indicated before the end of 1779 that it might be wise "at a future day" to form new states beyond the mountains. In the later months of 1780 Lee, Jefferson, James Madison, and Joseph Jones, conscious of the need for union, urged that their state do something toward meeting the wishes of the "landless" ones. Accordingly, on January 2, 1781, with certain restrictions, in part intended to destroy the private claims of Marylanders and others in the region, the Virginia Assembly formally ceded to the union the rights of that state north of the Ohio River. Soon afterward, Connecticut also abandoned, though with vexatious reservations, her dreams of trans-Appalachian empire. It then became evident that all the "landed" states would do likewise. Deprived of her public arguments against the Articles and unable to use the desires of her speculators as valid reason for not adhering to the union, Maryland abandoned the struggle. In February, 1781, that state authorized her men in Congress to sign the Constitution; and on March 1 it was possible, after nearly five years of effort, to announce that the union was complete.[17]

So it was that the union acquired control of the "Old Northwest," if the British were forced from it and if the Indians in the region were subdued, as they later were. In so far as the states were concerned, the union thus acquired a western empire. The consequences were vast, for the possession of that empire in common discouraged particularism within it and also in the regions already settled, supplying added and powerful bonds of interest and sentiment to the union. A long step was taken toward the creation of new states in that region. As other territories to the southward and westward became the property of the American people, they similarly served to strengthen national ties.

Before the end of the War of Independence another attempt to revise the Articles brought a less fortunate result. By 1783 it was obvious that the central government badly needed more efficient means to raise funds. In March of that year a committee on revenue, driven on by Alexander Hamilton, proposed an amendment by which the Congress would be permitted to levy certain import duties during a period of twenty-five years and also to change the system of state contributions to the common treasury. The assessment of values of lands and their improvements as the basis for contributions was causing no end of trouble, especially in New England, where the method of measuring

[17] Upon this struggle between the "landed" and "landless" states, see especially Jensen, *Articles of Confederation*, 150–59, 190–93, 196–218, 225–35.

quotas chosen by Congress had never been popular. As a remedy Hamilton and other members of the committee urged once more a return to contributions based upon numbers; and Northerners on the committee, led by Hamilton, once more sought to have Negroes counted. Again the Southern delegates resisted. In the debates which followed, James Wilson brought up as a substitute another scheme which the Southerners also found objectionable, a uniform tax of twenty-five cents per hundred acres on all land everywhere, regardless of value.

Reconsidering, the committee thought it necessary to use population as a basis and to find a compromise which would make the change palatable to the Southerners. Madison, a member of it, suggested that they would be satisfied if two Negroes were counted as one white, the solution put forth by Benjamin Harrison nearly seven years earlier, and the committee so recommended on March 28. There followed on the floor a fascinating game of fractions. Conceding that Negroes could not be numbered person for person, New Englanders argued that two for one was wrong; they liked four for three. Charles Carroll of Carrollton fancied four to one; John Rutledge thought three for one was about right, but said he would accept two for one. It was moved that the ratio be made three to two. All the Southern deputies voted against it, and the motion was lost. The Congress was weary of the argument and disposed to give up, when Madison offered a magic formula, five to three. Rutledge supported him. The Southern men, except for Georgia, which was not represented, voted unanimously for the Virginian's compromise, and it was adopted.[18]

For the moment Madison's arithmetical ingenuity was all in vain. The state legislatures, receiving the amendment, considered it in leisurely style. By 1786 only nine of them had ratified it, some with reservations; and four, including two Southern states, Maryland and Georgia, refused to give their consent. Both parts of the amendment were opposed, and there was indifference toward the desperate financial condition of the central government. By that time, indeed, it was evident to most public men that the Articles

[18] *Journals of the Continental Congress*, XXIV, 260–61; XXV, 915, 922–23, 926, 948–49.

needed a general overhauling, to many that a new constitution was required. When the federal convention of 1787 made a new constitution, its members discovered that Madison's formula was a very useful one.

It should be observed that the struggle between the Southerners and Northerners about counting Negroes in computing contributions did not lead to debate in Congress upon the merits of slavery as an institution. Such controversy would come, but as yet Northern representatives were not disposed to attack slavery, nor were Southern delegates eager to defend it. Indeed, many Southern leaders in and out of Congress believed that slavery must and should be ultimately ended—hence the rather remarkable sanction given by Congress in March, 1779, to a scheme to free and arm three thousand slaves for the defense of South Carolina and Georgia, though the patriots had vehemently condemned the British for using Negro troops and though Congress had earlier decided to discourage even the enlistment of free Negroes.

It was a brave young Continental officer, John Laurens of South Carolina, son of Henry Laurens, who furnished the impetus. Imbibing a dislike for slavery from his father, he wished to take steps toward extinguishing it. Toward that end he urged as early as 1776 that Negroes be permitted to earn their freedom by fighting in the patriot forces. He wished personally to lead Negro soldiers in battle. In the early months of 1779, after the British had captured Savannah, when they were invading South Carolina, he renewed his plea, and his father, sure the project would fail, nevertheless began to push it in Congress. General Isaac Huger, sent north from South Carolina by Governor John Rutledge to ask for help, lent his support, and William Henry Drayton, who then formed with the older Laurens the South Carolina delegation. Henry Laurens told Washington that with the aid of three thousand Negro troops the British could be driven back and even out of East Florida, and asked his opinion. The commander in chief expressed doubt, because the British had arms with which they could equip more Negroes than the patriots, also because he foresaw unrest among Negroes not permitted to win their freedom. However, Henry Laurens and Drayton proceeded, asking the

Congress to buy the release of three thousand slaves in South Carolina and Georgia and to help arrange for putting them in service, they to be free at the end of the war.

In the belief that the military situation in the far South was serious, if not critical, and in view of the fact that Huger and the two South Carolina deputies sponsored the scheme, the Congress unanimously endorsed it. Had it been carried through, slavery as an institution must have been greatly weakened. However, the Congress prudently refused to try to put it into effect without the consent of the two states concerned. When John Laurens, hastening to Charleston, placed it before the South Carolina Assembly, he was very coldly received. The South Carolinians at home were bitterly opposed to a measure so hostile to the institution of slavery, and they were not quite desperate. Only a few voices were raised in favor of the proposal, and it was "blown up with contemptuous huzzas." The scheme was dead for the moment. Three years later, after Yorktown, young Laurens again sought to persuade the South Carolina Assembly to raise and free Negro troops; and Nathanael Greene warmly supported the proposal, urging both South Carolina and Georgia to adopt it.[19] But the end of the war was approaching, and more soldiers, white or Negro, were not badly needed. The scheme then received many votes in South Carolina, but not a majority;[20] it was also set aside in Georgia. So ventures which might have given a powerful impulse toward gradual destruction of slavery failed.

[19] Greene to Governor John Martin, February 12, June 8, 1782, in Nathanael Greene Papers (Duke University Library, Durham).
[20] Wallace, *Life of Henry Laurens*, 447–52.

CHAPTER XIII

A CHAIN OF DEFEATS

SLIPPING sullenly out to sea after their disconcerting defeat at Sullivan's Island, the British forces under Henry Clinton and Sir Peter Parker sailed off to New York; and neither they nor other British contingents seriously menaced the Southern states for more than two years. By the fall of 1776 the power of the Cherokee was temporarily broken, their chiefs compelled to sue for peace. Meanwhile, the Creeks, though restless, remained neutral. There remained to vex the Southern patriots in their own region only the British garrison at St. Augustine, which was too weak to take the offensive, which was so remote and so little of a threat that the large expenditures of men and money necessary to reach and conquer it were not warranted. From St. Augustine the British were able to harass the Georgia frontier, but not seriously to injure. Accordingly, the Southern patriots, relieved of pressure at home, chiefly devoted their military efforts to the assistance of their Northern brethren until the British returned in strength to the lower South at the close of 1778. Thereafter they were required to defend their own homes.

As early as the summer of 1775 Maryland and Virginia began to send troops northward, the first contingents being four companies of riflemen, whose deadly shooting was expected by the Continental Congress to accomplish miracles. The sharpshooters arrived at Washington's camp outside Boston soon after the battle of Bunker Hill, and they were joyously welcomed. Their feats of marksmanship delighted the New England militia blockading General Gage and the British army in the city. Not overly pleased with their own weapons, muskets and shotguns which possessed neither range nor accuracy, the Yankees applauded enthusiastically when a rifleman brought down an unfortunate British sentry at two hundred yards and when another drove a red-coated officer to shelter in undignified haste. But the riflemen were boisterous and undisciplined; and they could not produce the wonders expected of them at Boston, since the British soon learned to make use of their entrenchments. They became disliked, especially by American officers toward whom they were something less than respectful. Eventually riflemen were to prove their value in woods fighting, and also in open battle, when properly led and supported. They were in the War of Independence less reliable than musketmen, who were the élite of both the British and American armies. They could not load rapidly enough to stop a determined attack with their firepower; they carried no bayonets, for they had not learned how to fasten them to their rifles; and their rifles, five feet and more in length, were not effective as clubs at close quarters. Accordingly, they could hardly stand against a bayonet charge in the open field. Some of the riflemen, and Daniel Morgan especially, performed heroically in Benedict Arnold's march against Quebec and in the desperate and unsuccessful assault upon that city at the end of 1775. The Southerners did not move northward in large numbers, however, until General William Howe, Gage's successor, and his brother Richard, Admiral Viscount Howe, appeared in New York harbor with large forces in the summer of 1776. Strengthened by the contingents which had failed at Sullivan's Island and also by Lord Dunmore's troops, the Howes possessed a fleet far stronger than the Americans could hope to build and an army of over thirty thousand men. They were to receive support from General Guy Carleton, who was sent ten thousand soldiers from England and was ordered to advance southward from Canada by way of Lake Champlain and the Hudson. The seriousness of the British menace was evident. Maryland sent a regiment, on paper something more than six hundred men, to assist Washington in defending New York against the Howes. It was rapidly followed by detachments of Maryland and Virginia riflemen, and then by several line regiments of Virginians, who joined Washington in time to fight at New York and to participate in his headlong flight across the Delaware and in his splendid victories at Trenton and Princeton. At Trenton both William

Washington and James Monroe were wounded. More Marylanders and more Virginians, enlisted as Continental troops, for three years or the duration of the war, appeared in Pennsylvania and New Jersey to take part in the campaign of 1777 in those states. They were followed by North Carolinians; that year, indeed, all the Continental troops of Maryland, Virginia, and North Carolina served outside the South. While Daniel Morgan and Virginia riflemen assisted New Yorkers and New Englanders in stopping on the Hudson the British army from Canada, the bulk of the troops from the upper South fought vainly with Washington to defend Philadelphia against General Howe and took part in Washington's unsuccessful surprise attack at Germantown. They also partook of the agonies of Valley Forge. Southerners were conspicuous in the last major engagement of the war in the North, at Monmouth in June of that year, and were among the Continentals who stormed the British fort at Stony Point in 1779. Washington was not embarrassed because his fellow Southerners in the ranks of his army performed less creditably than Jerseymen or Rhode Islanders. His Southern officers, including South Carolina's John Laurens, North Carolina's Abner Nash, Virginia's Light-Horse Harry Lee, William Grayson, William Woodford, and George Weedon, were inferior to none.

When Sir William Howe failed to crush Washington, when the British army from Canada under General John Burgoyne laid down its arms at Saratoga, the war assumed a new complexion. France, eager to secure advantage from the struggle between Britain and the patriots, very early in the conflict began secretly to send military material and cash to the "insurgents." Charles Gravier, Comte de Vergennes, foreign minister of Louis XVI, wished to enter the struggle openly on the side of the Americans. He saw an opportunity not merely to obtain revenge for the grievous defeats and losses of colonies which France had suffered in the Seven Years' War but to dismember the British empire and to reduce Britain to a second-class power. The French army and navy had been restored and were ready for combat. There were many reasons, however, why France should avoid hostilities, including the possibility that the Americans might be forced to abandon the struggle just as the French entered it. The news of

Germantown and especially of Saratoga decided the issue at Versailles. On February 6, 1778, His Majesty Louis XVI agreed to secret treaties which recognized the independence of the United States, created a Franco-American defensive alliance, and provided for joint prosecution of the common war with Britain, certain to result, until American freedom should be won. France forever renounced all claims to North America east of the Mississippi; the United States undertook indefinitely to help the French to defend their West Indian possessions against external attack. The Continental Congress joyfully ratified the treaties on May 4. The British, officially informed in March that France had welcomed the patriots into the family of nations, responded with gunfire against French ships, in mid-June. A French fleet was already en route to the American mainland. The war then spread rapidly, from the English Channel to the Mediterranean, to west Africa, to India, to the West Indies. A year later Spain, hoping to regain Gibraltar, entered the conflict as an ally of France, but not of the United States. Before the end of 1780 the British drove the Netherlands into the war; and that same year the League of Armed Neutrality, fomented by Vergennes and pushed by Catherine the Great, made its appearance. Accordingly, except for weak Portugal and her friends among the small states of western Germany, Britain was confronted during the latter years of the War of Independence by a Europe hostile or coldly neutral.

The British government was shocked by the news of Germantown and Saratoga and shaken by the approaching entrance into the war of France; and Lord North despairingly sought to resign. The British people clamored for new measures and an old leader, the Earl of Chatham. Pitt, however, was about to die, and George III remained vigorous and determined. The King kept North in office, and the cabinet and Parliament falteringly and tardily adopted new measures for America. A commission headed by the Earl of Carlisle was sent across the ocean to offer to the patriots peace and dominion status within the British empire. These emissaries arrived too late—after Congress had ratified the French alliance—and offered too little.[1] At the same time the

[1] In the New Bern *North-Carolina Gazette*, March 13, 1778, "A By Stander" predicted that Pitt and Rockingham would come into power in Britain and demanded

resignation of Sir William Howe was accepted, and orders were sent to his successor, Clinton. In view of the military situation in America and imminent war with France, Clinton was told to evacuate Philadelphia and to take the main British army to New York. He was, if possible, to hold on to New York and to wage a wasting war against the coasts of New England. He was to send part of his forces, if convenient, to seize the French island of St. Lucia in the West Indies, and another against the Southern states. These instructions roughly outline British strategy for most of the remainder of the war on the mainland, defensive operations in the North, coupled with ravaging raids, and limited offensive in the South.

The more modest military program which the British adopted for America as the result of the coming of France into the struggle was based on harsh realities. George III's instructions were followed across the Atlantic by Charles-Henri, Comte d'Estaing, admiral in the navy of Louis XVI, and a powerful fleet which made its way from Toulon through the Straits of Gibraltar and across the ocean without challenge from British warships in European waters. This fleet was far superior in gunpower to that of Admiral Howe, which lay in the Delaware when D'Estaing set sail from the Mediterranean. Had the French admiral hurried, he would have been able to blockade Lord Howe within the Delaware Capes and doubtless to strike a damaging, perhaps a fatal, blow to the British forces in the Thirteen States. As it happened, D'Estaing did not arrive at the mouth of the bay before the early days of July, by which time Clinton and Admiral Howe had returned to the British base at New York. D'Estaing followed in the wake of Howe's ships. He had with him about four thousand French troops. With Washington, who had harassed Clinton across New Jersey, he planned a joint assault upon the British base, but found reasons why it should not be undertaken, chiefly the fact that Admiral Howe, supported by land batteries, was obviously ready for battle. D'Estaing and Washington then projected and began a joint attack upon a British garrison at Newport. But

---

that the Americans fly into the loving arms of the mother country. Otherwise, Pitt would crush them. That "A By Stander" ventured to express such an opinion at that time is surprising; that the newspaper dared to print it is remarkable.

Howe, reinforced, though still inferior in guns, came to the rescue of the garrison. D'Estaing had no lust for engaging the intrepid British admiral; and a storm which scattered both fleets furnished him a plausible reason for abandoning the enterprise. Not long afterward he sailed off to the French West Indies, for he had business in the Caribbean.

While D'Estaing had won no victories, his presence on the coasts of the Thirteen States had created an ominous menace for the British. Sir Henry Clinton, who did not possess boundless faith in himself or in his star, did not fail to draw the obvious inference: thenceforth in all British operations on the American continent the French navy must be heavily taken into account. A superior French fleet co-operating with a patriot army would put into serious jeopardy any British forces caught between them, even those massed at New York. Accordingly, Clinton, who had on occasion earlier displayed audacity as a subordinate officer, was a very cautious commander in chief. Perhaps, since he lacked confidence in himself, he would have been such in any case.[2]

Keeping the chief part of the British army in America at New York until the war had substantially ended, Clinton was confronted there by Washington, who hovered about the city. The British general made no determined attempt to drive the Virginian away but sought instead to wear down American resistance by ruining the shipping of the patriots, ravaging their shores, bribing their leaders, enlisting the services of the loyalists, and occupying strategic points along the coast, especially in the South. After the departure of D'Estaing for the Caribbean, Clinton felt safe enough at New York to undertake the limited offensive in the far South, where the patriots were known to be relatively weak, where the loyalists were supposedly both numerous and pugnacious. In November, 1778, he sent Lieutenant Colonel Archibald Campbell with 3,500 men, redcoats, Hessians, and New York Tories, to Georgia. Accompanied by a naval squadron under Commodore Hyde Parker, Campbell was to be joined by troops under General Augustine Prevost from St. Augustine and to attempt the capture of Savannah. Prevost failed to come up

[2] For a superior analysis of Clinton and his generalship, see Willcox (ed.), *American Rebellion*, xliv–li.

quickly, but Campbell and Parker did not therefore delay the opening of hostilities which led ultimately and after many shifts in the tides of war to British disaster at Yorktown. They landed near Savannah in December, and were promptly opposed by General Robert Howe, who had been placed by Congress in command of the Continental troops in the South.[3]

Neither Savannah nor Howe was prepared for a struggle. The town, situated on a high bluff and containing about 450 houses, had been fortified in the Seven Years' War, but its defenses had been allowed to decay. Ten Continental regiments had been formed in South Carolina and Georgia in the early years of the war, but the ranks of these had never been full, and idleness, disease, and desertion had reduced some of them almost to skeletons. Howe had only seven hundred of these regulars to defend the town. With them and Georgia militia he could not man the extensive and dilapidated works. Accordingly, he occupied strong ground east of the town, where his flanks were covered by marshes. He probably did not have power enough to sustain a frontal attack, and he failed to guard against a flanking movement. Campbell came up, learned from a captured Negro slave of a path through the swamp on the American right, and sent troops by means of it to assail the militia men from the rear. They promptly fled, and a general attack routed Howe's little army. More than five hundred patriots were killed, drowned in the retreat, or captured; and Savannah fell to Campbell at trifling expense. The outcome was not altered because Howe's conduct was examined by a court of inquiry which found him innocent.

[3] It may be worth while to note that Congress in effect set up several military departments in the War of Independence. Washington normally commanded in the central division only. Officers such as Philip Schuyler and Horatio Gates operated quite independently of him in the Northern department, chiefly in upper New York. The same was true of American generals stationed in Canada. Similarly, Charles Lee, Robert Howe, Benjamin Lincoln, and Horatio Gates were successively responsible to Congress for the defense of the South. All of these men were, of course, subordinate in rank to Washington as commander in chief and were required to obey his orders when he was present. Congress changed this system in 1780 when it appointed Greene to the Southern command. Greene was specifically ordered to obey Washington's instructions. However, because of distance and poor communications, Washington could not direct the activities of Greene, who was in effect, like the other generals mentioned, an independent commander.

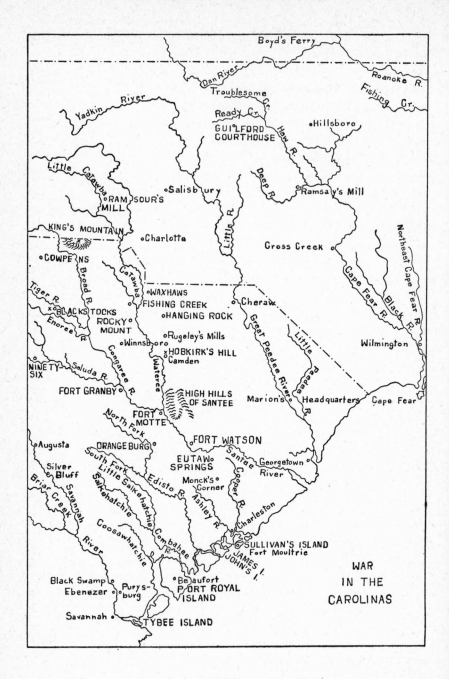

WAR
IN THE
CAROLINAS

The quick collapse of American resistance at Savannah gave the British a valuable base. Looting the town, they moved inland. Campbell was soon joined by Prevost, who assumed command. Augusta fell to the British in January, 1779; the Tories of Georgia flocked to join Prevost; and others as far away as North Carolina began to stir. About seven hundred supporters of the crown from the North State marched into Georgia to fight under the royal standard. They were routed in battle by patriot militia led by Andrew Pickens, and only half of them reached the British army. Five of them, captured by the patriots, were hanged as traitors in South Carolina. This unhappy event stimulated the internecine conflict which had already begun in the South. Thereafter bitter fighting between loyalists and patriots was frequent and atrocities not rare in the Carolinas and Georgia.[4]

The seemingly easy conquest of Georgia encouraged Prevost to meditate an invasion of South Carolina and an attempt upon Charleston. Meanwhile, General Benjamin Lincoln of Massachusetts, appointed to succeed Howe before the loss of Savannah, began to rally patriot forces in South Carolina; and Governor John Rutledge, given almost dictatorial powers by the South Carolina legislature, called up several thousands of militia. Lincoln, no great commander, had served creditably in the Saratoga campaign. Brave, abstemious, economical of words, he looked like a fighting general. His habit of taking naps amidst military business doubtless indicated to some patriots that he had confidence in himself; it also suggests a lack of aggressiveness. With five thousand men available, chiefly as the result of Rutledge's efforts, he moved toward Augusta in April. Prevost countered by crossing the lower Savannah River and marching toward Charleston. He correctly calculated that Lincoln would abandon his enterprise to go to the defense of Charleston. He had not expected to take the city, but was so weakly resisted that he reached its outskirts before Lincoln's men came to the rescue of its few defenders. Falling back, Prevost left a garrison of nine hundred

---

[4] The war, of course, had its lighter side. In 1778 a North Carolina gentleman entering the army advertised for a "companion," and received a prompt reply from "Belinda," who claimed no great beauty, but expressed her willingness to join him. New Bern *North-Carolina Gazette*, April 3, 1778.

Scottish Highlanders and Hessians under Lieutenant Colonel John Maitland at Beaufort on Port Royal Island. Summer and its heat approached, and neither the patriots nor the British thought it worth while to move in force for several months.

Nevertheless, Rutledge and William Moultrie were alarmed for the safety of the South. Should the British, perhaps reinforced, take the offensive in the fall, should the Tories of the Carolinas simultaneously take up arms, Charleston and the South to the border of Virginia would be in grave danger. They begged for help from D'Estaing, who was still cruising in the West Indies; and their pleas were supported by the Marquis de Brétigny, a French officer serving in South Carolina, who told D'Estaing that only he could save Charleston. The French admiral, receiving their urgent messages, had others from Washington's headquarters soliciting his aid in an attack upon New York or Newport. Indeed, Washington, expecting D'Estaing, long vainly watched for his appearance off Sandy Hook. The admiral later told his superiors in France that he chose to proceed to the Southern states because "the cruel task" of helping the patriots to deal with Prevost was "irrevocably imposed by national honor and by an irresistible train of events." [5] "National honor" might well have compelled him to return to the Northern states, where he had twice failed in great enterprises, where he had left behind him strong feeling against France, where there was opportunity to strike a mighty blow against Britain. It would seem that D'Estaing, soon to return to European waters, desired to add to his record in the New World a triumph on the mainland, that he saw an opportunity for quick success at Savannah. Whatever were his thoughts, the British at Savannah were startled and alarmed on September 8 when they learned that he was anchoring off Tybee Bar with twenty-two battleships of the line, ten frigates, several other craft, and four thousand troops. This mighty armament was much the same as that which he had led to New York and Newport the year before, except that his troops, besides regulars from France, now included

[5] Alexander A. Lawrence, *Storm over Savannah; The Story of Count d'Estaing and the Siege of the Town in 1779* (Athens, 1951), 21. The fine study by Mr. Lawrence is the basis for the account of the siege in this volume.

mulattoes and Negroes from the West Indies, among them Henri Christophe, long afterward King of Haiti and master of Sans Souci.

Were military issues decided by numbers and illustrious names, the British should have surrendered immediately. Aboard the French fleet were François Joseph Paul, Comte de Grasse, who must ever be remembered with Yorktown; Pierre André de Suffren, the ablest French naval officer of his generation, who was later to shake to its foundations British power in India; the Comte de la Pérouse and Louis-Antoine de Bougainville, famous explorers of the Pacific; the Marquis de Vaudreuil and the Comte de Colbert, bearers of names written large in the history of the French empire that had been virtually destroyed in the Seven Years' War; the Vicomte de Noailles, brother-in-law of Lafayette; and many French aristocrats more remarkable for their sonorous and mellifluous titles and the length of their genealogies than for their qualities of mind and heart. The British in Savannah were not, however, overwhelmed by nomenclature, nor had they need to dread bombardment by D'Estaing's ships, since most of the ships of the French fleet could not come close enough to use their guns upon the town. They feared that they would not be able to hold off the Bourbon troops and the Americans joyously hastening to join D'Estaing.

The Americans came on, Georgians, South Carolinians, and Virginians, among them many men also to be famous, at least in their own country: John Laurens, gallant and bold, once Washington's aide de camp; Francis Marion, later the "Swamp Fox"; the Pinckney brothers, Thomas and Charles Cotesworth, intelligent, trustworthy, and courageous; and Isaac Huger, Peter Horry, Andrew Williamson, William Thompson, and Lachlan McIntosh. At their head was Lincoln. With them was Count Casimir Pulaski, the Polish officer who commanded a cavalry detachment in Continental service. The Americans were, however, remarkable for quality rather than quantity. They numbered no more than 1,350, including Continentals and militia. With 3,500 men put ashore by D'Estaing, they made a formidable army.

The British had been caught napping. Ministers in London had been certain enough of the conquest of Georgia that they had sent back to Savannah Governor James Wright and other civil officials.[6] But Clinton had been unable to send reinforcements to Prevost, and the British commander in the town had available immediately for its defense no more than 1,700 troops. The appearance of the French fleet and army in the hurricane season was almost incredible to Prevost. He urgently begged Maitland to come to his aid from Beaufort, ordered James Moncrief, an able engineer, to repair the town's fortifications, and began parleys with D'Estaing in order to gain time. There is some reason to believe he considered surrendering in the face of greatly superior forces. He did not; and Maitland succeeded in a desperate attempt to come to the rescue, slipping rapidly through the unguarded inland waterways of South Carolina and making his way between the French fleet and the Franco-American army into the town on September 16 and 17. While D'Estaing and Lincoln, wavering between discouragement and hopes of easy victory, prepared to attack, Maitland brought new vigor to the British command. Moncrief, with hundreds of Negro slaves, solidified the British lines, fortified them with redoubts, and brought up cannon to cover those parts of Savannah not protected by the river on the east and marshes to the north. The river was blocked by sunken vessels and a boom of logs. The allies then had two choices—to assault the lines or to depart. With his fleet in open sea and exposed to hurricane, D'Estaing could not stay long on the Georgia coast.

Disappointed because Prevost failed to give up without a fight, D'Estaing and his men quarreled with the Americans and among themselves; brought ashore heavy guns from the fleet; and, with the patriots, began to approach the British entrenchments, on September 23. The guns, with others on small French craft in the river, began to bombard the town on October 4, but caused little damage and frightened only the women and children in it. It became apparent that the town must soon be taken by assault, or not at all. D'Estaing would not for the third time abandon a Franco-American project without a desperate effort. He laid

[6] William Bull II was asked to go back to South Carolina as governor, but delayed his departure. Bull to William Knox, July 3, 1779, in Sackville-Germain Papers (William L. Clements Library, Ann Arbor), ix. The request was doubtless later withdrawn.

plans to try to storm the British lines on October 9, Lincoln perforce acquiescing. Feinting to the right and left, he and Lincoln led French infantry and South Carolina Continentals forward at dawn against the weakest point in the British line, the Spring Hill redoubt and its vicinity. Informed by spies or deserters of the time of the attack, Prevost was ready, and Maitland was in command of the redoubt. The feints were easily repulsed; and after bitter hand-to-hand fighting and heavy losses, D'Estaing and Lincoln had to fall back from Spring Hill. Nearly half of the allies who engaged in the main attack were killed or injured; in all they had 244 slain, 584 wounded. Pulaski and many American officers had answered their last call to arms. D'Estaing, twice wounded, had fought like a grenadier. He was urged by the patriots to continue the siege or to take position at Charleston, but he could do neither. The allies raised the siege without molestation, and the admiral sadly set sail for France.

The news of the bloody defeat of the French and Americans at Savannah and of the departure of D'Estaing for Europe made it possible for Clinton to attack Charleston. When D'Estaing's fleet left American waters, New York, well fortified against assault from the land, became temporarily safe. In December, 1779, leaving his base under the command of the German general Baron William von Knyphausen, Clinton with 8,500 troops sailed southward. He was accompanied by Admiral Marriot Arbuthnot and a respectable squadron of five ships of the line and nine frigates. Surviving Cape Hatteras storms, though with serious losses, especially in horses and stores, Clinton and Arbuthnot collected their forces at Savannah and made a landing on Johns Island thirty miles south of Charleston on February 11, 1780. Slowly pushing northward, Clinton crossed the Ashley River on March 29 and began to besiege it. By mid-April, reinforced from New York, he had 10,000 troops outside the city. Meanwhile Admiral Arbuthnot closed in from the sea.

So slow was the British advance that the patriots had abundant time in which to prepare for defense. Governor Rutledge vainly called upon the militia of Upcountry South Carolina to take the field and fruitlessly begged Spanish officials at Havana—Spain having entered the war—to send a fleet and army to aid the patriots. Washington, however, ordered the remains of the Virginia and North Carolina Continental regiments with him to march as rapidly as possible to South Carolina. By April 6 these had reached Charleston, where Lincoln was gathering the American forces. By that time Lincoln had in and near the city almost 6,000 men, more than half Continentals, the remainder Low Country militia. Moreover, the works covering the city had been repaired and enlarged. The fort on Sullivan's Island, now called Moultrie, Fort Johnson on James Island, and a flotilla of small warships had been made ready in order to hold off the British fleet; and a well-fortified line of breastworks and redoubts protected by a water ditch and abatis work had been built across the Neck between the Ashley and Cooper rivers connecting the city with the mainland.

It would have been better for the American cause had the city been less prepared for defense, had there been fewer troops within it. There was little likelihood that Clinton and Arbuthnot could be held off. Prudence demanded that Charleston be evacuated and that the American troops be withdrawn to fight under more favorable circumstances. Lincoln, however, was reluctant to abandon the city, to give the British the prestige of a triumph and possession of the best seaport in the far South without a struggle; and the inhabitants of Charleston, led by Christopher Gadsden, insisted that the city could and must be held. Lincoln hesitated, while the British closed in. On April 8 British frigates easily forced their way between Forts Moultrie and Johnson into the harbor. By that time Clinton's army was preparing to bombard the city and to assault the American works on the Neck. An avenue of escape was still open to Lincoln. General Isaac Huger was in possession of Monck's Corner, and the bulk of the patriot troops might have fled across the Cooper River and northward by way of the Corner. The British bombarded the city on April 13. Lincoln then called together his officers and proposed that the Continentals depart, to fight another day. He was supported by General Lachlan McIntosh, but he decided to postpone a decision. Delay was fatal. The following morning at three o'clock, Lieutenant Colonel Banastre Tarleton and Major Patrick Ferguson, two British officers who had hitherto served unremarkably in the war, made their first bids for undying fame. Tarleton and Fer-

SIR HENRY CLINTON by Thomas Day. By permission of Frick Art
Reference Library

guson, at the head of British cavalry and Tory infantry, surprised and routed Huger's men. Two British regiments came up to join them, and the ring about Charleston was closed.

The ring was drawn more and more tightly. On April 19 and 20, in councils of war, Lincoln proposed treating with the British. He hoped to secure a convention something like that which Burgoyne obtained at Saratoga, an agreement allowing him to lead his Continentals away from the city in exchange for its surrender. Gadsden and other civilian officials demanded that the city be defended at all costs. Lincoln nevertheless sent his terms to Clinton, who promptly refused them. The siege went on, punctuated by a bloodless British capture of Fort Moultrie and one forward step after another by the British army on the Neck. Lincoln reopened negotiations with Clinton, to no avail. Meanwhile, John Rutledge strove vainly to raise militia for a stroke at the British rear.[7] In the afternoon of May 9 the defenders engaged the besiegers in an artillery duel. With their homes crashing down about them as the result of the British fire, the Charleston civilians at length recognized the uselessness of resistance. On May 12 Lincoln formally surrendered, the only concession he received being permission for his militia to go home as prisoners of war upon parole. Almost 5,500 patriots laid down their arms. Among their many leaders who fell into British hands and who were able to render no further service to the American cause were Charles Cotesworth Pinckney, William Moultrie, Christopher Gadsden, and Edward Rutledge. The British secured also several American ships, large quantities of ammunition and other supplies, and control of Charleston.

The Franco-American repulse at Savannah was a heavy blow; the loss of Charleston and especially of its garrison and supplies was a disaster. For the moment resistance to British arms in South Carolina almost vanished, and detachments of cavalry and Tory regiments sent out by Clinton easily overran the state. British garrisons occupied a chain of posts running from Cheraw to Ninety-Six, and also Georgetown. South Carolina loyalists came forth by hundreds to take oaths of allegiance to the crown, and many

[7] John Rutledge to Benjamin Lincoln, April 25, 1780, Revolutionary Collection (Duke University Library).

took up arms in behalf of the King. In Charleston 210 men signed an address welcoming the British to the city. Many patriots, offered a choice between serving under the British flag on the one hand and spoliation, imprisonment, and probably death through hardship and disease on the other, enlisted in the royal forces; and hundreds of the defenders of Charleston afterward fought for Britain in the West Indies, though not against their own people. General Andrew Williamson not only surrendered Ninety-Six to royal forces but also became a loyalist. When Clinton and Arbuthnot, because of news that a French fleet and army were on the Atlantic, hastened off early in June to New York, they left behind them a South Carolina seemingly conquered. Moreover, the Tories of North Carolina were again taking up arms. Two weeks after Clinton's sailing, John Moore of Ramsour's Mills was at the head of a body of 1,300 of them.

The appearance of things in South Carolina, and in Georgia, which was apparently even more firmly under British control, was not quite reality. John Rutledge would not give up the struggle,[8] nor Francis Marion and Thomas Sumter and many another patriot north and south of the Savannah. Plundering, ravaging, and abuse of civilians by Hessians and loyalists, and the brutalities of Tarleton, who refused quarter to patriots in the field, drove them to desperation and to bitter resistance. Unable to attack successfully the major British posts or to engage large British forces in open battle, the patriots began a harassing guerrilla warfare, interrupting communications, intercepting British supplies, smashing Tory detachments. Before long in South Carolina it was doubtful that the British and Tories controlled ground beyond that upon which they stood. In the North State the Tory threat simultaneously diminished, John Moore's men being routed and dispersed by patriot militia.

Help now again came to the Americans from the north. North

---

[8] Thaddeus Kosciuszko ardently testifies to the devotion, energy, and generous spirit which Rutledge displayed as he continued to mobilize the strength of South Carolina for the struggle. Kosciuszko to Gates, July 29, 1781, in Horatio Gates Papers (New York Historical Society). It is commonly not noticed that Francis Marion, Thomas Sumter, Andrew Pickens, and other Revolutionary heroes of South Carolina were Rutledge's militia officers.

Carolina and Virginia militia moved southward, and 1,400 veteran Maryland and Delaware Continentals under Baron Johann de Kalb, sent on by Washington to assist in the defense of Charleston. On July 25, 1780, Horatio Gates, the victor of Saratoga, appointed by Congress to succeed the captured Lincoln, took over the command of the Maryland and Delaware Continentals, a detachment of Continental cavalry under the French Major Armand de la Rouverie, and another of artillerymen, on Deep River in North Carolina. Gates had won undying fame by stopping the advance of Burgoyne from Canada and forcing him to lay down his arms at Saratoga; and there were men in and out of Congress who considered Gates to be an abler general than Washington. The commander in chief's opinion of that officer was far less favorable, and Washington had vainly hoped that the choice of Congress would fall upon Nathanael Greene. Washington's estimate of Gates was closer to reality than that of the admirers of the former British officer in Philadelphia. The son of an upper servant in an English household, Gates had risen far in the world. He reached the rank of major in the British regulars. Then, as a settler in the Shenandoah and a devoted adherent to the American cause, he entered Continental service and attained that of major general. He had gone so far, however, because of a pleasing personality, powerful friends, and good fortune rather than superlative abilities. He had displayed no more than good sense on the Hudson in 1777, digging in and letting Burgoyne rashly advance to his destruction.

Gates had been cautious in the Saratoga campaign, and there were many reasons why he should have been so in his new command. He had neither sufficient men nor enough supplies to undertake to drive the British from South Carolina. Indeed, his men were on short and unreliable rations, the commissariat services of Virginia and North Carolina being hopelessly inefficient. Yet Gates believed that he had to move forward, that his own situation and the patriot cause imperatively demanded action. The Baron de Kalb had formed a plan for the immediate future, to march to the southwest through Salisbury and Charlotte and thence against the British post at Camden. By taking this circuitous route the army would pass through country where patriot sentiment was strong, where supplies and reinforcements might be obtained. However, the slow approach of the patriots to Camden by this route would give the British ample time in which to bring up support to its garrison. Accordingly, despite protests from more than one officer, Gates decided to push directly and rapidly for Camden, even though he and his men were in consequence compelled to traverse an impoverished and desolated region. His was a bold decision if he attained success at Camden and eluded British counterthrusts, a rash one if he failed. His little army was so valuable to the patriot cause that such an audacious movement involved extraordinary risk. On the other hand, if Camden fell at no great cost, the Americans might reap rich rewards, especially in morale. The plan which Gates adopted was worthy of a Caesar or a Napoleon. He did not have the talents necessary to execute it, nor was he blessed by fortune.

Gates began his rapid march southward on July 27, and relentlessly drove forward in spite of summer heat and lack of food. There were days when his troops had nothing in their bellies but green corn, and that did not stay long. They murmured and threatened to mutiny. He would not alter his plan. On August 11 he reached Little Lynch's Creek, where he was confronted by Lord Rawdon, commander at Camden, who had come forth to oppose him. Rawdon was in an unassailable position. Gates accordingly moved westward, then resumed his progress, Rawdon falling back toward the village. At Rugeley's Mill, north of Camden, Gates was joined on August 14 by General Edward Stevens with 700 Virginia militia. With these men he then had under him 1,100 Continentals and about 2,350 North Carolina and Virginia militia supposedly fit for duty, a force large in numbers but unreliable except for the Continentals, who were weakened by their swift march. From Rugeley's, Gates sent 100 Continentals and 300 North Carolinians to the assistance of Thomas Sumter, who had learned of the approach of a British supply train toward Camden and wished to capture it. On August 15 he himself moved on toward the village, evidently unaware that the British garrison had been reinforced and that Lord Cornwallis, who had been placed by Clinton in command of the British troops in the far South and who had been informed in Charleston of Gates's ad-

vance, had reached Camden two days earlier. Gates marched by
night (to avoid the heat of the day?) and approached Sanders
Creek, seven miles outside Camden, about two o'clock in the morning of August 16. Suddenly he was confronted by the energetic
Lord Cornwallis, who had chosen not to wait for the Americans
in Camden, who had also moved at night, in the hope of surprising Gates. With Cornwallis were more than 2,200 troops, nearly
two thirds of them veterans, including Tarleton and his famous
British Legion. Advance guards fought vigorously but briefly in
the dark. Both commanders were astonished; both chose to wait
for dawn to take decisive action.

An American retreat was possible, but Cornwallis, almost invariably venturesome, would quite certainly pursue and attack;
and even a successful withdrawal would hardly bring strength to
the patriot cause. Gates occupied good ground, and he chose to
fight. Swamps covered his force on both flanks, and he drew up
his men between them in a thin pine wood, with Continentals
under De Kalb composing his right wing, militia under Stevens
his left, and Maryland Continentals under General William Smallwood his reserve in the rear. Cornwallis was similarly protected
by the swamps but had in his rear Sanders Creek, which rendered
retreat for him in case of need extremely hazardous. He was determined to win. He posted his line so that his best infantry faced
the American militia.

It was Gates who began the battle at dawn, sending his Virginia
militia forward in the hope of attacking the British right wing
before it was effectively formed. But the Virginians faltered in
their advance, the British regulars charged in solid formation,
and the Virginians fled, firing only a few shots. Panic-stricken,
most of the North Carolina militia also ran, apparently without
discharging one gun. In wild disorder they left the field, carrying
with them Armand's corps, Smallwood, and Gates himself. Only
the Continentals and a few North Carolinians were left on the
field. De Kalb withstood a first British onslaught and vigorously
counterattacked. The Continental reserve came up, formed at
his left, and tried to establish a solid line with him. It was unable,
however, to close a gap between and was before long so hard
pressed in front and flank that it was forced to give way and to

flee. De Kalb and the left wing, unaware of the flight of the bulk of the patriots—because of morning haze and gunsmoke—fought on and on. Assailed in front and then on their exposed left, they re-formed, drove the British back, and counterattacked with the bayonet. At length, however, they were also battered from the rear by Tarleton's British Legion. They could not withstand the entire British army. De Kalb was mortally wounded; and after a desperate resistance, the left wing also broke, its survivors taking to flight. Tarleton pursued them, and the patriots who had earlier fled the field, for twenty miles, capturing many prisoners. The American force had been completely routed and had sustained heavy losses, about 650 of the Continentals being killed, wounded, or captured.

Cornwallis did not escape without casualties, more than 300 men. Nevertheless, the battle of Camden was a shattering blow to the patriot cause in the South; and its effects were enhanced by a defeat which was inflicted upon Sumter two days later. Sumter captured the British wagon train he had set out to take, but was in turn surprised and driven off by Tarleton and his cavalry. Gates, making no effort immediately to gather the scattered remains of his army, rode rapidly away toward Hillsboro, North Carolina, where he appeared about three days after the battle, 160 miles from the field. There he was finally joined by 700 of his Continentals and a few of his militia. All thought of a major patriot offensive had to be abandoned; and Cornwallis was encouraged to move aggressively and to invade North Carolina.

CHAPTER XIV

TRIUMPH IN THE FAR SOUTH

IN HIS campaigns in the Carolinas as in his earlier ones to the northward, Lord Cornwallis was a fighting general. Resolute and sanguine, he preferred to beat the patriots in battle rather than slowly to wear down their resistance. When confronted by seemingly superior force, he did not avoid battle, was likely to attack. He was formidable in the field. After the War of Independence he made a brilliant military record in India. All of this does not prove, however, that he was an ideal leader for the British in the South, or even the best man available for the British command there. He chose to try to conquer the South; he encountered foes more dangerous than any he met in India; and he came ultimately to disaster at Yorktown.[1]

The chain of major British triumphs which began at Savannah, the easy British occupation of the interior of Georgia and South Carolina, the risings of the Southern Tories, and the confusion, seeming poverty, and low morale of the Southern patriots encouraged Cornwallis after Camden to try to overrun and subjugate the entire South. The task which he set for himself was far more difficult than he knew. The great distances within the South; its many geographical obstacles, including rivers, swamps, and mountains; its bad roads; its summer heat and malaria; the numbers and fighting qualities of the patriots; and the continuing danger that a French fleet and army would appear on the Southern coast might well have persuaded him to think of limited achievements.

---

[1] After Cornwallis left the Carolinas for Virginia, but before Yorktown, Greene described him as "a modern Hannibal." Greene to James McHenry, July 24, 1781, in Bernard C. Steiner, *Life and Correspondence of James McHenry* (Cleveland, 1907), 38.

He was painfully to learn that the patriots were more numerous than his loyalist allies in the South, that they would struggle desperately against both British and Tories, that Washington would come to their assistance, that the menace of French seapower was only too genuine.

When Sir Henry Clinton sailed from Charleston back to New York, he left instructions for Cornwallis. Above all, Cornwallis was to hold on to South Carolina, and especially Charleston. While Clinton did not forbid him to take the offensive, the British commander in chief warned Cornwallis not to undertake operations in the interior so expensive in men that the British grip upon Charleston and its vicinity would be imperiled. Clinton recommended that his subordinate send a small force to the neighborhood of Wilmington to encourage the North Carolina loyalists and to interrupt patriot trade, communications, and supply movements. In sum, Clinton counseled caution. At the same time, however, Sir Henry authorized Cornwallis to communicate directly with Lord George Germain in London as well as with himself. Cornwallis was second in rank among the British officers in America and would succeed his superior in the event that Clinton resigned or was unable to serve.[2] The commander in chief was talking frequently of quitting his post and had even sent in to Germain a qualified offer to resign, which had not been accepted. Moreover, Cornwallis was far more popular than he in the British army. Accordingly, Cornwallis was encouraged to think and to act independently.

Even before Camden, neglecting Clinton's advice to send a small force to the Cape Fear, Cornwallis was considering an invasion of interior North Carolina from the south. He believed this rather risky step was not inconsistent with his instructions. He was of the opinion that the cheapest and surest method to put an end to the activities of the patriot guerrillas in South Carolina and

[2] It is notorious that Cornwallis held a "dormant" commission designating him as Clinton's successor. Too much may be made of that fact. The purpose of the document, and of others like it issued to British officers during the war, was to make it as certain as possible that the supreme command would always be in the hands of a British officer. In the absence of such commissions Hessian officers such as Knyphausen might have had an opportunity to claim the right to command on the basis of superior rank.

Georgia was to deprive them of support and encouragement from the North State. He hoped, with the aid of the Tories of North Carolina, to form a base at Hillsboro, to overawe their patriot neighbors, and to cut off patriot supplies and reinforcements from Virginia. The cost of such an invasion he assessed lightly. He fancied he would be able to send a detachment northward to harass the Virginians after its execution. Three weeks after Camden he pushed forward toward Charlotte, calling upon the Tories to rise as he went. He easily brushed aside feeble patriot efforts to hinder his march and encamped at that place early in October. There he received staggering news from South Carolina.

Not that Charleston was in insurrection, nor that Camden had fallen. Cornwallis had left the garrisons behind him on the alert, and he had taken stern measures to quiet the South Carolinians. He had gone so far as to send off from Charleston to St. Augustine seventy-eight patriots, including Christopher Gadsden and many civilians, whose presence in the city he thought a menace; and he had proclaimed the death penalty for any American who took up arms for the patriots after enrolling in the King's militia. The bad news came from the west, from King's Mountain.

As Cornwallis marched northward, Major Patrick Ferguson and a Tory detachment, sent out by the British commander to deal with American partisans and to enlist Tories, moved to his left. Ferguson was to join Cornwallis in Charlotte. He failed to keep his rendezvous.

Ferguson, bold and brave, advanced steadily from Ninety-Six, he and his Tories arousing terror and antagonizing the backwoodsmen of Virginia and Tennessee. As he drove ahead, up the valley of the Broad River and into Rutherford County, North Carolina, patriots east and west of the mountains flew to arms. More than 1,000 riflemen collected by William Campbell, Isaac Shelby, John Sevier, and Charles McDowell gathered at the Sycamore Shoals on the Watauga on September 25. Proceeding rapidly eastward, they were joined at the Cowpens by 400 North and South Carolinians under James Williams. Informed of their coming, Ferguson hastily retreated toward Ninety-Six. Most of the patriots were mounted, and he could not escape by flight. Turning eastward, he established himself and his Tories, 1,100 of them, on the heights of King's Mountain. Sending out a plea for help to Cornwallis, he prepared for an obstinate defense. His men were both Northern and Southern loyalists, some of them veterans, all well armed. He was safe enough on the top of the mountain against formal assault but not against riflemen covered by trees and brush and swarming up the sides of the hill. The bulk of the backwoodsmen arrived at the base of the mountain in the afternoon of October 7. Led by Campbell, they immediately assailed Ferguson's position. Quickly reaching the summit of the mountain, they were more than once driven back by bayonet charges. But they continued to pour a heavy fire upon the defenders, and Ferguson fell, and many of the Tories. The remainder surrendered. The riflemen were so embittered by the raiding and marauding of Ferguson's force that they killed several Tories after quarter was asked and later hanged nine others.

Learning of Ferguson's danger, Cornwallis sent Tarleton to his assistance, but too late. The earl now became alarmed for his own safety. He envisioned the backwoodsmen sweeping down upon his posts in South Carolina; behind him Thomas Sumter and Andrew Pickens were already only too active. The British commander decided to fall back. Harassed by patriot detachments— Cornwallis himself was laid low by fever and had to be carried in a wagon—the British army retreated to Winnsboro. En route it subsisted for some days upon corn, riper, it is to be supposed, than that which Gates's Continentals ate before Camden. The backwoodsmen did not annoy Cornwallis's army. They had done their bit, and most of them had gone home.

Cornwallis was temporarily a chastened man, and lay quiet for some weeks. In December, however, he received reinforcements, more than 2,200 troops led by General Alexander Leslie. Leslie had been sent to Virginia by Clinton in October to raid the valley of the James River and to ravage Richmond and Petersburg, thus, among other objectives, to prevent supplies and troops from going to the American Southern army. Leslie failed to move energetically in Virginia. After receiving news of King's Mountain, Clinton planned to station Leslie's force at Wilmington, but Cornwallis, under whose command it had been placed, ordered it to Charleston. Although he did shortly afterward send a garrison to Wilmington, Cornwallis added the bulk of Leslie's contingent to his own army and thus had toward 4,000 troops, exclusive of garrison forces, under his command. It became possible for him then to take the offensive, and he soon did so, with the approval of Clinton, who was not opposed to an invasion of North Carolina, were it successful. It was not immediately necessary, however, that the British commander move northward to find his enemies, for the army which had been so badly beaten at Camden moved forward.

On December 3 Nathanael Greene assumed the direction of the Continental forces in the South, replacing Gates.[3] A Rhode Islander, Greene had served from the beginning of the war, had won the confidence of Washington, and had been appointed by Congress to the Southern command upon Washington's nomination. Greene came from a family of commercial Quakers, and he desired dollars, even Continental ones. He mingled his private ventures with public business, as did Robert Morris, the patriot "Financier." Like Morris, Greene has consequently been suspected, perhaps unjustly, of using his public offices for his personal profit.[4] In any case, he did not let his private interests interfere with his military duties; and he was no less the warrior for having been a Quaker. Experienced and cool, both thoughtful and bold, Greene was a commander of uncommon ability. It is idle to try to match his qualities against those of Washington and to

[3] When the crestfallen Horatio Gates, under threat of military punishment, appeared at Richmond, the Virginia House of Representatives, in a touching gesture, sent a committee to him to assure him that his earlier services had not been forgotten and to express sympathy. Gates rose to the occasion with dignity, promising loyalty and zeal. Williamsburg *Virginia Gazette* (Dixon and Nicolson), December 30, 1780.

[4] A thorough and reliable study of Greene has not yet appeared, although several scholars are now laboring toward that end. Among the documents which raise questions concerning Greene's financial transactions is a letter from the General to Griffin Greene, his cousin and friend, of December 21, 1778. Said the General, writing from Washington's headquarters: "It may not be amiss for you to lodge some good liquors at Albany in the course of the winter. This is a secret hint." Obviously, Greene, knowing early that an American army would march against the Iroquois in 1779, was giving a useful business tip to Griffin Greene. Moreover, there is a possibility that the General thought of personal profit, for he was a partner of his cousin in business. See Greene to Griffin Greene, December 21, 1778, June 18, 1779, in Marietta College Historical Collections (Marietta College Library, Marietta, Ohio, copies in the University of North Carolina Library).

attempt to prove, as some assert, that he excelled the Virginian in military talent. It is undeniable that Cornwallis and other British generals in the South found him to be, despite the fact that he never won a major battle in the field, a formidable antagonist. The first step which Greene took after succeeding Gates at Charlotte testifies both to his shrewdness and his daring.

At Charlotte, Greene faced much the same situation, though a more favorable one, largely because of King's Mountain and the continuing successes of Marion and Sumter, as Gates before Camden. He had about 1,500 men, two thirds Continentals, three thirds suffering from a lack of clothing, arms, and food.[5] While he could expect support from Southern militia and from the partisans, who seldom left the field, it did not seem prudent to march against Cornwallis. To retreat was obviously inadvisable, to stand still quite unprofitable. He chose to divide his small force. The Southern army had acquired a most valuable man, Daniel Morgan, who had left the Continental service because Congress had failed to promote him as he deserved, but who had come forward to serve in the Southern crisis. That December Greene gave Morgan a third of the army and directed him to march to the southwest, to the region between the Broad and Pacolet rivers. With the remainder Greene and General Isaac Huger soon made off to the southeast, to Cheraw Hill on the Pee Dee River. Both Greene and Morgan were soon joined by militia, and to Greene came a powerful reinforcement, Light-Horse Harry Lee's Legion, the equivalent of the British contingent which Tarleton had led to fame. Washington had sent Lee's men to Greene's assistance; his detachment, composed, like Tarleton's, of both horse and foot, and numbering nearly 300 men, was to achieve all that Washington could have expected.

Greene's rather remarkable division of forces and the simultaneous appearance of his two little armies in South Carolina offered opportunity to Cornwallis, of course, to deal separately with his enemies. Greene, however, relied upon the speedy movements of the Americans to evade disaster; and he had arranged for a junction with Morgan and had made preparations to retreat

[5] Some of his men were literally barefoot. William Smallwood to Gates, September 2, 1780, Gates Papers.

rapidly through North Carolina in case of need. The outcome was most fortunate for Greene. Cornwallis strengthened his garrison at Camden, sent Tarleton with 1,100 men to destroy Morgan, and himself moved northward to cut off Morgan's avenue of escape. Thereafter,

> *Cornwallis led a country dance,*
> *The like was never seen, sir,*
> *Much retrograde and much advance,*
> *And all with General Greene, sir.*

Early in the year 1781 Tarleton set forth, with his British Legion, two battalions of British foot, a party of dragoons, a few Tory militiamen, and a detachment of Royal Artillery with two cannon. He quickly found Morgan, who fled before him. At the Cowpens, however, Morgan turned about and offered battle on January 17. He then had nearly as many men as Tarleton, and he preferred to fight rather than to run. He took position in an open wood, his flanks exposed to the British cavalry, with the Broad River flowing behind him and making successful retreat very doubtful. Afterward he claimed he chose such dubious ground because he wished the militia in his force to know that they had no place to run and that they must do their duty. It is to be suspected that Morgan tired of retreating, that he did not desire to search for ideal ground, that he was determined to do or die. He arranged his men superbly—in front, two lines of militia, Carolinian and Georgian riflemen, behind them and based on a hill, his main line, composed largely of Continentals and Virginia militiamen who had seen much service. Behind a smaller hill to the rear he concealed 125 mounted men under William Washington. Morgan knew that the riflemen in his advanced line would not stand against bayonet or cavalry charge. He told them that he did not expect them to do so; that Tarleton would attack; that the first line was to shoot twice and fall back into openings left in the second one, under Andrew Pickens; that they were to continue firing as long as possible and then to follow Pickens to their left and to the rear of the main line, where, so Morgan said, they would be safe under the protection of the main line. To reassure them he had them tie their horses—all had mounts—in the rear, where they would be readily available. Morgan's preparations were masterful, and the riflemen in the front lines did more for him than he asked.

Tarleton reached the field early in the morning, drove the first line of riflemen back into the second, at some cost to his Legion cavalry. He then drew up his men, nearly all British regulars, in battle array, opened fire with two cannon, and immediately advanced in a general attack. Pickens and the riflemen waited until the enemy was in range, discharged their weapons again and again into the British ranks, inflicting heavy casualties. The British hesitated, came on, and the militia fled as Morgan had directed, with Washington and the American cavalry covering their retreat. Now Tarleton pushed forward to put an end to the battle, attacking the main American line. It stood firm, the Virginia veterans with the Maryland and Delaware Continentals. Tarleton brought up Highlanders from his reserve, extended his line to his left, sought to outflank the Continentals. Because of a mistake in executing orders they, and then the Virginians, withdrew slightly. The British commander, now sure of victory, ordered his men to charge. They did so, in their eagerness advancing in disorder. They were received with a heavy fire and halted. Then the Continentals counterattacked with the bayonet, and Washington struck the British from the flank and rear. Pickens and his men, having marched completely across the American rear, reappeared on Morgan's right flank and opened fire. Tarleton could not persuade his Legion cavalry to try a last charge. The British began to fall back, and finally to flee. Only a few of them, including Tarleton, escaped. More than 900 of his troops were killed or captured, and all of his equipment. Morgan was able to report joyfully that he had given Tarleton "a devil of a whiping." [6]

The American victory at Cowpens was a heavy blow to Cornwallis. True to himself, he sought to retrieve the damage by a quick offensive. He set off to the northwest to cut off Morgan, but the American general, aware of his danger, eluded him, retreating rapidly into North Carolina. At Ramsour's Mills in the North State Cornwallis learned that he had failed to intercept Morgan. He might have turned back, as he did from Charlotte

[6] Morgan to William Snickers, January 26, 1781, *ibid.*

after King's Mountain. He chose to plunge on. Destroying all his heavy baggage, even his supplies of rum, in order to increase the speed of his movements, he moved forward with almost 3,000 men. To evade him, Morgan considered flight to the mountains. But Greene arrived in Morgan's camp on January 30. Learning at Cheraw Hill of Morgan's triumph, he had anticipated Cornwallis's advance. Accordingly, he had ordered Huger to fall back into North Carolina and had hurried westward to lead Morgan's men to a junction with Huger. Greene insisted that Morgan retreat through relatively open country to the northeast, even though Cornwallis' chances of successful pursuit would be increased. He had made arrangements for ready crossing of the rivers as far north as the Dan. He hoped to elude the British commander, and eventually to turn about and give battle under favorable circumstances.

Cornwallis reached Salisbury on February 3, and was within ten miles of Morgan's men. Five days later, abandoning his close pursuit of Morgan, he crossed the Yadkin River, heading toward the upper Dan. Believing that the Americans lacked the boats necessary to cross the lower Dan, he concluded that both Morgan and Huger must use fords higher up on the river, and that he could intercept all of Greene's command. Greene, however, moved eastward and was joined by Huger near Guilford Court House on February 7. Huger's men were ill equipped; many of them are said to have marched barefoot from the Pee Dee. Greene considered offering battle, since a continued retreat would lower the spirits of the patriots and encourage the North Carolina Tories to flock to Cornwallis' assistance. He even studied the ground near Guilford. He had not received hoped-for reinforcements of patriot militia. He prudently chose to resume his retreat toward the lower Dan, seventy miles away. Cornwallis quickly followed. His advanced troops were soon threatening the American rear guard, led by Colonel Otho Holland Williams of Maryland, to no avail. The main body of the patriots passed the river on February 14 in boats made ready for them. Before midnight Williams' men crossed the river as the first British troops approached its south bank. Cornwallis could not hope to move immediately across the Dan without boats, and he had none. In any case, Greene was certain to receive support in Virginia; and Cornwallis could hope for none there. Although Benedict Arnold was on the Elizabeth River, he was too distant and in too small force to assist Cornwallis. The British commander's men were weary, worn, and suffering from sickness; and further pursuit was too risky even for that intrepid man. He could not stay where he was, distant from supplies. He marched away to the southward.

By easy stages Cornwallis retreated to Hillsboro. There he called upon the Tories of North Carolina to rally to the British flag. Some came to join him, not many, because it was soon apparent to the Tories that his strength was ebbing. Moreover, a party of 400 of them under Colonel John Pyle that sought to make its way to him was surprised and dispersed by Light-Horse Harry Lee. And Lee's Legion was quickly followed across the Dan by Greene. Greene's men were also suffering from exhaustion and illness, but Continentals and militia of Virginia and the Carolinas were finally coming forward to assist him, and he felt strong enough to return to North Carolina and to risk battle. Before the end of February Greene's light troops were busily attacking British detachments, interrupting Cornwallis' communications, driving the Tories to cover, and generally bedeviling the British commander. Cornwallis, despite his weakness, saw pitched battle as the solution of his many difficulties. He sought to compel Greene to fight. The American general evaded large-scale action until he had received all his reinforcements, until he could accept the challenge on ground of his own choosing. Finally, on March 14, with at least 4,500 men, Greene took position at Guilford Court House and awaited Cornwallis' onslaught.

Losses in the field, desertions, and especially disease had so reduced Cornwallis' army that he was able to muster fewer than 2,000 men for the struggle which took place on the following day. The disparity in numbers between his forces and those of Greene was remarkable, but Cornwallis had faith in his British and Hessian veterans and knew the bulk of the patriots to be green and unreliable. Of tried and true Continentals Greene could not muster 1,000. He had also 1,200 Virginia militia like those who had fought well at Cowpens—many of these had formerly been in Continental service. From the rest of his army Greene would receive little or great help, according to the finesse with which he used it and circumstances which he could not control. Even so, the Quaker general fought under highly favorable conditions. Moreover, he risked far less than Cornwallis. Should the Americans be defeated, they would flee in sufficient strength to resume the campaign later; should Cornwallis be driven from the field, the British grip upon the far South must be shaken. A drawn battle would be in effect an American victory.

In the morning of March 15 Cornwallis came up from the southwest, his men marching twelve miles to reach the battlefield. Early in the afternoon he studied Greene's dispositions as best he might —he could not secure full information about them, because the patriots were posted on rolling terrain and in thin woods—and prepared for action. Greene had chosen good ground and had drawn up his army in three lines, North Carolina militia posted in the most advanced one behind two open clearings and supported on the flanks by cavalry and veteran light troops under William Washington and Light-Horse Harry Lee; the Virginia militia in the second line four hundred yards or so to the rear, with riflemen behind them to shoot down any who should try to flee without fighting; the Continentals in the third line another four hundred yards back, occupying the brow of a hill near the courthouse. Greene's arrangements, except that he maintained an avenue of retreat, were in a very general way similar to those of Morgan at Cowpens. He asked his first line to fire at least twice before taking to flight; he hoped that the Virginia militia would hold for a time and inflict heavy casualties upon the enemy; he relied upon his Continentals ultimately to withstand and drive back the last assaults of the presumably weakened British troops.

The British formed in fine style, fusiliers, Highlanders, and the Von Bose Hessian regiment in front, two battalions of the Guards, some light troops, and Tarleton's horse behind them. The fusiliers and the Highlanders moved to the attack and drove the patriot first line into headlong flight, but not before its riflemen had delivered their two volleys. The Hessians and a few British troops engaged Lee's Legion, forced it away from the battlefield, and fought a separate and inconclusive engagement with it until after the issue of the day had been settled. William Washington, however, fell back to take post with the American second line. The redcoats had been galled and hurt by the fire of the militia, but they were joined by the Guards and pushed on. Edward Stevens, who commanded the Virginia militia that departed so hastily from the field at Camden, directed the American second line. Its right wing did not give way until it had inflicted at least two bayonet charges and fought steadily though unsuccessfully, long after the remainder of the militia had vanished. Lieutenant Colonel James Webster, a redoubtable officer leading the British attack, drove on behind the American militia scattering for cover on Greene's right and made a bayonet charge against the Continentals there. The third American line, both veterans and new troops, stood firm, counterattacked, and forced Webster back. Soon afterward the Virginia militia took to the woods. Now came the decisive time. Webster re-formed; part of the Guards came up; and the whole of the remaining British infantry, save for the Hessians and some Guards still busy with Lee and Stevens, advanced against the Continentals. A new Maryland unit broke and fled without firing a shot at the advancing grenadiers, who struck first. But William Washington swept completely through the Guards from the rear, and they were struck on the flank by the reliable Maryland and Delaware veterans of Camden and Cowpens. Living up to their magnificent reputation, the grenadiers, though halted, refused to be crushed, closed ranks, fought on. Joined by the fusiliers and Highlanders, they engaged the Continentals in close and furious combat. They received the worst of it and began to falter. Cornwallis saved the situation by the harshest of measures. He ordered his scanty artillery into action. He had his artillerymen load their three guns with grapeshot and fire them through the British ranks into the patriots. The redcoats suffered, but the Continentals were hit harder and were forced back to their original positions. Once again Webster re-formed and charged with the bayonet. He was driven back. Greene might then have counterattacked, although Cornwallis still had Tarleton's cavalry in reserve. The American general chose not to risk everything to win a complete victory, to let well enough alone. He began to withdraw in good order, Virginia Continentals steadily covering his retreat. He was followed for only a short distance by the weary British. At length Tarleton drove off Lee and the American riflemen engaging the Hessians, enabling the Germans to return to the main battleground.

Cornwallis had won, since he had compelled Greene to seek safety in flight and held the field. He was a technical victor only. Almost half of his Guards were killed or wounded, and the total of his injured and slain reached 532, about 28 per cent of his army. He also lost the brave Webster, mortally wounded near the end of the fighting. Greene's losses, except for vanished militia, most of which could be expected to return to service, were much smaller, 261 dead or wounded. It was impossible for Cornwallis to resume the offensive. Another such victory would mean the end of his army. Nor could he stay where he was, without supplies, without safe communications to the southward, without hope of early reinforcement. A prudent commander would have retreated into South Carolina to lend support to the British garrisons there and in Georgia, to save the early conquests of the British in the far South. Cornwallis moved away from Guilford Court House, but to the Pedee and thence to Wilmington, where he and the remainder of his army arrived on April 7. Greene followed him briefly, then turned southward.

At Wilmington Cornwallis considered his future course. That he would receive reinforcements sufficient to undertake a third invasion of the interior of North Carolina was highly unlikely. In any case he now knew the chances of completely subjugating the North State by such means were not too good. The orthodox thing to do was to hurry to Charleston and go to the support of his posts to the westward, for Greene was obviously moving against them. They would be gravely endangered, since Greene would have the assistance of Marion, Sumter, and other leaders of patriot irregulars, who could be expected to be more active than ever— they had been a menace before Cowpens, before Guilford Court House. But Cornwallis had no love for such defensive and limited operations, and his instructions from Clinton did not positively compel him to devote himself to them. They permitted him to remain on the offensive, as long as Charleston was safe against patriot attack. Moreover, Clinton had authorized him to move to the Chesapeake and to assume command of British troops in Virginia—after he had dealt with the patriots below the Dan. Major General William Phillips had recently arrived in Virginia from New York with more than 2,000 men. These, with Arnold's command and troops that Cornwallis might lead north from Wilmington, would make up an army large enough to do something big on the Chesapeake. Cornwallis knew that Clinton frequently talked of his own resignation, was doubtless aware that Clinton, quarreling with Admiral Arbuthnot, had told the cabinet that either he or Arbuthnot must go. His own prestige was great in London, because he had written home optimistically and had acted energetically. Cornwallis, in consequence, was encouraged to disobey Clinton's instructions in spirit and even in letter. Before the end of April he marched northward with 1,500 men toward Petersburg.

It is clear that Cornwallis intended to substitute his strategy, at least in part, for that of Clinton, and it is equally certain that he was far more responsible than Clinton for the British disasters that followed. He wrote to Clinton from Wilmington on April 10, "I cannot help expressing my wishes that the Chesapeake may become the seat of war—even, if necessary, at the expense of abandoning New York.[7] Until Virginia is in a manner subdued, our hold of the Carolinas must be difficult if not precarious." In a letter to Lord George Germain signed eight days later, Cornwallis expressed himself less recklessly, saying that "a serious attempt upon Virginia would be the most solid plan, because successful operations might not only be attended with important consequences there, but would tend to the security of South Carolina and ultimately to the submission of North Carolina."[8]

Hastening off to Virginia, Cornwallis was well aware that he left the British behind him in an ugly predicament. He expressed alarm for them, left under the command of Lord Rawdon. He feared that "Rawdon's posts will be so distant from each other,

---

[7] The letter is in Benjamin Franklin Stevens (ed.), *The Campaign in Virginia, 1781; An Exact Reprint of Six Rare Pamphlets on the Clinton-Cornwallis Controversy* (London, 1888), I, 395–99. That Cornwallis could even consider evacuating New York in order to operate on the Chesapeake suggests that his intellectual powers were not impressive.

[8] *Ibid.*, 417–18.

and his troops so scattered, as to put him into the greatest danger of being beat in detail, and that the worst of consequences may happen to most of the troops out of Charleston." [9] Momentarily he considered marching toward Hillsboro, in the hope of inducing Greene to return to North Carolina. Instead he went on to Petersburg. His estimate of the situation in the far South, with which he was familiar, was quite accurate; the strategy which he hoped to push upon Clinton was not so well calculated. In Virginia he encountered an ever memorable destiny.

Precisely eight months after the defeat and rout of Gates near Camden, Continentals again approached that town. There were only 1,250 of them, and they were accompanied by no more than 250 North Carolina militia. But they were well fed, healthy, momentarily well equipped, and they moved confidently forward. It was full spring in Carolina; they had learned that they could rely upon Greene; they knew that the British before them were not invincible; and they could count upon receiving effective aid from the patriots of South Carolina and Georgia.

Watching Cornwallis slip off to Wilmington, Greene chose, as Cornwallis had expected, not to pursue the earl, but to seek to drive the British from the interior of South Carolina and Georgia, and ultimately, if possible, to force them to depart from the ports of the far South. He called upon Sumter to join him, near Camden, asked Pickens to threaten Ninety-Six, and urged Marion to join Henry Lee in an attack upon Fort Watson on the Santee River halfway between Camden and Charleston. His principal immediate objective, of course, was Camden, the strongest post of the British outside Charleston.

Even after the departure of Cornwallis for Virginia the British forces in the deep South far outnumbered Greene's men. Yet Rawdon was in a most uncomfortable position, because his men were scattered about in no fewer than ten garrisons, at Charleston, Savannah, and Georgetown on the coast; at Camden, Ninety-Six, Augusta, and Fort Granby on the Congaree River, far in the interior; and at Orangeburg, Fort Watson, and Fort Motte, the last near the junction of the Congaree and Wateree rivers, connecting links between Charleston and the more distant British posts. On

[9] *Ibid.*, 428–29.

paper Rawdon had more than 8,000 men, many of them Tories. He could not immediately bring the bulk of them together, nor could he hope to hold all his stations against both Greene and the patriot partisans in defensive and piecemeal operations. If he could deal effectively with Greene in pitched battle, of course, most of his various positions would be relatively safe as against the partisans.

Lord Rawdon was early informed of Greene's approach, secured reinforcements from Ninety-Six, and rapidly prepared for combat. He was still in his twenties, though a veteran of many engagements. He had the energy and daring of Cornwallis, and he promptly displayed both qualities. Informed that Greene, posted on Hobkirk's Hill, just north of Camden, had sent his cannon and his militia to his rear, Rawdon chose to attempt a surprise attack rather than to await the Americans in his entrenchments. By arming his musicians, drummers, and every man who could carry a gun, he collected about 900 men, most of them loyalists. In the morning of April 25 he marched quietly out of Camden. Greene was unaware of the British movement until his pickets were driven in, but was well prepared for battle, had with him his militia and his three cannon, and occupied advantageous ground on the hill. Indeed he felt himself to be so strong that he preferred to abandon his positions and to attack Rawdon rather than to await the British onslaught. Observing that Rawdon's line was narrow, he sent forward his Continental infantry to assail the British in front and on both flanks and ordered William Washington with his cavalry to ride around them and strike them from the rear. He entertained high hope of destroying Rawdon's force. He misjudged his opponent, and fortune was not with him. Rawdon saw his danger, extended his line so as to protect his flanks, and poured bullets and grapeshot from his two cannon upon the patriots. The Continentals came on, but never reached the British line. A company of the First Maryland regiment, containing troops as reliable as any in the American armies, lost its captain, and began to fall back. An adjacent company was also struck by panic, also began to retreat. Colonel John Gunby, the regimental commander, made a mistake, choosing to try to withdraw and re-form his men rather than to rally them and push on. As he moved back, the panic spread along the patriot line. Rawdon saw his opportunity, sent his men forward, drove it from the field. Only the Fifth Virginia Regiment, standing firm and covering the flight, prevented a complete rout. Washington, having delayed in his encircling movement to pick up some prisoners among British camp followers who had come out to see the battle, arrived on the field too late to be of service. The losses in men were about equal, more than 250 in each army.

Rawdon was unable immediately to pursue Greene because he lacked sufficient cavalry. While the American commander was "almost frantic with vexation at the disappointment," Rawdon was planning to retire south of the Santee River.[10] His communications and his supply line were collapsing behind him. Reinforced, he offered battle to Greene, but Greene prudently fell back. On May 10 Rawdon evacuated Camden, at the same time sending out orders for abandoning Ninety-Six and Fort Granby. He did not stop until he reached Monck's Corner.

Greene could not win victories in pitched battles, but he did not need to win them. Two days before Hobkirk's Hill, Francis Marion and Henry Lee, using a high wooden tower, "a Maham Tower," with riflemen on top to threaten its defenders from above, forced the surrender of Fort Watson and its garrison of 120 men. On May 11 Sumter, who had failed to join Greene before Camden, captured Orangeburg and 85 men. The following day Fort Motte and more than 150 troops fell to Marion and Lee, just as Rawdon approached on his way to Monck's Corner. On May 15 Lee easily secured possession of Fort Granby by offering its commander and strong garrison terms permitting them to carry off plunder they had acquired and to go to Charleston as prisoners of war. Lee immediately hurried off to Augusta, where he joined Pickens, Elijah Clarke, and other partisans of the Carolinas and Georgia in besieging two British forts there. A smaller one fell quickly. The larger was bitterly defended by Colonel Thomas Browne, able and desperate. He was not overawed by a Maham tower and made courageous sallies. At last, however, threatened by a general assault, he surrendered, with 300 men, on June 6. Two weeks later the British garrison fled from Georgetown by

[10] Willcox (ed.), *American Rebellion*, 513–15.

sea to elude attack by Marion. Less than two months after Hobkirk's Hill the British held in South Carolina and Georgia only Charleston and Savannah, their environs, and Ninety-Six, their principal interior post, except for Camden.

Greene himself, afterward joined by Lee and Pickens, undertook the capture of Ninety-Six, garrisoned by 550 loyalists under Lieutenant Colonel John Harris Cruger of New York. Cruger had failed to receive orders from Rawdon instructing him to retire toward Charleston. He resisted ably and obstinately within strong fortifications. His men, Northern and Southern Tories, had indulged in devastation, looting, and rape, and they hated and feared the patriots. They fought with extraordinary zeal; and neither Maham tower nor fiery arrows on the roofs of their buildings nor formal assault nor capture of their water supply compelled them to abandon the defense. They fought on, thirsty and ferocious, and their bravery was rewarded. Meanwhile, British reinforcements from Ireland arrived at Charleston, and Rawdon came forward to their relief at the head of 2,000 troops. Rawdon eluded Sumter, sent to delay him, and moved rapidly upcountry. Greene was not strong enough to meet him in the field, gave up the siege in disappointment on June 20, and retreated northward.[11] Rawdon followed briefly, but there was little hope of coming up with him, and summer heat was taking its toll of his own men, tired from their swift marches. Rawdon ordered the evacuation of Ninety-Six and withdrew to Orangeburg. Greene and several partisan corps followed, could not prevent his successful retreat. Again Greene had been unable to win victory; again he had its fruits.

The British were not yet prepared to give up all their conquests outside Charleston. Rawdon sailed for Europe because of ill health, but his successor, Lieutenant Colonel Alexander Stuart, sought to hold Orangeburg and set up camp on the south side of the Congaree River. Greene tried to compel him to withdraw by sending light troops who raided to the outskirts of the city. Stuart refused to take alarm. Meanwhile, Greene himself rested in the High Hills of Santee north of that river, avoiding as much as pos-

[11] During the siege Greene was meditating a joint Spanish-American attack on Savannah. Greene to Bernardo de Galvez, June 12, 1781, General Nathanael Greene Papers (Duke University Library).

sible the heat of summer, gathering supplies, calling in reinforcements. On August 22, assured that he would have strength
enough to face Stuart, he moved against him. Forced to march up
to Camden in order to cross the flooded Santee and Wateree, he
came down upon Stuart from the northwest. Meanwhile, the new
British commander had fallen back to Eutaw Springs in order to
protect and receive supplies en route to him from Charleston.
Greene followed. By September 7 he was within seven miles of
Stuart, with 2,400 men, of whom perhaps 1,000 could be described
as militia. With him were Marion, Pickens, Henry Lee, William
Washington, Jethro Sumner, and many another veteran and
trusted officer. He was stronger than he had ever been before.
Stuart, with 2,000 troops, largely British regulars, was so harassed
by Greene's scouting parties that he did not know his opponent
was near at hand until the morning of September 8. The news
reached him in a most unpleasant manner; 100 men he had sent
out to gather sweet potatoes had been captured, and a covering
party had been routed by the patriots, coming up in great force.
He promptly put the remainder of his force in line, with his left
flank protected by Eutaw Creek. He was unable to anchor his
right flank, but covered it as best he could by placing the few
horsemen he possessed in its rear. The ground which he occupied
was wooded. Cornwallis or Rawdon might have advanced to attack the patriots; Stuart, perhaps prudently, awaited their onslaught.

Greene came up and deployed in a formation similar to that
which he had used at Guilford Court House, a first line of militia
supported on its wings by light troops including cavalry, and a
second of Continentals, with Washington's cavalry and Delaware
Continentals in reserve. At midmorning he sent forward his first
line. It performed well for some time, inflicted serious losses upon
the British, was driven back by a charge of the redcoats. Greene
sent up a detachment of North Carolina Continentals under
Sumner to fill the gap. They also fought well, and were forced
back. The British pushed on to finish the job, were struck by the
bulk of the Continentals, and were driven back and away from the
field. Most of Stuart's center and left began to flee in disorder.
And then, for it seems it was foreordained that Greene should not

win a battle, many of the Continentals stopped to pillage the British camp. Some of the redcoats rallied in a brick house under Major Henry Sheridan; Stuart checked the flight of the others. Meanwhile, Major John Marjoribanks, in command on the British left, though forced back, withstood infantry and cavalry assaults, and opened a counterattack. The disorganized Americans gave way, and Greene was compelled to abandon the struggle, which had gone on for three hours. Both sides had suffered extremely heavy losses, and Stuart could not pursue his advantage. He had 436 killed and wounded, and more than 400 of his men were prisoners. Greene's injured and slain reached nearly 500. He withdrew from the field. But Stuart did not follow; he moved away toward Charleston. Retracing his steps, Greene sought to intercept him, but vainly.

Immediately after Eutaw Springs the British held below the boundary of Virginia only Wilmington, Charleston, and Savannah. Greene was unable to proceed against any of the three places. His militia went home, and his Continental veterans, long suffering and long unpaid, began to murmur. Camped once more on the High Hills of the Santee, Greene was faced with the threat of mutiny. He put an end to it by executing one of his malcontents, but he was unable to do more than engage in desultory operations until after the British surrender at Yorktown. Then General Arthur St. Clair, with Virginia, Maryland, and Pennsylvania Continentals, marched southward to his assistance. The British garrison at Wilmington fled to Charleston as St. Clair approached. Greene was still far too weak to attempt the capture of Charleston, but he drew close to the city and cut off its land communications. Meanwhile, however, "Mad" Anthony Wayne, who had accompanied St. Clair, moved against Savannah. He was unable to do more than blockade the town. It was unnecessary for him to do more. General Guy Carleton, who succeeded Clinton at New York in the spring of 1782, had been ordered to discontinue hostilities, and the British chose to evacuate Savannah rather than try to defend it. On July 11, 1782, its garrison moved off to Charleston.

Nor was there any point thereafter in trying to take Charleston, which Greene was far too weak in any case to attempt. In April he had again been forced to deal sternly with mutiny. His army was afflicted by malaria, war-weariness, and poverty in money, equipment, clothing, food, and medicines. Behind it, nevertheless, civil government was in resurrection in South Carolina and Georgia. Greene managed to keep together a more or less respectable force while the British prepared to abandon Charleston. At last, on December 14, a British fleet carried away from the city the British army, about 4,000 loyalists who preferred exile, at least at the moment, to patriot vengeance, and 5,000 Negro slaves, too valuable to be left behind. In the morning the British embarked from Gadsden's Wharf; in the afternoon John Matthews, newly elected governor of South Carolina, with Greene at his side, proclaimed at the Town Hall the restoration of civil government throughout South Carolina.

The services of Nathanael Greene were deeply appreciated in the South, and the legislatures of the Carolinas and Georgia proved their gratitude by giving him very handsome presents. There were some, however, who believed that he received too much acclaim, that his Continentals, especially those of Maryland and Delaware, were too generously praised, that the contributions and sacrifices of the partisans and the militia were valued too slightly. A hot and continuing debate sprang up over the question

> *Who clipped the lion's wings*
> *And flea'd his rump and pared his claws?*

It is clear that the patriots of the lower South, although they might have been able to continue guerrilla fighting indefinitely, could hardly have dealt effectively with the British and their Tory allies without the assistance of the regulars from the upper South and Delaware. On the other hand, Greene could hardly have kept the field without the aid of Marion, Sumter, Pickens, Clarke, Huger, and the partisans. Those militiamen who so often fled without fighting made their contribution. There was glory enough for all. As for Greene, it may be doubted that the commander who was unable to win a pitched battle was a general of the very first order. It is hardly to be believed that any other American officer could have achieved more than he.

CHAPTER XV

THE SOUTHWESTERN FRONT

AT THE beginning of the War of Independence the West of that time, the region between the Great Lakes and the Gulf of Mexico, between the Mississippi and the established settlements of the Thirteen Colonies, was still largely no white man's land; and at the end of that struggle the red men remained its most numerous occupants. However, as a result of the war, the British hegemony in the region, save for the Floridas, which became Spanish properties, was replaced by American domination. Except for the peninsula of Florida and a strip of territory stretching westward from it to the Mississippi, the United States was acknowledged to be the owner of the vast area extending from the Atlantic to the Mississippi and the Great Lakes in the treaties of peace of 1783. Moreover, by that time American settlers were firmly planted on the south bank of the Ohio as far west as the great river, and East Tennessee was effectively occupied. Thereafter it was most unlikely that the Americans could long be prevented by European powers or Indian resistance from putting themselves down in any of the other parts of the empire conceded by the Europeans to be theirs in 1783. Indeed, it was safe to predict that Spanish rule in the Floridas and western Louisiana could not stand indefinitely against the burgeoning United States, hence that these too must fall under American sway unless France or Britain should intervene; and it is evident, now at least, that neither of those powers, burdened with their own rivalry and many troubles in and outside of Europe, could easily have withstood American pressure.

In 1775, nevertheless, the immediate future looked dark for the American frontier settlers, especially those in the thin buckskin line moving below the Ohio toward the Mississippi. They had feared attack since the very opening of hostilities in Massachusetts, and with good reason. Not that they expected to be promptly assailed by British warships or even by British regulars in large numbers, but that they could hardly escape Indian onslaught. From Lake Champlain to Lake Maurepas the red men were restless, resenting the intrusions of white settlers upon their hunting grounds and those of their neighbors. They knew their homes and their freedom were at stake, and they were likely to strike, without British urging, even despite efforts of the British to persuade them to remain quiet. And it could not be hoped that the British would try heartily to keep them neutral. Rather, the worst was to be anticipated, that British civil officials and army officers, and loyalists, too, would supply the red men with arms and liquor and instigate them to take the warpath. Hence the Tories in the interior of the Southern colony-states and the British redcoats in St. Augustine, Pensacola, Mobile, and Detroit were dangerous, not in their own strength, but in the mischief they could create.

Conscious of the peril at their rear, the patriots sought to appease the Indians, and the Continental Congress and other patriot bodies in areas most seriously threatened appointed agents to soothe them with soft words and gifts. They at first sought chiefly the neutrality of the red men, although semidomesticated Stockbridge Indians served in the investing army about Boston in 1775, and Massachusetts early enlisted others to serve as scouts in an expedition against Canada. When it became apparent that unfriendly Indians were preparing to take up arms, the patriots strove to enlist the aid of others; and some warriors of smaller tribes, such as the Catawbas and Oneida, eventually fought for the Americans. The British hesitated briefly, for there were among them men like General Guy Carleton and Indian Superintendent John Stuart, who were familiar with the horrors of Indian fighting and who knew that the use of the warriors of the woods was ultimately of dubious military value. In the summer of 1775, however, Lord Dunmore, seeking help wherever he could find it, plotted with Dr. John Connolly, a loyalist, an attack upon Virginia in the spring of 1776 by a force of Ohio Valley Indians, supported by Tories from the vicinity of Pittsburgh and a detachment of redcoats from the British garrison at Detroit. Dunmore hoped that this force would make junction with his own at that time at Alexandria. Connolly secured the consent to this scheme of General Gage at Boston, but was captured en route to Detroit by Maryland patriots near Hagerstown. The Dunmore-Connolly enterprise then collapsed. That same summer, however, the British cabinet also called for employment of Indians; thereafter it was certain that tomahawk and scalping knife would be joined to British musket and bayonet, but the time and manner remained unsettled.

Had the power of decision rested entirely in John Stuart, Indian warfare must have been long delayed. He, however, had no authority whatever north of the Ohio, and could neither dictate policy to the cabinet and British generals nor impose his will upon the Indians south of the river. No white man had greater personal knowledge of Indian bestialities than he; and he shrank from visiting them upon a people among whom he had lived for more than a quarter century. Moreover, he knew that the many loyalists in the Southern backsettlements must suffer with their patriot neighbors in the event of Indian raids, for the red men could not easily distinguish between the one group and the other. Accordingly, at the beginning of the war he strove to preserve his own influence and that of the crown among the Southern Indians, but to prevent them from taking the field. Driven by the patriots to St. Augustine, he continued to urge the red men to remain quiet. After his flight he had added reason to be cautious, for the South Carolina patriots seized and held his wife as a hostage until 1777. However, Gage urged him to turn loose the Indians, and Lord Dartmouth; and he had to comply or resign his post. He obeyed, but tried to lessen atrocities by insisting that the red men should be employed only in conjunction with white troops and under white leadership in operations directed toward specific military objectives. His superiors, especially Lord George Germain, for some time agreed with him; and the ferocity of warfare in the Southern interior was as a result moderated for a time, but only in minor degree. He was unable to hold back the Cherokee, who took up the hatchet in the summer of 1776 despite his urging to the contrary. Fear of losing their lands and their independence, coupled with the desire of their young men to secure scalps and recognition of their manhood, and the machinations of Tories and trans-Ohio tribesmen impelled them to that decision.[1]

The Cherokee were the first Indian nation to strike as such. The struggle which they began was a major one, enduring until the treaty of peace. The British supported them from St. Augustine, Pensacola, and Mobile; and when Creeks, Choctaw, and Chickasaw ventured into the fray, they likewise found encouragement, arms, and supplies at the British bases on the shores of the Gulf of Mexico. Ultimately, as a result there developed a major threat to the Southern patriots from the southwest. Meanwhile, another sprang up from the northwest, the British post at Detroit doing for Shawnee, Mingos, and Wyandots what those at Pensacola and Mobile did for the Southern tribesmen. The newly formed and scanty white settlements in East Tennessee and Kentucky were thus doubly exposed to attack.

The Cherokee poured down upon the frontiers of the Carolinas and Georgia at the beginning of July, and soon afterward struck at the Watauga pioneers. Their onslaught was not unexpected, although some of them protested until the last moment that they intended to be neutral. Not surprised, the patriots were not ready to meet them, for they were unable to protect every possible point of assault. Isolated families and small groups of whites were butchered by the enraged Indians, among whom moved Tories who proclaimed themselves savages by redskin disguise and bloody deeds. Slaughtering men, women, and children, whites and Negroes, patriots and Tories, the Cherokee spread blood from the Watauga to the south bank of the Savannah; and reports of their onslaughts poured down to Tidewater. Ninety-Six, well within the South Carolina settlements, was described as having become a frontier post.[2] Sending out frantic calls for aid, the buckskinned

[1] Philip M. Hamer, "John Stuart's Indian Policy during the Early Months of the American Revolution," in *Mississippi Valley Historical Review*, XVII (1930–1931), 351–66.

[2] Drayton, *Memoirs of the American Revolution*, II, 368.

folk of the interior rallied desperately, gathered in small wooden forts, and defended themselves as best they might until help should come.

Of special importance was an attempt by the Cherokee to overrun and destroy the new settlements in East Tennessee. These outposts of white advance were inevitably a major target, and 700 warriors swept forward against them after the middle of July. The borderers had been warned, however, and were as prepared for them as might be. On July 20 near Eaton's Station in a hot fight at close quarters 170 backwoodsmen routed double their number of Cherokee and wounded their leader, the chief Dragging Canoe. The following day a dawn attack upon the Watauga fort near the Sycamore Shoals was repulsed. Thereafter, although the Indians continued for some time to invest the fort and to capture and slay isolated whites, the redskinned tide began to recede in that quarter. The riflemen of East Tennessee, led by James Robertson, John Sevier, and other noted fighters, stood firm, protecting not only themselves but the communication of the Kentuckians with the seacoast by way of the Wilderness Road.

In 1760, sixteen years earlier, when their frontiers were assailed by the Cherokee, the Southern colonies had begged for and had obtained the help of British regulars; now the Southern patriots must save themselves. They responded to the emergency with extraordinary zeal. Georgia militia under Major Samuel Jack drove back the Cherokee within their state, and Virginia and the Carolinas undertook offensives to crush the Indians in their own country. Toward that end the Carolinas sent out troops to invade and destroy Lower, Middle, and Valley towns of the Cherokee, while the Virginians pushed forward through their Overhill settlements.

Despite many difficulties and hazards this plan was executed with remarkable success. Colonel Andrew Williamson, the same officer who rendered excellent service against the Tories in 1775 and who afterward went over to the British, drove into the Lower Cherokee villages in August, collecting men as he went until he had gathered a force of 1,800, with some Catawba scouts. Brushing aside opposition, he razed town after town, destroying huts and cornfields. The Lower Cherokee, routed and deprived of homes

GENERAL HORATIO GATES by Charles Willson Peale.

and sustenance, fled southward for refuge. The Middle and Valley townsmen encountered no better fortune. Their towns were over-run in September by Williamson and General Griffith Rutherford, who led 2,500 North Carolinians into their rugged fastnesses; the torch was put to their homes and crops. They made but one brief stand in large force against Williamson, and another against Rutherford, and then fled westward. They found little comfort among the Overhills, for 2,000 Virginians and North Carolinians under Colonel William Christian entered the Overhill country from the Holston and ravaged it. The mother town, or "capital" of the Overhill Cherokee, Choté, was not entered, but the Over-hills also suffered severely. There was little hope of securing effec-tive help from the British, and they and their fellows were forced to beg for peace. In treaties signed with South Carolina and Georgia at Dewitt's Corner, South Carolina, on May 20, 1777, and with Virginia and North Carolina at the Long Island in the Holston River on July 20 of the same year, the Cherokee acknowl-edged their weakness and their humiliation, ceding all their lands east of the Blue Ridge and conceding their claims to territory north of the Nolichucky River.

But not all the Cherokee accepted the treaties. Dragging Canoe and other chiefs and warriors haughtily withdrew to Chickamauga, and continued the war. Gradually they were joined by more and more warriors, some of them Creeks, who formed new towns and nearly a new nation. Occasional supplies sent by Stuart reached them from Pensacola. So dangerous were they by 1779 that Vir-ginia and North Carolina sent 900 men under Evan Shelby to crush them. Floating down the Clinch, Powell, and Tennessee rivers, Shelby surprised the Chickamaugas, routed them, and de-stroyed their villages. Even then Dragging Canoe persevered, re-settling his people about Lookout Mountain. Encouraged by the British and later the Spanish, he remained for another decade the inveterate and indomitable enemy of the Americans.

Nevertheless, the handwriting was on the wall for the young chief and his people, both at Lookout Mountain and in the re-maining older Cherokee towns. Early in 1779 James Robertson explored the valley of the Cumberland. Less than a year later Robertson and Colonel John Donelson, pushed on by Richard

Henderson, undertook to found a colony within it. Robertson and a party of pioneers marched overland through Kentucky and founded Nashborough, later Nashville, at the end of 1779; and another group led by Donelson, containing many women and children, floated down the Tennessee, pushed its way through the Chickamaugas despite many casualties, and moved up the Cumberland from the Ohio to reach the new settlement in 1780. Desperate, Dragging Canoe and many Overhills who had laid down their arms in 1777 strove to take advantage of the absence of the frontier riflemen during the King's Mountain campaign and once more began to gather for a great effort. They encountered disaster swiftly. John Sevier and 250 riflemen routed a Cherokee party in the valley of the French Broad on December 8, 1780; and Colonel Arthur Campbell of Virginia, coming up with 400 men, drove into the Overhill towns at the head of 650 backwoodsmen. There was no resistance; even Choté fell without a fight; and the Overhill chiefs once more begged for peace. But Dragging Canoe continued the struggle with desultory fighting, and some of the Cherokee east of the Appalachians resumed hostilities in 1781, when the British star was ascendant in the Carolinas. Andrew Pickens drove them back into the mountains in 1781 and again in the following year; John Sevier led another punitive expedition into the Chickamauga country in 1782, where he destroyed several villages, but failed to reach those of Dragging Canoe. In the fall of that year, except for that intrepid chief and his followers, the Overhill Cherokee signed another treaty which definitely ended the war for them. Their great chief Ouconnostotah, he who "had never run from an enemy, but . . . had walked fast up a branch once," now old and almost blind, witnessed this final act.[3] In 1783 their brethren east of the Appalachian divide also signed a treaty, at Augusta, in which they ceded all claims south of the Savannah River and east of the Chattahoochee.

It was a happy circumstance for the Southern states, suffering as they did from Cherokee onslaughts, that the belligerent Creeks never threw their full weight into the war on the Southern fron-

[3] John P. Brown, *Old Frontiers; The Story of the Cherokee Indians from Earliest Times to . . . 1838* (Kingsport, 1938), 162–204, offers a good account of the struggle with the Cherokee after 1777.

tier. The Creeks, somewhat less alarmed for their lands than the Cherokee, but unhappy nevertheless, harbored little love for the backwoodsmen of South Carolina and Georgia. Early in the war the Seminole branch of the nation did begin hostilities as allies of the British. Encouraged and supported by the British in St. Augustine, they staged several raids into southern Georgia with Tory and British contingents. But the Lower Creeks remained neutral, and the warriors of the Upper towns were long largely inactive, because of the labors of George Galphin. Galphin, giving his support to the patriot cause and appointed Indian commissioner by the Continental Congress, wielded all his great influence among the Creeks to dissuade them from taking the warpath. He and other patriot leaders gave them liberal presents and managed to supply them with trade goods. John Stuart was unable to match Galphin's gifts, and British traders could not easily bring them goods from Pensacola. Moreover, Stuart had fewer friends among the Creeks than with the Cherokee; and his agent among them, David Taitt, was unable to match Galphin's wiles. The Lower Creeks uneasily observed the distresses of their Cherokee neighbors and gave some of them asylum, but would not themselves stir. Discouraged by their example, the Upper townsmen, at a greater distance from the Southern frontier, were also generally quiet for several years.

Ultimately, the Upper Creeks, pushed on by Thomas Browne, who succeeded Stuart in 1779 as superintendent in the eastern part of Stuart's district, took up the hatchet. By that time, however, Spain had entered the war and the British bases in West Florida were menaced by Bernardo de Galvez, governor of Louisiana. Accordingly, the British strove to bring Creek warriors, and also Choctaw and Chickasaw, to their assistance on the shores of the Gulf of Mexico rather than to send them against the patriots.[4]

Had the British been firmly established in the Floridas, the Cherokee and Creeks must have been more potent enemies of the patriots than they were. But the forces they were able to main-

[4] The role of the Creeks in the War of Independence has not been thoroughly studied. Useful information concerning it may be found in Helen Louise Shaw, *British Administration of the Southern Indians, 1756–1783* (Lancaster, 1931), Chaps. III–IV.

tain at St. Augustine, on the shores of the Gulf of Mexico, and the Lower Mississippi were few, heterogeneous, and weakened by heat, disease, and boredom. In those regions where

Sometime too hot the eye of heaven shines

troops lost their vigor and commanders their energy. Moreover, supplies needed to keep the friendship of the Indians and to arm them were often unavailable. Further, the British garrison forces faced danger after 1775 not only from the patriots but by the Spanish. Ultimately, indeed, they were driven from West Florida by the dons, who displayed unusual aggressiveness under the leadership of the young Galvez.

Had it been possible, the patriots would early have seized West Florida. However, that province was remote; and they had no more success in a feeble attempt to reduce it than they had in its sister colony to the eastward. Oliver Pollock, Ulsterman, patriot, and merchant of New Orleans, who gave powerful assistance to the American cause west of the Appalachians, long urged an attack upon West Florida by way of the Ohio and Mississippi. He thought 3,000 men sufficient to take the colony.[5] Success in such a venture would have dealt a blow to Britain, would have brought the Southern Indians to their knees. In consequence Spanish reconquest might have been forestalled, an American stronghold secured on the lower Mississippi, and American power in trans-Appalachia generally enormously strengthened. The patriots in the Continental Congress seriously meditated an attack in 1776 and 1777, George Morgan pushing it energetically. However, the Congress, impressed by the need for Spanish help, proposed to turn the colony over to Spain in return for Spanish entrance into the war and free use of the Mississippi and the harbor of Pensacola. This scheme collapsed, since the patriots lacked men and means to execute it.[6] The only patriot effort in the region was the expedition of Captain James Willing, who came down the Mississippi to trade and raid in 1778 with 27 men in *The Rattletrap*, an armed boat. Landing at Natchez and pushing on southward, Willing overran and plundered British plantations on the

[5] James A. James, *Oliver Pollock* (New York, 1937), 127–28.
[6] *Ibid.*, 105–16.

east bank of the river. With help from Pollock and from Galvez, he also attacked British shipping. Before British superior force asserted itself, he caused panic and terror in Mobile and beyond.[7] The Willing raid was only an episode. It was otherwise with the activities of Galvez, who undertook to regain West Florida for Spain; he acted with the blessing of the patriots, since they continued to desire Spanish aid and saw little opportunity of securing the coveted colony for themselves. Congress approved of his efforts, even though Pollock warned that the Spanish hoped to gain control not merely of West Florida but of the entire Mississippi Valley.[8]

In Louisiana the Spanish were by no means powerful, but Galvez hoped to secure support from the French inhabitants and also from Cuba. In August, 1779, he boldly led a motley force of Spanish regulars, militia, Americans, and Indians against the English outposts on the lower Mississippi, at Manchac, Baton Rouge, and Natchez. All fell almost without a struggle, though the Spanish advance was not unexpected, though the British were strong enough to meditate an attack upon New Orleans. Flushed with success, Galvez intrepidly moved against Mobile early in 1780 by sea. Storms severely injured his shipping and deprived him of supplies, but he persevered. Joined by troops and ships from Havana, he marshaled 1,400 men and attacked Fort Charlotte at Mobile in the first days of March. It was garrisoned by 300 men under Elias Durnford, and 1,100 more, sent forward by General John Campbell, were coming from Pensacola to their assistance. The relieving force was unable to reach the fort, however, and Durnford surrendered after two days of fighting. Galvez proposed to move on immediately against Pensacola, the center of British power in West Florida, but lacked strength for the attempt and was forced to be content for the moment with his conquest of Mobile. He was determined, nevertheless, to have Pensacola. In October he sailed from Havana with a fleet and a large army, but a storm wrecked the enterprise. With stubborn persistence he gathered another fleet and army and appeared off Pensacola

[7] John W. Caughey, "Willing's Expedition down the Mississippi, 1778," in *Louisiana Historical Quarterly* (New Orleans), XV (1932), 5–36.

[8] James, *Oliver Pollock*, 191.

in March, 1781. General Campbell hoped to hold off Galvez. He had about 1,600 men in Fort George, the strong place of the town, and there were many hundreds of Southern Indians, especially Creeks and Choctaw, at hand. But Galvez had collected an overwhelming force, estimated at more than 7,000 men, together with a well-armed fleet. Campbell resisted, but his Indians failed to fight. He endured the pounding of Spanish artillery for a month and then surrendered, on May 9.[9]

West Florida thus fell into Spanish hands, and the British were thereafter able to supply their allies among the Southern Indians only from Savannah and St. Augustine. They could hardly reach the Choctaw and Chickasaw, nor the Cherokee in the valley of the Tennessee. Their prestige had also been greatly damaged, and the Southern Indians accordingly became lukewarm toward them. They continued even after the collapse of their West Florida position to receive some help from the Creeks, who assisted them in the defense of Augusta in 1781 and of Savannah in 1782. Their efforts were vain. Emistisiguo, still the leader of the Upper Creeks, was slain in combat outside Savannah. When the English withdrew from Savannah and St. Augustine after the peace of 1783, the Creeks were forced, save for assistance from the feeble Spanish Floridas, to stand alone against American expansion. They had lost finally, and without a real struggle, the balance-of-power position they had so long enjoyed among the French, Spanish, and English. The future for the Choctaw and Chickasaw was equally dark.

Almost as gloomy was the outlook for the Indian tribes above the Ohio after 1783. They long refrained from seizing the hatchet. When they did so, the Ohio Valley became a bloody battleground. They shook the new settlements in Kentucky, but could neither destroy them nor loosen the American grip upon the regions to the eastward. Ultimately, the backwoodsmen south of the Ohio, aided by Virginia authorities and the Continental Congress, withstood all attacks; and in the end the Shawnee, Delawares, Mingos,

---

[9] Concerning Galvez and the Spanish conquest of West Florida, see John W. Caughey, *Bernardo de Gálvez in Louisiana, 1776–1783* (Berkeley, 1934). Additional information on the campaigns in West Florida from British sources may be found in Shaw, *British Administration of the Southern Indians,* Chaps. III–IV.

and other red men reluctantly gave up the conflict, abandoning forever the southern banks of the river.

The trans-Ohio tribes were tardy in taking the field for various reasons, one being swift action by the patriots to secure their neutrality. Virginia sent agents to visit and make presents to the Shawnee, Delawares, and Mingos in the summer of 1775, and these, with the aid of an agent sent by the Continental Congress and that of Dr. John Connolly, who undertook to help the Americans preserve peace, successfully soothed the red men, restless and unhappy after Lord Dunmore's war. At Pittsburgh, which the Virginians promptly occupied to defend the frontier, these tribes signed a treaty in the autumn in which they promised to remain neutral, the whites pledging in return not to settle north of the Ohio. A quarrel between the Delawares and the Iroquois, which the patriots sedulously permitted to continue, also helped to keep the Indians at home. Even more important in preventing outbreaks on the Ohio was the American invasion of Canada in 1775–1776, which closed the upper St. Lawrence to the British for many months and made it impossible for the British to supply the Indians with guns, ammunition, and rum.

Peace could not, however, be preserved indefinitely in the troubled valley. The Mingos, originally Iroquois, but independent and warlike, were unable to think of the lands south of the Ohio as permanently lost. By 1776 they were raiding across it in small divisions; and they infected their neighbors with a desire for conflict. Some Shawnee assisted the Cherokee in the battle of Long Island that year, and a Shawnee-Cherokee party fleeing from that defeat killed two whites and captured three girls at Boonesborough. The Shawnee did not love the backwoodsmen the more because Daniel Boone and other Kentuckians pursued the party and killed two of the Indians, releasing the girls. Messengers and belts passed about among the Wyandots, Mingos, Iroquois, Shawnee, and Delawares. As usual, the young men lusted for war; the older ones, as customary, urged that it be avoided. American agents and presents temporarily calmed the Indians, even the Mingos, in the fall of 1776. In the following year, however, the storm broke. The young braves could no longer be restrained. In February, 1777, warriors from several of the trans-Ohio tribes ravaged the south bank of the river from Pittsburgh to Louisville, besieging Boonesborough, Wheeling, and other forts, creating terror and confusion. The backwoodsmen struck back as best they could, and slew Indians guilty and innocent of the attacks. The Shawnee chief Cornstalk, who had done everything within his power to prevent war, was murdered in mistaken reprisal in November at Fort Randolph. Thereafter, the Shawnee and their neighbors waged war to their full strength.[10]

That same year Henry Hamilton, lieutenant governor of Detroit, immortalized as "The Hair-Buyer," became a major figure in the conflict. He had hitherto advised the Indians to remain neutral, partly for the sake of humanity, partly because he lacked means to supply the Indians and to make use of them. He received goods from Britain, and he was told to incite the Indians to action. He was also ordered to send white men with the savages to prevent barbarities, a vain precaution, since Tories who accompanied Indians were unable to restrain their allies and were often more brutal than the red men. He obeyed. It is doubtful that Hamilton bought scalps; and it is not certain that he approved of the orders from the British cabinet.[11] Nevertheless, the warfare which he fomented and encouraged was inhumane; and his name must ever be stained, more so than those of John Stuart and Alexander Cameron, whose records, despite extenuating circumstances and their own sufferings at the hands of the patriots, are not beyond reproach. Hamilton not only urged on the Indians already at war with the patriots but sent forward tribesmen from the Great Lakes region who had not suffered at American hands. Detroit became a haven, a base, and a source of inspiration for the Ohio Valley tribes. Hamilton was never able to execute a project he entertained to seize Pittsburgh, nor smash the pioneer strongholds in Kentucky, but the furious assaults of his red allies and Tory troops caused agony from the forks of the Ohio to its Falls. Frontier forts shuddered under the impact of their attacks. The tomahawk, the

[10] Randolph C. Downes, *Council Fires on the Upper Ohio* (Pittsburgh, 1940), 179–207, describes clearly the approach to war on the Ohio.

[11] John D. Barnhart (ed.), *Henry Hamilton and George Rogers Clark in the American Revolution with the Unpublished Journal of Lieut. Gov. Henry Hamilton* (Crawfordsville, Ind., 1951), Chap. II.

torch, and the scalping knife did their bloody and lurid work; and proud Indians brought to Detroit from the lands across the Beautiful River scores of scalps, ghastly and pitiful evidence of slain men, women, and children.

For the Americans there was an almost certain remedy for their ugly predicament in the Ohio Valley, the capture of Detroit. Were that town in patriot hands, the Indians dependent upon it for trade and supplies must yield or starve. The Americans were well aware of the singular importance of that strategic spot, and action against it was urged early in the war and late. A successful expedition against it, expensive though it would have been in men and money, would have been cheap in terms of results and ultimate cost; and George Morgan, experienced Indian agent, began clamoring for a great effort in the first days of open hostilities. But Morgan's employers, Federal Indian commissioners and the Continental Congress, failed to take quick action, and Morgan disappointedly resigned his post. The Congress was not indifferent to his pleas; it could not spare men, money, and supplies in 1777, when Sir William Howe and General John Burgoyne posed grave threats on and near the seaboard. It did send Brigadier General Edward Hand to Pittsburgh to defend that place and to push forward across the Ohio into the Indian country. Hand was unable to move until February, 1778. By that time Congress hoped he could proceed even to Detroit. Hand, less optimistic, made Sandusky, an advanced British post, his objective, and set out with 500 militia. He did not reach it, snow, rain, and flooded streams forcing him to abandon his "Squaw Campaign." Censured for his failure, he resigned in disgust. Lachlan McIntosh, the Georgia general who was unpopular in his own state because he had slain Button Gwinnett in a duel, was sent by Congress to replace him, supplied with 500 Continentals and some money. McIntosh had no better fortune than Hand. He moved out toward Lake Erie, traversing one hundred miles of Indian country. Then militia with him chose to go home, supplies ran short, and the expedition collapsed. In 1779, a third American commander at Pittsburgh, General Daniel Brodhead, was more successful. Believing that Detroit, at least for the time being, was beyond his reach, he marched into and ravaged the country of the Seneca, westernmost, most numerous, and most dangerous of the Iroquois. His exploit, however, by no means assured American success in the Ohio Valley as a whole. Happily for the frontiersmen on the Kanawha and the Kentucky, Virginia came to their aid.

When Lord Dunmore fled from Williamsburg and the royal régime in Virginia vanished, the new patriot leaders there were soon faced by many problems in trans-Appalachia, among them Judge Richard Henderson and his bold effort to establish a proprietary domain south of the Kentucky River. With little hesitation the Virginians undertook to assert authority both south and north of the Ohio and to send help across the mountains.

Judge Henderson, after successfully defying the colonial governments of Virginia and North Carolina and Britain herself, was faced by new and ultimately more formidable enemies, the states of Virginia and North Carolina. In 1775 he organized in Kentucky the colony of Transylvania, consisting of four small posts, Boonesborough, Harrodstown, Boiling Springs, and St. Asaph, together with a few scattered homesteads; and a convention which he arranged undertook to legislate for the settlers. He and his proprietary associates then sought legal recognition from Virginia, and one of the latter, James Hogg, proceeded to Philadelphia to secure the approval of the Congress. But the Virginia authorities, after a brief hesitation, refused to acknowledge the legality of Henderson's proceedings; asserted the full control of Virginia as far west as the Mississippi; established the county of Kentucky, stretching to the mouth of the Tennessee River; and successfully demanded that Hogg's pleas be rejected in the Congress. The enterprising Henderson was quite unable to stand against Virginia, partly because many of the Kentucky settlers had quickly turned against him. In the end he had to accept as compensation for his efforts in Kentucky a grant from Virginia of two hundred thousand acres at the mouth of the Green River. When the state of North Carolina followed the example of her neighbor and denounced his claims in the valleys of the Tennessee and Cumberland, he was again forced to yield; and again he received land for his reward, two hundred thousand acres near Nashville.[12]

[12] Judge Henderson's striking career has been sympathetically narrated and his importance in the settlement of Kentucky and Tennessee established by Archibald

One of the chief opponents in Kentucky of Henderson was George Rogers Clark, land speculator, Indian trader and fighter, and extraordinary leader of men. It was apparently he who discredited Henderson by taking advantage of the fact that the Transylvania Company charged more for land than Virginia; it was certainly he that was a tower of patriot strength in Kentucky and gave the United States its first foothold in the Old Northwest.

Struggling with his fellow pioneers against Indian forays in Kentucky, Clark, like every thoughtful American west of the Appalachians, saw salvation in seizing Detroit. In 1777, knowing that the British base between the lakes could not be easily taken, he conceived a brilliant idea, to seize the Illinois country as a first step toward the march upon Detroit. The Illinois country, the region between the Wabash, Miami, Ohio, Mississippi, and Illinois rivers, was inhabited by only a few hundred whites, chiefly of French origin, who would hardly fight for Britain and who might assist American invaders. Its towns, Kaskaskia, Prairie du Rocher, Cahokia, and Vincennes, were almost undefended, and the neighboring Indians were the chief immediate obstacle to conquest. Even if Detroit remained unattainable, possession of the Illinois country would be valuable, for it would give the Americans control of the Ohio, open a communication with the Spanish at St. Louis, close the Mississippi to the British, dampen the ardor of the Indians, and increase American opportunities to trade.

Spies sent into the Illinois region by Clark early in 1777, Benjamin Linn and Samuel Moore, returned with good news. The British did not even have a garrison at Kaskaskia, which had earlier been their stronghold. In the fall Clark hurried over the mountains to Virginia to seek help. Jefferson, George Mason, and Richard Henry Lee were impressed with the possibilities of the scheme, and they saw in Clark the man who might be able to

Henderson in "Richard Henderson and the Occupation of Kentucky, 1775," in *Mississippi Valley Historical Review*, I (1914–1915), 341–63; "The Creative Forces in Westward Expansion: Henderson and Boone," in *American Historical Review*, XX (1914–1915), 86–107; and *The Conquest of the Old Southwest . . . 1740–1790* (New York, 1920). The legality of Judge Henderson's operations remains, however, dubious. One may begin to study the knotty problems of law involved by consulting Alden, *John Stuart and the Southern Colonial Frontier*, 293, and references there cited.

take both the Illinois country and Detroit. Further, they found in it and him a chance to assert Virginia's claim to the Old Northwest. They, with the support of Patrick Henry, who was then governor, persuaded the Virginia Assembly to support the man and his project without telling the members what he intended to do. He was given £1,200 and was empowered to secure boats, to enlist seven companies of men, and to call for additional funds. Publicly, he was commissioned to defend Kentucky; secretly, he was to proceed to Kaskaskia, and thence, if possible, to Detroit.

Floating down the Ohio and gathering boats and men as he went, Clark established a base near its falls in the spring of 1778. The men and means he was able to assemble were scanty, but he did not lose heart. Leaving behind a small garrison to defend a blockhouse and supplies on an island near the falls, he set out down the river on June 26 for Kaskaskia, with only 179 men, in a fleet of flatboats. Ten miles below the mouth of the Tennessee, because they could not proceed further by water without discovery, Clark and his men hid their boats and set out overland toward their first objective, about a hundred miles distant. They pushed on through forests and across prairies, waded streams, became lost, found their way again, arrived outside the town hungry and tired. Luck was with the bold. The Chevalier de Rocheblave, in command for the British of the local militia, had been informed of their approach and had turned out his men to meet them, had then decided Clark's force was not near at hand, and had sent the militia home. Clark's appearance was therefore a surprise, and he occupied the village without the firing of a shot. The French inhabitants of Kaskaskia, except for Rocheblave, who was sent to Virginia as a prisoner of war, actually welcomed Clark; and they secured for him the surrender, also bloodless, of Vincennes. A delegation of Frenchmen headed by Father Pierre Gibault went to Vincennes and persuaded its villagers—no British troops were there—to permit the Americans to occupy both the village and Fort Sackville, its strong place. In August Clark was able to place a garrison in the fort under Captain Leonard Helm.

In control of the Illinois villages, Clark was nevertheless in a desperate situation. His scanty force, without supplies, was exposed to hostile Indians and British attack from Detroit. He called upon Oliver Pollock at New Orleans for aid, and Pollock generously and effectively responded. Meanwhile, Clark conferred with thousands of Ottawa, Chippewa, Miami, and Fox warriors at Cahokia, adroitly securing at least temporary neutrality from them. He was as well prepared as could be when the British moved, as they did. Detroit was menaced by Clark's presence above the Ohio, and it seemed prudent to them to march against and destroy him before he obtained reinforcements. Hamilton, whatever his defects, was neither slothful nor lacking in courage. He left Detroit on October 7 with 175 troops, mostly Frenchmen, and 60 Indians. Gathering red allies as he went until there were 500 with him, he approached Vincennes in December. Capturing small parties sent out by Captain Helm to scout and to warn Clark, he arrived there on December 17. Helm then had only one American soldier with him, and the French would not help him. He was forced to surrender.

The news of Hamilton's appearance at Vincennes alarmed the French at Kaskaskia, and Clark, too. Many of his riflemen had returned to Kentucky upon the expiration of their enlistments, and he had no more than 100 with him. While Hamilton prudently rested in Vincennes before resuming his march, Clark meditated upon his troubles and resolved that prudence for him meant offensive action. Early in February he sent off an armed row galley to the Wabash to prevent Hamilton from escaping southward, and set out with 127 men, nearly half of them Frenchmen, to attack Vincennes, about 180 miles away by trail. That audacious man, who was even thinking of moving on from Vincennes against Detroit, must have seemed merely foolhardy to many of his American and French followers. It was extremely doubtful that he could reach Vincennes, much less force the surrender of Fort Sackville. But fortune was again with the dauntless. Clark and his men trudged through sucking mud, waded creeks and rivers, endured cold, wet, and hunger, and camped outside Vincennes on February 23. Completely surprising Hamilton, he moved into the town in two columns so as to impress the British officer, his red allies, and the French inhabitants with his numbers. Some of the pro-American French in Vincennes gave him powder and shot, which he desperately needed; many of Hamilton's Indians, impressed by Clark's obvious determination, vanished into the woods. Clark had still another piece of luck. Hamilton had fewer than 100 men in Fort Sackville, for he had sent 40 up the Wabash to hurry forward supplies en route from Detroit. In the morning of February 24 Clark surrounded and opened fire on the fort, his men alternately chewing their first substantial food in many days and firing their rifles. The British responded from their stout wooden walls with cannon and small arms, but were quickly silenced by the riflemen, who killed or wounded all those who came to the portholes. Before sundown Hamilton and 79 men still alive within the fort put down their arms, and the 40 men he had sent up the river also surrendered shortly afterward. One of Clark's men was wounded.

The Illinois country thus came under American domination, and remained so until the close of the war. Clark, however, regarded his work as incomplete so long as the British held Detroit. He yearned to march against that place, but even he considered such a venture in 1778 foolhardy. It remained so. Repeatedly he tried to collect the necessary men and means, in 1779, 1780, and 1781, but was never successful, although Jefferson as governor of Virginia was eager to add the Old Northwest to the "Empire of Liberty" and attempted to furnish Clark with the means to do it. Indeed, the Americans west of the mountains were subjected to heavy attacks from the north, and were ultimately assailed even by the Choctaw and Chickasaw. Clark, who continued to direct the protection of Kentucky for Virginia through the remaining years of the war, was reduced to the defensive and local offensives.

The year 1779 brought Brodhead's successful invasion of the Seneca country, but also a counterbalancing success of the British, the wiping out of an American convoy on the Ohio by Simon Girty and Indian marauders. Moreover, frontier riflemen who endeavored to drive their way into the Shawnee towns were forced back.

In 1780 the British and Indians resumed the offensive on a large scale. In May they tried to storm Spanish St. Louis, but were driven off. A little later Chickasaw and Choctaw came up from the south and besieged Fort Jefferson, which Clark had built at the mouth of the Ohio. After a six-day struggle they, too, were beaten away. In a third and larger effort Colonel Henry Bird with 150 whites and 1,000 Indians pushed into the valley of the Licking River, where he captured two American posts, Ruddle's and Martin's, and more than 100 prisoners, many of whom were brutally slain before Bird returned to Detroit. This ghastly raid brought prompt reprisal. Clark led 1,000 riflemen across the Ohio to punish the Shawnee and Delawares, the latter having entered the war as allies of Britain. He was unable to reach the Delaware villages, but ravaged the Shawnee country. In August he put Chillicothe, their "mother town," to the torch, and moved forward against Piqua, on the Big Miami River, also one of their principal places. At Piqua he was confronted by the Shawnee and other tribesmen, supported by Simon Girty and a Tory contingent. He routed them after bitter fighting and burnt Piqua. The spirit of the Shawnee was not, however, broken; and they continued to fight rather than sue for peace.

The year of Yorktown brought no American triumph in the Ohio Valley. Again trying desperately to gather forces to assail Detroit, Clark suffered keen disappointment. A detachment of more than 100 Pennsylvania militia pushing down the Ohio to join him was surprised and destroyed near the mouth of the Big Miami River by a party of Tories and Indians, among whom the redoubtable Joseph Brant was conspicuous. Joined by other Indians and Tories, Brant then moved against Clark himself and another patriot body on the lower Ohio. The Indians would have no part in a fight with Clark, and they forced a retreat upon Brant and the Tories. They had nevertheless inflicted a heavy blow, and Clark grieved because he could not strike back. There were only two bright spots in the gloom for the Americans. The new Fort Nelson, built by Clark at the falls of the Ohio, gave some protection to the Kentucky settlements, and the Spanish presented the British in Detroit food for thought by staging a successful raid on Fort St. Joseph in southwestern Michigan.

Even after Yorktown bloody war went on along the Ohio. Indian attacks actually increased, for the Delawares, driven into the conflict by an American attack upon them, gave the enemies of the patriots added strength and ferocity. Colonel William Crawford with 300 troops marched from Pittsburgh into the valley of the upper Sandusky River in an attempt to surprise the Shawnee and Wyandots, and was attacked and routed after fierce fighting by Indians and Tories on June 4; more than 50 Americans were slain in battle or were afterward as prisoners gruesomely slaughtered, one of the latter being Crawford himself. In mid-August 300 Indians with Tory allies besieged Bryan's Station in Kentucky. The stockade held out against their attacks, and the marauders retreated. As they fell back, however, they laid a trap for the backwoodsmen, who were certain to gather and pursue. Two hundred of these, without waiting for others en route to join them, followed and came up with the Indians and Tories on the Lower Blue Licks. Impetuously attacking, the riflemen were driven back and fled in wild confusion, losing almost half their number. This bloody affair and other Indian incursions caused panic among the pioneers. Once more Clark moved. He urged General William Irvine, commander at Pittsburgh, to march into the Sandusky Valley from the east while he himself moved up from the south. Irvine, learning that the United States and Britain were making peace, did not stir. But Clark advanced from the mouth of the Licking River with 1,050 mounted riflemen. He also carried some small cannon. The Shawnee, learning of his approach, fled before him. He destroyed Chillicothe and five other Shawnee towns before falling back to the Ohio. He struck the last major blow in the war, for hostilities had already ceased east of the mountains.

In the end the efforts of the red men to protect themselves and to push back the patriots below the Ohio, supported though they were by the British, were fruitless. They had ravaged, burnt, and slain from Virginia to Georgia. They had brought torture to thousands of frontier families. They had not forced back the tide of American expansion. Kentucky and eastern Tennessee were firmly occupied by the backwoodsmen in 1783. The power of the Cherokee was nearly broken, and that of the Shawnee and Delawares was waning. Thereafter the other tribes east of the Mississippi continued to fight effectively, but also ultimately in vain. Moreover, the Americans had not only held and increased their grip south of the Ohio; they had secured, thanks to George Rogers Clark, a foothold in the Old Northwest. In the Peace of Paris of 1783 both that region and the Old Southwest to the borders of the Floridas became American soil.

CHAPTER XVI

YORKTOWN AND THE PEACE

VIRGINIA, like the other Southern states, suffered little from the depredations of British troops during the early years of the war. From the departure of Lord Dunmore in 1776 until the spring of 1779 Virginia was unmolested by redcoats, suffering attacks only by Indians and Tories on her distant western frontiers and by British warships upon her overseas commerce. The state made large contributions to the patriot cause, giving powerful support to Washington in both men and food, and tobacco shipped from its rivers to Europe bolstered the credit of the United States abroad. Virginia escaped invasion, however, only because primary objectives of the British lay elsewhere. After the withdrawal of the British fleet and army from Philadelphia to New York in the summer of 1778, Sir Henry Clinton gave increasing attention to the Chesapeake area. He did not think of trying to overrun Virginia nor even of major operations in the state until his other plans had been executed. He hoped, however, seriously to injure the patriot cause by raids from the bay, which would not only weaken the Virginians but might prevent them from giving vigorous assistance to the American forces in the Carolinas and Georgia. Should fortune smile upon the British, he meditated securing bases between Albemarle Sound and the Chesapeake and also a stronghold on the peninsula between it and Delaware Bay. Were the latter project successful, a force established on that peninsula might move against Philadelphia from the south with the support of other British forces pushing out from New York. However, Lord Cornwallis had his own schemes, and Virginia ultimately became a major seat of warfare against Clinton's wishes and to his deep sorrow. The surrender of Cornwallis at Yorktown substantially ended the war on the American mainland and assured the independence of the United States.

It was in May, 1779, that Clinton turned his attention to the Chesapeake, sending General Edward Mathew there with 1,800 men in company with a fleet commanded by Admiral Sir George Collier. Clinton hoped that Mathew and Collier would be able, among other things, to destroy stores gathered in Virginia for the American army to the southward and also to discourage recruiting for Washington's forces. The expedition was extraordinarily successful, for the general and the admiral seized Portsmouth on May 10 without opposition. They plundered it and neighboring towns with little hindrance. The patriots destroyed a few ships and some supplies to prevent capture of them by the British. Even so, the British set on fire several towns, captured 130 vessels and 3,000 barrels of tobacco, and sailed hurriedly away to New York without losing a man. Had Collier had his way, Portsmouth would then have been turned into a British base. Mathew, however, felt that his orders compelled him to hasten back to New York so that his men would be available for service there.[1]

For various reasons, Clinton was unable to strike again in the Chesapeake for many months. The campaign in the far South which he began late in 1779 required too much of his strength to permit other operations; and the establishment of a French fleet and army at Newport under the Chevalier de Ternay and General Count Rochambeau in the summer of 1780 seriously embarrassed him. Both his army and the British fleet at New York, however, were reinforced soon after the appearance of the French. Begged for help by Cornwallis, he undertook to make diversions in his behalf by raiding Philadelphia with one force and Richmond and Petersburg with another. The British fleet was not strong enough to carry out both schemes, but he sent General Alexander Leslie to the Chesapeake in mid-October with 2,500 men. Leslie occupied Portsmouth. Fearing strong opposition, he did not follow his orders to move up the James to destroy the American magazines at Richmond and Petersburg. Instead,

[1] Willcox (ed.), *American Rebellion*, 122–24.

having been placed under the command of Cornwallis and being instructed by him to proceed to South Carolina, he took his army to Charleston, where it was absorbed into Cornwallis' forces. Virginia again escaped serious injury.

Persevering, Clinton sent still another expedition to the Chesapeake two months later. For its leader he chose Benedict Arnold, whose ability and energy could not be doubted; there was some question in Clinton's mind about Arnold's loyalty, and he prudently ordered Arnold to consult Colonel Thomas Dundas and Colonel John Graves Simcoe, who accompanied him, in all important decisions. He gave the great traitor 1,800 men, with the same instructions as those he had furnished Leslie, except that he strongly urged the creation of a post at Portsmouth. With characteristic vigor and audacity Arnold swept into the valley of the James at the end of 1780, looting, destroying, and terrifying. Particularly hurtful to the Americans was his destruction of stores gathered in and near Richmond. Falling back as patriot troops under General von Steuben gathered about him, he retreated safely to Portsmouth, and dug in at that place. There he was suddenly threatened with entrapment.

Washington, hovering about New York, saw an opportunity to capture Arnold's force and its general, upon whom he would have liked to lay hard hands. He hurried off to Virginia by land the Marquis de Lafayette [2] with 1,200 New England and New Jersey Continentals; and Captain Sochet Destouches, who had succeeded De Ternay at Newport, co-operated by sending a ship of the line and two frigates to the Chesapeake in February, 1781. The plan was clear enough: to catch Arnold between the French ships and American troops and to force his surrender before he could secure relief. The French vessels could not remain long enough in the bay to bring pressure on Arnold; they returned to Newport on February 25. On March 8, however, the entire French squadron sailed for the bay, and Arnold was put in grave peril. He was rescued by Admiral Arbuthnot, who hastily pursued with the bulk of the British fleet based on New York, caught up with the French before they reached the Chesapeake, and worsted

[2] Lafayette's career in Virginia is fully described in Louis R. Gottschalk, *Lafayette and the Close of the American Revolution* (Chicago, 1942).

them in battle on March 16, forcing their return to Rhode Island. Although Arnold was saved, Clinton learned by example what he well knew in theory, that a powerful French fleet in command of the bay would very likely bring the destruction of a British army stationed in Tidewater Virginia. The example was, however, lost upon Lord Cornwallis.

As a result of this crisis, the British force in Virginia was strengthened, for Clinton sent there Major General William Phillips with 2,000 men, following on after Arbuthnot. Before the end of March Phillips appeared off Portsmouth. There, joining Arnold's men to his own, he resumed ravaging and raiding, doing great destruction, especially at Petersburg. Meanwhile, Clinton, hoping to carry out his scheme to seize the peninsula between the Chesapeake and the Delaware, sent Phillips further reinforcements. He proposed either to execute that scheme or, if it were not feasible, to continue desultory operations in the Chesapeake and to bring most of the British troops there back to New York. Before he could act, Cornwallis arrived at Petersburg with his small army from Wilmington, assumed command of all the British forces in Virginia, and developed his own strategy, such as it was.[3]

Stunned by the news that the earl had appeared in Virginia and had taken over Phillips' men, Clinton, after some hesitation, laid before Cornwallis in June, 1781, two plans which took into account the fact that Washington and the French were meditating a major attack upon one or the other of the British generals. Cornwallis should either move northward with his troops to meet Clinton advancing southward by way of Pennsylvania or leave a garrison force at a base in Virginia and bring the bulk of his army to New York by sea. Unfortunately for the British, he merely

[3] William B. Willcox, "The British Road to Yorktown: A Study in Divided Command," *American Historical Review*, LII (1946–1947), 1–35, searchingly analyzes the behavior and thought of the various British officers involved in the Yorktown disaster. He contends cogently that Cornwallis and Admiral Sir George Rodney were peculiarly responsible for it, with Clinton bearing a smaller share of the onus. His views have been adopted by the writer. Extensive use has also been made in this chapter of Professor Willcox's "Rhode Island in British Strategy, 1780–1781," in *Journal of Modern History* (Chicago), XVII (1945), 304–31, and his notes in *American Rebellion*.

recommended these alternatives to Cornwallis; he did not order either of them carried out. At the moment the British commander in chief rather expected to be relieved, with Cornwallis succeeding him. Not forced to adopt one of these policies, the earl chose neither. He fancied that British efforts ought to be concentrated upon Virginia. He agreed that a base was necessary, not only for the use of the British navy but also for the protection of the British troops in the state. He believed, however, that one could not be held unless he were permitted to keep all of his men. At length, Clinton, against his own judgment, ordered his subordinate to proceed with the base, allowing him to keep part or all of his army, as Cornwallis should think wise; but he continued to urge that Cornwallis did not need his whole force.

Engaged for many weeks in the summer of 1781 in correspondence at cross purposes with Clinton and in efforts to find a proper station, Cornwallis was simultaneously active in the field. He raided Richmond, and a detachment he sent out under Tarleton drove the Virginia Assembly from Charlottesville and almost captured Thomas Jefferson, then governor of his state. Virginia was ill-prepared for his onslaughts, although Jefferson had doubtless done everything possible to hold him off. Particularly hurtful to the cause of the patriots was further destruction of supplies destined for Greene's army. However, Greene's forces managed to survive. Moreover, Pennsylvania Continentals under General Anthony Wayne sent southward by Washington came to the assistance of Lafayette and the Virginia militia. The patriots gathered strength, and Lafayette even dared to assail Cornwallis' rear guard at Jamestown Ford on July 6. The French nobleman was driven off, but escaped heavy punishment and managed thereafter to limit British raiding without risking full combat. At last, Cornwallis, having found his base, established himself on the York River, occupying and fortifying Yorktown and Gloucester. He had not chosen an ideal spot, if there was one on the Virginia coast. There he remained while Washington, Rochambeau, Admiral De Barras, Admiral De Grasse, and Lafayette made arrangements for his capture and the destruction of his army.

Washington, largely inactive outside New York after 1778, received splendid news late in May, 1781, that Admiral De Grasse was sailing with a powerful fleet from France to the West Indies and that De Grasse would come to the American mainland in late summer. Colonel John Laurens and Benjamin Franklin had warmly urged in Paris that the French make a great effort in the American theater of war, and they had been successful. The Virginian rejoiced. Admiral D'Estaing's fleet had earlier been of little service; he hoped for better fortune with De Grasse. He conferred with Rochambeau and other officers at Wethersfield, Connecticut; it was agreed to attack New York, with De Grasse crowding in from the sea and the combined American and French armies assailing from the land. Rochambeau did not like the plan, and consented to it with the greatest reluctance. Nevertheless, he moved his troops from Rhode Island to the Hudson and began to consider with Washington early in July what might be done to breach the defenses of the city. The difficulties they faced were enough to daunt the boldest commander. Fortunately, De Grasse forced them to choose another objective. Taking a hint from Rochambeau, he informed the two generals that he would sail on August 13 from the West Indies, not for Rhode Island or New York but for the Chesapeake. He said he would bring 3,000 troops with him from the French garrison at San Domingo. His message, received on August 13, spurred Washington to take a bold step. Leaving behind him scanty forces to cover the Hudson, he started 2,000 Continentals together with Rochambeau's French regulars, nearly 5,000 men, for Virginia on August 19. He wrote to De Grasse to ask him to place transports for the troops at the northern end of Chesapeake Bay; he would with De Grasse attack Cornwallis. He ordered Lafayette to do what he could to prevent Cornwallis from escaping by land. Trying to deceive Clinton, he made gestures toward New York. Not until September 2, when the allied soldiers were passing through Philadelphia, did Clinton become fully aware that they were headed for Virginia. By that time the French Rhode Island squadron, under the command of Admiral De Barras, who had succeeded Destouches, was also en route to the bay.

Franco-American planning was executed with almost astonishing efficiency and good fortune. De Grasse reached the Chesapeake on August 30, put ashore 3,000 French troops under the Marquis de Saint-Simon on September 5. These promptly joined the Continentals and Virginia militia under Lafayette. The French admiral also sent up the bay transports that loaded the troops of Washington and Rochambeau and brought them to the James River on September 18. Before the arrival of the French regulars from the West Indies, Cornwallis had a good chance to escape by land, for Lafayette had not strength enough to pen him in. To be sure, the British general could hardly have made his way southward or northward without losses. In any case, he did not try. After the appearance of De Grasse's troops, he might still have been able to flee by pushing aside either Lafayette or Saint-Simon before the other could come to his aid. Again he did not try, working instead upon fortification of his positions. With the coming of the Franco-American contingents from the north, only the most desperate effort and the greatest good fortune would have enabled him to reach safety by land. Meanwhile, his last real hope, for flight by sea, vanished. By September 20 the French fleets had combined in the bay and were in full command of it.

The recklessness of Cornwallis, abetted by the indecision of Clinton, created a menace for the army of Cornwallis from which only the British navy could ultimately rescue it; and the navy failed to come effectively to its aid. Admiral Sir George Rodney was largely responsible for that failure. In command of a British fleet in the West Indies, he knew the strength of De Grasse and the Frenchman's intention to sail for the American mainland. It was his duty to send enough of his own fleet to the American coast so that the British naval forces there, decidedly inferior in strength to those of De Grasse and De Barras, should not be overwhelmed. He did not do so. He sailed for England with three ships of the line and three frigates, ordering Admiral Sir Samuel Hood to collect a squadron and to proceed northward. He too casually trusted in Admiral Sir Peter Parker, stationed at Jamaica, to supply Hood with additional ships, but Parker delayed doing so until they were too late to be of service to Hood, or to Cornwallis. Thus Hood was given only fourteen ships of the line to the twenty-eight heavier ones of De Grasse. Had Admiral Thomas Graves, commanding the British fleet based at New York, hurried to the Chesapeake as soon as he learned that De Grasse was sailing from the West Indies, had he joined his ships to those of Hood and occupied the bay before De Grasse's arrival, the French admirals might have been checkmated. Graves made no such bold and hazardous move. He waited for Hood, who stopped in the Chesapeake, saw no sign of the French, and hastened on to New York. On August 31, knowing that De Barras had left Rhode Island, the two British admirals put to sea with nineteen ships of the line, hoping to deal with De Barras or with De Grasse before they could join. They encountered De Grasse off the mouth of the bay on September 5 in far greater strength than they expected, engaged him indecisively, and after a week's maneuvering abandoned the contest and returned to New York. Meanwhile, De Barras had entered the bay. The French were in full control of it.

At New York Clinton had been desperately considering schemes to save Cornwallis. He could find no feasible plan. Nor were Graves and Hood after their return able to hit upon one which had a good chance of success. On September 23 Clinton received an ominous warning from Cornwallis. "If you cannot relieve me very soon, you must be prepared to hear the worst." [4] A week later the British commander in chief wrote unhappily, " 'I see this in so serious a light, so horrible, that I dare not look [at] it.' " [5] The admirals gathered and repaired ships, determined to sail again for the Chesapeake, despite doubt they could force their way to Cornwallis, despite even greater doubt that once in the bay they could safely depart from it. Finally, on October 19, they left New York harbor, with Clinton and 7,000 troops. The same day Cornwallis' army laid down its arms. Clinton and the British admirals heard the dismal news long before they reached the bay and mournfully turned about for New York.

It was on September 28 that the Franco-American army approached, and began the siege of Yorktown. While the fleets of De Grasse and De Barras rode the bay, about 7,800 French troops and about 8,800 Americans, of whom 3,000 were Virginia militia, established themselves so as to cover Yorktown and Gloucester from the land, the bulk of the allied army being directed against

---

[4] Stevens (ed.), *Campaign in Virginia*, II, 158.
[5] Willcox, "British Road to Yorktown," in *loc. cit.*, 32.

Yorktown itself, a detachment under General De Choisy being entrusted with the task of holding in Tarleton's Legion and some British infantry stationed in Gloucester. De Choisy accomplished his mission, entrenching close to his British opponents. Meanwhile, Cornwallis evacuated his outer works at Yorktown, on September 30, and tried to resist from his inner fortifications. The allies, amply supplied with engineers and heavy guns, began approaches on October 6, and began to bombard the British three days later. In the night of October 14 the French stormed one redoubt and the Americans another. British sorties at dawn on October 16 were repelled after achieving little. After dark of the same day, with his army of more than 6,000 men dwindling away, Cornwallis decided that Yorktown could not be held. He undertook to slip across to Gloucester with as many men as possible, sweep aside De Choisy, and flee northward. It was unlikely that a large part of his army could thus escape. However, he had nought to lose, so he thought. A portion of his army actually crossed the river, but the boats which carried the men were swept down the river in a storm. Unable to continue ferrying, Cornwallis abandoned all hope. The next morning he had the men he had sent to Gloucester brought back across the river. The allied bombardment resumed, with shattering force. The British general requested a parley. Exactly four years earlier Burgoyne had laid down his arms at Saratoga.

Cornwallis asked for a twenty-four-hour armistice while terms of surrender were discussed. Washington gave the British commander two hours in which to propose conditions. Cornwallis asked that his men be permitted after abandoning the struggle to go to England, pledging themselves in return to take no further part in the war unless they should be exchanged. The American commander insisted that the British yield completely, and Cornwallis bowed to his fate. Two days later, in the early afternoon of October 19, General O'Hara, acting for Cornwallis, formally handed his sword to Benjamin Lincoln serving for Washington—the British commander gave out that he was ill—and the British redcoats and Hessians, together with hundreds of sailors, put down their weapons at Yorktown. Meanwhile, at Gloucester Tarleton escaped the most grievous humiliation by surrendering to De Choisy rather than to an American officer.

Ten years afterward Clinton wrote to Earl Percy, who had served with him at Boston and New York: "Trent town shook us, Saratoga staggered us quite, and established the French alliance." [6] He might have added that Yorktown decisively put an end to all British hope of crushing the American rebellion. Washington wished De Grasse to join in an attack upon New York or upon Charleston, but the admiral refused, because his presence was required in the West Indies. The admiral had done enough. The British were able to hold on at their two major bases. That they continued to occupy New York and Charleston for many months meant very little. Sir Guy Carleton, who soon succeeded Clinton as commander in chief, was ordered to prepare for evacuation rather than to continue the war. On March 4, 1782, the British House of Commons denounced as an enemy to his country any Britisher who should advise offensive war against the patriots and demanded that negotiations for peace be undertaken.

The war dragged on for some months between Britain and the Bourbons, for Spain was determined to have Gibraltar. But Franco-Spanish assaults upon that bastion failed. As exhausted as the British, the Bourbons finally, in 1782, decided to abandon the struggle.

A British band played "The World Turned Upside Down" at Yorktown. It remained, however, for the diplomats to describe in detail how it had been altered; and it was not at all certain that it would be changed as remarkably as the musicians declared. In the end, nevertheless, they were correct in their estimate: the Americans were as successful in the bargaining as they were in the fighting.

The Continental Congress had long been preparing for the contest of wits at the conference tables. Early in 1779, when its members fancied the end of the war to be near, they had begun to define the demands they would make—and they had fallen into grievous sectional controversy. They agreed that they would accept

[6] Clinton to Earl Percy [1791], Sir Henry Clinton Papers (William L. Clements Library, Ann Arbor).

299

nothing less than complete independence, that all British forces must be withdrawn from American territory, that that territory should be generously outlined on the map. Concord also reigned with respect to various minor questions. It was otherwise when the delegates talked about the Newfoundland fisheries and the Mississippi River, free access to both being desired by all, but in greater and lesser degree. New Englanders insisted that peace ought not to be made unless they were guaranteed the right to chase cod, haddock, and mackerel on the Grand Banks of Newfoundland; many Southerners believed that the right to fish in those cold waters was not so vital that it should be made a *sine qua non*. They were not convinced that the noblest work of man was cod. On the other hand, Southerners contended that free use of the Mississippi, including port facilities near its mouth which would permit the passage of American goods into and from the Gulf of Mexico, was vital, while New Englanders fancied that unhindered navigation of the great river was merely desirable.

Debate over the fisheries began in February and continued for six months. The contest was as sharp as any which had earlier occurred in Congress. Passions flamed; infinite argument proceeded; intricate maneuvers abounded; the delegates voted on this and that compromise which was no compromise. The New Englanders steadily clung to their position; the men from below the Mason-Dixon line, save for Richard Henry Lee and Henry Laurens, as steadily opposed them; the delegates from the Middle states divided. The result was a frustrating and infuriating stalemate that endured week after week. The clash was so bitter that it could not be confined to the Congress. It spread to the newspapers, and was taken up by private persons, who contributed rancor rather than help.

So intense was feeling among the Southern delegates that Richard Henry Lee and Henry Laurens were looked upon as "monsters" betraying their constituents.[7] Lee escaped the turmoil when he returned temporarily to private life, but Laurens was hotly assailed by his colleague, William Henry Drayton, and by John Penn, Thomas Burke, and Whitmell Hill, the representatives of North Carolina. Laurens had doubtless voted for the best

[7] Burnett (ed.), *Letters of Members of the Continental Congress*, IV, 262.

interest of all, as he saw it. However, his vote counterbalanced that of Drayton, since South Carolina had only two representatives in Congress at the time, with the result that the state was recorded on the issue as divided. Drayton turned against him; and the two men engaged in oral and written debate, with nasty aspersions offered by both. The behavior of the North Carolina trio was especially bad. They addressed, with Drayton's approval, an abusive and threatening letter to the South Carolina delegation which was really intended only for Laurens. Commenting that South Carolina was supposedly "feeble" in men and resources and that neighboring states, especially North Carolina, had come to her assistance in the past, they asserted that her powers must have been larger than had been thought. Otherwise, said they, how could South Carolinians insist upon the American right to exploit the Newfoundland fisheries, when insistence upon it was likely to prolong the war? Surely they would not seek to protect a conflict in which they relied upon North Carolinians and others for their defense! The three men also prepared a letter to Richard Caswell, governor of North Carolina, of which they supplied Laurens with a copy, in which they urged that Tarheel troops be withdrawn from South Carolina and kept at home, unless Laurens changed his vote.[8] Laurens bitterly protested against the sneer, the insinuation, and the threat offered by the men from the "Land of Turpentine"; accused Drayton of collusion with them; and forced them to retain their message to Caswell and to withdraw the threat of withholding aid from South Carolina.[9] Happily, the quarrel went no further, and tempers abated.

At length, indeed, feeling on the issue in the Congress generally subsided. The New Englanders, believing that their purpose could be achieved through the appointment of peace emissaries who would defend their interests, consented on August 14 to make free exploitation of the fisheries a goal for American negotiators, but not an ultimative one.

If the bulk of the Southerners in Congress were not disposed to risk too much to make sure that the cod catchers could go freely to the Newfoundland fishing grounds, the New Englanders were not at all eager to hazard their interests in order to secure

[8] *Ibid.*, 129–33.   [9] *Ibid.*, 134, 137–41, 145–49, 158, 199, 210–11.

free navigation of the Mississippi, greatly desired by the Southerners. The unobstructed use of the great river was of the greatest importance to the new settlers beyond the Alleghenies, who could hardly send their products by land over the mountains. To export by way of the river and the Gulf of Mexico was almost vital to them. Should they not be able to do so, they might throw themselves into the arms of Spain, or seek independence. Accordingly, the Virginians and other Southerners pressed hard for arrangements which would open the river to Americans. They pushed for the extension of American territory westward to the river and assurance of free passage through New Orleans, where both banks of the river were under Spanish control. The New Englanders were not opposed to claiming the Mississippi as a boundary, but they balked at bringing pressure upon Spain to force that power to open the lower stretches of the river to American shipping. They wanted financial and military assistance from Spain, and they were averse to action which would seriously jeopardize it. Most Southerners, on the other hand, believed free passage through the river was so necessary that it must be obtained, even at heavy cost.

The question whether or not the United States should insist upon freedom to send shipping through the lower Mississippi was before Congress even longer than that of the cod fisheries. It was complicated by the fact that the right must be extorted from Spain rather than Britain, from Spain, a neutral at the beginning of the debate and later on a participant in the war against Britain. Further difficulties arose from patriot designs upon the Floridas, which Spain sought for herself. Congress vacillated. On March 24, however, the proposition that free use of the Mississippi be made a *sine qua non* in the peace negotiations was put to a vote. Drayton and Thomas Burke tried to obtain support for it, by pushing for an amendment which would have made it an ultimative matter only in the event that American allies were able to continue the war. But both the amendment and the main proposition were lost by heavy votes.[10] Nevertheless, it was agreed among the delegates that free use of the river was most desirable and that the Floridas were valuable properties. Ul-

[10] *Journals of the Continental Congress*, XIII, 369–70.

timately, in September, a solution was worked out. M. Conrad Alexandre Gérard, the first French minister to the United States, declared that the patriots could expect no help from Spain, if they asked for both the Floridas and the free navigation. Accordingly, the Congress undertook to abandon claim to territory below the thirty-first parallel, to help Spain conquer the Floridas so defined, and to guarantee them to Spain in return for the right to use the river.[11]

In November, 1780, George Walton and Richard Howley, Georgia delegates, reopened the whole question. They indicated that they were willing to sacrifice the use of the Mississippi to secure other gains. They then proposed to Congress to abandon all territory west of the Mobile River to Spain and to cease attempts to secure the river passage through Spanish territory in exchange for a Spanish loan and a promise from Spain not to oppose American interests in peace negotiations. It should be observed that their proposal would have left the Floridas east of the Mobile River open to American—rather, Georgian—occupation. The Virginia delegation promptly protested, and the Georgia scheme was set aside. However, James Madison was thoroughly convinced that concession had to be made so as to win Spanish friendship. Should Spain oppose American independence, should Spain support Britain in an effort to keep possession of the places British troops occupied at the end of the war—both were dangers —the United States must suffer. Accordingly, Madison persuaded the Virginia Assembly and the Virginians in Congress to sacrifice the state's special interest in the Mississippi, if necessary, for the common good. Accordingly, Congress, on February 15, 1781, sent new instructions to John Jay, who had been sent as emissary to Spain, to give up the right of navigation, if doing so would secure Spanish good will and assistance.[12]

In the debate over the cod fisheries and the Mississippi River question, the general good had again triumphed over sectional selfishness, as it did in the quarrel over quotas to be contributed

---

[11] *Ibid.*, XV, 1047–48, 1081–82. A motion to reduce the demand from unrestricted navigation to a free port or ports was lost on October 13, 1780. *Ibid.*, 1168–69.

[12] *Ibid.*, XVIII, 1070–71; XIX, 151–54; Gaillard Hunt (ed.), *The Writings of James Madison* (New York, 1900–1910), I, 157.

by the states for common expenses; and again Virginia supplied a generous statesmanship. It was evident, however, in the later years of the War of Independence that difficulties would continue to develop from sectional differences. The Southerners were sufficiently alarmed lest they be outvoted in the Congress that they vigorously opposed the acceptance of Vermont as a fourteenth state.[13] Had it been necessary to admit Vermont, they would have pressed for the formation of a balancing fifteenth state in the South, probably out of the territory of Virginia.[14]

To negotiate the peace Congress eventually chose a delegation nicely balanced in terms of sectional interests, John Adams, John Jay, Benjamin Franklin, Thomas Jefferson, and Henry Laurens. Jefferson, however, felt himself compelled to refuse appointment, and Laurens, captured on the ocean by the British, was not free to act until the bargaining was well under way. Accordingly, Franklin, Jay, and Adams assumed the burden, with the Philadelphian playing the principal role. There was, accordingly, no Southerner in Paris, where the business was chiefly done, to assert vigorously Southern claims as opposed to those of the New Englanders. None was needed, for Franklin and Jay eagerly pushed for ample boundaries on the west and south and for the free navigation of the Mississippi. The interests of the South were at least as well cared for as those of New England, which received only a dubious "liberty" rather than a "right" to fish off Newfoundland.

In Madrid, Jay discovered long before Yorktown that the Spanish King and his advisers were by no means friends of the United States. They refused to recognize American independence, at least until the British had done so, and they were disposed to limit American territory as rigidly as possible. They disliked republicanism; they feared that a successful republican régime in the United States would spur revolution in Spain's New World colonies; and they foresaw danger from American expansion in the future. The Spanish crown claimed the Floridas, by right of part conquest after Bernardo de Galvez' campaigns in West

[13] Burnett (ed.), *Letters of Members of the Continental Congress*, VI, 433; VII, 32; Hunt (ed.), *Writings of James Madison*, I, 174–75.
[14] Burnett (ed.), *Letters of Members of the Continental Congress*, VI, 253.

GENERAL NATHANAEL GREENE by Charles Willson Peale. Courtesy of City of Philadelphia, Department of Public Works

Florida, would make no concession to American shipping on the Mississippi, in fact sought to obtain the whole area between the Appalachians and the river, or at least overlordship of the Indians in that region. Happily, when Jay tried to placate the Spanish by offering to give up the right to use the lower stretches of the river, they hesitated. Before they could reply, Jay hastily withdrew the offer.

Treated as a nuisance in Spain, in Paris Jay ardently supported Franklin in asserting American claims against both Britain and Spain. Indeed, Jay turned against France, because he suspected that the French Bourbon secretly supported the Spanish one where there was clash between American and Spanish interests. Nothing could be done at Paris toward opening up the lower end of the great river. But the American delegates negotiated separately with the British emissaries, ignoring a command by Congress that they seek and ultimately follow French advice. They secured from Britain not only an acknowledgment of independence but very favorable boundaries. They obtained all the territory between the mountains and the Mississippi. Moreover, ceding to Spain the Floridas, the British agreed that the American limits on the south should run eastward from the river along the thirty-first parallel to the Chattahoochee River and thence generally eastward to the Atlantic, thus cramping the Floridas as closely as possible. That Spain would long be able to deny the citizens of the new union the right to traverse the lower Mississippi was doubtful; that she could cling permanently to the Floridas was equally unlikely.

The United States, recognized as independent in 1783 by the European powers and given a generous territory, were thereafter easily strong enough to defend their independence, at least until the twentieth century had passed mid-point. There was, however, real danger that the union would collapse because of sectional divisions; and the winning of the war, leaving unsettled a host of problems, created others. The millennium had not arrived, either for the nation or for the South.

CHAPTER XVII

THE SOUTHERN STATES:
POLITICAL RECONSTRUCTION

THE American Revolution was more than a war for independence. It is said, in fact, that the term includes two revolutions, the one national, the other domestic. The phrases External Revolution and Internal Revolution, used to designate these, have acquired vogue. Internal Revolution is a rather extravagant description of the domestic changes which came during and immediately after the war. Many of these would doubtless have proceeded had there been no military struggle; and their scope and importance have been magnified.[1] Nevertheless, the violent separation from Britain made possible and stimulated major political and social shifts within the American union. These may be collectively designated as a Reformation rather than a Revolution, but they richly deserve analysis. There was conspicuous change in the Southern states as well as in those to the northward; and the American central government which developed during and after the war varied strikingly from the British one which it largely replaced.

The power to rule was, of course, rapidly assumed by the Continental Congress and the patriot legislatures in the several colonies during the period 1774–1776. The colonial assemblies were steadily pushed into the background, the last of them dying at the time of the Declaration of Independence. They could not be used effectively as patriot instruments, especially because they were able to function only with the permission of imperial governors. Moreover, their very existence implied continuation of the authority of the crown and Parliament. Accordingly, they were

[1] J. Franklin Jameson's thought-provoking *The American Revolution Considered As a Social Movement* (Princeton, 1926), enlarges the significance of some of the changes that took place.

replaced by the conventions or Provincial Congresses which usurped their powers, the memberships of the new bodies being strikingly similar to, even identical with, those of the old. The imperial governors, of course, were replaced during the same period by patriot Councils of Safety, which seized control of the executive.[2]

The new régimes in the colony-states, although they were quite efficient except in the administration of justice, were illegal and hastily contrived, in the South as elsewhere, and the patriots soon undertook to replace them with better and more permanent systems of government having a legal foundation. They achieved both purposes by making written constitutions, to the use of which, particularly in the form of colonial charters, they had long been accustomed. Such a constitution was produced in New Hampshire in the first days of 1776, and a governmental system based upon it was promptly organized. The Continental Congress expressed its approval of this procedure, and advised the patriots in other colony-states to do likewise. In May, 1776, it urged all of the Thirteen which had not yet organized such governments to act, because they were needed to meet the problems of the moment and because they would be even more necessary in the event of a final separation from Britain. Thus encouraged, the patriots throughout the Thirteen, and in Vermont as well, prepared constitutions and put them in operation. Much of the work was done in the years 1776–1777. Several of the instruments then formed, however, were intended for only temporary use, and constitution-making continued in some states beyond the war. In the South the first to act was South Carolina, which declared a temporary constitution in effect on March 26, 1776. Georgia and Virginia soon did likewise, the Virginia instrument being approved on June 29 of the same year. Maryland and North Carolina did not follow their example until after the Declaration of Independence.

The first state constitutions in the South, as elsewhere, were not made by bodies specially and exclusively chosen for the purpose. Although it was universally believed among the patriots that

[2] Rhode Island and Connecticut offer exceptions, of course, to these general statements. The imperial governor and legislature in both being American, political transition from colony to state was a simple process.

a constitution was basic and that its provisions must be obeyed, it was generally then thought that a legislature could prepare one and declare it in effect in the same way that it made laws. The voters of Concord town in Massachusetts contended in 1776 that the fashioning of a document describing the framework of the government of a state and the rights of the individual within it was far more important than ordinary legislation, that it should be entrusted only to men elected by the voters to do that specific task. Toward the end of the war their view acquired popularity, and the constitutional convention soon afterward became an American institution. The Concord men, and others in Massachusetts, and Thomas Jefferson in Virginia, urged also that no constitution should be promulgated without the consent of the voters; and the constitutional referendum likewise became an American institution soon after the close of the war. During the conflict, however, constitutions were freely constructed and declared in operation without resort to new machinery. Indeed, in many cases, they were designed by men who had been sent to the legislature in elections in which constitution-making was not an issue. Those of South Carolina and Virginia of 1776 were so formulated. In Maryland, North Carolina, and Georgia it was otherwise. The Continental Congress had urged late in 1775 that a legislature try to avoid creating a constitution unless its members had been chosen by "a full and free representation" of the people, these having had an opportunity to think about the matter.[3] The three states followed the recommendation of the Congress.

The constitution-makers were not without models, and one offered by John Adams in his "Thoughts on Government" was widely circulated and used, in the South and elsewhere. Conscious of the defects of mankind and averse to domination by the many as well as tyranny of the few, Adams urged both balance and separation of powers. Toward these ends he called for a bicameral legislature, a lower house annually elected, a relatively independent senate chosen by the lower house. A governor and other officials should be selected by the two chambers; however, if experience indicated the wisdom of the change, popular election

[3] Burnett, *Continental Congress*, 122–23.

of the governor might later be substituted, with the stipulation that he should not enjoy two successive terms. The governor was neither to pardon nor to veto bills without the consent of a privy council. The judges should be elected by the legislature and should occupy the bench during good behavior, subject to removal only by impeachment. He advised that county dignitaries be directly responsible to the voters.

The system proposed by Adams was generally acceptable to most patriot leaders and doubtless to the majority of plain folk. It was in accord with the prevailing current of political philosophy among the Americans and with their political experience; and its influence may readily be observed in the constitutions adopted in Maryland, Virginia, and South Carolina. To be sure, the Adams plan was nowhere used as a blueprint to be slavishly followed; rather it was a convenient arsenal of ideas.

The South Carolina Provincial Congress, making a temporary constitution in the spring of 1776, established a central governmental structure very similar to that proposed by Adams. A major difference was that the president, i.e., governor, was given the veto power. In 1778, however, that structure was altered, the president losing his veto and the upper house, or senate, being thereafter elected by the voters. The basic document put into effect in Maryland in 1776 also deviated with respect to the upper house, in a very different way. Its members were chosen by electors, who were in turn elected by the voters for five-year terms, an indirect system which won the admiration of conservative-minded people. The Virginia constitution of 1776, one which long endured, though intended to be temporary, likewise called for an elected senate, its members being chosen, however, for four-year terms by the voters directly. Virginia failed to follow Adams' philosophy in another respect, for power in that state was heavily concentrated in the lower house. South Carolina, Maryland, and Virginia alike, and North Carolina, substantially ignored the advice of the Massachusetts man to provide for the election of local officials.

The Revolutionary constitution of North Carolina, drawn up toward the end of 1776, was not one to please Adams, nor any other believer in balanced government. Its authors had the benefit of the experiences of constitution-makers in neighboring states, and profited somewhat from them; they gave some heed to the advice of the crusty gentleman of Massachusetts. They arranged for a bicameral system, both houses elective, the governor being chosen by them each year, together with a council of state. The governor was permitted few powers, and he exercised those only with the consent of the council of state. He became accordingly a figurehead who could insist upon receiving his salary and who might exert personal influence.

Balance and separation of powers were almost completely lacking in the "Rules and Regulations," Georgia's emergency constitution, adopted in April, 1776, and in the presumably permanent one prepared in the following year. Indeed, the form of government established by these documents may be called bizarre. The "Rules and Regulations" placed almost all power in a unicameral Assembly, which elected from its own membership a council headed by a president. The president could not act without the consent of the council; his term was for six months. The basic document of 1777 was even more extraordinary, since it was intended to endure. Declaring that "the legislative, executive, and judiciary departments shall be separate and distinct, so that neither exercise the powers properly belonging to the other," it also placed virtually complete authority in a one-house legislature. A governor and council chosen by this gathering were almost entirely deprived of a share in the making of laws but were given a few trifles of executive power. The governor was not permitted even to preside over the council nor to address the legislature. The chief justice of the state was to be chosen by that body annually, and other magistrates were to hold office during its pleasure.[4] Such a remarkable concentration of power ensured bad government in Georgia for years to come.

The forms of state government which thus appeared in the South were not developed without contest and quarrel among

[4] Saye, *New Viewpoints in Georgia History,* 157–95, offers a valuable history and analysis of the two Georgia documents. Fletcher M. Green, *Constitutional Development in the South Atlantic States, 1776–1860* (Chapel Hill, 1930), Chaps. I–III, is very helpful with respect to all of the Revolutionary constitutions made in the South.

the patriots. They did not all seek the same goals, and their conflicting purposes led them to favor differing structures. In general, the Southerners, like other Americans, fell into three groups, all of them favoring independence but otherwise at odds. Some patriots, whom we may call Conservatives, believed that separation from Britain was the only major objective of the Revolution, hence that there should be few changes beyond those made necessary by the erasure of the British element in government. Had they had their way, the power previously in the hands of the British would have been inherited by those Americans who had earlier shared authority with the British. Of such were Edmund Pendleton, James Iredell, and Thomas and Charles Cotesworth Pinckney. An opposing element, the Democrats, who are often called Radicals, demanded majority rule, social equality, and the destruction of privileges, even, on occasion, of their own. Conspicuous among them in the South were Willie Jones, Thomas Person, and Griffith Rutherford of North Carolina, and Isaac Peronneau of South Carolina. Between these wings were the Liberals, men like George Mason, Jefferson, and Madison, who favored change but could not immediately accept complete political and social leveling.[5]

Seeking majority rule, the Democrats desired to concentrate power in the lower house and to install white manhood suffrage. They were opposed to independent judiciaries, powerful senates, strong executives, indirect elections, plural voting, long terms for offices, and property qualifications for them. The wishes of the Conservatives ran quite uniformly to the contrary. The Liberals, urging balanced government, wished neither to enthrone the

[5] There were also, of course, the uninterested. Scholars who have analyzed the internal struggles of the patriots customarily find only two groups. These are often called Conservatives and Radicals, as in Allan Nevins, *The American States during and after the Revolution, 1775-1789* (New York, 1924). Elisha P. Douglass, *Rebels and Democrats; The Struggle for Equal Political Rights and Majority Rule During the Revolution* (Chapel Hill, 1955), prefers Whigs (or Whig leaders) and Democrats. Such classifications are at best inevitably crude, and it is very difficult to place within them Franklin, Jefferson, and many others. Hence the use of three divisions in the text. Some may wish to designate the middle group Moderates. These classifications bring up problems of semantics, which interested persons may solve to their own pleasure. It should be added that the clashes among the patriots have sometimes been exaggerated.

men possessing wealth and superior social standing who were the backbone of the Conservatives, nor to put their trust in mass opinion.

In this struggle the Conservatives were at a disadvantage, even though they occupied entrenched positions developed in the colonial period. They were weakened because the loyalists, many of whom would have been their natural allies, were barred from the lists. They had orated and written in behalf of the "rights of mankind," and now found difficulty in defining those rights narrowly. Moreover, the suffrage had been broadened in the conventions and Congresses of 1774–1776 so as to secure popular support, and it was awkward to try to withdraw the vote once given. Besides, the support of the Liberals and Democrats was essential to the winning of the war. And in the heat of the war some Conservatives were rather less disposed to defend their special interests than they afterward were. They gained or maintained control in Maryland and South Carolina. The Radicals were victorious in Georgia. The Liberals had their way in Virginia and North Carolina. However, none of the triumphs of either the Conservatives or Radicals was complete and permanent.

The convention which drew up the constitution of Maryland was dominated by planters and prosperous lawyers, such as Charles Carroll of Carrollton, Edward Lloyd, Robert Goldsborough, Matthew Tilghman, William Paca, and Thomas Johnson. They largely ignored feeble complaints from Liberals and Radicals. The indirectly elected senate which they established has already been mentioned. Toward ensuring the independence of that body they provided for staggered terms of five years. They erected another and stronger defense against "mob rule" by stipulating that the vote should be given only to those possessing at least 50 acres of land or property worth £30, a requirement only slightly lower than that in vogue in colonial Maryland. They built other barriers by requiring that members of the lower house own property valued at £500 or more, that those of the senate have possessions worth at least £1,000. They also gave to eastern Maryland larger representation than it deserved on the basis of numbers, thus offering advantage to the planters and their allies of the east over the farmers of the west. While they provided for election rather than appointment of sheriffs, barred plural officeholding, and called for rotation in office, they otherwise did about everything that was possible to make certain that they and their kind should rule in Maryland.[6]

The patricians of South Carolina also strove to secure a constitution which would permit them to dominate their state, with almost equal success. In the winter of 1774–1775, conscious of the need of enlisting the support of the Upcountry in the approaching struggle with Britain, their leaders in the Provincial Congress gave 40 seats out of 184 in that body to the backsettlers. A measure of justice was thus accorded to the long restive Upcountry folk.[7] The Tidewater aristocrats, however, did not intend to let power slip from their hands into those of the farmers of the interior or into those of the tradesmen and workmen of Charleston. They continued easily to control the Congress, and the temporary constitution of 1776 was their creation. It gave increased representation to the Upcountry, 64 members in the lower house, but that number was far less than a majority of the whole. Moreover, the high colonial qualifications for voting and officeholding were not altered. These arrangements, coupled with the choice of the president and the upper house by the lower and the presidential veto, assured Low Country and oligarchic dominance. Largely because this instrument was so drawn, it was widely attacked. The Low Country aristocracy felt forced to make further concessions; and the constitution of 1778 contained several. The president lost his veto power; the senate became elective; the suffrage was given to all men possessing 50 acres or a town lot, or paying taxes equivalent to those levied upon such properties. It was stipulated, however, that the presidency should go only to a man owning a freehold worth £10,000, and senatorships exclusively to those having a £2,000 freehold. Plural voting was sanctified; and residence qualifications were described so as to permit the election of Low Country magnates in Upcountry dis-

[6] Francis N. Thorpe (ed.), *The Federal and State Constitutions, Colonial Charters, and Other Organic Laws* (Washington, 1909), III, 1691–1701; Philip A. Crowl, *Maryland during and after the Revolution* (Baltimore, 1943), 17–40; Bernard C. Steiner, *Western Maryland in the Revolution* (Baltimore, 1902), 19–20.

[7] McCrady, *South Carolina under the Royal Government*, 757–62.

tricts. Moreover, Charleston and its environs continued to enjoy representation far beyond their deserts in terms of numbers, although reapportionment was to be made in 1785 and thereafter at intervals of fourteen years "in the most equitable and just manner on a basis of both numbers and taxable property." [8] Since the Low Country had the property and the Upcountry the people, this formula meant only that the demands of the latter for larger representation would be considered again in the future. The Rutledges, Pinckneys, Lowndeses, and their kind remained in the saddle.

Probably because so many of those who might have been Conservatives were Tories and barred from participating in public life, the Democrats had their way almost utterly in the making of the Georgia instruments of 1776 and 1777. The seats in the all-powerful unicameral Assembly were apportioned in accordance with numbers except for sops thrown to Savannah and Sunbury because of their commercial importance. A property qualification for voting was set at the small figure of £10, and one for members of the Assembly was put at £250, or 250 acres of land. Voting was to be secret, and any qualified person who failed to use his ballot was declared subject to a fine of £5. It will be recalled that state officials were to be chosen by the Assembly. Local ones were to be elected. Juries were permitted to rule upon the law as well as the facts, and also to ignore statutes conflicting with the constitution. Amendment by popular petition was also provided for; a demand for a constitutional convention signed by half of the voters in half of the counties would compel the Assembly to call one into session. The principle of majority rule was thus enthroned, even in the courts, with jurymen serving as interpreters of the constitution.[9] So ill contrived was the system, particularly

[8] Thorpe (ed.), *Federal and State Constitutions*, VI, 3241–57.

[9] See again Saye, *New Viewpoints in Georgia History*, 157–95. It is hardly surprising that the Democrats who controlled Georgia flatly refused to consider a scheme proposed by the legislature of South Carolina in the winter of 1776–1777 to unite the two states. With many other objections, the Georgia politicians must have feared that they and their constituents would come under the heels of the South Carolina aristocracy. William Henry Drayton, who made a brief visit to Georgia to push the scheme, secured very little support; and the governor of Georgia offered a reward for his arrest. Gibbes (ed.), *Documentary History of the American Revolution*, 77–87; Jones, *History of Georgia*, II, 275–78.

in its arrangements for judicial anarchy, that the complete collapse of patriot government which took place in Georgia in the later years of the war was by no means entirely a curse.

The North Carolina constitution of 1776, made by a body in which Democrats and Conservatives were almost evenly represented, with Liberals holding the balance, also had its defects, but fewer and less serious ones. It was sufficiently well made to endure for a half century. In this "corner stone of all law" the executive was far too weak; the judiciary was independent only in theory; the legislature was nearly all-powerful in practice. The requirements for the suffrage and for officeholding were, however, generous and well suited to a state in which most men were small farmers. All taxpayers could vote for members of the lower house, all men owning fifty acres of land could participate in the election of senators; a representative had to own a hundred acres, a senator three hundred acres. The governor must own a thousand acres. The popular will thus became dominant, with the men of greater property having power to delay the execution of that will and to force compromise. Moreover, the grievance of the Piedmont with respect to representation was partly removed. Henceforth, each county was to elect two representatives and one senator, with six "boroughs" being given the right to choose one representative each. While the Tidewater retained more power in the Assembly than its numbers warranted, the people of the Piedmont were no longer at the mercy of those of the coastal plain. The constitution could not satisfy Conservatives such as Samuel Johnston and William Hooper; it did not, however, ignore their wishes and those of their kind.[10]

In essence the Virginia instrument of 1776 was almost surprisingly like that later adopted by North Carolina, having fundamentally the same virtues and the same defects. The Virginia convention, in which George Mason played the principal role, was directed by the Liberals. The document, hastily produced in the summer of 1776, put large powers in the lower house of the Assembly. It had complete control over appropriations and the right to initiate all legislative measures. A popularly chosen senate was given little authority, and the governor, also severely limited in

[10] Lefler and Newsome, *North Carolina*, 205-11.

his functions, was elected annually, with a privy council, judges, and other officials, by the Assembly. The governor was required to secure the consent of the privy council before acting, even in the limited sphere accorded to him. There were no property qualifications for office, and the suffrage was generously given, as in colonial times, to all men who owned one hundred acres of unimproved land, or twenty-five acres with a house, or a house and lot in a town. Each county sent two members to the lower house, Williamsburg and Norfolk electing one each, with the senators being chosen in twelve specially designed districts.[11] As a result, the more heavily populated and generally larger counties of the Piedmont and to the westward suffered from discrimination, although Tidewater was not given a majority in the lower house. Perhaps an equally serious defect was that local government remained in the hands of the appointive county court, oligarchy continuing at the county seats.[12] On the whole, the constitution was not ill made. Its chief shortcoming lay in the fact that the judiciary and the executive, especially the latter, were too weak. This deficiency was strikingly shown in the later years of the war, when Jefferson as governor was unable to move effectively to thwart British raids and attacks by Benedict Arnold, Tarleton, and Cornwallis.

Too much may be made of the shortcomings of the first state constitutions made in the South, and elsewhere. They were hurriedly made, often in the midst of pressing business, sometimes when British forces immediately threatened. Moreover, the many problems faced were extraordinarily difficult. It is surprising, not that the framers failed at this point and the other, but that they were so successful. Certainly the lowering of requirements for voting pointed toward majority rule in the future, if it was not

[11] The document is conveniently available in Boyd *et al.* (eds.), *Papers of Thomas Jefferson*, I, 377–83. Dr. Boyd proves that a few parts of it came from Jefferson. *Ibid.*, 337–65, 384–86.

[12] Charles S. Sydnor's scholarly and delightful *Gentleman Freeholders; Political Practices in Washington's Virginia* (Chapel Hill, 1952), points out the merits of the system of local government in Virginia, emphasizing that it produced honest and efficient administration. Professor Sydnor's view does not quite take into account the fact that the system was almost ideal only if the status quo were acceptable.

316

established at the moment. The concessions made to the back-settlers, especially in the Carolinas, led in the same direction. The grievances of the Piedmont people were not entirely removed, and inequalities in representation long lingered, but it is significant that during and after the war the capitals of all the Southern states except Maryland moved westward, from Williamsburg to Richmond, from New Bern to Raleigh, from Charleston to Columbia, from Savannah toward Augusta.[13]

Every American state promptly acquired a Bill of Rights as well as a constitution. The patriots, from Massachusetts to Georgia, so feared tyranny—hence, in the main, the weak executives established by those constitutions—that they strove to put their personal rights beyond question by listing them and declaring them to be fundamental law untouchable by governor, legislature, or judge. They might be described in a constitution, as they were in South Carolina and Georgia, or they might be embodied in a separate document as in Virginia, Maryland, and North Carolina. In either case they were presumed to be inviolable, although they were hardly so in fact, then or later. Believing in natural rights granted by the Creator and accustomed to safeguards of them in British laws and colonial charters, the patriots considered Bills of Rights as necessary as—even more important than—provision for legislatures and courts.

Again it was Virginia that led the van, with the Declaration of Rights unanimously voted by her convention on June 12, 1776. George Mason supplied most of its statements. The first clause forthrightly asserted that: "all men are by nature equally free and independent, and have certain inherent rights, of which when they enter into a state of society, they cannot, by any compact, deprive or divest their posterity; namely, the enjoyment of life and liberty, with the means of acquiring and possessing property, and pursuing and obtaining happiness and safety." All power was "vested in, and consequently derived from, the people." The "magistrates" were "their trustees and servants, and at all times

---

[13] The change was not complete in the case of South Carolina, which divided governmental functions between Charleston and Columbia, for some years. Immediately after the war Georgia's capital was at Savannah for nine months of the year, for three months at Augusta.

amenable to them." The "majority of the community" had "an indubitable, unalienable, and indefeasible right, to reform, alter, or abolish" government "in such manner as shall be judged most conducive to the public weal." Other clauses proclaimed that all men who had a "permanent common interest with, and attachment to, the community" should be allowed to vote, that the military power should always be inferior to the civil. Jury trial and freedom of the press were guaranteed. A person tried for crime was entitled to confront his accusers and witnesses, to present evidence in his own behalf; he was not to be "compelled to give evidence against himself." No man could be "deprived of his liberty except by the law of the land, or the judgment of his peers." Excessive bails and fines, cruel and unusual punishments, and general warrants of search and seizure were forbidden. A final trenchant article, sponsored by Madison, declared

"That religion, or the duty which we owe to our Creator, and the manner of discharging it, can be directed only by reason and conviction, not by force or violence; and therefore all men are equally entitled to the free exercise of religion, according to the dictates of conscience; and that it is the mutual duty of all to practise Christian forbearance, love, and charity towards each other." [14]

The charter of liberty of Virginia was widely circulated and used as a model, with additions and deletions, in other states. The Maryland Bill of Rights, adopted on November 3, 1776, contained further protections for the person, denouncing *ex post facto* laws and bills of attainder; however, it guaranteed religious liberty only to Christians, at the same time providing that no one was to be molested because of his faith, or lack of it.[15] That established in North Carolina in the following month added a denunciation of imprisonment for debt, and was remarkably forthright in proclaiming religious freedom, asserting that "all men have a natural and unalienable right to worship Almighty God

[14] The Declaration is conveniently reprinted in Thorpe (ed.), *Federal and State Constitutions*, VII, 3812–14; and in Robert A. Rutland, *The Birth of the Bill of Rights, 1776–1791* (Chapel Hill, 1955), 231–33. George Mason and Patrick Henry called merely for religious toleration; Madison demanded religious freedom. Irving Brant, *James Madison, The Virginia Revolutionist* (Indianapolis, 1941), 245–50.

[15] Thorpe (ed.), *Federal and State Constitutions*, III, 1686–91.

according to the dictates of their own consciences." [16] Georgia specifically protected the right to the writ of *habeas corpus*, and also provided for religious liberty "not repugnant to the peace and safety of the State." [17] The South Carolinians, in their constitution of 1778, declared Protestantism to be the official religion of the state, but gave freedom to worship to all those who professed belief in one God and in "a future state of rewards and punishments." No person was to be forced to pay toward the support of any church. They also inserted a provision demanding that no one be deprived of life, liberty, or property except by the judgment of his peers or by "the law of the land." [18]

The provisions of the first constitutions of the Southern states and of their Bills of Rights make it evident that the Southern patriots, like those to the northward, were moving in the direction of religious freedom. In each of them the Anglican Church, which had been established, either lost, or was threatened with the loss of, its favored position. It is a striking fact that practicing clergymen were barred from office in the Carolinas and from the legislature in Georgia. Religious liberty had not, however, arrived, and it was not to be won without struggle. The right of believers in a Christian God to worship as they wished was, to be sure, generally recognized. Such was not the case with reference to Roman Catholics, deists, Mohammedans, agnostics, Jews, atheists, and other religious minorities. Besides, Georgia, preventing clergymen from taking part in the making of laws, insisted that members of her Assembly be Protestant; and North Carolina, also barring the men of the cloth, demanded of all holders of "office or place of profit or trust" that they be Protestant, acknowledge the existence of God, accept the divine authority of the Old and New Testaments, and entertain no "religious principles incompatible with the freedom and safety of the state." Maryland required all lawmakers and civil officers to declare their loyalty to a Christian faith. Taxation for "the support of the Christian religion" was specifically made possible, provided that each taxpayer retained the right to specify to what clergyman or church his contribution should go. Should he prefer to give it to the poor, he was to possess that alternative. In South Carolina the official establishment

[16] *Ibid.*, V, 2787–89. [17] *Ibid.*, II, 784–85. [18] *Ibid.*, VI, 3255–57.

of Protestantism was supported by a requirement that the state president swear to "maintain and defend the laws of God and the Protestant religion." Such stipulations, together with the fact that generous promises of religious freedom, or at least toleration, in fundamental laws were not always kept, indicate that complete religious liberty was desired by few rather than many. Nevertheless, it substantially came, and within a few years, after hard contest.

In Virginia, where the Anglicans—later Episcopalians—formed perhaps half of the body of orthodox believers, where almost all gentlemen and ladies were Anglican, although not nearly all Anglicans were aristocrats, the year 1776 marked the beginning of a dramatic conflict over religion. The Anglican clergy were loath to give up their privileged position and that of their church, and they were supported by many of their parishioners. They contended that the Virginia Declaration of Rights merely gave to other sects the right to worship freely, that the Anglican Church remained the official church of Virginia, that taxes should continue to be levied for its maintenance. Presbyterians, Lutherans, and Baptists would not have it so, interpreted the Declaration to mean that the Anglican Church had been reduced to the level of their own. In the fall of 1776 they and their communicants urged the Virginia Assembly to pass laws which would definitely carry their wishes into effect. The majority in that body was Anglican. However, the dissenters had justice on their side. And Jefferson, Madison, and George Mason came forward immediately as allies of the dissenters.

Jefferson, returning to Virginia from the Continental Congress in order to reform the institutions of his native state, assumed command of the anti-Anglican forces. Like so many Revolutionary leaders, he was religiously unorthodox, unitarian and deistic.[19] He

---

[19] Such men, when their opinions were known, were often attacked as infidels. Cornelius Harnett, one of them, announced what his views had been by providing for an epitaph over his grave, lines from Pope:

> Slave to no sect, he took no private road,
> But looked through Nature up to Nature's God.

He was, as might be expected, thought by the thoughtless to be an atheist. Robert D. W. Connor, Cornelius Harnett (Raleigh, 1909), 198–201.

believed utterly in religious freedom, and was therefore at variance with many of his allies. Neither he nor they had their way in the Assembly. A bill disestablishing the Anglican Church outright would have been defeated, for Pendleton and Robert Carter Nicholas mobilized strong opposition. Jefferson secured what he could. The non-Anglicans were freed of religious taxation and were relieved of other legal restrictions; and religious taxation even upon Anglicans was suspended for one year. No more could be done until 1779, except to continue the suspension year by year. Then it was possible to forbid forever public levies for the support of the Anglican Church, which thus, in effect, was disestablished.

But Jefferson's struggle for religious liberty was by no means won in 1779. A bill which he prepared and which called for a complete separation of church and state was defeated. Many of his former allies among the Protestant sects now joined the Anglicans in pushing a scheme of establishment like that made possible by the constitution of Maryland, by which all taxpayers would be forced to contribute to the support of all the Christian churches. This plan was popular, particularly because many persons believed that religion should be encouraged as a means of combating a current rise in crime. Moreover, leaders like Washington, John Marshall, Richard Henry Lee, and Patrick Henry saw in the scheme a compromise which might satisfy most of the sects. They thus committed themselves to the defense of existing religious organization and thought. Nor were they concerned because their "general assessment" might be paid by the indifferent and the agnostic. Henry vigorously championed the proposal, and it was sanctioned by the lower house in 1784 by a majority of two to one. But Madison fought against it with skill and determination, and secured postponement. With George and Wilson Cary Nicholas he then embarked upon a campaign to persuade the Presbyterians to turn against it, with marked success. The Baptists also gave him steady support. In 1785 petitions of protest poured into the Assembly, and the scheme was abandoned.

In January, 1786, Madison led the Liberal forces to final and overwhelming victory in the legislature, securing the passage of Jefferson's bill for separation of church and state which had been set aside more than six years earlier. The preamble of the Statute of Religious Liberty asserted the very sanity of sanities that "truth is great and will prevail if left to herself." Accordingly, it was enacted "that no man shall be compelled to frequent or support any religious worship, place, or ministry whatsoever, nor shall be enforced, restrained, molested, or burthened in his body or goods, nor shall otherwise suffer, on account of his religious opinions or belief; but that all men shall be free to profess, and by argument to maintain, their opinions in matters of religion, and that the same shall in no wise diminish, enlarge, or affect their civil capacities." [20] Jefferson had reason to be proud of his magnificent phrases. He shares with Madison the glory of leading a splendid cause which more than once seemed lost.

Nowhere in the South outside Virginia was sharp struggle over religious freedom so long continued. The Anglicans were far too weak to fight for exclusive special privilege in North Carolina and Georgia; and they were in a decided minority in Maryland and South Carolina. The scheme of "general assessment" plagued the public in Maryland as well as Virginia, but it was decisively beaten at Annapolis in 1785. It was not pushed in the other Southern states.[21] Instead, this religious restriction and that gradually vanished in the South and throughout the American union, until the principles of the Statute of Religious Liberty were uniformly put into practice. One form of tyranny over the mind of man received its American deathblow as a result of the Revolution.

[20] For the drafting of the act, see Boyd *et al.* (eds.), *Papers of Thomas Jefferson*, II, 545–47. The standard account of the struggle for religious freedom in Virginia is Hamilton J. Eckenrode, *Separation of Church and State in Virginia* (Richmond, 1910).

[21] This illiberal scheme, however, had wide appeal. As originally drawn, the basic Land Ordinance of 1785, which provided for the distribution of nationally owned lands beyond the Alleghenies, gave a section of land in each township "for the support of religion, the profits arising therefrom . . . to be applied for ever according to the will of the majority of male residents of full age" within the township. In a vote taken on April 23 seventeen members of the Continental Congress supported the provision, and but six opposed it. Happily, there were only five state delegations in favor of it, and the measure, "smelling so strongly of an antiquated Bigotry," as Madison said, was defeated. Burnett, *Continental Congress*, 624.

Striving to assure to themselves the "rights of mankind," however those might be defined, the patriots were reluctant to concede any of them to the Tories until the passions roused by the war had waned. The loyalists, supporting Britain in word and in deed, with propaganda, with military information, and with arms, were feared and detested by the patriots everywhere. During the war every state struck at them, and some even after arms had been laid down. The Tories were refused the vote, barred from the professions, specially taxed, restricted in their movements, deprived of their property, imprisoned, and banished. More than one was executed for treason. Official action was accompanied by private, and except for those who were both cautious in behavior and fortunate, the American supporters of Britain suffered grievously. Often the path of the Tory led but to the wave.

The loyalists were not, of course, a homogeneous group. They were united only in giving their allegiance to Britain. They came from all social classes and groups, including aristocrats, poor and unlettered farmers, tradesmen, royal officials, clergymen, Germans, Scotch-Irish, Highlanders, English, Irish, and Negroes. Some were devoted and would have supported Britain in almost any circumstances; others, like the Reverend John Joachim Zubly of Georgia, were quitting images of patriots, men who took part in the Revolutionary movement to the point where independence became the great objective and then turned back; a third element, doubtless a large one, neither automatically supported Britain nor waited until the summer of 1776 to make up their minds. There were Tories who were disposed to do little or nothing against the patriots. However, they were commonly in the South a fighting folk, and they were a genuine and even formidable danger to the patriots.

Virginia, which contained relatively few adherents of Britain, but among them men of repute such as Attorney General John Randolph, William Byrd III, Richard Corbin, and Ralph Wormeley, proceeded against them with vigor. As early as 1776 men active in behalf of the crown were declared to be subject to penalties of imprisonment or death and loss of property. In the following year those who merely refused to take an oath of allegiance to the

323

state were deprived of the suffrage, denied the right to sue for debts. They were not permitted to acquire land, and were taxed doubly, later triply. In 1779 the state began the general confiscation and sale of property belonging to Tories and British-born persons alike, which netted little profit to the public, did injustice to many who were not enemies of Virginia, and enriched some shrewd patriot purchasers who proffered depreciated paper currency for solid lands and structures. When the war was over, however, Virginia quickly abandoned all effort to punish the Tories; and in the fall of 1783 her Assembly, pushed on by no other than Patrick Henry, declared that all loyalists who had fled the state— and many had—might return, except for those who had borne arms with the British. Those who took advantage of this act were not usually molested by unforgiving patriot neighbors, probably because the Tories had been less dangerous in Virginia than in states to the southward.[22]

The treatment accorded to the loyalists of Maryland was similar to that they received in Virginia. In that state there was strong opposition to seizure of their property, as immoral and valueless to the patriot cause, because Britain would force its return in the peace treaty. "A Sentry" answered the first argument in the *Maryland Gazette* of March 3, 1780. "Good God! What is this state come to . . . we cannot take the property of our enemies to pay our taxes, when, if it was in their power, they would take our lives?" A week later "A Maryland Officer" dealt with the second objection in the same newspaper. "Let the assembly give it to us, and all the devils in hell shall not take it from us." Confiscation and sale of property was undertaken in 1781. Once begun, forfeitures and sales proceeded rapidly, and the state collected something like £500,000 as a result. However, the Maryland patriots chose to forgive and forget soon after the end of hostilities.[23]

The Tories fared far worse in the Carolinas and Georgia, where they were numerous, vigorous, and dangerous. It has been asserted,

[22] The basic facts about Virginia's treatment of the Tories may readily be found in Hamilton J. Eckenrode, *The Revolution in Virginia* (Boston, 1916), 114–22, 126–56, 175–94, 232–60, 284–92. Isaac S. Harrell, *Loyalism in Virginia; Chapters in the Economic History of the Revolution* (Durham, 1926), offers a fuller account.

[23] Crowl, *Maryland during and after the Revolution*, 42–60.

perhaps correctly, that North Carolina contained more Tories in proportion to her numbers than any other state.[24] If so, those of South Carolina and Georgia formed a proportion almost as large. When the British evacuated Charleston in 1783, about four thousand South Carolina loyalists departed with them, as has been mentioned, and South Carolinians who later asked the British government to compensate them for their losses were more numerous than those of any other state except New York.[25] Certainly, the loyalists south of the Dan River were bold, warlike, and determined. Even after the departure of Cornwallis for Virginia, they continued to struggle. In September, 1781, David Fanning led a band of them against Hillsboro, capturing Governor Thomas Burke. And Fanning and other Tories did not drop their weapons when they learned of Cornwallis' surrender. As late as the spring of 1782 Fanning's men took part in bitter and cruel partisan warfare in North Carolina, and other Tory detachments were similarly engaged in South Carolina and Georgia.

The North Carolina patriots early in the war sought to persuade the Tories of that state rather than to punish them, and many months after the battle of Moore's Creek Bridge promised pardon to all who would take an oath of allegiance. The offer was, however, accepted by few or none of the loyalists. Thereafter, the patriots resorted to the usual methods of coercion. In April, 1777, persons who refused to take the oath were ordered banished, and those who gave active support to the British were declared subject to imprisonment for the duration of the conflict and the loss of half of their property. Two years later the Assembly ordered

[24] Robert O. DeMond, *The Loyalists of North Carolina during the Revolution* (Durham, 1940), vii.

[25] Robert W. Barnwell, "The Loyalists of South Carolina, 1765–1785" (Ph.D. dissertation, Duke University, 1941), 405–10. Numbers of Tories and patriots cannot be accurately computed. The latter were doubtless more numerous in the Carolinas; they were certainly stronger in the field. It is significant that the large British forces sent into the area after 1779, with the aid of the Tories, were unable to make progress against the smaller American contingents sent there, helped by the local patriots. Certainly many in all three states were neutral, or nearly so; and many wavered from one side to the other. A special difficulty in estimating the number of loyalists arises from the fact that the patriots were apt to class neutrals with them.

the confiscation of the estates of sixty-eight named individuals who were conspicuous for wealth as well as Tory principles. There was then a disposition to deal harshly with the "imps of hell," as Griffith Rutherford described the loyalists. After the close of the war, sentiment among the patriots moderated, with men of the Conservative cast urging relaxation of punitive measures. In 1783 an act of pardon extended relief to many of the humbler, less active, and less obdurate Tories. Even they were often unable to secure return of their possessions. Sales of Tory properties went on until 1790. A recommendation from the Continental Congress, made in accordance with the peace treaty of 1783, that confiscation cease and restitution be made, was ignored. The conspicuous, the wealthy, the inveterate loyalists, together with those who had committed atrocities, were not forgiven.

The Georgia patriots were, in the end, slightly more generous than those of North Carolina. In 1778 they banished and declared forfeit the property of dozens of loyalists, among whom they included James Wright. In 1782, they condemned more Tories to the same punishments; others were fined 8 or 12 per cent of the value of their estates. A few loyalists who had fled the state were then authorized to return to it. In the following year, however, the list of the banished was shortened, and fines were substituted in several cases for confiscation. So furious against the supporters of Britain were many Georgians that Tories who sought to go back to their homes soon after the end of the war were mistreated and mobbed. Popular feeling gradually subsided, however, and the Assembly continued to reduce and remove the penalties inflicted upon the losers.

Nowhere was the problem of the treatment to be accorded the loyalists a more serious one than in South Carolina. The state was slow to act against them. Property was sequestered early in the war, but not forfeited. However, when the legislature met at Jacksonborough toward the end of 1781, with British troops still in Charleston, only a few miles away, John Rutledge urged confiscation. Gadsden, who had suffered as a British prisoner, urged instead forgiveness, but other patriots who had been imprisoned, whose fortunes had been diminished or destroyed, who had lost friends and relatives, supported Rutledge. One group of persons, British citizens and Tories who had zealously struggled for the crown, was both banished and deprived of property; another, composed of men who had accepted the protection of the British and had aided them financially, was fined.[26] As in Georgia, the end of the war brought a softening of feeling. The laws were not rigidly enforced, and were steadily relaxed for Tories who got on the "stool of repentance." In 1787 Lieutenant Governor Bull was given permission to return to his native country, though only after warm dispute.[27] But the giving of mercy was bitterly opposed by Radicals of Charleston and the Upcountry. Four Tories who dared to return to Charleston in 1783 were slain. One named Love who was accused of atrocities and who was legally acquitted at Ninety-Six because of a technicality was lynched in 1785. The Radicals of Charleston were especially opposed to the return of wealthy planters and merchants who had sided with the British. Composed principally of tradesmen and workmen, they found a leader in Isaac Peronneau. They hoped "to level the spirit of aristocracy," to destroy the power of the Low Country "nabobs." The return of the wealthy Tories would be a serious blow to them, for those loyalists would certainly ally themselves with the aristocrats among the patriots, with whom they shared ties of interest and blood. The Charleston Radicals wished to destroy the "family compact." [28] They were well organized in two societies which served as engines for propaganda and for action. They failed, however, to prevent the return of the loyalists, and they were unable to secure control of the Charleston city government.[29] Resorting to violence, they were equally unsuccessful.

[26] After the fall of Charleston many South Carolinians hitherto considered patriots announced their attachment to Britain, taking an oath of allegiance to the crown. It was difficult to deal with these persons, for their motives were diverse. Some did so to save their property and themselves, in the belief that the patriot cause was lost. One of these was Henry Middleton, formerly president of the Continental Congress. Others, like Charles Pinckney and Daniel Horry, apparently took the oath without reservation. The motives of Rawlins Lowndes, who also resumed British allegiance, cannot be surely ascertained. Barnwell, "Loyalists of South Carolina," 212–15, 232–34.

[27] Charleston *Morning Post and Daily Advertiser,* February 3, 7, 9, March 27, 1787.

[28] A reference to the family compact between the Bourbon rulers of France and Spain. See Lewis Morris to Greene, July 17, 1784, General Nathanael Greene Papers (William L. Clements Library).

[29] Nevins, *American States during and after the Revolution,* 397–403, offers a good brief account of the Peronneau movement, in which Commodore Alexander Gillon was for a time conspicuous.

Mobs of Radicals led by Peronneau paraded in the streets of the city during three successive nights in July, 1784. They were ultimately broken up by militia under William Washington, commissioned by the governor and his privy council to restore order.[30] Peronneau was knocked down and arrested.[31] By the end of that year the Low Country aristocracy was again firmly in the saddle.

The Tories, once so hated, are no longer assailed by American historians merely because they gave their devotion to the British empire. Much was said in the twentieth century about their travails and their distresses, about their loyalty, which led or forced tens of thousands of them into permanent exile in the West Indies, Canada, and the British Isles. Much was also made of the indignities and punishments heaped upon them by the patriots. Had the Tories triumphed with their British allies, the patriots would hardly have escaped harsh treatment. It is a striking fact that the only American legislature composed of Tories which met during the war, that of Georgia, in 1780 declared the patriots of that state guilty of treason and their property forfeit, at the same time asserting that 151 patriot leaders should be forever barred from public office.[32] In revolutions passions rise. It is perhaps remarkable that the patriots were so lenient,[33] especially in the South, where the loyalists fought bitterly and were guilty, with the patriots, of many atrocities. It is assuredly remarkable that the Tories who remained in or came back to the United States made no effort after 1783 toward resurrecting union with Britain, that they were quickly and completely lost among their neighbors.

[30] Minutes of South Carolina Privy Council, July 12, 1784, Journals of the Privy Council of South Carolina (South Carolina State Archives).

[31] William Washington to Greene, July 8, 1784; Nathaniel Pendleton to Greene, July 10, 1784, General Nathanael Greene Papers (William L. Clements Library).

[32] Jones, History of Georgia, II, 421-23.

[33] They were certainly generous to Andrew Williamson, whose defection had been a serious blow. Greene, Commodore Gillon, and Governor George Mathews pleaded for him. He was permitted to stay in South Carolina, despite the opposition of Pickens and Edward Rutledge. Even his estate was relieved of amercement at his death. Williamson to ———, June 24, 1782; Williamson to [Greene], December 22, 1782, Revolutionary Collection; Charleston Morning Post and Daily Advertiser, January 2, February 10, 1787. It is a striking fact that William Cunningham, a well-known Tory partisan leader, died in Charleston early in 1787. Ibid., January 30, 1787.

CHAPTER XVIII

THE SOUTHERN STATES:
SOCIAL FERMENT

MOVING unevenly and uncertainly during and immediately after the War of Independence toward political democracy, which definitely came into being in the United States, at least for white males a half century later, the patriots also undertook and carried through social reforms which were ultimately of paramount importance. To Radicals, Liberals, and Conservatives alike "the rights of mankind" for which they struggled against Britain were more than political, however differently they might interpret that beloved phrase. "There is a rage for all kinds of reformation," wrote Nathaniel Pendleton to Nathanael Greene from Charleston in 1784.[1] Pendleton might justly have made the same remark then and earlier at any of the state capitals. There was widespread among the Liberals and Radicals the belief that the Americans could build a new and better society, that America, "removed, spacious, composite, sound" was destined to lead the world toward a happier order. Even Conservatives who feared innovations in general were often in favor of specific social changes. In consequence schemes of all sorts were brought forth, some of them commonly adopted, for improving the lot of the American people, including even the Negro. Demands were made for codification of laws, for softening penalties imposed for crime, for prison reform, for the extirpation of hereditary privileges and titles, for the erasure of primogeniture and entail, for free public education, for free public libraries, for the destruction of the African slave trade, for the abolition of slavery itself—these along with campaigns for religious freedom, for other

[1] Pendleton to Greene, January 30, 1784, General Nathanael Greene Papers (William L. Clements Library).

329

personal rights, for a wider suffrage, for more truly representative government. Occupying the central place among the reformers was Jefferson, one of those extraordinary men of the eighteenth century

Whose sympathetic mind
Exults in all the good of all mankind.

Jefferson's statute of religious freedom, remarkable as it was, formed only one part of a vast program for improving his much loved Virginia. On October 12, 1776, he celebrated the anniversary of Columbus's appearance in the New World by bringing before the Assembly at Williamsburg two bills directed toward the making of a new Virginia. He saw that the change from dependence to independence and from monarchy to a republic offered a chance to secure new laws "friendly to liberty and the rights of mankind," and he clutched at it. One of these bills called for the abolition of entails, the other for the appointment of a committee to report upon revision and codification of the laws of the state. The second bill, by far the more important of the two, received ready assent, since the Assembly did not thereby pledge itself to action; and a committee consisting of George Wythe, George Mason, Edmund Pendleton, Thomas Ludwell Lee, and Jefferson himself was chosen.

Not so with the bill of the long-limbed gentleman from Albemarle to crop entails. In Europe the institutions of entail and primogeniture were twin props of aristocracy, and they threatened to serve the same function in America. Entail was sanctioned legally in all the states except South Carolina. It was therefore possible in Virginia, and elsewhere, for the owner of property to assure its continuance in the possession of his descendants. Entailed property could not be alienated by its owner, and usually passed from eldest son to eldest son. In Virginia slaves as well as land could be entailed. The stipulated heir was thus favored generation after generation at the expense of his kindred. What was far worse, entail tended to confine social position and power as well as wealth to one line of descent, and so to create and perpetuate a privileged class. Striking at entail, Jefferson was aiming a blow at a hallowed device of social injustice, and at the principle of aristocracy which

330

it supported. In Britain, where privilege was buttressed by law and by custom, a measure like that offered by Jefferson would have been hooted down in the House of Commons. Pendleton and others fought it in the Assembly at Williamsburg, but it quickly became law.

The "Committee of the Revisors" established at Jefferson's urging began its labors early in 1777. Mason and Lee soon dropped out of it on the ground that they lacked the legal knowledge necessary for its tasks. Two years later Jefferson, Wythe, and Pendleton presented their reforms to the Assembly in 126 bills. These were never passed as a whole, but 56 of them were substantially enacted within the seven years following. In the 56 were a revised criminal code and a law abolishing primogeniture, these being largely the work of Jefferson, together with his Statute of Religious Liberty.

The criminal code of Virginia at the beginning of the War of Independence was much like that of Britain, demanded harsh and savage punishments for many misdeeds, the death penalty even for stealing. Jefferson, supported by Pendleton and Wythe, urged that the courts take the lives only of traitors and murderers, including among the latter those who killed in duels and those who were twice guilty of manslaughter. They would have swept away a host of cruel and barbaric practices. As punishment for rape and buggery, however, they—Jefferson reluctantly—advised castration for males and nose-boring for females.[2] They also counseled the use of the *lex talionis* for maiming and disfiguring. For all other crimes they proposed as punishment, hard labor, the pillory, reparation to the injured, and fines. Long afterward Jefferson was amazed that he had once recommended the exaction of an eye for an eye and a tooth for a tooth. Greater cause for surprise lies in the fact that the changes proposed by the Revisors were as enlightened as they were. The Assembly eventually accepted most of the reforms pushed by the committee; horse steal-

[2] Nathan Schachner, *Thomas Jefferson* (New York, 1951), I, 150–151. Afterward Jefferson commented that excusable homicide, suicide, apostasy, and heresy were "to be pitied, not punished." Thomas Jefferson, *Notes on the State of Virginia*, ed. by William Peden (Chapel Hill, 1955), 145.

ing, however, a grievous crime during and after the war, continued to be a capital offense until 1786, when Jefferson persuaded the Assembly to lessen the penalty for it.[3]

The abolition of primogeniture must be considered, of course, as a companion measure with that destroying entail. In all the new states in 1776 law gave preference to the first born, especially to first-born sons, in distributing the real estate of persons who died without leaving a will. In the South and in New York the eldest son in such cases inherited all the lands of the parent; elsewhere, he received a double portion of such properties. The law sponsored by Jefferson, Wythe, and Pendleton [4] stipulated that the children were to share equally. It thus struck at the perpetuation of wealth, position, and power which the principle of primogeniture forced, perhaps against the wish of the deceased person. With laws compelling the equal distribution of land among the heirs of intestate persons and permitting free partition by will, the way was opened for a broader, a more general ownership of property, and hence ultimately for the creation of a less sharply stratified society and an evener division of political power. The new system, of course, permitted unequal division by will; and it did not positively prevent the perpetuation of wealth, position, and influence. Henceforth, for several generations, whether or not an estate remained intact depended largely upon the wisdom and the wishes of its possessors.[5]

[3] Williamsburg *Virginia Gazette* (Dixon and Nicolson), May 9, 1780, chronicles the execution of three men for that crime.

[4] In the discussions of the Revisors, Pendleton suggested that the eldest son ought to have a double share. Jefferson asked ironically whether the eldest son ate twice as much as his brothers and sisters, whether he worked twice as hard as they.

[5] The significance of the destruction of primogeniture and entail in Virginia, and elsewhere, was at one time too greatly enlarged. Recently scholars have pointed out that there were means before the Revolution of setting aside and of circumventing entails, and they have emphasized that primogeniture was not too serious an evil, because propertied persons who failed to make a will were in a minority. Jefferson's contribution has also been depreciated on the score that the changes were in the very air, that they were certain to come in America. See the careful analyses by Richard B. Morris, in "Primogeniture and Entailed Estates in America," *Columbia Law Review* (New York), XXVII (1927), 24–51; and in *Studies in the History of American Law* (New York, 1930), Chap. I; also Douglass, *Rebels and Democrats*, 300–303. For a more traditional account of the changes in Virginia, consult Dumas Malone, *Jefferson the Virginian* (Boston, 1948), 247–60. It should not be denied

Perhaps the most far-reaching of all the measures drawn by Jefferson was one which the Assembly refused to pass, the bill for the "more general diffusion of knowledge." Jefferson believed profoundly and ardently in the efficacy of education, and insisted that its benefits be more liberally spread. He urged that schools be established throughout the state to provide free instruction for all children in reading, writing, and arithmetic. The most gifted children of the poor were also to be given free tuition in grammar schools and at the College of William and Mary, the number of these being competitively and sharply diminished as they progressed upward—Jefferson was not at all ready to urge advanced education for the many at public expense. He also proposed wholesale alteration of the college. He would have placed it under the direction of "visitors" chosen by the Assembly and would have provided it with eight professors. The latter were to teach philosophy, history, political science, mathematics, languages, biology, anatomy, medicine, and the arts. Theology was to be dropped. Here were the basic elements of the modern state university.[6] The bill also called for the sending of a "missionary" to the Indians by the college faculty. He would have been not a spreader of the Gospel but an anthropologist. Further, Jefferson asked for the creation of a state library for public use. The bill encountered heavy opposition, partly from those who had a vested interest in the College of William and Mary, partly on the score of expense. Doubtless, Jefferson's scheme was also unpopular for many other reasons, because it ignored theology, because education was less loved by some than it was by him, because taxpayers would be forced to help pay for the education of their own and other children. The bill was defeated. Only at long last were its principal purposes achieved, one of them in the founding of the University of Virginia.[7]

---

that the changes brought social improvement, that they made possible far greater social advance, that Jefferson did supply leadership. That he did not solve all the legal and social problems arising from inheritance is hardly to his discredit.

[6] One "B.R." in the Williamsburg *Virginia Gazette* (Purdie and Dixon) urged as early as May 12, 1774, that William and Mary be turned into a university like Oxford and Cambridge. He said it could be done at a cost of only £5,000 per annum to the public.

[7] An event little noticed at the time was the founding of Phi Beta Kappa at

One far-reaching reform measure which Jefferson, Wythe, and Pendleton favored was not even presented to the Assembly, a bill for the gradual emancipation of the Negroes of the state. Jefferson was thoroughly convinced that slavery was a vicious institution and that it should be destroyed. He had vainly supported a similar bill offered by Richard Bland in the House of Burgesses in 1769.[8] He did not believe that the Negro was the equal of the white man in mental endowment, fancied he was so with respect to "memory," but not with regard to "reason" and "imagination." He acknowledged, however, that his opinion was based on little evidence and that he might be mistaken. In any case, the black man and the white were the same in the sight of the Creator, and the one was entitled to no privilege at the expense of the other. Moreover, slavery injured master as well as man and balefully affected society as a whole. Convinced that slavery must go, he also took the view that the Negroes must be deported as soon as freed, for he was certain that whites and blacks could not live side by side in equality and friendship. The differences between them were too sharp; and in any event, the Negroes would be unlikely to forget or forgive the wrongs they had suffered as slaves.[9]

The emancipation bill prepared by the Revisors, which provided for the freedom of all Negroes born after a fixed date and also for their deportation, was not introduced because it was certain to fail. While many prominent Virginians condemned Negro bondage and were disposed to put an end to it, majority opinion among the whites ran to the contrary. When Mason's Declaration of Rights was before the Virginia convention in 1776, it was bitterly opposed because of its assertions "That all men are by nature equally free and independent, and have certain inherent rights, of which they cannot, by any compact, deprive or divest their posterity; namely, the enjoyment of life and liberty. . . ." Members saw in those phrases a condemnation of slavery, perhaps even

William and Mary in 1776. For early records of the first chapter, see Edgar W. Knight (ed.), *A Documentary History of Education in the South before 1860* (Chapel Hill, 1949-1953), II, 242-59.

[8] Paul L. Ford (ed.), *The Writings of Thomas Jefferson* (New York, 1892-1899), I, 5.

[9] See Jefferson's fascinating analysis of the racial problem in Jefferson, *Notes on the State of Virginia*, ed. by Peden, 139-43. Jefferson's opinions are substantially declared therein, and they varied little throughout his life.

its legal outlawry, and came forward to defend it. They forced the inclusion of the words "when they enter into a state of society" after "which," thus depriving the Negroes of the rights secured for the whites—it was assumed that the blacks had not entered into "a state of society." It doubtless seemed prudent to the Revisors to withhold an unpopular measure which might strengthen opposition to other parts of the reform program.

If nothing could be done toward tearing up slavery by its roots, it was nevertheless possible to do something toward lessening its evils. Jefferson successfully urged that the Assembly prevent by law the further importation of slaves, even from other states. This proposal pleased the Assembly, appealing perhaps even on the score of economic interest, since it would tend to enhance the prices of slaves then held within the state. In 1782 the Assembly took another forward step, removing legal restrictions which had made it difficult for owners to free their slaves, thus encouraging manumission. Many planters took advantage of the opportunity, and thousands of slaves were freed, including those of Horatio Gates, for whom manumission was not inconvenient, since he had married a wealthy woman and was removing from Virginia to New York. Slavery then seemed on the road to gradual extinction in Virginia. It was not. The Assembly gave a very chilly reception three years later to Methodist and Baptist petitions calling for the abolition of slavery. Before long manumission was again discouraged by law.

Many of the reforms sponsored in Virginia by Jefferson, and others, were carried through in the Southern states generally, and outside them, including the erasure of primogeniture and entail. Both were outlawed by the first permanent Georgia constitution.[10] Entail was destroyed by the legislature of Maryland in 1783, and primogeniture by the same body three years later.[11] North Carolina abolished both institutions by law in 1784.[12] Entail was on the way to extinction in South Carolina even before the war, but primogeniture was still part of the established order. It perished

[10] Thorpe (ed.), *Federal and State Constitutions*, II, 784.

[11] Virgil Maxcy (ed.), *The Laws of Maryland* (Baltimore, 1811), I, 468; II, 16.

[12] Walter Clark (ed.), *The State Records of North Carolina* (Goldsboro, 1895–1905); XXIV, 572–77.

there in 1791,[13] the legislature putting an end to it as the result of an instruction placed in the state's constitution of the preceding year at the urging of Governor Charles Pinckney.

The patriots detested titles of nobility even more heartily than primogeniture and entail. Few native Americans had ever borne European titles, and the special American orders created by the proprietors of the Carolinas in the seventeenth century had vanished. There was relatively little desire for titles, even among the planters and wealthy merchants. They seemed "un-American." Accordingly, it was unlikely that they would soon appear. But some patriots wished to be certain for all future time that these sobriquets which so decisively exalted their possessors above the ruck of human beings in the Old World should be barred in the New. Accordingly, the Georgia constitution of 1777 denied the privileges of voting and officeholding to any person claiming a title; [14] and that of Maryland of 1776 declared that "no title of nobility, or hereditary honours, ought to be granted in this State." [15] The North Carolina Revolutionary instrument asserted that "no hereditary emoluments, privileges or honors ought to be granted or conferred in this State." [16] Other states would doubtless have inserted preventive provisions, had it seemed necessary. It did not seem so because the Articles of Confederation contained a general prohibition, forbidding the acceptance of foreign titles by state and Federal officeholders and denying to both the states and the central government the right to establish American ones.[17] Moreover, the Federal Constitution of 1787 contained similar prohibitions, except that a Federal officeholder was permitted to receive a foreign title with the special consent of Congress.[18] So strong was the feeling against hereditary honors that Congress refused when passing a law affecting the Baron von

[13] Thomas Cooper and David J. McCord (eds.), *Statutes at Large of South Carolina* (Columbia, 1836–1841), V, 162.

[14] Thorpe (ed.), *Federal and State Constitutions*, II, 780.

[15] *Ibid.*, III, 1690.　　　　　　　　[16] *Ibid.*, V, 2788.

[17] Art. VI, sec. 1. Jefferson tried to insert a clause forbidding the use of titles in the Land Ordinance of 1784, but the Continental Congress thought it superfluous.

[18] Art. I, secs. 9, 10. Apparently state officials were not granted the same privilege. In ratifying the Constitution, Massachusetts and New Hampshire vainly urged an amendment withdrawing it from Federal officers.

THOMAS JEFFERSON by Charles Willson Peale. Courtesy of Independence National Historical Park, Philadelphia

Steuben in 1790 to give him his title, "for we hold it that no man in our land shall have a title, since the president has none." [19] The Congress was all the more justified in that Steuben's "Baron" and "von" were his own creations. After 1795, following an amusing debate in which New England Federalists, who were less averse to titles than others, spoke slightingly of them and Republicans, who were much opposed to them, stressed their importance, Congress also demanded that aliens abandon titles upon becoming American citizens.

Hereditary honors were so disliked that even the Order of the Cincinnati was vigorously attacked, although its members were pledged "to preserve inviolate those exalted rights and liberties of human nature for which they had fought and bled." It was suspect because membership was confined to officers and was inherited by the eldest son in each generation. Judge Aedanus Burke of South Carolina vehemently assailed it on the grounds that it was an incipient order of nobility, that it placed the military above the civil, that it sanctioned the vicious principle of primogeniture.[20] The fears voiced by Burke and shared by Jefferson, John Adams, and New England legislatures, proved to be unfounded, for the order failed to flourish.[21] Less exclusive societies ultimately appeared in America, the Daughters of the American Revolution, the Benevolent and Protective Order of Elks, Phi Beta Kappa, the Independent Order of Odd Fellows, Rotary International, the Royal Order of Lady Bugs, the Mystic Knights of the Sea, and others, in astonishing variety and abundance. The offices and honors derived from these have doubtless served to a degree as harmless substitutes for those of the European caste system.

Had there been as a result of the American Revolution a vast

---

[19] Clark (ed.), *State Records of North Carolina*, XXII, 798.

[20] The King of Sweden forbade Swedish officers in French service who were eligible for membership to join the Cincinnati because it was *republican*. Fitzpatrick (ed.), *Writings of George Washington*, XXVII, 458.

[21] Washington asked Jefferson's opinion of the order, and Jefferson urged that it be remodeled. In accordance with his advice Washington pushed for amendments, one of them discarding the hereditary feature, which was not uniformly adopted. Some of the state chapters continued to permit membership by birth. Boyd *et al.* (eds.), *Papers of Thomas Jefferson*, VII, 105–10.

economic leveling, it would be entirely appropriate to use the label of Internal Revolution. No such leveling occurred. There was neither general expropriation nor general partition of land. The patriots, including many men of wealth, largely retained their property, with some profiting from the conflict and others losing. Redistribution did come, as the result of the seizure and sale of the lands of the Tories, in Southern as well as in Northern states. Tenants, farmers, and artisans bought them, often with depreciated currency, and in consequence moved upward in terms of wealth, social status, and political power, while Tory aristocrats were reduced and exiled. The effects were doubtless substantial, but should not be overstressed. Most loyalists were not aristocrats; many of them did not lose their property; and the purchasers of that which was seized included rich as well as poor patriots. Ownership of land shifted, but only moderately, and without far-reaching consequences.[22] It is possible that the humbler Americans ultimately found it easier as a result of the Revolution to obtain land in the West. Such was probably not the case immediately. The speculators in Western lands, favored during the colonial period at the expense of the homestead settlers, continued to hold advantage over them under Federal law until 1820; and the Ohio and Yazoo companies differed in no essential way from the Loyal and Indiana companies. It may be, however, that the later generosity of government to the American homesteader was to a degree brought about by the separation from Britain. It may also be that there was economic leveling as the result of the disappearance of the British bounty upon indigo. Without that bounty the Low Country aristocracy could no longer profitably produce it, and that aristocracy was deprived of one of its sources of revenue before 1800. But the loss was hardly fatal to that aristocracy; and indigo-growing probably would not have long continued to be important in any event. On the whole, economic shift was limited, in the South and elsewhere.

Joining Virginia in the general attack upon hereditary wealth, privilege, and power, the other Southern states failed to follow her lead immediately in improving their criminal codes. There

[22] Close and fruitful studies of the seizure and sale of Tory property in the South have not been made, perhaps cannot be.

were few men like Jefferson, combining legal knowledge, zeal for reform, political acumen, and aggressiveness. The lower house in Maryland proposed in 1778 that a thorough revision be undertaken, but the senate merely consented to a study of the matter, which was then forgotten in the press of war business. A similar project was pushed in the South Carolina Assembly early in 1784,[23] and a committee of three, Aedanus Burke, Henry Pendleton, and John F. Grimké, was appointed in the following year to prepare a draft of a new code. It completed its task. Its product did not, however, please the legislature.[24] Criminal codes, except in Virginia, therefore tended to retain their severities, cruelties, and injustices for several generations. Mutilation, branding, whipping, ducking, and pillorying remained in vogue in North Carolina well into the nineteenth century, and twenty-eight offenses continued to be capital. In that state imprisonment of women for debt was not ended until 1823, and the branding and whipping of females was not outlawed until 1855. As late as 1829 a former governor died in prison while confined for debt.[25]

Lagging behind Virginia in reform of criminal codes, the other Southern states hardly surpassed her in educational advance. There were within them, as there were throughout the union, men who urged the necessity of spreading the benefits of education, many of them pushing for its public support, and even for public schools, academies, and universities. Leaders of the Revolutionary generation, Madison, John Jay, George Clinton, and John Adams, along with Jefferson, contended that popular education was indispensable to good government in a republic. In his "Defense of the Constitutions," written in 1786–1787, Adams declared that the instruction of the American people in their moral, civil, and political duties "ought to be the care of the public, and of all who have any share in the conduct of its affairs, in a manner that never yet has been practised in any age or nation." [26] Almost simultaneously Dr. Benjamin Rush was counseling national sup-

[23] Nathaniel Pendleton to Greene, February 3, 1784, General Nathanael Greene Papers (William L. Clements Library).

[24] Robert H. Woody, "The Public Records of South Carolina," *American Archivist* (Menasha, Cedar Rapids), II (1939), 262.

[25] Lefler and Newsome, *North Carolina*, 353–54.

[26] Adams (ed.), *Works of John Adams*, VI, 168.

port for institutions of advanced learning.[27] Public money was lacking, however, to put into practice such large and liberal views; and the enlightened vision of such leaders was not always shared by others. Private and denominational instruction continued to be the vogue in the South for some years, and the war seriously interfered with learning of all kinds, except mastery of the arts of straight shooting and skillful bayoneting. Nevertheless, the foundations of the public schools and the state universities and the outlines of their structures appeared, at least in blueprint, not only in Virginia, but in the other Southern states. Moreover, instruction in private institutions, especially beyond the grammar school, continued and, when the travail of the war had ended, increased.

When the War of Independence began, Maryland already had on paper one public school in each of her twelve counties; some of these were functioning, others were dormant. No change occurred in that system for some years. However, three colleges appeared soon after the close of hostilities. Much fruitless planning for one went on in the colonial period. In 1782 the legislature finally acted, offering an annual grant to Washington College, which was established at Chester on the Eastern Shore in that year. It then became necessary to provide a like institution with similar support west of the Chesapeake—to assuage sectional jealousy, if for no other reason—and St. John's College was founded at Annapolis three years later. The two were then linked in a "University of Maryland," a handsome description of the sister schools,

[27] Jefferson shared with others a dislike of the practice of sending young American males abroad for their schooling. An American learned in Europe, the Virginian said in 1785, to abhor the "lovely equality" of his own country, and to favor aristocracy and monarchy. Moreover, he was led "by the strongest of all the human passions, into a spirit for female intrigue destructive of his own and others happiness, or a passion for whores destructive of his health, and in both cases learns to consider fidelity to the marriage bed as an ungentlemanly practice and inconsistent with happiness." Boyd *et al.* (eds.), *Papers of Thomas Jefferson*, VIII, 636–37. The legislature of Georgia seems to have agreed heartily with Jefferson. That same year it deprived any Georgian who went abroad before the age of sixteen for his education of the right to hold civil or military office in the state for at least three years after his return. Candler (ed.), *Colonial Records of the State of Georgia*, XIX, Pt. II, 378.

which did not long flourish. Within a generation public funds were withdrawn, and the "University of Maryland" collapsed. Decades passed before the modern university with the same name appeared. Even more short-lived was Cokesbury College, established in 1784 by the Methodists for the education of their youth. Its building burned soon after it was erected, and the project, always a dubious one in the eyes of Bishop Francis Asbury, for whom the college was named in part, was abandoned. Educational advance in Maryland was more a matter of schemes than of students.

And so it was in South Carolina. Both private and publicly supported schools appeared early in the Low Country, and there were about two dozen of these in operation at the time of the Revolution. These, however, were insufficient for the needs of the public; and there was no provision for higher learning in the state until 1785. It will be recalled that Lieutenant Governor Bull's bill for creating a college at Charleston, and also for increasing the number of free schools, failed in the Commons House in 1770. But private gifts for the college accumulated. Despite economic troubles the state legislature in 1785 determined that higher education must be made more readily available in the state, and created three new colleges, at Charleston, Winnsboro, and Cambridge, and two more within the next twelve years. These were to be financed in part by the funds saved since 1770. Only two of them, however, opened their doors, the one at Winnsboro, which evolved into a training school, the other at Charleston, which ultimately became the municipally supported College of Charleston and which thrives in the twentieth century. But instruction even at the Charleston institution was long chiefly at the elementary and secondary levels. The University of South Carolina and the religious colleges of the state were not founded until after the turn of the century, and students desiring sound advanced instruction continued for many years to go outside the state for it. Nor did it become generally easy even to obtain a good elementary education, for the legislature was not disposed to spend money for it. "We see," declared a citizen in the Charleston *Courier* in 1803, "great incomes made and great incomes wasted, great grandeur in equipage and household circumstances . . . but we do not see the country studded up and down with those precious jewels of a state, *free schools.*" [28]

The small state of Georgia made a better record than her richer neighbor across the Savannah, although plans ran far ahead of achievements there as elsewhere in the South. A magnificent program inserted in the Georgia constitution of 1777 declaring that "Schools shall be erected in each county, and supported at the general expense of the State, as the legislature shall hereafter point out," [29] was hardly executed. However, in 1783 the legislature, pushed on by Governor Lyman Hall, empowered the governor to endow a free school in every county with a thousand acres of public land, and provided for a school at Washington and academies at Waynesborough and Augusta; and five years later that body supplied funds for academies at Savannah and Sunbury. Unfortunately, there was strong opposition against provision for free elementary education, except for the children of the poor; and Georgia during several generations compelled her children either to secure it privately or suffer the stigma of receiving public charity. The academies at Augusta and Sunbury flourished and performed splendid service. In the winter of 1784–1785 the legislature also laid the foundations for the University of Georgia. Urged to act by Abraham Baldwin, a Yale graduate, the Assembly reserved forty thousand acres of frontier land for its endowment, and then formally chartered it. It was to be operated by a *Senatus Academicus,* which was also to control all schools in the state receiving public funds. The members of this board were to exclude no one from the benefits either of the university or of the other schools because of religion. Unfortunately, the forty thousand acres of land given to the university could not profitably be sold until the eighteenth century had ended, and it remained without professors, students, and buildings. The *Senatus Academicus* did not even meet until fourteen years had passed. In 1801 the university opened modestly in the form of Franklin College.

[28] Colyer Meriwether, *History of Higher Education in South Carolina with a Sketch of the Free School System* (Washington, 1889), 111.
[29] Thorpe (ed.), *Federal and State Constitutions,* II, 784.

For more than a generation before the War of Independence there was agitation in North Carolina for schools supported by the public. Nothing, however, was achieved. In 1754 the Assembly voted £6,000 "for founding and endowing a public school," but the money was soon permanently borrowed for military uses. Seventeen years later the Assembly passed an act to incorporate Queen's College in Mecklenburg County, to be financed in part by a tax on rum brought into the county. The college was opened, but the law was disallowed in England, and the result was a private academy at Charlotte, which became "Liberty Hall" in 1777 and vanished in 1780. Private teaching was inadequate, and the patriots took up the cudgel for public action. The legislature was ordered to act by the constitution of 1776, which declared "That a school or schools shall be established by the Legislature, for the convenient instruction of youth, with such salaries to the masters, paid by the public, as may enable them to instruct at low prices; and all useful learning shall be duly encouraged, and promoted, in one or more universities." [30] These phrases, however, called only for public assistance to private institutions, and the state made no effort to organize public schools for many years. Instead, it merely gave moral support to many academies which sprang up immediately after the war, offering exemption from taxes and militia duty to male teachers. Nevertheless, the legislature did take one long forward step, chartering the University of North Carolina in 1789. It received no cash, but a loan of $10,000 from the state, later converted into a gift, made it possible to welcome students at Chapel Hill six years later. Thereafter the university received no public funds for almost fifty years, but it continued to exist. It was thus the first state university in the South to begin continuous operation, and it ultimately became as well the most distinguished one in the South.

The steps taken by the Southern states toward using public money to remove intellectual bondage were short and uncertain, and it is conceivable that illiteracy was as common throughout the region in 1825 as it was fifty years earlier. Even less progress was made toward destroying the physical bondage of the Negroes. The institution of slavery was condemned not only by Jefferson,

[30] *Ibid.*, V, 2794.

343

Mason, and Edmund Pendleton but by virtually all the great Virginians of the Revolutionary time, including Washington, Patrick Henry, Richard Henry Lee, and Madison. It was also denounced by Marylanders, among them Charles Carroll of Carrollton and Samuel Chase, and by James Iredell in North Carolina. It is well known that in 1776 and afterward Henry and John Laurens expressed hatred of it and were willing to make great personal financial sacrifices to help put an end to it. Citizens of Darien in Georgia in 1775, moved by "a general philanthropy for All Mankind," declared their abhorrence "of the unnatural practice of Slavery in *America* . . . a practice founded in injustice and cruelty, and highly dangerous to our liberties, (as well as lives,) debasing part of our fellow-creatures below men, and corrupting the virtue and morals of the rest." [31] But sentiment in the Southern states supporting slavery was so powerful that legislation to abolish it was introduced in only one of their legislatures, that of Maryland. Nor was manumission readily permitted except in Maryland, and in Virginia for a few years after 1782. Between 1785 and 1791 various bills to provide for the gradual abolition of slavery were introduced in the Maryland legislature. They were supported by Carroll of Carrollton and William Pinkney, but were uniformly defeated. A bill to make it easier for Maryland owners to free their slaves, although it was eloquently supported by Pinkney, was lost in 1788, but another to the same purpose was passed two years later.[32] Manumission was common in the state, and Maryland's slave population actually diminished between 1790 and 1860. However, the bill pushed by Pinkney would have had no chance whatever in the assemblies of the Carolinas and Georgia. In only one other legislature did Southerners demand abolition of slavery—the Continental Congress—and then only with respect to the Old Northwest, where Negro bondage did not yet exist. Below the Mason-Dixon line slavery continued to receive legal protection rather than injury.

[31] Force (comp.), *American Archives*, 4th ser., I, 1136.

[32] Jeffrey R. Brackett, *The Negro in Maryland* (Baltimore, 1889), 52–54, 151–52. In the *Maryland Journal and Baltimore Advertiser*, March 31, 1789, "Benevolus" applauded a master who had freed seventy-five slaves and asked, "Why has the pride of American youth been immolated on the altar of Liberty, if all her sons are not to taste her blessings?"

Had there been few Negroes owned in the South, abolition of slavery in that region would doubtless have proceeded promptly. Throughout the Northern states, where Negroes were comparatively uncommon, the institution was either dead or dying thirty years after the patriots took up arms in defense of the rights of mankind. It was not difficult for legislatures and courts north of the Mason-Dixon boundary to extinguish slavery by law and by constitutional interpretation, for there could be as a result little economic loss and, for the time at least, no harassing problems of relations between whites and masses of free Negroes. It was otherwise south of the Susquehanna, where slaves were numerous, forming in some counties of Virginia and the Carolinas the bulk of the population. While it could be contended that slave labor was in the long run unprofitable [33]—the argument would certainly have been contested in the realm of the rice swamps and indigo fields—it was obvious that too-rapid emancipation, which was inevitably feared, would be a serious financial blow to the owners. A far greater obstacle to abolition was dread of a future in which the Negroes would be free, burdensome, aggressive, and even vengeful. Hence, Jefferson, and much later Abraham Lincoln, coupled colonization with emancipation. Since mass deporting of the Negroes was seemingly impossible, many Southerners preferred to keep them in chains, vicious though the effects might be both for Negroes and for whites, rather than face the uncertainties and difficulties of a society in which the two races would live in freedom and intimacy. These barriers against action, reinforced by a general belief among the whites in their own superiority, made abolition almost unthinkable in the far South, in those areas where the Negroes were most numerous.

The Southerners did not, however, object to the extinction of slavery in the Northern states. When Jefferson tried to insert in the Land Ordinance of 1784 a statement forbidding slavery and involuntary servitude after 1800 everywhere in the Federal regions beyond the Alleghenies, other Southern members of the Continental Congress came forward to oppose him. He was unable

[33] See the interesting comment upon the value of Negro labor by Philip Fithian in Hunter D. Farish (ed.), *Journal & Letters of Philip Vickers Fithian, 1773–1774* (Williamsburg, 1943), 23.

to carry with him the Virginia delegation, and that of North Carolina divided on the issue, with those of South Carolina and Maryland voting against his measure. Had one Southern delegation voted favorably, it would have been enacted. It was instead lost. However, when men from the Northern states urged that slavery and involuntary servitude be barred in the Old Northwest by the great Ordinance of 1787, every Southerner in Congress agreed. It was said that they did so "for the purpose of preventing tobacco and indigo from being made on the northwest side of the Ohio, as well as for several other political reasons." [34] In any case, they were not disposed to demand that slavery be permitted to spread into that region, even in principle.

Sentiment against the oceanic slave trade was far more powerful in the South than feeling against slavery itself, and its eradication helped to solve problems rather than to substitute new ones for old. Its destruction was actually profitable to some slaveowners. It was therefore possible to strike at it, and every Southern state except Georgia did so before 1789. The notorious brutalities of the oceanic trade shocked the sensibilities of all merciful whites. Moreover, the destruction of the overseas traffic would limit the growth of the Negro population and stimulate white immigration, thus making it easier to deal with racial difficulties, including slavery. Those whites who owned Negroes might even derive an immediate profit because prices of slaves would tend to advance as they became more difficult to obtain. Virginians and Marylanders were especially in a position to gain, because their slaves were increasingly less valuable in the fields. Were the oceanic trade stopped, they could hope to sell their Negroes into the far South at better prices.

The maritime traffic in slaves was under attack in the Southern colonies and others long before the outbreak of the War of Independence. The Virginia Assembly tried on several occasions during the decade prior to the war to put an end to the importation of slaves into Virginia by imposing a prohibitive duty, but was unsuccessful because the crown, partly at the urging of British slave traders, disallowed such taxes; and South Carolina, prin-

[34] Andrew C. McLaughlin, *The Confederation and the Constitution, 1783–1789* (New York, 1905), 116–26.

cipally because her people were alarmed by the vast increase of Negroes in the Low Country, successfully used the same weapon during the periods 1740–1751 and 1766–1768.[35] Maryland also employed it after 1771 by putting a duty of at least £8 per head upon every slave brought into that colony. Heavier blows against the traffic were struck, however, by the Southern nonimportation agreements of 1769–1770, and by the Continental Association, which brought the commerce to a complete halt. Although Jefferson deleted from the Declaration of Independence his denunciation of Britain as the promoter of the slave trade from a desire to avoid displeasing South Carolinians [36] and Georgians, and New Englanders, the Continental Congress had already urged that the boycott upon the importation of slaves be continued, voting on April 6, 1776, that "no slaves be imported into any of the thirteen United Colonies." [37] The trade did not revive during the war, the war itself making Congressional fiat and state action superfluous.[38]

The states did not wait, however, until the end of the war to act. Delaware led the way with a positive prohibition in 1776, and her example was rapidly followed by the Northern states, with those of New England a decade later forbidding their citizens even to participate in the trade. Virginia, of course, was the first state in the South to act. Maryland permanently barred the traffic in 1783. Below the Dan River adverse legislation came less rapidly, but North Carolina imposed a prohibitive duty three years later. The slave population had greatly diminished during the war in South Carolina and Georgia, and planters in those

---

[35] Motivation in South Carolina was partly economic. McCrady, *South Carolina under the Royal Government*, 377–81; Elizabeth Donnan (ed.), *Documents Illustrative of the History of the Slave Trade to America* (Washington, 1930–1935), IV, 400–402. Said merchant Josiah Smith, Jr., in 1774, commenting on the arrival of many slaves at Charleston, "I should be heartily glad that an everlasting stop was put to the future importation of such into any part of America, and then many a poor white person could have room to get employment, which is not the case at present in Carolina." Smith to Poyas, January 25, 1774, Letterbook of Josiah Smith, Jr.

[36] Jefferson's explanatory statement is incorrect in that he asserts South Carolina "had never attempted to restrain the importation of slaves."

[37] *Journals of the Continental Congress*, IV, 258.

[38] W. E. Burghardt Du Bois, *The Suppression of the African Slave-Trade to the United States of America, 1638–1870* (New York, 1954), 47–48.

states eagerly demanded imported Negroes, offering high prices. Charleston and Savannah again became centers of the traffic, but even in the far South it continued to be a hateful business. In 1793 Georgia restricted the oceanic trade; five years later it was positively forbidden there by constitutional provision. The Southern states, unfortunately, did not unanimously and permanently bar the ugly traffic. South Carolina prevented it by law during the years 1787–1804. Then, however, the door was reopened to slaves from Africa, though not from the West Indies. It was soon closed again by the Federal prohibition act of 1807.

Had human slavery in the United States disappeared promptly as a result of the social ferment which was stimulated by the Anglo-American conflict, it would indeed be proper to think in terms of an Internal Revolution. As it was, there was insufficient political, economic, and social change during the quarter century after the onset of that struggle in 1763 to justify the use of the name. Further shifts came later, and it may be appropriate to ponder over a continuing revolution which began in 1607 and which moved more rapidly during that period than it did in earlier and later eras.

CHAPTER XIX

THE SOUTHWEST AGAIN

WHEN historian John Fiske came to choose a title for his history of the United States from the peace with Britain to the inauguration of President Washington, he hit upon *The Critical Period of American History*, an extraordinary phrase. Impressed by postwar economic difficulties and the weakness of the American central government, he saw the United States emerge from a morass and find solid and almost sacred ground when the Federal Constitution of 1787 was ratified and put into use. It is evident enough that the decade of the 1780's was less filled with peril for the Americans than other periods, including that of the War of Independence. What he took for symptoms of raging disease were often merely the chicken pox and growing pains. The union was sinking, to stronger foundation; and the American people were building mightily in the eastern valley of the Mississippi. The door was opening for the occupation of the Old Northwest, which began with the founding of Marietta in 1788. Even more remarkable in the years immediately after the Peace of Paris was expansion south of the Ohio, which soon led to the creation of two new states beyond the Alleghenies. Kentucky and Tennessee were not states when Washington assumed the presidency, but the United States were then solidly planted in the fertile Bluegrass country and the valleys of the Tennessee and Cumberland rivers.

Kentucky and Tennessee were settled by Southerners who brought with them Negro slavery and the plantation, and they became part of a larger and more heterogeneous South. But the Old Northwest did not become Southern, although Virginians and Carolinians in large numbers eventually found new homes north of the Ohio. The region was ill suited to the production of indigo, rice, and tobacco—and cotton—and to slavery and the plantation. It is doubtful in any case that the Old Northwest could have become Southern. Certainly Virginia cut one important tie between the South and the Old Northwest in 1783 when she definitely abandoned her claim to the lands north of the Ohio and urged that new states be founded upon them. Another measure which tended to separate the region from the South was, of course, that part of the Northwest Ordinance which forbade slavery north of the river.

The settlements of Virginia expanded remarkably after 1783, despite cession of her claim to the Old Northwest, despite an agreement of 1779 whereby she ceded her pretensions to Pittsburgh and adjacent areas to Pennsylvania. Even before the end of the war migration westward by way of the Ohio, the Wilderness Road, and other routes was impressive; soon it became almost astonishing. Settlers poured into what is now West Virginia by thousands, rapidly forming farms and plantations on the south bank of the Ohio and in the Kanawha and Big Sandy valleys. By 1790 there were in the area as many as 55,000 persons. Even more startling was the growth of Kentucky. Boats and flatboats on the Ohio, horses, pack horses, and human foot power on the overland trails carried men, women, children, Negro slaves, and goods into the Bluegrass, an Eden almost too fertile for raising corn. Swarming through Cumberland Gap and streaming down the Ohio, Virginians, Marylanders, and North Carolinians swept into the Dark and Bloody Ground in almost unbelievable numbers to find new Kentucky homes. By 1790 Kentucky contained 73,000 inhabitants, of whom 12,000 were slaves.

On a smaller scale the story is the same for North Carolina and her Tennessee country. North Carolina powerfully stimulated westward emigration by a law of 1780 and others of 1782 and 1783 which gave vast quantities of land beyond the Appalachians to her soldiers, and Virginians continued to enter Tennessee from the northeast. The settlements on the Holston and Watauga spread into the valley of the French Broad, and the Cumberland River communities also increased and widened. By 1790 there were about 28,000 pioneers in East Tennessee and perhaps as many as

7,000 in Nashville and its vicinity. The influx might have been far greater, had it not been that the Cumberland colonies remained isolated and attainable only by journey through Indian country. A more formidable barrier to the rapid occupation of Tennessee was the hostility of the red men.

As usual, land speculators were extremely active in the 1780's, in Kentucky, Tennessee, and the region south of the Ohio generally; and as usual some of them coveted and sought to secure lands far beyond white settlements. Those of North Carolina were bold and enterprising, and were sometimes extraordinarily successful, although their best-known project was a failure. In 1782 William Blount, Richard Caswell, Joseph Martin, and Colonel John Donelson formed a company to secure the lands between the southern boundary of Tennessee and the Great Bend of the Tennessee River. Taking in Griffith Rutherford, John Sevier, and others, they purchased the region from some Cherokee in the fall of the following year. Early in 1784, since Georgia claimed the area, Blount persuaded the Assembly of that state to establish it as the County of Houston and to organize a government for it in which members of the company were the conspicuous officials. Because South Carolina also had pretensions to control over the region, Wade Hampton and other South Carolinians were brought into the company to ward off hostile action from that state. But the scheme languished, and the company ultimately collapsed, after Sevier had vainly tried to secure Spanish support for it. Other North Carolina ventures of the 1780's, including one of James Robertson to colonize the area about modern Memphis and one of Joseph Martin to establish a colony on the Tombigbee River in what is now Alabama, also failed. Robertson went so far as to put surveyors to work, but they found Chickasaw in their sights. The Chickasaw drove them off.[1]

[1] The activities of the speculators of the Southern states in the 1780's are well described in Arthur P. Whitaker, *The Spanish-American Frontier, 1783–1795* . . . (Boston, 1927), Chaps. IV, VII–IX. Professor Whitaker's valuable study deals with all the involved problems raised by American southwestward advance, Indian resistance, and the conflicting interests of the United States and Spain. The writer has made extensive use of it in this chapter. Thomas P. Abernethy, *From Frontier to Plantation in Tennessee* (Chapel Hill, 1932), Chaps. III–XI, offers much useful material and comment upon the pioneers, speculators, and postwar development of Tennessee.

The westward advance of South Carolina after 1783 was steady and unspectacular, for the Cherokee had been rather effectively driven from her territories east of the mountains.[2] That advance was limited by the Appalachians, since the state could claim only a very narrow strip of land between the mountains and the Mississippi. Indeed, South Carolina did not actually own any territory beyond the divide.[3] Accordingly, except for the region east of the mountains, South Carolina speculators were compelled to seek support for their projects outside South Carolina, to associate themselves with those of other states. They ultimately became extremely active at the capital of Georgia.

Georgia settlements did not move rapidly westward immediately after the war, although pioneers pushed forward to and across the Oconee and Ocmulgee rivers. However, Georgia contained an ample supply of speculators of her own, and was hospitable to South Carolinians and others who sought her favor and assistance. She was generous to the Muscle Shoals Company, and was kind to people who wished to speculate in lands on the lower Mississippi. In 1785 Georgia created by act of Assembly Bourbon County, which included Natchez and all the district along the great river between the thirty-first parallel and the mouth of the Yazoo. Organized government in the area would be useful, of course, to dealers in and settlers on lands in the new county. So eager to assert sovereignty and to please expansionists were the Georgia lawmakers that they treated as a minor matter the fact that the area had been conquered by and contained Spanish troops, set aside Spanish ownership, and ignored a claim to authority in it of the United States. The legislature sent four commissioners to establish the new régime, enjoining them, however, to commit no act of hostility against Spain. Two of them, en route overland, seized the opportunity to urge the Choctaw and Chickasaw tribes to resume trading with Georgians, and rumors began

[2] In 1786 South Carolina pioneers were expanding their holdings at the expense of the Catawbas. The procedure was to give an old horse or saddle to a warrior as "rent" for a tract of land. Joseph Kershaw to William Moultrie, February 24, 1786, General Nathanael Greene Papers (William L. Clements Library).

[3] Robert S. Cotterill, "The South Carolina Land Cession," in *Mississippi Valley Historical Review*, XII (1925–1926), 376–84.

to fly to the effect that they intended to use force, if necessary, to execute their mission, that George Rogers Clark and backwoods riflemen from Kentucky and Tennessee would come down the Mississippi to support them. At Natchez the Georgia emissaries demanded that "Bourbon County" be abandoned to them; and one of them threatened violence if the Spanish refused to surrender it. Esteban Miró, governor of Louisiana and West Florida at the time, must have been somewhat astonished by their highhandedness and their braggadocio, since Georgia's pretensions were so dubious and since the commissioners had no troops at hand. He did not act hastily, but put the matter before his superiors and assessed opinion among the occupants of the region, chiefly former loyalists. He was instructed to expel the intruders; the loyalists promised to help him in case of need; and he did so. Georgia was not prepared to resent the insult and easily denied responsibility for the acts of her agents. They had disobeyed her instructions. Nor was the Continental Congress disposed to complain.

But the Bourbon County fiasco was only the beginning of Georgia's attempts to help speculators occupy the eastern shore of the lower Mississippi. After 1787 James Wilkinson, Patrick Henry, John Sevier, Isaac Huger, and many other Americans, casting covetous eyes upon the region, sought to obtain lands in it with the help of both Georgia and Spain. The Georgia legislature assisted them generously. In 1789 it sold a strip of land in what is now northwest Mississippi to a Virginia company, another district running to the southward from the first as far as the mouth of the Yazoo to a South Carolina Yazoo company, and in addition the Muscle Shoals area to a Tennessee company, altogether about fifteen million acres. The price was low, and it was to be paid in cheap paper. Nathaniel Pendleton, a former Continental officer from Virginia who had settled in Savannah and who observed the transaction, commenting that "corruption pervades every public department," asserted that the lawmakers had sold the lands to "a parcel of jobbers" with whom "it would have disgraced a man of character to have had dealings." The price was three farthings per acre "in a species of our depreciated paper money and securities that reduces it to a fraction that wants a name." [4] Six years later, after wholesale bribery, another Georgia legislature was again to sell lands on the Mississippi.

The swift expansion of settlements south of the Ohio and the schemes of the speculators inevitably stimulated hostile passions among the Indians, especially the Creeks and Chickamaugas. The red men must have been alarmed in any case by the advance of the pioneers. Because North Carolina, Georgia, and even the State of Franklin, during its brief existence after 1784, hastened occupation and encouraged speculation, giving little heed to Indian protests, that advance was more rapid and less orderly than it might have been; and the resentment of the tribesmen was correspondingly increased. There was little concern at the Southern state capitals about the sad fate of the Indian, and not much more about his wounded feelings, even though the sense of injury sustained was likely to take him to the warpath. Only in Congress was there powerful sentiment for making and keeping peace with the warriors of the woods.

The Congress, in truth, assumed during and immediately after the War of Independence the role formerly played by the British crown in Indian affairs. Toward preventing border wars, it began to send agents to the Indians, to hold conferences, to offer presents, to make treaties, to negotiate boundary lines. Before long, in fact, Congress was also to undertake the regulation of their trade. By a law of 1786 it provided for two Indian superintendents, one Northern and one Southern, with jurisdictions and powers much like those formerly granted to Sir William Johnson and John Stuart. And Congress, using the same weapons as the crown, faced the same fundamental difficulties encountered by British officials and had no better fortune in dealing with them than they had. While the authority over Indian affairs of Congress under the Articles of Confederation seemed to be handsomely stated, it was limited by the legislative authority of the states; and in practice the states, and individuals, both white and red, were able to defy it. [5]

[4] Pendleton to Mrs. Catharine Greene, December 30, 1789, General Nathanael Greene Papers (William L. Clements Library).

[5] How Congress sank into the shoes of the crown with respect to Indian problems appears clearly in Walter H. Mohr, *Federal Indian Relations, 1774–1788* (Philadelphia, 1933).

After the Peace of Paris the Congress and its servants strove to assure both the peace and the protection of the Western frontiers. Again and again the agents of the central government made agreements with the Wyandots, Shawnee, Ottawas, and other tribes of the Old Northwest in the hope of ending warfare on the Ohio and making feasible a pacific penetration across the river. It was impossible, however, either to soothe the northwestern tribes or to persuade them to cease raiding settlements south of the river; and Kentuckians could not be prevented from retaliating. And when General Henry Knox proposed establishing forts and using troops to quiet the antagonists, there was no money for the forts and little for troops. Ultimately, Kentucky and western Virginia generally were freed of border warfare, but only by the exertion of military force that pushed the Indians away from the Ohio.

The story was quite similar in the Old Southwest. In 1785 the Congress appointed commissioners, Benjamin Hawkins, Andrew Pickens, Joseph Martin, and Lachlan McIntosh, to negotiate agreements with all the major Southern Indian nations. They were to be financed in part by the Southern states and were to work with emissaries of those states. But Georgia, failing to supply her share of the funds, did everything possible to obstruct the Federal agents. Her people urged the Creeks not to meet the commissioners; and the "king of the Creeks," Alexander McGillivray, used his influence toward the same end. The Georgians and McGillivray had their way. At the same time Georgia separately dealt with the Creeks and secured treaties to her liking. Not content with this success, the Assembly of that infant state solemnly declared that "all and every act and thing done or intended to be done within the limits and jurisdiction of this state by the said commissioners" in violation of "the sovereign, territorial and legislative rights and privileges to which each citizen is entitled by the confederation and the rights of the land" was "null and void." [6] Georgia had not ceded her claims beyond the Appalachian divide to the Congress; and by virtue of charter and legislative right the state argued that her western boundary lay on the Mississippi, that her limits on the south ended only at the boundaries of the Spanish Floridas—which had been pushed as near

[6] *Ibid.*, 147–48.

to the Gulf of Mexico as possible. Accordingly, Georgia was challenging the authority of the United States in a vast territory in which lived the Creeks, Choctaw, and many of the Cherokee. The commissioners proceeded to negotiate with representatives of the Cherokee, Choctaw, and Chickasaw at Hopewell in South Carolina in the winter of 1785–1786, and entered into treaties with all of them. Each of these agreements contained a guarantee of Indian territory which could not but displease all those eager to occupy or speculate in the lands of those tribes. Bitter protest therefore came from North Carolina as well as from Georgia, so violent that Congress decided to avoid trouble by failing to ratify the treaties. James White, the first Indian superintendent in the South, discovered that he could achieve nothing. Indeed, his heart was probably not in his work, for he was himself interested in land speculation. He resigned after a few months in office; and his successor was also inactive.

Little was done by the Americans in the period 1783–1789 to placate the red men, and much to offend them. Most of the western tribes accordingly remained hostile, the distant Chickasaw, who found advantage in American friendship, being a singular exception. Border warfare therefore continued; and it was aggravated by British and Spanish officials and civilians who encouraged the Indians from the forts on the Great Lakes, Louisiana, and the Floridas.

The British, clinging to Detroit, Niagara, and Michilimackinac, despite the fact that they were on American territory, in order to continue the fur trade with the northwestern Indians, found it to their advantage not to discourage their clients from undertaking marauding raids across the Ohio. Rather, British traders supplied those Indians with the weapons, ammunition, and firewater which made such raids possible and likely. After 1783 groups of them continued to slip over the river, stealing horses and killing unwary settlers. They were joined in these activities by a band of Chickamaugas who found a convenient base of operations north of the river, and by other Chickamaugas who came up from the Tennessee Valley. These raids so alarmed the Kentuckians that they begged the Virginia Assembly to build forts on the Ohio, vainly. In 1786 the Long Knives once more took the field in force—rather, in two forces. A detachment of one thousand men led by George Rogers Clark moved against the northwestern warriors by way of Vincennes, while another of about eight hundred under Benjamin Logan drove into the Shawnee country. Clark achieved nothing, was forced to turn back from the scene of his earlier triumph at Vincennes because of mutiny and lack of supplies. Logan was successful, inflicting serious injury upon the Shawnee. Thereafter, the Kentuckians were less molested by northwestern Indians,[7] and the victory of Anthony Wayne at Fallen Timbers and subsequent American occupation of the forts on the Great Lakes put an end to the raids over the river. Indian attacks from the southward, never major, except on the Wilderness Road, also subsided by 1790.

The Tennesseans suffered far more at the hands of the red men than did the Kentuckians in the years immediately after 1783. Indeed, Tennessee was not freed of Indian attack until Andrew Jackson occupied Pensacola thirty-five years later. From the fast-nesses of his Chickamauga retreat Dragging Canoe continued desperately to struggle against the onrushing Americans until his death in 1792. He dreamed of forming a great confederacy among the Southern Indian nations which would force them to halt. He was never able to persuade them to common action. However, his Chickamauga warriors spread havoc among the Cumberland settlements; the Cherokee in their old haunts in East Tennessee also eventually took the field in force; and some of the Upper Creeks at times gave him support. His people received supplies after 1785 from the British firm of Panton, Leslie, and Company, sent forward from Pensacola and Mobile, and he and his Chicka-maugas bravely withstood all counterattacks.

The Cumberland settlements about Nashville underwent a trial by fire as the result of assaults of the Chickamauga warriors, sup-ported on occasion by Upper Creeks. Their frequent raids might well have discouraged strong men. But James Robertson and his fellow colonists, though they suffered heavily in lives and goods,

---

[7] Nevertheless, during 1787 and 1788 reports like the following, taken from the Lexington *Kentucky Gazette*, June 21, 1788, frequently appeared in that paper: "Yesterday a party of Indians came in on the north fork of Elkhorn creek, and murdered a young man, and took a negroe girl prisoner."

resolutely clung to the lands they occupied and even expanded their holdings. He called upon North Carolina for help, and received some. Major John Evans, leading three hundred militiamen, appeared in Nashville in 1787 and gave useful service. But the Cumberland colony remained substantially isolated, and its people had to rely largely upon themselves for their salvation. They stood off the assaults of Dragging Canoe, counterattacked when possible, survived, and grew ever more numerous and more powerful.

In May, 1788, Dragging Canoe's Cherokee brethren to the eastward also began open hostilities, attacking both on the Tennessee River near Chattanooga and on Little River south of present-day Knoxville. John Sevier promptly collected a body of frontiersmen and swept into the old Cherokee villages, burning and destroying as he went. At Chilhowee town one of his followers, John Kirk, Jr., whose family had been slain by the Cherokee, murdered five of them who were under a flag of truce. Among the slain was Old Tassel, the great chief of the nation. Shortly afterward Sevier again invaded the Cherokee country. Old Tassel's followers bitterly sought revenge, capturing Gillespie's Station on the Holston in October and desperately attacking others, though not successfully. On January 9, 1789, "Nolichucky Jack" struck a decisive blow. He managed to surround a large body of Cherokee led by John Watts at Flint Creek. In a savagely fought battle that followed, the red men were routed, and only a few of them escaped unhurt. Sevier's men buried on the field 145 warriors, probably the greatest loss ever sustained by the Cherokee in a single engagement. Thereafter, the war died down in eastern Tennessee. The Cherokee no longer had any heart for it. Soon they removed their capital from Choté to northern Georgia.

But the Chickamaugas were more fortunate. They, too, were assailed in large force, in August, 1788, by militia under General Joseph Martin who gathered in East Tennessee and rapidly pushed on to Lookout Mountain in the hope of surprising Dragging Canoe's people. Instead, Martin's men were ambushed. Only three of them were slain, but the remainder were overcome by panic and compelled Martin to retreat. The Cherokee in general were glad to make peace after the battle of Flint Creek; not the

Chickamauga warriors, who continued to fight on even after the death of Dragging Canoe.

The distant Choctaw, though not so friendly toward the Americans as their Chickasaw neighbors, brought no serious trouble to the pioneers. The Creeks, however, engaged in desultory warfare not only against the Cumberland colony but also on the frontiers of Georgia, partly because Georgia leaders cared little whether they were at war or at peace with the Muskogee warriors.

The Creeks after 1783 were under the domination of a most remarkable man, Alexander McGillivray, who was known as their "king." [8] He was actually three-quarters white and one-quarter red, the son of Lachlan McGillivray, a Georgia Indian trader. Well educated, generous-minded, and astute, he lived in grand style on the Coosa River. Both he and his father were loyalists, and he suffered as the result of Georgia's confiscation of Tory property. Accordingly, for some years he nourished a grudge against the Americans that affected his judgment and his policy, which was to preserve his own lordly independence and that of the Creeks. A master of Indian psychology, he was as well an adept in the wiles of the whites. Toward strengthening his own position and that of his followers, he placed the nation under Spanish protection in 1784. He also, with the permission of Spanish officials, assured weapons and supplies for his people by opening an extensive trade with Panton, Leslie, and Company. He was thus able to secure in large measure freedom from American pressures. He paid a price for that freedom, since he became subject to the influence of the company, all the more so because he lived extravagantly and secured funds from it, as well as a small salary from Spain.

Georgia challenged the Creek nation, and Georgia traders threw down the gauntlet to Panton, Leslie and Company; and McGillivray was persuaded and driven into waging war. Between 1783 and 1786, ignoring Congress, Georgia negotiated no fewer than three treaties with small and unrepresentative bands of Creeks to secure dubious cessions of lands east and south of the Oconee River. These, with the Bourbon County and Muscle Shoals enterprises, alarmed the bulk of the Muskogees. Meanwhile, Georgia traders competed rather effectively with Panton, Leslie, and Com-

---

[8] John W. Caughey (ed.), *McGillivray of the Creeks* (Norman, 1938), is helpful.

pany; and possible other rivals for the British firm loomed in the Cumberland colony. The company urged McGillivray to act, and he did so. The Georgia traders were killed or driven from the Creek towns, and in April, 1786, McGillivray sent his warriors against both Georgia and Cumberland. The war which followed was one of sporadic raids rather than major blows, and Mc-Gillivray discovered before long that Panton, Leslie and Company could not supply enough arms to wage it. He therefore appealed to Governor Miró, who reluctantly and secretly assisted him, at the same time urging him to make peace. In 1790, when President Washington sought eagerly to restore calm on the Southern frontier, McGillivray was able with grace and dignity to drop the hatchet. Invited to visit the President in New York, he made peace with and accepted the protection of the United States, keeping that of Spain.

But McGillivray, like Dragging Canoe, could not arrest the American advance. His people continued to struggle bravely after he was gone—McGillivray died in 1793—in vain. Like the Cherokee, the Creeks were strong enough to exact a heavy price in blood for their lands and waters. Within thirty years they would go down under the onslaughts of Andrew Jackson; and even the Seminole, the outthrusts of the Creeks in the Everglades, were reduced to subordinate status within two generations.

Nor was Spain ultimately strong enough to stand against American westward and southward expansion. Failing in the peace negotiations of 1782–1783 to keep the Americans away from the Mississippi, the Spanish crown actively sought to protect its holdings in Louisiana and the Floridas. Hence Governor Miró's treaty of 1784 with the Creeks, in which the latter accepted Spanish protection, and similar agreements of the same year with the Choctaw and Chickasaw. Hence also came permission from Spain to Panton, Leslie, and Company to operate in Spanish territory, although the partners were British subjects and dealt with merchants in Britain, because the Spanish could not supply Indian goods and wished to keep American traders away from the three tribes. There were few Spanish civilians in Louisiana and the Floridas, and the scantiest of garrison troops. Miró and his superiors in consequence sought to erect an Indian barrier against the aggressive Americans. Toward holding off the Americans, Spain in addition put forth a claim that West Florida's true boundary on the north was the Tennessee River as far east as its junction with the Hiwassee, a claim that was supported by the protectorates established over the three Indian nations. Further, in 1784, in order to cramp the Americans, the Spanish crown, which had hitherto permitted them freely to use the lower Mississippi, declared it closed.

Spain's attempt to push northward the boundary of West Florida and her closure of the Mississippi aroused a storm of American protest, Indian traders, land speculators, Western settlers, and politicians at the state and central capitals joining in it. To them the Spanish were at once indolent, insolent, and belligerent. The barrier placed on the lower Mississippi was an especially detestable measure, for Kentuckians, Tennesseans, and others living west of the Appalachian divide; though they had as yet little to sell, they knew that they must send their products to market by way of the great river and the Gulf of Mexico. They could not profitably carry them eastward across the mountains. They were determined to use the Mississippi. They thought, said George Mason in 1783, that they had "a natural right to the free, though not the exclusive navigation of that river." Should they not obtain it, Mason predicted "another war in less than seven years" and that the Westerners would be "strong enough to enforce that right." [9] Moreover, by American interpretation of the peace treaties of 1783, the United States had acquired from Britain the right to use the lower stretches of the river and also that part of West Florida lying north of the thirty-first parallel.[10]

The Spanish crown was willing to pay a price for American acquiescence in the closure of the river, and Don Diego de Gardoqui was sent to the United States with the rank of chargé d'affaires to secure formal American consent. He was authorized

[9] Niles (ed.), *Principles and Acts of the Revolution in America*, 306.

[10] American claims were not without fault. Britain had acquired the right to navigate the Mississippi freely in the Peace of 1763. It was doubtful that she could transfer it to the United States. It was also doubtful that she could put the boundary of West Florida at the thirty-first parallel—it had been placed far to the northward in 1764—after that province had been quite effectively conquered by Spain.

to offer in exchange commercial favors, a defensive alliance, and a mutual guarantee of territory. The Spanish ministers were prepared even to consider the cession of St. Augustine and of part of West Florida below the Tennessee to obtain a treaty by which the United States withdrew its claim to navigation. Gardoqui reached New York in the early summer of 1785 and opened discussions with John Jay, secretary for foreign affairs. He did not succeed. Jay was bound by instructions from Congress to make no concessions with regard either to the river or to the boundary. After months of fruitless discussion, Jay, who was as eager to sign a treaty as Gardoqui, became convinced that the United States could not obtain the opening of the river and that concession had to be made in order to secure the commercial privileges. He believed that the right to use the river was not yet essential to the Westerners. Accordingly, he became willing to withdraw the claim to it for a period of twenty-five years.

However, when Jay sought permission from Congress to make this concession, he roused a storm. Delegates from New England and the Middle states supported his request, those from the South stoutly opposed it. Delegates from commercial states quite understandably agreed with Jay that the use of the river was not yet vital. But they had other reasons for backing him. At least some of them were opposed to expansion south of the Ohio, partly on the score that it would denude the older states of people. Rufus King of New York fancied that the mountains were so great a barrier that the settlers beyond them could not be kept within the union. James Monroe, then a delegate from Virginia, became convinced, in fact, that the New Englanders preferred to form a separate union with the Middle states rather than to encourage occupation of the lands south of the Ohio. If the confederation should collapse, Monroe was determined that Pennsylvania be part of a Southern union. He was willing, if necessary, to use force to wrest Pennsylvania from the Yankees. After furious debate in Congress a motion to permit Jay to make concessions both with respect to the river and the boundary was carried by a vote of seven states to five, the South voting solidly against it, the other states, except for Delaware, which was not represented, giving it unanimous approval. But, in view of the fact that treaties under the Articles of Confederation required the votes of nine states, was the motion carried? Certainly any agreement resulting would require the consent of nine delegations. Jay chose not to exacerbate the sectional passions which had been excited, continued negotiations, did not come to terms with Gardoqui.

In the fall of 1787 the Spanish crown adopted a new policy. The ministers of Charles III told Gardoqui Spain was willing to cede to the United States all of West Florida north of the thirty-first parallel (save for Natchez) and to refer the American claim to the use of the river to a commission for study. They now believed that the safety of Louisiana and West Florida could best be assured by taking a moderate stand toward the United States, encouraging Westerners to settle in Spanish territory and to become Spanish subjects, and fomenting discontent among Westerners who remained on American soil. They would caress rather than try to strangle Kentuckians, Tennesseans, and Georgians. Had Gardoqui been able to offer such terms two years earlier, he probably could have secured an agreement. By the spring of 1788, however, opinion in Congress was shifting. Stories of seizure and confiscation of goods sent down the river despite the Spanish closure had aroused bitterness in the West and also among the delegates. Several of those of the Northern states were no longer willing to make concessions to Spain. Moreover, the Congress came to feel that it ought not to act, since its own existence might soon be ended. In the fall of 1788, it once more asserted the American right of navigation and referred the question of a Spanish treaty to "the federal government which is to assemble in March next." [11]

Efforts on the part of Spain immediately after 1787 to attract within her colonies American settlers who would strengthen her grip upon her possessions in Louisiana and Florida also failed. That year the notorious James Wilkinson, who had migrated to Kentucky in 1784, began at New Orleans his long continued intrigues with Spain, and soon became a Spanish agent. Other frontier leaders, including James Robertson and John Sevier, also opened negotiations. But these, even Wilkinson, had no desire

[11] Burnett, *Continental Congress*, 654–59, 679–80; Whitaker, *Spanish-American Frontier*, 68–86.

to become Spanish subjects. Wilkinson hoped to secure the separation of Kentucky from the United States and financial gain for himself. Robertson merely wished Spanish aid for the better protection of his Cumberland colony; and Sevier wanted it only to support his land speculations. Sevier and Robertson were no more interested in trying to secure the independence of East and Middle Tennessee with Spanish encouragement than they were in becoming subjects of the Spanish crown; and whatever Wilkinson desired, few Kentuckians really wanted independence with Spain's blessing, even if Spain used the waters of the lower Mississippi in the ceremony of bestowal. Toward attracting settlers and toward easing tension in the valley Spain declared the river open at the end of 1788 to Americans paying substantial duties upon the goods they carried. Westerners who became Spanish subjects would, of course, be exempt from those tariffs. This scheme to invite in and "to tame the Goths" failed. And after 1789 Spain was forced to deal with a new and far stronger American central government which could not be treated casually, which in the end compelled a settlement of river and boundary questions in the American way.

Of course, both the closure of the river and the later Spanish campaign to win friends and to influence people west of the Appalachians encouraged division between them and Americans dwelling east of the mountains, even though the men of the Western waters could hardly think of themselves as Spanish citizens under Spanish domination. The Westerners were unhappy after 1784 because the Congress failed to force open the river, and they knew that Jay was willing to let it remain closed for a generation. They also resented the efforts of the Congress to secure peace with the Southern Indians, since those attempts involved protection of the lands of the Indians. Moreover, Kentuckians believed that Virginia was slack in aiding them against the red men, and Tennesseans entertained the same sentiment regarding North Carolina. The distance between the new settlements and the capitals of the two states, the intervening mountain wall, poor communications, and the fact that the Westerners had often occupied their lands without the consent and even against the will of those states, likewise stimulated division. Western discontent was directed more against Virginia and North Carolina than it was against the Congress, and soon led to attempts to create new states in the Mississippi Valley, attempts which were supported by a philosophy of home rule and by land speculators and politicians who fancied they would do better in capitals west of the mountains than in the older ones to the eastward. Hence arose a separatist movement in what is now West Virginia and others in Kentucky and Tennessee, the stillborn state of Franklin, and, a little later, the commonwealths of Kentucky and Tennessee.

As early as 1776 inhabitants in the later West Virginia urged Congress to establish for them a fourteenth state of Westsylvania, without success, partly because the state of Virginia opposed the scheme, partly because it was not ardently supported in the region of its origin. While there was separatist sentiment between the Shenandoah and the Ohio, clash between that region and the older Virginia was not yet strong enough to make possible a formal division. Indeed, separation did not come until the Civil War, and then under extraordinary circumstances.[12] It was otherwise with Kentucky, populous, independent-spirited from her beginnings, remote enough from Richmond to stimulate her people to seek statehood and to persuade Virginians that it was not worthwhile to strive to maintain control over them. As early as December, 1784, an assembly of militia officers held at Danville called for separation. Thereafter, convention after convention— nine of them in all—asked independence from Virginia, and Virginia after 1786 passed enabling act after enabling act—a total of four. Virginia insisted that separation must be accompanied by the admission of Kentucky as a state and upon other conditions protecting the rights of Virginia, reservations which were not entirely pleasing in the Bluegrass country. The stipulations were not finally met until 1792, when Kentucky became the fifteenth state.[13]

[12] George H. Alden, *New Governments West of the Alleghanies before 1780* (Madison, 1897), 64–70; Frederick J. Turner, "Western State-Making in the Revolutionary Era," *American Historical Review*, I (1895–1896), 70–87, 251–69; Ambler, *Sectionalism in Virginia.*

[13] Robert S. Cotterill, *History of Pioneer Kentucky* (Cincinnati, 1917), 198–228, offers a clear and concise description of the movement for statehood in Kentucky and apt comment upon the part played in it by James Wilkinson.

The state of Franklin—originally Frankland, but later renamed in honor of Benjamin—had a brief, stormy, and unofficial history. It had its origins in an act of the North Carolina legislature of the spring of 1784 which ceded the western lands of the state to Congress, under certain conditions. That law gave opportunity to Arthur Campbell, a conspicuous figure of Southwest Virginia who had been pushing since 1782 for a new state composed of eastern Tennessee and part of western Virginia. It was easy enough for him and others to convince the settlers in eastern Tennessee that they had been cast off by North Carolina and that they ought to form their own state; and an assembly held at Jonesborough in August called for a convention to meet in December and to prepare a constitution. Before the convention met, North Carolina repealed her action of cession. However, the delegates proceeded with their work, and a constitution, legislature, and a governor, John Sevier, had appeared by 1785. Franklinites hoped to include in their proposed state eastern Tennessee, part of western Virginia, and also the Muscle Shoals country. But Sevier, who apparently never was entirely committed to separation, failed to struggle strenuously for it; a faction within Franklin led by John Tipton steadily urged continued union with North Carolina; and that state clung to her authority beyond the mountains, offering to sanction separation under certain conditions, including acceptance of her over-mountain region as a state by Congress. Riven by dissension and failing to secure support in Congress— and also from Benjamin Franklin—the state of Franklin collapsed before the end of 1788. Even during the short existence of the phantom commonwealth sponsors of it served in the North Carolina Assembly, and Sevier and other principals in it were quickly forgiven.[14] Eight years later, however, under happier conditions arose the greater and permanent state of Tennessee.

In the end separatist sentiment in Southern trans-Appalachia led neither to the strengthening of the Spanish empire nor to the weakening of the American one. Instead, it moved toward the creation of two new states and strengthened the United States.

[14] Abernethy, *From Frontier to Plantation in Tennessee*, Chap. V, argues cogently that land speculation is the key to the history of Franklin.

CHAPTER XX

TOWARD A MORE PERFECT NATION

" **A**MERICA after this seven years war will relish peace like a new mistress adorned with every charm," predicted Nathanael Greene at the end of the Revolutionary conflict. Yet Greene was worried, and also prophesied "new convulsions" unless more authority were given the American central government. There was, he said, too much "local" power and not enough "general." There must be created, he asserted, a better balance between the two; he wanted an excess neither of "local" nor of "general." [1] Greene both posed the great American problem of the postwar period and gave its answer. For many Americans, including Southerners, the problem was not vital, indeed hardly then existed. Labors, joys, and perplexities personal and immediate absorbed their thoughts and energies; and it did not become urgent until several years had passed. Some, in fact, never felt a need for a stronger union. By 1789, nevertheless, a new national constitution providing for a strong central government had been made and put into practice. In the spring of that year Washington soberly assumed office as the first American president.

The years between the final departure of the British troops and the inauguration of the towering Virginian, although they were not without troubles and alarums, were years of economic progress in the South. The British sailing off from the Southern coasts left behind them in Virginia, the Carolinas, and Georgia lands ravished of slaves and livestock, a dislocated economy, many an empty patriot pocket, and many a filled patriot grave. When

[1] Greene to John Collins, April 22, 1783, General Nathanael Greene Papers (Duke University Library).

Washington traveled northward to New York to take up his new duties, he saw prosperous and happy regions from which evidences of the war had almost vanished. When he made a tour of the South two years later he gazed upon similar scenes. So rapid was recovery in the Southern states, so remarkable was increase within them in numbers, that the South seemed likely in 1789 to surpass the remainder of the new union in both population and wealth. As we have observed, the startling growth of the Southern states had even earlier aroused jealousy above the Mason-Dixon line which had persuaded some Yankees and Yorkers that it was unwise to try to force Spain to open the Mississippi quickly.

The soil was peculiarly the source of Southern economic health, and the British did not bear off very much of it. Only tillage and markets for its produce were required for early prosperity, since the devastation and debts resulting from the war, although they were impressive to some, were relatively small. Cultivation of the land was somewhat hindered by lack of capital, and by a shortage of slaves in the far South, but these difficulties were overcome. Markets were more abundant than they had been before the war, partly because it was no longer so necessary to obey or even to circumvent the British laws of trade, partly because American tobacco, rice, wheat, and naval stores were wanted in France, Holland, and Germany. Exports to Britain remained smaller than they had been before the war, but only because the South was no longer forced to send tobacco and rice there; and trade with the West Indies flourished, despite the fact that British ports in the Caribbean were theoretically closed to American ships. The British even continued for a decade after the peace to buy American indigo in preference to French and Spanish dyestuff; and, although the British no longer gave a bounty upon it, the Low Country planters managed to profit from growing it until the British found a new source for it in the East Indies.

It was common observation in 1789 that the South, with the rest of the union, was once more prosperous. If that prosperity be measured in terms of exports of tobacco, wheat, rice, indigo, and naval stores, the Southerners were nearly as well off as they were in the years of abundance immediately before the war, with a brighter future ahead of them. Virginia and Maryland shipped as

368

CHARLES COTESWORTH PINCKNEY by James Earl. Courtesy
of Worcester Art Museum

much tobacco annually during the years 1783–1789 as they did prior to the conflict,[2] and they also sold away large quantities of wheat and flour, for the planters of the Chesapeake were prudently turning from the weed to wheat. In the year ending September 30, 1792, 63 per cent of the wheat, 38 per cent of the flour, and 60 per cent of the corn exported from the United States came from the South, principally from the Chesapeake states.[3] By 1789 the exports of North Carolina were double those of the prewar period.[4] Those of South Carolina steadily mounted after 1783, being worth in 1786 almost twice as much as imports for that year.[5] Although South Carolina sent forth annually until 1786 no more than one half as much rice as was earlier shipped, the prewar level was regained in 1788, with prices high. Despite the fact that indigo planters no longer received a British bounty, more dyestuff was produced in the year ending September 30, 1792, than in the year 1771.[6]

There was, to be sure, a dark cloud or two on the economic horizon. The lands of Maryland and Virginia long devoted to tobacco culture were wearing out, and one could no longer easily see great riches in rows of tobacco plants beside the Chesapeake. However, many planters followed the example of Washington, who had turned to wheat before 1775, with surprising success. Without an assured British market and British bounties, the production of indigo had also become a dubious enterprise, and it virtually ceased in the Low Country before the end of the century. However, indigo was not essential to the well-being of South Carolina and Georgia. And these were Tidewater troubles, which had little or no effect upon the Piedmont and the new settlements beyond the mountains.

Indeed, the Southern prospect was even more alluring than customhouse papers indicate, for the South was moving rapidly toward general farming, the full values of which do not appear in papers kept at the ports, although the numbers mentioned above

[2] Gray, *History of Agriculture in the Southern United States*, II, 605.
[3] *Ibid.*, 610.
[4] Crittenden, *Commerce of North Carolina*, Chap. X.
[5] Charles G. Singer, *South Carolina in the Confederation* (Philadelphia, 1941), 23–26.
[6] Gray, *History of Agriculture in the Southern United States*, II, 610.

in connection with wheat are impressive. The flood of settlers from the northeast to the rolling upper country of the Carolinas and Georgia which had begun more than a generation earlier and which had been dammed by the war, resumed after its close; and thousands of farms appeared on the Piedmont, together with those carved out beyond the Appalachians. These farms, with their wheat, corn, livestock, and tobacco gave a new stability to the Southern economy. Moreover, the postwar settlers, many of them from Northern states, including veterans, brought with them vigor and enterprise peculiarly useful to Southern society. Unfortunately for the South, that tide of migration before long turned from the Southwest to the West, and plantations producing cotton with slave labor began to compete only too effectively with small general farms.

If, on the whole, the Southern economic outlook was bright in 1789, it does not follow that the six years preceding were ones of steady and untroubled progress. Immediately after the end of the war an optimistic spirit reigned in South Carolina and Georgia. In 1784 Negroes and goods worth nearly £2,000,000 were imported into South Carolina. But they were purchased largely upon credit at heavy interest, and the crops which were to pay for them were insufficient, those of 1783 and 1784 together bringing in no more than £700,000, and that of 1785 being little better than its predecessors.[7] By 1785 additional credit was difficult to obtain. In fact, the British merchants who supplied it were then in straits, many of them going into bankruptcy. Returning to Savannah after the war, the merchant Joseph Clay resumed business with enthusiasm and high hopes. He reported that crop acreage was three times greater in 1784 than it was in the preceding year. Not long afterward, however, Clay discovered that he had to struggle even to continue in business, that a plantation which he owned was his chief means of livelihood.[8] It is evident

[7] Edward Channing, *A History of the United States* (New York, 1905–1925), III, 410–11.

[8] *Letters of Joseph Clay, Merchant of Savannah, 1776–1793*, in *Collections of the Georgia Historical Society* (Savannah), VIII (1913), 190 ff. Tobacco culture attained surprising importance in Georgia immediately after the war. Between September, 1791, and September, 1792, the state exported 5,471 hogsheads of it, about one tenth as much as Virginia. Gray, *History of Agriculture in the Southern United States*, II, 606.

that the years 1785–1786 were full of stress in the far South, as they were, indeed, generally throughout the union. Recovery was, however, prompt and enduring.

In the postwar period of restoration and economic revival, debts private and public were, of course, a burden, and the citizen was eager to pay neither the one nor the other with his own hard-earned cash. In 1783 all of the Southern states owed money borrowed to carry on the war, and all of them owed money to the Congress toward their shares of the expenses of the general government, both past and current. Private obligations to British merchants incurred before the war were large, amounting to hundreds of thousands of pounds, those of the Virginians being especially impressive.[9] They had not been paid, and they were increased by optimistic postwar purchases of slaves and goods on credit. Private debts weighed heavily, and taxes levied to meet current expenses and past outlays added to the load upon the shoulders of the citizen, until it seemed almost staggering in the depression of 1785–1786. Ways of lightening it and escaping it were eagerly sought and found.

There were three principal means by which the burden of private debts could be removed or evaded, laws preventing collection by British creditors, refusal to pay them, and currency inflation; and all of these were used in the Southern states and the others.

Laws to make it impossible for the British merchants to proceed against their American debtors were very popular. It was argued, and believed, that the debts had been enhanced by extortionate

---

[9] The figures cannot be accurately estimated. Often cited are those offered by British merchants to the British ministry in 1791. The merchants then asserted that the debts were approximately £2,305,000 for Virginia, nearly £688,000 for South Carolina, over £517,000 for Maryland, £379,000 for North Carolina, and almost £248,000 for Georgia. But these numbers included interest between 1776 and 1791, more than £2,000,000 of it, some of it apparently for the war period. The original debts were doubtless also inflated by the merchants, who would hardly have asked only their due, since they hoped to be paid by government. In 1794 the creditors were willing to accept 40 per cent of the amount they stipulated three years earlier, that fraction including interest for ten years. Samuel F. Bemis, *Jay's Treaty* (New York, 1923), 103, 315–17. The debts were doubtless smaller than they are commonly said to have been. It should be noted that payments made between 1783 and 1790 should also be included in any attempt to assess the size of the obligations in the earlier year.

charges for goods, services, and interest, and by unjustly low prices paid for American exports; that British citizens ought to suffer because of the losses inflicted upon America by the British government in its efforts to beat down the rebellion. Such contentions were all the more convincing to their makers because the merchants demanded interest upon the debts, even for the war period, when payment could not be offered. The preventive laws were passed both before and after 1783, despite the treaty of peace, which declared that no hindrance was to be placed upon the creditors. They were remarkably popular in Virginia, where the debts were the largest. In 1785, however, Jefferson and John Adams persuaded the British merchants to abandon all claims for wartime interest and to accept payment by installments; and the Congress called upon the states to execute the treaty and to repeal their hostile legislation. The justice of the request was evident, and all the states, except for Virginia, promptly complied. Patrick Henry bitterly opposed it, was strongly supported; and Virginia, finally acceding in 1787, did so upon condition that the British abandon the posts they still held on the Great Lakes and pay for the slaves they had carried off from Virginia during the war. Thus the British creditors were kept out of the Virginia courts until after 1789, when Federal action forced the opening of those courts to them.[10]

Deprived of their legal barriers, except in Virginia, many debtors, unable or unwilling to pay, continued to deny and evade their obligations. Access to American state courts by no means assured collection to the British merchants. Ultimately, in order to persuade Britain to abandon the forts on the Great Lakes passageway and to secure other concessions, the United States, in the Jay treaty of 1795, undertook to pay those private debts still outstanding. The sum was substantial, a large part of it doubtless the debts of Southerners.

Inevitably, debtors also turned to the time-honored device of printing paper money as a means of inflating the currency, stimulating economic activity, and lessening the weight of their obligations. Such paper could also be used to pay public debts and

[10] Merrill Jensen, *The New Nation; A History of the United States during the Confederation, 1781–1789* (New York, 1950), 68, 276–81.

expenses, and could therefore be substituted for taxation. While it was not usually liked by creditors, and others who sought financial stability, it appealed on occasion and for special reasons even to stable merchants and planters, and almost invariably to small farmers who were often in debt and only too frequently pressed for money with which to meet their taxes. Just after the war insistent demands for emissions of paper currency pervaded most of the Thirteen States, and the assemblies of three Southern ones responded, despite the fact that it had been necessary throughout the South to repudiate large amounts of it placed in circulation during the war. North Carolina put forth £100,000 of paper in 1783, making it legal tender, and £100,000 more two years later, ignoring furious protests from some of her merchants, who talked of leaving the state, if they did not do it. The paper before long sank in value, but it improved the financial condition of the state and of many of its people, though hardly that of the creditors of either. South Carolina's performance was far more statesmanlike. In 1785 her governor proposed the issuance of £400,000 in paper, and he was stoutly backed by men who wished it to be made legal tender. In the end, however, opposition from the merchants forced a reduction of the amount to £100,000, to be lent on land mortgages, and a stipulation that the paper was to be tender only for future payments to the state. The result was happy; the currency stimulated, circulated at par, and gave the state a handsome profit. Georgia was far less fortunate. Her Assembly in 1786 put forth £30,000 of bills, legal tender, to be repaid from the proceeds of the sale of lands still in the possession of the Creek nation. The paper depreciated rapidly; by 1787 it was worth only one quarter of hard money; and it was necessary to deprive it of its tender quality three years later. That it profited a few perhaps even without the loss of their souls, may be; that it materially benefited the state or many of its citizens is doubtful.

Maryland and Virginia neither gained from paper currency, nor lost, save in wasted time and perturbed spirits, for creditors and advocates of sound money were able in both states to fight off the champions of the fiat stuff. The contest was violent in Maryland in 1785 and 1786. All kinds of money were scarce, and public opinion called for action. The lower house of the legislature responded. Led by Samuel Chase, it proposed an emission of £200,000 based on land mortgages. The Maryland senate, dominated by Charles Carroll of Carrollton, John Eager Howard, and other wealthy conservatives, resolutely denounced the scheme; and it was dropped by its sponsors when prosperity returned to the state. Virginia had hardly called in her wartime paper currency at the rate of one dollar for $1,000—Maryland had paid one dollar for $40 for her emergency paper—when clamor began for another supply. Money was so scarce in Virginia, commented a wag, that poverty-stricken people, elegantly clad and betting freely, thronged about race-tracks and cock-fights, and that many had been forced to exchange sedan chairs for coaches. Irony had no effect; and indeed, the tax collector frequently discovered that those from whom he sought to extract cash had none of it or had departed "over Allegheny," and to other vaguely described habitats and climes. In the Assembly in the winter of 1785–1786 there was a "considerable itch" for paper money. A large majority in the lower house, led by Madison, refused to apply any salve to it, instead asserted that an emission would be "unjust, impolitic, destructive of public & private confidence, and of that virtue which is the basis of republican government." [11] Nevertheless, the lawmakers felt it necessary to supply remedies for the taxpayers, forgiving part of several levies and making it possible to meet others with hemp, flour, and warehouse receipts for tobacco.[12]

With and without new paper currency the Southern states began putting their economic houses in order. Revenue was extracted from sales of confiscated Tory properties and of western lands; taxes were imposed in great variety—in Georgia even a special levy upon lawyers and physicians—but chiefly upon real property, polls, and imports; costs of government were kept low; and ar-

[11] Hunt (ed.), *Writings of James Madison,* II, 277.

[12] The contest over paper money in the several states is described in some detail in Nevins, *American States during and after the Revolution,* 515–43. Jensen, *New Nation,* Chap. XVI, offers a briefer account, pointing out that emissions well conceived had merit. See also Crowl, *Maryland during and after the Revolution,* 86–110; Irving P. Brant, *James Madison the Nationalist, 1780–1787* (Indianapolis, 1948), 317–18, 361–63; Lefler and Newsome, *North Carolina,* 251–52; Amanda Johnson, *Georgia as Colony and State* (Atlanta, 1938), 174–75.

rangements were made toward liquidating both local debt and that owed to the central government. By 1789 Maryland, Virginia, and South Carolina had achieved stability, and the outlook for North Carolina and Georgia had greatly improved.

The economic progress of the Southern states after the war, their increases in numbers, their expansion to the westward, and their political and social reforms and advances form an impressive record. It was not, however, achieved without harassing political strife. Parties did not appear, but factions did. The Conservatives, who sought to confine power to a minority, including often themselves, were also commonly those who favored leniency to the Tories, those who fought against paper money, those who called for the payment of private and public debts. The Radicals, on the other hand, were likely to desire punishment for the loyalists, to push for paper currency, to support measures reducing or canceling obligations, and to desire office for themselves. They were also apt to dislike taxation, with the Conservatives demanding it. The two groups also struggled over types of taxation, with the Conservatives evincing a fondness for poll taxes and levies on land in proportion to acreage rather than value, and the Radicals calling for taxation in accordance with wealth and ability to pay. The Liberals veered to one side and the other, and fortune also, amidst cries of triumph and groans of anguish. Contests between East, more Conservative, and West, more Radical, spiced and enriched political warfare, which inspired vigorous epithets and occasionally included resort to pistols at dawn and fists at more convenient hours.

There were also conflicts among the Southern states, and between them and Congress. Georgia and South Carolina squabbled about the boundary between them and about navigation of the Savannah River. Virginia feuded with Maryland concerning the free use of the Potomac; and both North Carolina and Georgia resented South Carolina import duties upon goods which ultimately went to her neighbors. At the same time Georgia and North Carolina bristled because Congress tried to restore peace on the Southern frontier by protecting Indian lands; and all the Southern states were angered by the failure of Congress to force open the Mississippi. Requisitions for money from Congress, whether met or not, aroused jealousy both toward that body and among the Southern states.

As the decade wore on, Southern Conservatives, and Liberals too, became ever more convinced, for their own benefit and for the general welfare, personal and public advantage being doubtless inextricably associated in their thought, that the central American government should be strengthened. The Conservatives, who had suffered defeats as well as gained victories in factional warfare in the several states, could not expect to win and to hold continuous sway in the state capitals. In alliance with their fellows to the northward they had a better chance to dominate a powerful central government, especially if they were able to secure a Federal constitution less "democratic" than those in vogue in Virginia, North Carolina, and Georgia. Such a constitution, and a government based upon it, might be used to prevent the issuance of cheapening paper money, compel the execution of contracts, supply a stable currency, prevent state interference with commerce, maintain internal order, and solve the problems arising from westward expansion. A robust régime at New York or Philadelphia or on the Potomac might also provide more effective defense, strengthen the United States in foreign affairs, bind the American people more closely together, and enable them to take pride in their country. It might even bring, and probably did, direct financial profit to some Conservatives, those who were creditors of the existing central government and who were more likely to collect from a richer and stronger one.[13] Many of these considerations also moved Liberals.

[13] Charles A. Beard, *An Economic Interpretation of the Constitution of the United States* (New York, 1929), especially pp. 150 and 290, pointed out that no fewer than forty members of the fifty-five who attended the Federal Convention were creditors (or at least holders of Federal securities) in 1791, and that there were many of these among the persons who pushed for ratification of the Constitution of 1787. He believed that economic interest in the securities "must have formed a very considerable dynamic element, if not the preponderating element, in bringing about the adoption of the new system." Beard laid stress upon the fact (p. 289) that fourteen of the thirty-one Low Country men who voted for ratification in the South Carolina convention held such securities four years later. However, the Low Country delegates were unanimously for ratification, including seventeen other Low Country representatives without such interest. Crowl, *Maryland during and*

Until 1786 those who sought to form a sturdier central government labored to achieve it by altering the Articles of Confederation so as to enlarge the powers of Congress. A favorite device
was to give that body authority to levy import duties. But an
amendment proposed for the purpose in 1781 was defeated because the legislature of Rhode Island, and then that of Virginia,
refused consent—unanimous approval of the states being required.
Another proposal of 1783, which would have authorized Congress
to levy such duties for a period of twenty-five years only, also encountered opposition and indifference, notably in New York,
where the legislature accompanied approval with clogging pro-
visos which Congress could not accept. Many persons, especially
those of the Radical persuasion, feared to give that body power;
it might become tyrannical.

An attempt to bestow upon Congress the right to regulate interstate and foreign commerce and to levy import and export duties
toward that end, the proceeds going to the states in which they
were gathered and the states retaining the power to interdict
commerce, also failed, in this instance principally because of
Southern opposition. Southerners in Congress were alarmed lest
the authority be used to drive British and other foreign ships from
their ports and so to confer a monopoly of Southern overseas traffic
upon Northern shipowners. Southern interests were threatened,
and Southern jealousy aroused. An amendment toward the purpose, since it could not possibly secure sanction and because it
could only add to sectional discord, died in Congress. Another
which would have given to that body a limited right to control
shipping was referred to the states, but was neglected in the far

---

after the Revolution, 124-27, offers valuable evidence regarding the influence of
the securities in Maryland. There, of sixty-three men who voted in the state convention for ratification, eleven were holders, and at least four candidates who were
defeated in the election of that body were also holders. However, at least two unsuccessful candidates who were hostile to it likewise held the paper. The possessors
of the paper seem to have been more numerous proportionately in South Carolina
and Maryland than in the other Southern states. Professor Beard, after the publication of his great book, lowered his estimate of the importance of the securities
(which did not always belong to the man in whose name they were listed and which
were doubtless in some instances acquired after 1787). His later opinion was doubtless better founded.

South, and elsewhere, because both particularist and sectional sentiment were arrayed against it. Even though they failed, these proposals hurt sectional feelings, in the South because they had been pushed, in the North because they had not succeeded. The contests over them, together with that upon the Mississippi question, stimulated the schemes for division of the United States which thoughtless and narrow men had conceived. In November, 1785, Rufus King of New York suggested that the states north of the Mason-Dixon line might form a separate confederacy unless those to the southward conceded to Congress the right to regulate commerce,[14] a scheme which was also put forth by Theodore Sedgwick of Massachusetts in the following August.[15]

In the spring of 1786 Congress considered a batch of amendments that would have enabled it to govern, but did not push them; it also decided not to try to arrange for a special convention to submit amendments. Weariness and a hope that the Annapolis convention would lead to action doubtless contributed to these decisions. If members did so hope, they were not disappointed. Commissioners of Maryland and Virginia had met at Mount Vernon in the preceding year to try to settle disputes between the two states. They came to terms which both accepted; and Maryland then proposed that the commissioners, of whom Madison was one, invite representatives of all the states to Annapolis in September, 1786, to consider the trade of the union and "a uniform system in their commercial regulations." Emissaries from only five states—those of two others failed to arrive in time— appeared at the Maryland capital, and there was no hope of achieving its official purposes. But Alexander Hamilton, who was one of the New Yorkers present, saw in the Annapolis gathering a splendid opportunity. With the support of Madison, and doubtless of Washington, he introduced a resolution of far-reaching importance which was unanimously approved by the men present. It called upon the states to send delegates to Philadelphia in May, 1787, "to devise such further provisions as shall appear to them necessary to render the constitution of the federal government

[14] Charles R. King (ed.), *Life and Correspondence of Rufus King* (New York, 1894–1900), I, 113.
[15] Burnett (ed.), *Letters of Members of the Continental Congress*, VIII, 415.

adequate to the exigencies of the Union; and to report such an act for that purpose to the United States in Congress assembled, as, when agreed to by them, and afterwards confirmed by the legislatures of every state, will effectually provide for the same." [16] This invitation, separately repeated by the Congress in February, 1787, brought to Philadelphia men from twelve states, including all the Southern ones. They spent a long summer drafting a new constitution.

The men who made their way to Philadelphia from the South on horseback, by coach, and by sailing ship in the late spring and early summer of 1787 were, except for those sent by Virginia and South Carolina, not remarkably impressive. Maryland's leading men remained at home, partly because they feared a drive for paper money might succeed in their absence, partly because they believed the convention would achieve little or nothing. The state was represented by James McHenry, Daniel Carroll, John Francis Mercer, Daniel of St. Thomas Jenifer, and Luther Martin, respectable but not distinguished characters, Martin being by far the most active in the convention. From North Carolina came Dr. Hugh Williamson, William R. Davie, Richard Dobbs Spaight, Alexander Martin, and William Blount, Williamson being by far the most talkative of the group at Philadelphia. He offered some useful suggestions there. Georgia sent three Williams, Few, Houstoun, and Pierce, and Abraham Baldwin. Far superior was the group that appeared from South Carolina, John Rutledge, Charles Cotesworth Pinckney, Pierce Butler, and Charles Pinckney, the last a son of the gentleman of the same name who turned Tory but himself an ardent patriot and a young man of ability.[17] The South Carolinians, although no one of them was of the stature of Jefferson, Franklin, or Washington, were uniformly able, solid, and broadminded. Most remarkable of all the delegations which entered the Pennsylvania Statehouse was that of Virginia, its members, Washington, Madison, Edmund Randolph, George Mason, George Wythe, John Blair, and Dr. James Mc-

---

[16] Elliot (ed.), *Debates in the Several State Conventions*, I, 118.

[17] Recently he has been the target of severe censure, and has been described as an intellectual "sponger and a plagiarist." Irving Brant, *James Madison, Father of the Constitution, 1787–1800* (Indianapolis, 1950), 27–29, 132.

Clurg. Mason, who eventually turned against the Constitution prepared by the convention, nevertheless contributed genuinely to its making; Randolph also rendered very useful and similar service, later taking position against it and then again reversing his stand; Madison was, of course, the principal designer of the new Constitution; and Washington, no deviser of political machinery, no debater, no subtle manager in committee, gave dignity, prestige, and high purpose to the body over which he presided and to the Constitution which it made.

In the convention the Virginians, as usual, led the way. Arriving early in Philadelphia, they discussed the ills of the nation and agreed upon a remedy, largely conceived by Madison, the "Father of the Constitution." The medicine was not a collection of palliatives, but powerful stuff calculated to cure. The Virginians presented it to their fellow delegates for consideration. The changes which they proposed in their "Virginia Plan" were so vast that they compelled the making of a new basic document. Madison and his associates called for a national Congress of two houses, the lower elected by the people, in proportion to wealth or to numbers, the upper house chosen by the popular chamber. The executive was to be elected by the legislature. There should be also a national judiciary to decide cases involving "the national peace and harmony." The Congress was to have impressive powers, all those vested in the existing body, plus the right to make laws in whatever fields where the "separate states" were "incompetent" and in those where state action might threaten the harmony of the union. Further, it would be authorized to veto state laws violating the national Constitution and to use force against "any member of the union failing to fulfill its duty."

It is evident that the "Virginia Plan," if carried out, would have reduced the states to secondary units, and that Madison and Washington, if not the rest of the Virginia delegation, desired a powerful central government, that they were little concerned about "state rights," that they were devout nationalists. They could hardly have placed more severe limits upon the states without destroying their authority. Nor was nationalistic fervor lacking in the other Southern delegations. The South Carolinians, indeed, were almost as united in demanding large powers for the central government as were the Virginians. Not that the Southerners were prepared to sacrifice all sectional interests. They wanted to be sure that they had their full share of power in that government, even hoped to dominate it, since they rather expected the South to surpass the remainder of the nation in numbers; they were averse to the use of its authority in behalf of commercial interests and against their own; and they sought assurance that Federal taxation would be no more injurious in the South than to the northward. Men from South Carolina and Georgia were also opposed to national action against the oceanic slave trade. Among the Southerners there was, however, a general willingness to make concessions, if necessary, with respect to their special interests in order to build a more binding union.

Although sectional interests were formidable obstacles in the path of those pushing for the powerful central government urged by the Virginians, the first great clash over their plan, and a spectacular one, arose from another quarter. The states had been equally represented in Congress under the Articles of Confederation, and the plan would destroy that equality. The delegations from New Jersey, Delaware, and New York, with some support from Connecticut and Maryland, protested violently, forming a "small state" party. Led by William Paterson of New Jersey and Luther Martin, the "small state" men professed to see in the plan a scheme to put power into the hands of the "large states," which would use it to their own benefit and at the expense of their sisters. They claimed that representation in the lower house of Congress based on wealth or numbers, together with the plan's arrangements for choice of the upper chamber and the executive, would enable Virginia, Massachusetts, and Pennsylvania, with little help from other states, to control the central government. They were moved not only by the jealousy of the small toward the large but by fears of economic discrimination—it will be recalled that New Jersey, Delaware, and Maryland had long striven for equal, or better than equal, treatment for their people with respect to the lands beyond the mountains. They were the stronger because some of them, and other members, disliked centralized power for other reasons. To no avail, Madison and other members sensibly urged that only sectional and economic interests, rather than those of states, large or small, would create keen contest under his system. In the end, the so-called Great Compromise, which assured to the smaller states equal representation in the upper house, satisfied Paterson and most of his associates. Thereafter, many of the "small states" men ardently championed centralization of power, and those who believed that as much authority as possible should be preserved to the states were left in a small minority.

Meanwhile, the less colorful and basically far more important struggle between the sections had begun. Early in June when the nature of the executive was discussed, George Mason urged that there be three heads of the national government, chosen by the Northern, Middle, and Southern states. Thus, since the executive would have some sort of veto power, the varied interests of the nation would be protected. Mason also contended in behalf of this scheme that a single executive would tend to become a monarch.[18] Although Hugh Williamson a little later voiced similar statements, Mason received no solid support from the South. Indeed, only the delegations of New York, Delaware, and Maryland voted against the single executive in committee of the whole, and none afterward. The Southerners were willing to risk the creation of a powerful president, Charles Pinckney and John Rutledge joining with James Wilson of Pennsylvania in pushing for one. Presumably they believed the South would not lose by the arrangement.

But the Southern delegates were not so easily satisfied when the manner of choosing the lower house was debated. Toward pleasing them Wilson proposed on June 11 that representation in the lower house be based upon the number of free citizens plus three fifths of the number of Negro slaves, Indians not taxed to be excluded—Wilson was suggesting the fractional formula Madison had championed for taxation in 1783. Wilson's generous scheme encountered little sectional opposition when he put it forth, and was accepted.[19] But South and North became entangled in bitter argument three weeks later, when Gouverneur Morris of Pennsylvania, an ardent Conservative, reopened the matter,

[18] Max Farrand (ed.), *The Records of the Federal Convention of 1787* (New Haven, 1937), I, 110–14. Mason's proposal brings to mind that of John Calhoun in the crisis of 1850 that there be two presidents, one Northern, the other Southern, each with a veto power.
[19] *Ibid.*, 193.

urging that representation be based upon wealth as well as persons. "Life and liberty," he contended, "were generally said to be of more value, than property. An accurate view of the matter would nevertheless prove that property was the main object of society." [20] Rutledge, Charles Cotesworth Pinckney, and Pierce Butler enthusiastically agreed, not only because they too valued wealth, but also because they fancied that slaves might be counted as property and that South Carolina would thus acquire a larger share of the membership of the house than it would under the Madison-Wilson formula. A special committee, in which Morris and Rutledge were conspicuous, was appointed to consider the proposal, and recommended on July 9 that both riches and numbers be taken into account, with Congress to have power to decide the representation of new states upon those bases.

The way was thus cleared for Congress to limit seriously the representation of new states beyond the Alleghenies, an arrangement desired by Rutledge and many Northerners, including Morris, who feared that the West would be Southern rather than Northern. However, the committee report did not indicate whether or not slaves were to be considered as property; and it soon became apparent that Morris also hoped to limit representation in the existing Southern states. When Randolph urged a periodic census, with representation fixed in proportion to the wealth and numbers discovered, the South Carolinians urged that slaves be fully counted; and Morris angrily demanded that they be omitted. Madison penetrated Morris' plans and insisted upon and secured a constitutional provision requiring both the census and apportionment accordingly, thus assuring equal treatment for the West.

Whether or not slaves were to be counted was not so easily settled. William Paterson contended with Morris that they should be omitted. Charles Cotesworth Pinckney talked about "the superior wealth" of the South and said it must have its due weight. Pierce Butler supported him, but a motion to count the blacks with the whites was supported only by South Carolina, Georgia, and Delaware, men from the upper South joining Northerners to defeat it. Northerners then put their motion, to drop the three-

[20] *Ibid.*, 533.

fifths formula. It carried, six to four, on July 11, with Virginia, North Carolina, Georgia, and Connecticut voting nay, with South Carolina—because her people wanted slaves fully counted—joining five Northern delegations to form a majority.[21] But that decision could not stand. William R. Davie, in one of his few speeches in the convention, made it clear on July 12 that Morris, Paterson, and their followers could not have their way. Davie was sure that North Carolina "would never confederate on any terms that did not rate them [the Negroes] at least as 3/5. If the Eastern states meant, therefore, to exclude them altogether the business was at an end." [22]

If there was to be a stronger union, compromise was indispensable. And Morris himself, on that same July 12, took the first step, moving that "direct taxation shall be in proportion to representation." Thus he would prevent the presumably poor of the West from taxing unjustly the presumably rich of the East, and would impose a tax burden upon the South which would be larger or smaller in accordance with the number of slaves counted. His proposal was unanimously approved. Randolph then urged that the convention adopt representation on the basis of numbers, with the three-fifths formula for the slaves, after each census. The South Carolinians, partly because they were tax conscious, agreed, and Northerners also. Accordingly, compromise was arranged, without violent dissent in any quarter. Thus the three-fifths formula was to be used in computing both representation and direct taxation.[23]

Other sectional issues had already appeared, and new ones were soon added. The convention perforce apportioned the members for the first House of Representatives. When a committee recommended that the Southern states be given twenty-nine seats and the others thirty-six, the men from the far South objected. They tried to cut down the votes of New Hampshire and to add to those of South Carolina and Georgia, but were unsuccessful.[24] Madison struggled against equal representation of the states in the Senate,

---

[21] *Ibid.*, 575–88.　　　　　　　　　　[22] *Ibid.*, 593.

[23] *Ibid.*, 589–97. In the event the South made no great concession with regard to direct taxes, since levies of that type were seldom imposed by Congress.

[24] *Ibid.*, 563–65.

because he feared the South would be in a minority in that body.[25] When the method of choosing Federal judges was debated, he urged appointment by the president with the approval of two thirds of the Senate. Were a mere majority required in that body, judges might be placed in office by a Northern minority of the people, though by a majority in the Senate; as a result, "a perpetual ground of jealousy & discontent would be furnished to the Southern States." [26] He lost the contest. Similarly, other Southerners ardently insisted that the Senate, in ratifying treaties, must do so by a two-thirds majority of senators present. Thus a Northern president and a Northern majority in that body would not be able to cede the right to navigate the Mississippi or Western territory without Southern support. They had their way, particularly because Northerners feared codfishing interests might conversely be bargained away by the Southerners.[27] Again, the convention was split over the question of giving to Congress a broad grant of authority in general terms or enumerating its powers in detail. The men from the far South were willing to approve a general grant only if it were specifically asserted that the Congress was to be without authority to interfere with slavery or impose an export tax. They preferred, however, toward safeguarding their special interests, to have both enumeration and the specific limitations.[28] Their wishes with regard to the principle of listing the powers of Congress were rather readily met, because enumeration permitted a more exact description of them, also because some delegates from all parts of the country feared that a general grant would permit the creation of an excessively strong central government. However, when the men from South Carolina and Georgia sought to curb that government by omitting grants of power and by specific limitations (on export taxes, on interference with the oceanic slave trade, and on encouragement of the Northern merchant marine at the expense of the South), they were less successful. A second great struggle between the sections resulted.

Nicholas Gilman, a delegate from New Hampshire, reported in

[25] Brant, *James Madison, Father of the Constitution*, 99–100.
[26] Farrand (ed.), *Records of the Federal Convention of 1787*, II, 80–81.
[27] Charles Warren, *The Making of the Constitution* (Boston, 1929), 651–58.
[28] Brant, *James Madison, Father of the Constitution*, 34–35, 102–104, 111–12.

a letter to a relative on July 31 that "Great wisdom and prudence, as well as liberality of sentiment and a readiness to surrender natural rights and privileges for the good of the Nation, appears in the Southern delegates in general"; and he devoutly wished that "the same spirit may pervade the whole Country." [29] Presumably, Gilman did not expect the Southerners to make needless special sacrifices, and they did not do so. In the important Committee of Detail, which had been appointed a week earlier and which was then functioning, Rutledge, its chairman, Randolph, Wilson, Nathanael Gorham of Massachusetts, and Oliver Ellsworth of Connecticut worked out three basic prohibitions upon Congress to satisfy the South, which were offered to the convention on August 7. These forbade export duties; interference with the oceanic slave trade; and navigation acts, save when passed by two-thirds majorities in both houses of Congress. It is evident that Ellsworth allied himself with Rutledge and Randolph in the committee, for he later stood firmly for the prohibitions on the floor of the convention.

The limiting clauses aroused hot debate in the convention. Wilson strenuously fought the prohibition against taxation of exports, and was joined by several Northerners, and by Madison and Washington, who felt that the power to levy duties upon exportations was essential to the national government and who did not fear that it would discriminate against the South. However, Ellsworth, his colleague Roger Sherman, and Elbridge Gerry of Massachusetts sided with the bulk of the Southerners, and the prohibition was approved.[30] It was far more difficult to reach a decision upon the other limitations. Sentiment against the slave trade was powerful in the upper South as well as in the North. George Mason denounced "this infernal trafic" which added to the number of slaves, injured the arts and manufacturing in the South, and discouraged white immigration into it; and Luther Martin vehemently attacked it. But the men from the Carolinas and Georgia insisted upon the prohibition. Rutledge asserted that "religion and humanity had nothing to do with the question." Charles Cotesworth Pinckney suggested that South Caro-

[29] Warren, *Making of the Constitution*, 374.
[30] Farrand (ed.), *Records of the Federal Convention of 1787*, II, 359–64.

lina might "by degrees do of herself what is wished," but she positively would not permit Federal action against the trade; and Abraham Baldwin indicated a belief that Georgia might also abolish it, if left freedom to make the decision locally. The two-thirds requirement for navigation acts also caused contention, for many Northerners found it unpalatable. It became evident on August 22 that there must be bargaining regarding the three prohibitions, and they were referred to a select committee containing one member from each state.[31] The key figure upon it was Charles Cotesworth Pinckney.

The select committee found a way out, offering on the floor a compromise which was substantially approved on August 29. The prohibition upon taxation of exports was retained, to the pleasure of the far South, and the men of that region also secured a bar against Federal interference with the slave trade before 1808. However, they conceded power to regulate it after that year, and also the right to levy a tax up to ten dollars upon each slave imported both before and after that year. Moreover, they gave up the two-thirds provision with regard to navigation acts, at that time a remarkable concession, since a Congress desiring to encourage the American merchant marine might bar foreign ships from Southern ports, despite Southern opposition.[32] Presumably, Northern shipowners would thus be enabled to secure a monopoly of the carrying trade of the South, to the disadvantage of the South, since freedom of trade best suited Southern economic interest. Northerners eager for a settlement and for the opportunity to seize that carrying trade had been offered a good bargain, and they accepted it. Southerners were reluctant to concede the special protection they had asked against a sectional navigation act, but Pinckney astutely, generously, and effectively urged that they do so. In an able speech he said: "it was the true interest of the S. States to have no regulation of commerce; but considering the loss brought on the commerce of the Eastern States by the revolution, their liberal conduct towards the views of South Carolina, and the interest the weak Southn. States had

[31] *Ibid.*, 364–65, 369–75, 378.
[32] A minor part of the compromise required that poll and other direct taxes be levied in accordance with census returns.

in being united with the strong Eastern States, he thought it proper that no fetters should be imposed on the power of making commercial regulations; and that his constituents though prejudiced against the Eastern States, would be reconciled to this liberality—He had himself, he said, prejudices agst the Eastern States before he came here, but would acknowledge that he had found them as liberal and candid as any men whatever." [33] Rutledge supported Pinckney, as did Butler, perhaps reluctantly, for he thought Southern and Northern interests to be as different as those "of Russia and Turkey"; and the weight of South Carolina was thus cast for the compromise, despite the opposition of Charles Pinckney. Charles Pinckney, once thought to be a principal architect of the Constitution of 1787, played a smaller role in its making than Charles Cotesworth Pinckney, whose major contribution is not generally known.[34] The stature which he displayed in the convention and the opinions which he voiced explain in some part why New England Federalists supported him for the vice-presidency in 1800 and for the presidency in 1804 and again four years later.

There were no further difficulties between North and South. Both Northerners and Southerners who disliked slavery recognized that the institution could not be directly attacked in the Constitution, and it was not. Indeed, the words "slave" and "slavery" were carefully avoided. Moreover, there was no opposition to a provision requiring the return of slaves fleeing across state lines. The problem of slavery was largely left to the states, and to the future.

Whether the new Constitution prepared at Philadelphia, with the strong central government for which it provided, would be approved in the states was doubtful when the convention broke up on September 17. The single and powerful chief executive, the Congress with ample powers, and the independent Federal judiciary which it envisaged, all of these exerting authority directly over the people, were certain to arouse distrust in many quarters

[33] Farrand (ed.), *Records of the Federal Convention of 1787*, II, 449–50. Earlier, Pinckney had done what he could to assure that Congress would do nothing to favor Northern at the expense of Southern ports. *Ibid.*, 418–19.

[34] *Ibid.*, 420, 445–53.

and for diverse reasons. Moreover, the document deprived the states of the power to issue currency and to "impair" the obligations of contracts, and it contained no bill of rights protecting the person against Federal tyranny. Further, it was certain that sectional interests, harmonized in the convention, would form a bar against approval in the states. That there would be a sharp struggle in some of the Southern ones was indicated even before adjournment when Randolph, Mason, John Francis Mercer, and Luther Martin indicated that they were opposed to the Constitution which they had helped to make. Before adjourning, the delegates called for a decision upon the document by state conventions specially chosen for the purpose, and declared that the Constitution should be put into operation when nine of those bodies voted aye.

CHAPTER XXI

THE SOUTH ENTERS
THE NEW UNION

THE convention of 1787 asserted that its Constitution should be put into motion as soon as nine states had approved it, and the old Congress, sending it on to the state capitals, took the same view. Actually, the consent of more than nine, and especially of the large states, was required before the new machinery could begin to turn. A union without Virginia was very doubtful; and one without Virginia and South Carolina was almost impossible. Happily, the conventions of both states, and those of Georgia and Maryland also, promptly gave assent. Only North Carolina in the South and Rhode Island in New England hung back, and a new central government commenced to move in the spring of 1789.

Georgia, rather surprisingly, was the first Southern state to act. Why it was so is not known, but sentiment for the Constitution was almost overwhelming. It may be that the Georgians ardently desired the protection which a powerful central government could give them against their Spanish and Indian neighbors.[1] In any case, the legislature of Georgia quickly arranged for the election of her convention, and that body unanimously gave assent at the beginning of the year 1788.[2]

Nearly four months passed before a second Southern state, Maryland, followed Georgia's example, after a sharp but one-sided contest. The Constitution was keenly attacked by Samuel

[1] Orin J. Libby, *The Geographical Distribution of the Vote of the Thirteen States on the Federal Constitution, 1787–8* (Madison, 1894), 44–45.

[2] E. Merton Coulter (ed.), "Minutes of the Georgia Convention Ratifying the Federal Constitution," in *Georgia Historical Quarterly* (Savannah), X (1926), 229.

Chase, Luther Martin, John Francis Mercer, and others—men who occupied debtor positions and who would profit personally from its defeat. They received support from the Maryland advocates of cheap paper money. But Washington, aware that the decision of Maryland would affect that of Virginia, powerfully intervened. South of the Potomac, Patrick Henry was preparing to fight the Constitution to the last ditch, and was talking about a Southern union to force economic concessions from the Northerners before ratification. Should Maryland act affirmatively, Henry's scheme would lose some of its appeal in Virginia. Pushed on by Washington, the friends of the Constitution in Maryland— the Federalists—campaigned for it with great vigor and secured an overwhelming majority in the state convention, which met at Annapolis late in April. In that body the Anti-Federalists, led by Chase, strove to postpone a decision until Virginia had spoken, and failed; he and his cohorts then tried to add crippling amendments in committee, and they were rejected. The Federalists, who would not even assert the merits of the Constitution upon the floor, forced its approval by a vote of 63 to 11.[3]

Less than a month later South Carolina also gave her solid endorsement. Debate upon the Constitution began early, in the state legislature in January, with Charles Pinckney, Charles Cotesworth Pinckney, John Rutledge, and Robert Barnwell ably defending it. There was no opposition to calling for the election of a convention to consider it, but Rawlins Lowndes, with little support from other members, denounced it, chiefly because it did not sufficiently defend Southern interests. Praising the Articles of Confederation, surely a tactical error, he attacked the parts of the Constitution giving Congress the power to regulate commerce and to put an end to the foreign slave trade. Too many concessions had been made, against the interests of South Carolina and Georgia. Moreover, he was sure that Northerners would dominate Congress and secure the presidency, after Washington should be no longer available for that office; that the election of a South Carolinian or Georgian was unlikely; that the Northerners would use their authority against the South. He believed that,

[3] Crowl, *Maryland during and after the Revolution*, 116–63, offers a splendid account of the contest.

"when this new Constitution should be adopted, the sun of the Southern States would set, never to rise again." [4]

The Pinckneys, the Rutledges, and others answered Lowndes. They belittled the concessions made regarding the slave trade and national control over commerce. They argued the far South would lose little as the result of navigation acts; the North might gain, to the common good; in any case, the North had also yielded at several points. They did not fear Northern tyranny. Barnwell made possibly the most effective appeal, for he spoke to the emotions as well as to reason. In a fervently nationalist appeal he ridiculed efforts to arouse jealousy of the "Eastern states." "When the arm of oppression lay heavy on us, were they not the first to arouse themselves? When the sword of civil discord was drawn, were they not the first in the field? When war deluged their plains with blood, what was their language? Did they demand the southern troops to the defence of the north? No! Or, when war floated to the south, did they withhold their assistance? The answer was the same. When we stood with the spirit, but weakness, of youth, they supported us with the vigor and prudence of age. When our country was subdued, when our citizens submitted to superior power, it was then these states evinced their attachment. He saw not a man who did not know that the shackles of the south were broken asunder by the arms of the north." [5] Barnwell's listeners could not fail to remember that Lowndes had given up the patriot cause in that time of crisis, that he had taken an oath of allegiance to Britain when other patriots persevered. Receiving only uninformed help from Upcountry members, Lowndes was borne down. That the men from the back country were not made happy by this result was shown to a degree in a vote upon the meeting place of the convention. Charleston was chosen, 76 votes to 75.

At Charleston in May the contest was resumed in the state convention, with the outcome certain. The overrepresented Low Country was almost solidly for the Constitution, the bulk of the Upcountry was against it. Thomas Sumter, who apparently led

[4] Elliot (ed.), *Debates in the Several State Conventions*, IV, 265–66, 271–74, 287–91, 308–11.
[5] *Ibid.*, 292–93.

the Anti-Federalists, was no more able than Lowndes to withstand the orators of the seaboard aristocracy. John Rutledge put the issue squarely. "The true question at present is, whether the Southern States shall or shall not be parties to the Union." The vote, on May 23, was 149 to 70.[6] The foes and doubters of the Constitution did win one concession. It was agreed that South Carolinians in Congress were later to support amendments to the Constitution, chiefly certain ones proposed by Northern conventions, including a declaration reserving to the states "every power not expressly relinquished by them." [7]

If Virginia did not join the new union, the states in the lower South could hardly be, or at least remain, parts of it. Indeed, it was doubtful that the Constitution would be put into operation without her assent. And Virginia was all the more important because eight conventions had voted aye when her delegates gathered at Richmond early in June. New Hampshire was about to make up her mind, and Virginia, if she ratified, would be the ninth or tenth state to do so. Moreover, her example might prove decisive for North Carolina, where the issue was very much in doubt, and would exercise influence in New York and Rhode Island, where the enemies of the Constitution were also numerous. In view of Virginia's past record, the Old Dominion might well have been expected to answer quickly and positively in the affirmative. Instead, there was a furious struggle. Patrick Henry looked squarely at the Constitution and heartily disliked it. What he did want— the existing union; the existing union with minor changes; a Southern federation; or the new system proposed, with massive amendments—is not entirely clear. That he had no clear-cut and sound program of his own to present did not prevent him from

---

[6] *Ibid.,* 316–17.

[7] *Ibid.,* 325. By the summer of 1789 Pierce Butler as a United States senator was wondering whether he had made a mistake in pushing for a strong central government. He was then urging that North Carolina enter the Union "as the only chance the Southern interest had to preserve a balance of power. Col. Davie and Mr. Williamson can witness for me that I was strongly federal; and that I conceded many points for the purpose of bringing about the union . . . but I could not suppose that those concessions would be so soon abused and taken advantage of." Pierce Butler to Iredell, August 11, 1789, Griffith J. McRee, *Life and Correspondence of James Iredell* (New York, 1857–1858), II, 264–65.

condemning the one offered. Henry retained all of his pristine magic as a persuader, and he rallied about him all the men and forces opposed to the Constitution.

In the winter and spring that preceded the Virginia convention, Henry formed an alliance of those who favored the Constitution with changes and those who were flatly opposed to it. He himself pretended to seek amendments. He posed as the champion of the common man against aristocrats who were seeking to create a government which they would control; he appealed to men indebted to British creditors and to advocates of paper money, whose personal interests would be cramped or defeated by the adoption of the Constitution; he contended that it would mean to the Kentuckians permanent loss of use of the Mississippi; he invoked sectional jealousy—the Northerners would dominate the union under it and would injure the South. He played upon the doubts, fears, and jealousies of the Virginians in masterly fashion. He claimed before and during the convention that majority opinion was with him, a doubtful pretension. Certainly, nearly half, if not a majority, of the delegates who gathered at Richmond were with him. He had failed, however, to win the support of Edmund Randolph, who long wavered, long sought both the Constitution and prior amendments to it. In the end Randolph determined that the Constitution was vital, amendments merely very desirable. Nor could Henry rely upon the help of any other Virginia leader then of the first rank, save for George Mason. He and Mason did obtain energetic assistance from William Grayson and James Monroe, two of Virginia's war heroes, and John Tyler. They were faced, however, by Madison, Randolph, and Edmund Pendleton, who were warmly backed by Light-Horse Harry Lee and John Marshall, also war veterans; and behind the Federalists was the pervasive influence of the absent Washington, whose wishes were well known, although they could hardly be trumpeted, since the first president under the Constitution would almost certainly be the man of Mount Vernon.

The conflict in the convention consumed more than three weeks, the 168 delegates who made the decision being exposed to lengthy, exhaustive, and enervating debate. When a thunderstorm put an early end to one session, it must have been greeted by many as an act of Heavenly mercy. Henry and his cohorts asked to be allowed to examine the Constitution point by point, a tactical error, since Henry spoke much more effectively to the general than to the specific. However, their wish was granted, and the document was combed with care. Henry, with astounding ingenuity, found the Constitution filled with flaws; and Mason, Grayson, and Monroe, not so fertile in argument, steadily backed him. The great orator posed as the champion of liberty, of the common man, of the states, and of the South. The Constitution was so formed that the president would become a king; the Senate was too small, and the House of Representatives also; the South would be outvoted; the new government would abandon the right to navigate the Mississippi, would favor Northern shipping at Southern expense; the slave trade could not be federally prevented for twenty years, but the new government could abolish slavery; the union was to be "consolidated" rather than federal; there was no clause specifically protecting the authority of the states; the Constitution did not contain a Bill of Rights; Federal taxation would discriminate against the South; treaties would be made without Southern consent; the members of Congress would vote themselves excessive salaries, would create for themselves plums in the shape of lucrative offices; the Federal district would form a stronghold for tyranny; escaped slaves would not be returned from it; national authority over the militia was dangerous; and so on and on. Henry went so far as to compare the Constitution unfavorably with that of monarchist Britain. It should not be asserted that Henry's fears for Southern interests were without foundation. They were given point by John Tyler, who asserted that "so long as climate will have effect on men, so long will the different climates of the United States render us different."

The burden of answering Henry and his allies fell chiefly upon Madison, who countered thoughtfully and quietly, often speaking in such a low voice that the reporter of the convention was unable to hear him. Madison gave logical replies to many of the Anti-Federalist arguments, which were to a degree chimerical and contradictory. If Henry was persuasive, Madison was often convincing. The Constitution was the best that could be secured; a strong central government would better protect American rights on the Mississippi than they had hitherto been, powerfully assert American interests against foreign ones, ensure sound military defense;

no one planned or desired a central tyranny; the powers of the states were sufficiently guarded; individuals would not be abused; both Northerners and Southerners sacrificed in making the Constitution; it was likely that Southerners would become more numerous than Northerners and that they would dominate the central régime; and both would continue to compromise on sectional interests. If the Constitution required altering, changes should be undertaken after adoption, not before; attempts to secure prior amendment would cause confusion and thwart a solid union.

Randolph, George Nicholas, Pendleton, and Marshall rallied behind Madison and debated effectively. Light-Horse Harry Lee doubtless contributed to the Federalist cause by personal attacks on Henry, steeled his party. His friends were uniformly polite to Henry, even when answering his most trivial objections. The young cavalryman, instead, was rough-handed. He challenged the orator's frequent claims to special championship of "liberty." Lee reminded his listeners that he himself had fought for it, and invited comparison of his own record with that of Henry. He attacked Henry's "windings and turnings," and voiced a low opinion of Henry's intellect. "The honorable gentleman is so little used to triumph on the grounds of reasoning, that he suffers himself to be quite captivated by the least appearance of victory." No one more emphatically spoke for the Constitution than Lee. "In the course of Saturday, and some previous harangues, from the terms in which some of the Northern States were spoken of, one would have thought that the love of an American was in some degree criminal, as being incompatible with a proper degree of affection for a Virginian. The people of America, sir, are one people. I love the people of the north, not because they have adopted the Constitution, but because I fought with them as my countrymen, and because I consider them as such. Does it follow from hence that I have forgotten my attachment to my native state? In all local matters I shall be a Virginian: in those of a general nature, I shall not forget that I am an American." [8] It was almost as if the master of Mount Vernon had spoken.

[8] For Henry ("Light-Horse Harry") Lee's speeches, see Elliot (ed.), *Debates in the Several State Conventions,* III, 41–43, 176–87, 272–73, 333–34, 405–407.

Henry and his associates were worsted in debate, but it long remained doubtful that they formed only a minority. Most of Virginia south of the James was with them, and also Kentucky. However, the Northern Neck, the Shenandoah, and the Virginians settled on the upper Ohio voted for the Constitution; and Henry's opposition was weakened by the fact that some of the Federalists indicated they were willing to push for amendments after ratification. It has been said that Randolph, who was then governor as well as a delegate, gained the victory for the Federalists by withholding from the convention, until after it had voted, a letter from Governor George Clinton of New York declaring that New York would ratify the Constitution only with prior and clogging amendments. It has been asserted that Henry's party would have been strengthened had the contents of the letter been known, that the example of New York would have had an effect. Whether it would have changed votes must remain unknown.[9] In any case, on June 25, prior amendments were voted down, eighty-eight to eighty, and the Constitution was approved, eighty-nine to seventy-nine.[10]

Sanctioning, the Virginia convention also asserted the right of revolution and insisted that the powers remaining to the states be respected. Moreover, it unanimously called for a list of amendments to protect personal rights. Further, a few who had voted for the Constitution joined with the Anti-Federalists to push through another group of proposed changes, principally intended to defend Southern interests. It was urged that no "commercial" treaty be ratified except by two thirds of the whole membership of the Senate; that no treaty ceding territory or rights of navigation be ratified by the Senate except in extreme necessity and that such an agreement be valid only when confirmed by three fourths of the states; that "no navigation law, or law regulating commerce, shall be passed without the consent of two thirds of

[9] Moncure D. Conway, *Omitted Chapters of History Disclosed in the Life and Papers of Edmund Randolph* (New York, 1888), 110–12.

[10] Elliot (ed.), *Debates in the Several State Conventions*, III, may be consulted for the speeches and actions of the convention. Hugh B. Grigsby, *The History of the Virginia Federal Convention of 1788*, in *Collections of the Virginia Historical Society* (Richmond), new ser., IX–X (1890–1891), is helpful.

the members present, in both houses." [11] There was, of course, no chance that the amendments intended to create special bulwarks for the South would be adopted, either in Congress or by the states. Those which were devoted to safeguarding personal rights had a happier fate, and were largely incorporated into the Constitution three years later.

The Virginians pushed the keystone of the new union into place. New Hampshire, although the fact was not known in Richmond, had already responded favorably; and a few weeks later New York gave grudging consent. Rhode Island and North Carolina still held out, but Rhode Island was small, and her adherence was not necessary; moreover, the people of both Rhode Island and North Carolina were certain to feel a "band-wagon" impulse and to find it to their advantage to slip in under the Federal roof.

The North Carolinians battled orally and even physically over the Constitution in the latter months of 1787 and until August of the following year. Thomas Person, an Anti-Federalist leader, condemned Washington as "a damned rascal and traitor to his country for putting his name to such an infamous paper as the new Constitution"; and Archibald Maclaine described Person and his party as "a set of fools and knaves." William Hooper, who did not look through Anti-Federalist eyes, had his own blacked by an enemy of the Constitution. In December, 1787, the document was subjected to bitter criticism in the legislature, and Person tried to prevent the calling of a convention. He lost his point. Delegates were chosen in March, and they met at Hillsboro on July 21.

In the elections the Anti-Federalists, with Person, Willie Jones, Samuel Spencer, Timothy Bloodworth, and David Caldwell guiding them, won an overwhelming victory. Hooper and Richard Caswell were defeated. Only on Tidewater, where the planters and merchants prevailed, were the Federalists in a majority. Elsewhere, their opponents were almost uniformly victorious. The farmers of the interior feared the Constitution and those who made it. In the convention there were 184 opposed to it, only 84 for it. The debates were similar to those in Virginia, but less protracted, because the Anti-Federalists contented themselves

[11] Elliot (ed.), *Debates in the Several State Conventions*, III, 656–63.

with brief replies to the arguments of James Iredell and others who spoke for the document. On August 2 they put through their program. They urged a second Federal convention to reconsider the Constitution, demanded a Bill of Rights, and submitted a long list of other amendments, chiefly to protect Southern interests, these being literally the same as those proposed by Patrick Henry and his followers in Virginia.

The decision of the Hillsboro convention could not stand. When the other Southerners proceeded to take their part in launching the new national government, the North Carolinians found themselves outside the American nation, their state becoming an independent republic, and they were not happy. The majority of them had sought federation on their own terms; it now became only too evident that they could not impose conditions. Assurances of a Federal Bill of Rights had an effect,[12] and also the possibility of economic warfare with the United States. There was a rapid shift of sentiment which led to a call for a second convention late in 1788; and a year later that body ratified by a large majority, 195 to 77.[13] The South had entered the new union.

While North Carolina cheerfully reversed her stand,[14] Patrick Henry vainly sought ways and means to retrieve his defeat. Under his leadership the Virginia Assembly called for a second national convention to propose amendments, but to no avail. He was able to secure the choice of two enemies of the Constitution, Richard Henry Lee and William Grayson, for the new Federal Senate in the elections of 1788. He also backed Monroe in a campaign against Madison for the lower house, but Monroe lost. And Washington was unanimously selected for the presidency by the electors,

[12] The news that Madison was pushing a Bill of Rights in Congress reached Carolina in June, 1789, and had a great effect. Some of the Anti-Federalists were not so concerned with the protection of Southern interests as they had appeared to be, and indicated that they were satisfied with Madison's amendments. William R. Davie to Madison, June 10, 1789, William R. Davie Collection (University of North Carolina Library).

[13] Louise I. Trenholme, *The Ratification of the Federal Constitution in North Carolina* (New York, 1932), competently deals with its subject.

[14] The Anti-Federalists in the second convention accepted its verdict in good spirit. William J. Dawson to Iredell, November 22, 1789; Samuel Johnston to Iredell, November 23, 1789, in McRee, *Life and Correspondence of James Iredell*, II, 272.

Northern, Southern, Eastern, Western.[15] The Virginia Dynasty began to emerge. Few will say that its princes did not deserve the dignities accorded to them. Certainly the Virginians of the Revolutionary generation, including Henry himself, specially contributed to the making of the wide arch of the American republic.

Much has been said, and rightly, about the splendors of the Constitution of 1787, about the fine statecraft of its makers in the convention. It is not always observed that the manner in which the document was confirmed was even more remarkable, that the people of thirteen different states eventually gave their consent, without the loss of a single life. That all the Americans should always be content with the new arrangement was not, of course, to be expected. Westerners, more New Englanders, and many Southerners were to seek to leave the new union. During the War of Independence and immediately thereafter, the South, emerging as a section with interests opposed to those of a North, set aside fears of domination by that North and freely joined in making it. The decision, seriously questioned at the time below the Susquehanna, was afterward widely regretted in the South. However, much as they venerate their forebears who sacrificed so generously and so enormously for the Lost Cause of a Southern nation, nearly all Southerners have accepted with Robert E. Lee the verdict of Appomattox and offer fidelity to that larger nation for which Washington, Jefferson, Madison, the Rutledges, and the Pinckneys, and a host of other Southern leaders, together with Southern planters, merchants, and plain folk, in alliance and comradeship with their brethren above the Mason-Dixon line, laid the foundations.

---

[15] The love and admiration which the American people gave to Washington were so great that it is difficult to describe their sentiments. They may be deduced from verse which appeared in the Annapolis *Maryland Gazette*, November 29, 1781. The general was tumultuously received at Annapolis after Yorktown.

> *You would have thought the very windows spoke,*
> *So many greedy looks of young and old*
> *Through casements darted their desiring eyes*
> *Upon his visage; and that all the walls,*
> *With painted imagery, had said at once,*
> *GOD SAVE THEE, WASHINGTON.*

CRITICAL ESSAY ON AUTHORITIES

GUIDES TO MANUSCRIPT COLLECTIONS

AMONG the more useful guides to the manuscript materials for Southern history during the Revolutionary period is Lynette Adcock (comp.), *Guide to the Manuscript Collections of Colonial Williamsburg* (Williamsburg, 1954). Charles M. Andrews, *Guide to the Materials for American History, to 1783, in the Public Record Office of Great Britain,* 2 vols. (Washington, 1912–1914), and Charles M. Andrews and Frances G. Davenport, *Guide to the Manuscript Materials for the History of the United States to 1783, in the British Museum, in Minor London Archives, and in the Libraries of Oxford and Cambridge* (Washington, 1908), are indispensable for the effective use of relevant British documents. Henry P. Beers, "The Papers of the British Commanders in Chief in North America, 1754–1783," in *Military Affairs* (Washington, 1937–), XIII (1949), 79–94, offers helpful comment on the location and content of the papers of the successive British military commanders. The *Calendar of the General Otho Holland Williams Papers in the Maryland Historical Society* (Baltimore, 1940) gives a list of and extensive quotations from the papers of an important Revolutionary officer. The *Catalogue of Archival Material, Hall of Records, State of Maryland,* in *Publications of the Hall of Records Commission,* No. 2 (Annapolis, 1942), and the *Calendar of Maryland State Papers,* in *Publications of the Hall of Records,* Nos. 1, 3, 4, 5, 6, 7, 8, 9, and 10 (Annapolis, 1943–1950), cover documents of the Revolutionary period. David L. Corbitt (ed.), *Calendars of Manuscript Collections . . . of the North Carolina Historical Commission* (Raleigh, 1926), is helpful, as is Norma B. Cuthbert, *American Manuscript Collections in the Huntington Library for the History of the Seventeenth and Eighteenth Centuries* (San Marino, 1941). Robert B. Downs (ed.), *Resources of Southern Libraries: A Survey of Facilities for Research* (Chicago, 1938), and

James H. Easterby, *Guide to the Study and Reading of South Carolina History* (Columbia, 1950), offer useful introductions. William S. Ewing, *Guide to the Manuscript Collections in the William L. Clements Library* (Ann Arbor, 1953), describes the rich holdings of Revolutionary documents in that repository. Curtis W. Garrison (comp.), *List of Manuscript Collections in the Library of Congress to July, 1931,* in American Historical Association, *Annual Report,* 1930, I (Washington, 1931), 123–233, offers a guide to additions made during the period 1918–1931. Evarts B. Greene and Richard B. Morris, *A Guide to the Principal Sources for Early American History (1600–1800) in the City of New York* (2d ed., New York, 1953), is thorough and reliable. Grace G. Griffin, *A Guide to Manuscripts Relating to American History in British Depositories Reproduced for the Division of Manuscripts of the Library of Congress* (Washington, 1946), serves as a pilot to the large collection of copies of British documents in that institution. The *Guide to the Manuscripts in the Southern Historical Collection of the University of North Carolina,* in *James Sprunt Studies in History and Political Science,* XXIV, No. 2 (Chapel Hill, 1941), is very helpful, and also the *Guide to the Records in the National Archives* (Washington, 1948). *The Handbook of Manuscripts in the Library of Congress* (Washington, 1918) is of the first value. Historical Records Survey, *Guide to the Manuscript Collections in the Archives of the North Carolina Historical Commission* (Raleigh, 1942), offers a helpful introduction, as does Hugh T. Lefler, *A Guide to the Study and Reading of North Carolina History* (Chapel Hill, 1955). Helen G. McCormick, "A Provisional Guide to the Manuscripts in the South Carolina Historical Society," in *South Carolina Historical and Genealogical Magazine* (Charleston, 1900–), XLV (1944), 111–15, 172–76; XLVI (1945), 49–53, 104–109, 171–75, 214–17; XLVII (1946), 53–57, 171–78; XLVIII (1947), 45–53, 177–80, is inconveniently published, but useful. Howard H. Peckham, *Guide to the Manuscript Collections in the William L. Clements Library* (Ann Arbor, 1942), remains excellent. C. Percy Powell (comp.), *List of Manuscript Collections Received in the Library of Congress, July 1931 to July 1938,* in American Historical Association, *Annual Report,* 1937, I (Washington, 1939), 113–40, is helpful with respect to acquisitions of the Library during the period covered. Alice E. Smith, *Guide to the Manuscripts of the Wisconsin State Historical Society* (Madison, 1944), and Nannie M. Tilley and Norma Lee Goodwin, *Guide to the Manuscript Collections in the Duke University Library,* in Trinity College Historical Society *Papers,* Ser. XXVII–XXVIII (Durham, 1947), are well done. The

Catalogue of Manuscripts in the Collection of the Virginia Historical Society (Richmond, 1901), is a good guide. Library of Congress, *Manuscripts in Public and Private Collections in the United States* (Washington, 1924), is helpful. University of Virginia Library, *Annual Reports of the Archivist* [Charlottesville], 1930–1940 (I–X), *Annual Reports on Historical Collections* [Charlottesville], 1940– (XI–) and Virginia State Library, *Reports* (Richmond), 1903–1904—lead one to valuable Virginia papers. Robert H. Woody, "The Public Records of South Carolina," in *American Archivist* (Menasha, Cedar Rapids, 1938–), II (1939), 244–63, is extremely useful, especially since publication of South Carolina documents of the Revolutionary period has been scanty.

MANUSCRIPT COLLECTIONS

The manuscripts concerning the history of the South during the Revolutionary period would, if collected, form an immense body. The largest holding is that of the Public Record Office of Great Britain, which houses official documents relating generally to America and specifically to each of the Southern colonies, including the Floridas. Manuscripts in the British Museum, such as the General Frederick Haldimand Papers, are also useful.

The public records of the Southern colony-states are also, with some exceptions, preserved either in original documents or copies in American institutions. The Library of Congress contains a vast collection of copies of official papers secured in Great Britain and other countries. One important set of Board of Trade documents is similarly available in the Historical Society of Pennsylvania; and the New York Public Library houses a large body of transcripts concerning the American loyalists. All of the older Southern states have tried to secure complete files, by means of originals and copies, of the papers dealing with their colonial and Revolutionary history, with uneven results. The holdings of the Maryland Hall of Records are incomplete. The bulk of the records of Virginia are available in her State Archives, the Virginia State Library, and the University of Virginia Library. Correspondence of the later British governors of Virginia is to be found in the Library of Congress; and institutions in Virginia are now sponsoring an attempt to make available in Virginia all British documents relating to the Old Dominion. The Historical Commission of North Carolina and the South Carolina State Archives have secured virtually complete colonial archives for their respective states, in both of which the Revolutionary records are also preserved in quantity. The Georgia State Department of Archives and History houses transcripts of the bulk of British colonial papers concerning Georgia, and rather scanty Revolutionary records have been preserved at Atlanta.

The immense body of Papers of the Continental Congress is now preserved in the National Archives, with some other materials for Revolutionary history.

Large collections of personal papers relevant to the South during the era of independence are, alas, rather few. The Library of Congress contains the George Washington Papers, together with very important Thomas Jefferson, James Madison, and James Monroe collections. The South Carolina Historical Society holds the papers of Henry Laurens. The William L. Clements Library of the University of Michigan contains the papers of General Thomas Gage, Lord George Germain, and General Sir Henry Clinton, British leaders who had much to do with the Revolutionary South, and also a valuable collection of General Nathanael Greene Papers. Documents of the Virginia Lees and other Nathanael Greene documents are in the possession of the American Philosophical Society. A third Greene collection of importance is in the Henry E. Huntington Library and Art Gallery. The General Horatio Gates manuscripts are with the New-York Historical Society. The Wisconsin State Historical Society has the Lyman Copeland Draper Papers, valuable for the history of the Southern frontier. With the Maryland Historical Society are the General Otho Holland Williams Papers. The Virginia State Library serves as repository for many George Rogers Clark documents. The University of Virginia Library has an important Jefferson collection.

NEWSPAPERS

While files of Southern newspapers of the Revolutionary period are often incomplete, long runs of several are preserved, especially of the Annapolis *Maryland Gazette* (1745–1777, 1779–1839), the Williamsburg *Virginia Gazettes* (1736–1780), the Charleston *South-Carolina Gazette* (1732–1775), and the Charleston *South-Carolina and American General Gazette* (1764–1775). As a guide to these, Clarence L. Brigham (comp.), *History and Bibliography of American Newspapers, 1690–1820*, 2 vols. (Worcester, 1947), is indispensable. Lester J. Cappon and Stella F. Duff (comps.), *Virginia Gazette Index*, 2 vols. (Williamsburg, 1950), is also helpful. Hennig Cohen, *The South-Carolina Gazette, 1732–1775* (Columbia, 1953), offers a good introduction to that publication.

GUIDES TO PRINTED MATERIALS

A Bibliography of the Virginia Campaign and the Siege of York-town, 1781 (Yorktown, 1941) is helpful. Thomas D. Clark (ed.), *Travels in the Old South; A Bibliography,* 2 vols. (Norman, 1956), is thorough and very useful. Easterby, *Guide to the Study and Reading of South Carolina History,* serves as a good introduction to printed as well as manuscript materials. Charles Evans (ed.), *American Bibliography; A Chronological Dictionary of All Books, Pamphlets and Periodical Publications Printed in the United States . . . 1639 . . . 1820,* 12 vols. (Chicago, 1903–1934), needs no comment. Grace G. Griffin *et al.* (eds.), *Writings on American History,* 1902– (Princeton, New York, New Haven, Washington, 1904–), is indispensable for both contemporary and noncontemporary writings. Oscar Handlin *et al., Harvard Guide to American History* (Cambridge, 1954), is helpful, as is Lefler, *Guide to the Study and Reading of North Carolina History.* William Matthews (ed.), *American Diaries: An Annotated Bibliography . . . to the Year 1861* (Berkeley and Los Angeles, 1945), is an important guide. Stanley Pargellis and D. J. Medley (eds.), *Bibliography of British History: The Eighteenth Century, 1714–1789* (Oxford, 1951), contains listings of value. Joseph Sabin *et al.* (eds.), *Bibliotheca Americana: A Dictionary of Books Relating to America, from Its Discovery to the Present Time,* 29 vols. (New York, 1868–1936), is standard. Earl G. Swem, "A Bibliography of Virginia," Virginia State Library, *Bulletin* (Richmond), VIII (1915), X (1917), XII (1919), XVII (1932), and Earl G. Swem (comp.), *Virginia Historical Index,* 2 vols. (Roanoke, 1934–1936), save the student much time and trouble. Justin Winsor (ed.), *Narrative and Critical History of America,* 8 vols. (Boston, 1889), covers the older literature and is too often ignored.

PRINTED PUBLIC DOCUMENTS

The most important printed British records for the Revolutionary South are William Cobbett (ed.), *The Parliamentary History of England from the Earliest Period to the Year 1803,* 36 vols. (London, 1806–1820); Danby Pickering *et al.* (eds.), *Statutes at Large from Magna Charta* (Cambridge and London, 1762–1814); Sir John Fortescue (ed.), *The Correspondence of King George the Third from 1760 to December, 1783,* 6 vols. (London, 1927–1928); *Journal of the Commissioners for Trade and Plantations from April 1704 . . . to May 1782,* 12 vols. (London, 1920–1938); and William L. Grant and James Munro (eds.), *Acts of the Privy Council of England, Colonial Series,* 6 vols. (London,

1908–1912). Among the most useful American collections of a Federal nature are Worthington C. Ford *et al.* (eds.), *Journals of the Continental Congress, 1774–1789,* 34 vols. (Washington, 1904–1937); Edmund C. Burnett (ed.), *Letters of Members of the Continental Congress,* 8 vols. (Washington, 1921–1936); Max Farrand (ed.), *The Records of the Federal Convention of 1787,* 4 vols. (New Haven, 1911–1937); *Heads of Families at the First Census of the United States Taken in the Year 1790,* 12 vols. (Washington, 1907–1908); Francis Wharton (ed.), *The Revolutionary Diplomatic Correspondence of the United States,* 6 vols. (Washington, 1889); and David Hunter Miller, *Treaties and Other International Acts of the United States of America,* 8 vols. (Washington, 1931–1948).

A considerable part of the public records of Revolutionary Maryland is published in William H. Browne *et al.* (eds.), *Archives of Maryland* (Baltimore, 1883–). Included are papers of Lieutenant Governor Horatio Sharpe, 1753–1771, VI, IX, XIV (1888, 1890, 1895); the proceedings and acts of the General Assembly, 1764–1774, LIX–LXIV (1942–1947); the proceedings of the council, 1761–1770, XXXII (1912); journal of the Convention, 1775, XI (1892); journal and correspondence of the council of safety, 1775–1777, XI, XII, XVI (1892, 1893, 1897); and journal and correspondence of the state council, 1775–1784, XVI, XXI, XLIII, XLV, XLVII, XLVIII (1897, 1901, 1924, 1927, 1930, 1931). *Proceedings of the Conventions of . . . Maryland . . . 1774, 1775, & 1776* (Annapolis, 1836), is also useful, together with "Correspondence of Governor Eden [1769–1777]," in *Maryland Historical Magazine* (Baltimore, 1906–), II (1907), 1–13, 97–110, 227–44, 293–309; Helen L. Peabody (ed.), "Revolutionary Mail Bag: Governor Thomas Sim Lee's Correspondence, 1779–1782," *ibid.,* XLIX (1954), 1–20, 122–42, 223–37, 314–31; L (1955), 34–46, 93–108; and Virgil Maxcy (ed.), *The Laws of Maryland,* 3 vols. (Baltimore, 1811). For Virginia there are available H. R. McIlwaine and John P. Kennedy (eds.), *Journals of the House of Burgesses of Virginia,* 13 vols. (Richmond, 1905–1915); H. R. McIlwaine (ed.), *Legislative Journals of the Council of Colonial Virginia,* 3 vols. (Richmond, 1918); "Proceedings of Virginia Committee of Correspondence," in *Virginia Magazine of History and Biography* (Richmond, 1893–), IX (1902), 355–60; X (1903), 337–56; XI (1903–1904), 1–25, 131–43, 346–57; XII (1904–1905), 1–14, 157–69, 225–40, 353–64; *Proceedings of the Convention of Delegates . . . in . . . Virginia, 1775–1776* (Richmond, 1816); *Journal of the House of Delegates, 1776–1790* (Richmond, 1827–1828); *Journal of the Senate of the Commonwealth of Virginia, 1778–1790* (Richmond, 1828); H. R. McIlwaine (ed.), *Journals of the Council of State of Virginia, 1776–1781*, 2 vols. (Richmond, 1931); W. P. Palmer *et al.* (eds.), *Calendar of Virginia State Papers and Other Manuscripts,* 11 vols. (Richmond, 1875–1893); H. R. McIlwaine (ed.), *Official Letters of the Governors of the State of Virginia,* 3 vols. (Richmond, 1926–1929); *Letters of Thomas Nelson, Jr., Governor of Virginia,* in Virginia Historical Society, *Publications,* new ser., No. 1 (Richmond, 1874); and William W. Hening (ed.), *The Statutes at Large; Being a Collection of All the Laws of Virginia, from the First Session of the Legislature, in the Year 1619,* 13 vols. (Richmond, 1819–1823). Basic for North Carolina are William L. Saunders (ed.), *The Colonial Records of North Carolina,* 10 vols. (Raleigh, 1886–1890); Walter Clark (ed.), *The State Records of North Carolina, 1777–1790,* 16 vols. (Goldsboro, 1895–1905); and Stephen B. Weeks, *Index to the Colonial and State Records of North Carolina,* 3 vols. (Goldsboro, Raleigh, 1909–1914). South Carolina records of the Revolutionary period are largely unpublished. Useful are "Correspondence of Charles Garth," in *South Carolina Historical and Genealogical Magazine,* XXVIII (1927), 79–93, 226–35; XXIX (1928), 41–48, 115–32, 212–30, 295–305; XXX (1929), 27–49, 105–16, 168–84, 215–35; XXXI (1930), 46–62, 124–53, 228–55, 283–91; XXXIII (1932), 117–39, 228–44, 262–79; "Miscellaneous Papers of the General Committee, Secret Committee and Provincial Congress, 1775," *ibid.,* VIII (1907), 132–50, 189–94; IX (1908), 9–11, 67–72, 115–17, 181–86; "Journal of the Council of Safety for the Province of South-Carolina, 1775," in *Collections of the South-Carolina Historical Society* (Charleston, 1857–1897), II (1858), 22–64; "Journal of the Second Council of Safety, Appointed by the Provincial Congress, November, 1775," *ibid.,* III (1859), 35–271; "Papers of the First Council of Safety of the Revolutionary Party in South Carolina, June–November, 1775," in *South Carolina Historical and Genealogical Magazine,* I (1900), 41–75, 119–35, 183–205, 279–310; II (1901), 3–26, 97–107, 167–93, 259–67; III (1902), 3–15, 69–85, 123–38; "Papers of the Second Council of Safety of the Revolutionary Party in South Carolina, November 1775–March 1776," *ibid.,* III (1902), 193–201; IV (1903), 3–25, 83–97, 195–214; A. S. Salley, Jr. (ed.), *Journal of the General Assembly of South Carolina, September 17, 1776–October 20, 1776* (Columbia, 1909); A. S. Salley, Jr. (ed.), *Journal of the House of Representatives, January–February, 1782* (Columbia, 1916); and Thomas Cooper and David J. McCord (eds.), *Statutes at Large of South Carolina,* 10 vols. (Columbia, 1836–1841). For Georgia there are Allen D. Candler (ed.), *The Colonial Records of the State of*

Georgia, 26 vols. (Atlanta, 1904–1916); Allen D. Candler (ed.), *The Revolutionary Records of the State of Georgia,* 3 vols. (Atlanta, 1908); "Letters from Sir James Wright," in *Collections of the Georgia Historical Society* (Savannah, 1840–), III (1873), 157–375; Lilla M. Hawes (ed.), "The Proceedings and Minutes of the Governor and Council of Georgia, October 4, 1774, through November 7, 1775, and September 6, 1779, through September 10, 1780," *ibid.,* X (1952); Lilla M. Hawes (ed.), "Letters to the Georgia Colonial Agent, July, 1762, to January, 1771," *Georgia Historical Quarterly* (Savannah, 1917–), XXXVI (1952), 250–86; C. C. Jones (ed.), *Acts Passed by the General Assembly of the Colony of Georgia, 1755 to 1774* (Wormsloe, Ga., 1881); E. Merton Coulter, "Minutes of the Georgia Convention Ratifying the Federal Constitution," in *Georgia Historical Quarterly,* X (1926), 223–37; and William H. Crawford and Horatio Marbury (eds.), *Digest of the Laws of the State of Georgia, from . . . 1755, to . . . 1800* (Savannah, 1802). A small part of the records of West Florida is published in Dunbar Rowland (ed.), *Mississippi Provincial Archives: English Dominion, 1763–1766* (Nashville, 1911).

PERSONAL COLLECTIONS

Among the more important published collections of personal papers is James A. James (ed.), *George Rogers Clark Papers, 1771–1784,* in *Collections of the Illinois State Historical Library* (Springfield, 1903–), VIII (1912), XIX (1926). *Letters of Joseph Clay, Merchant of Savannah, 1776–1793,* in *Collections of the Georgia Historical Society,* VIII (1913), throws light upon the economic and political history of Georgia during and after the Revolutionary War. Clarence E. Carter (ed.), *The Correspondence of General Thomas Gage,* 2 vols. (New Haven, 1931–1933), contains valuable sidelights on the South during the period 1763–1775. Materials of value on Georgia during the same period are available in *The Letters of Hon. James Habersham, 1756–1775,* in *Collections of the Georgia Historical Society,* VI (1904). Griffith J. McRee, *Life and Correspondence of James Iredell,* 2 vols. (New York, 1857–1858), is of first importance for Revolutionary North Carolina. Julian P. Boyd *et al.* (eds.), *The Papers of Thomas Jefferson* (Princeton, 1950–), far surpasses the earlier Jefferson collections. Thomas Jefferson, *Notes on the State of Virginia,* ed. by William Peden (Chapel Hill, 1955), is a recent scholarly edition. Awkward to consult, but extremely valuable, is the Henry Laurens correspondence in *South Carolina Historical and Genealogical Magazine,* III (1902), 86–96, 139–49, 207–15; IV (1903), 26–35, 99–107, 215–20, 263–77; V

(1904), 3–14, 69–81, 125–43, 197–208; VI (1905), 3–12, 47–52, 103–10, 137–60; VII (1906), 3–11, 53–68, 115–29, 179–93; VIII (1907), 3–18, 57–68, 123–31, 181–88; IX (1908), 3–8, 59–66, 104–14, 173–80; X (1909), 49–53. It is supplemented by William G. Simms (ed.), *The Army Correspondence of Colonel John Laurens in the Years 1777–8* (New York, 1867). *The Lee Papers,* in *Collections of the New-York Historical Society for the Year 1871 . . . 1872 . . . 1873 . . . 1874* (New York, 1872–1875), offers the papers of General Charles Lee, the originals being largely lost. James C. Ballagh (ed.), *The Letters of Richard Henry Lee,* 2 vols. (New York, 1911–1914), is a valuable compilation. John W. Caughey (ed.), *McGillivray of the Creeks* (Norman, 1938), offers interesting documents of the "King of the Creeks." Lilla M. Hawes (ed.), "Collections of the Georgia Historical Society and Other Documents: The Papers of Lachlan McIntosh, 1774–1799," in *Georgia Historical Quarterly,* XXXVIII (1954), 148–69, 253–67, 356–68; XXXIX (1955), 52–68, 172–86, 356–75; XL (1956), 65–68, 152–89, is an important collection. Gaillard Hunt (ed), *The Writings of James Madison,* 9 vols. (New York, 1900–1910), is not yet superseded. John Bennett (ed.), "Marion-Gadsden Correspondence," in *South Carolina Historical and Genealogical Magazine,* XLI (1940), 48–60, and "Francis Marion's Correspondence with General Nathanael Greene [1781–1782]," in *South Carolina Historical Association Publications,* XI (1907), 186–207, are helpful with respect to Francis Marion. The more important because Middleton materials are scanty is the "Correspondence of Hon. Arthur Middleton," in *South Carolina Historical and Genealogical Magazine,* XXVI (1925), 183–213; XXVII (1926), 1–29, 51–80, 107–55. Stanislaus M. Hamilton (ed.), *The Writings of James Monroe,* 7 vols. (New York, 1898–1903), is valuable, though a new edition is needed. Though small in quantity, the "Correspondence of John Rutledge," in *South Carolina Historical and Genealogical Magazine,* XVII (1916), 131–46; XVIII (1917), 42–49, 59–69, 131–42, 144–67, is important. John C. Fitzpatrick (ed.), *The Writings of George Washington . . . 1745–1799,* 39 vols. (Washington, 1931–1944), is the standard edition, easily superior to its predecessors.

DIARIES AND JOURNALS

Lida T. Rodman (ed.), *Journal of a Tour to North Carolina, by William Attmore, 1787,* in *James Sprunt Historical Publications,* XVII, No. 2 (Chapel Hill, 1922), contains interesting social commentary. John Bartram's journal in William Stork, *An Account of East Florida* (London, 1769), and Francis Harper (ed.), John Bartram, "Diary of a Journey through the Carolinas, Georgia, and Florida . . . 1765 to . . . 1766," in American Philosophical Society, *Transactions* (Philadelphia, 1769–1809, 1818–), new ser., XXXIII, Pt. I (1942), 1–120, offer interesting comment on natural phenomena. Jean B. Bossu, *Nouveaux Voyages dans l'Amérique Septentrionale* (Amsterdam, 1777), offers a Frenchman's view of Louisiana in the third quarter of the eighteenth century. [Andrew] *Burnaby's Travels through North America,* ed. by Rufus R. Wilson (New York, 1904), is a recent edition of the work of a discerning traveler in the colonies. In the "Diary of Col. Landon Carter [1774–1776]," in *William and Mary Quarterly,* 1st ser., XIV (1906), 181–86, 246–53; XV (1906), 15–20; XV (1907), 205–11; XVI (1908), 149–56, 257–68; XVII (1908), 9–18; XVIII (1909), 37–44; XX (1912), 173–85; XXI (1913), 172–81, we are given a part of the fascinating diary of a shrewd Virginia planter and politician. François Jean Chastellux, *Travels in North America in the Years 1780–81–82* (New York, 1827), contains valuable comment on the Southern states. *The Journal of Nicholas Cresswell, 1774–1777* (New York, 1924), Hunter D. Farish (ed.), *Journal & Letters of Philip Vickers Fithian, 1773–1774* (Williamsburg, 1943), and Robert G. Albion and Leonidas Dodson (eds.), *Philip Vickers Fithian: Journal and Letters,* 2 vols. (Princeton, 1900–1934), describe life in Virginia and Maryland and upon their frontiers. The hitherto unpublished journal of "Hair-Buyer" Hamilton in John D. Barnhart (ed.), *Henry Hamilton and George Rogers Clark in the American Revolution with the Unpublished Journal of Lieut. Gov. Henry Hamilton* (Crawfordsville, Ind., 1951), puts that individual in a somewhat more favorable light. Fred Shelley (ed.), "Ebenezer Hazard's Travels through Maryland in 1777," in *Maryland Historical Magazine,* XLVI (1951), 44–54, is interesting. *Mémoires du duc de Lauzun* (Paris, 1880), offers comment by a French officer serving in Virginia. J. G. de Roulhac Hamilton (ed.), "Revolutionary Diary of William Lenoir," in *Journal of Southern History* (Baton Rouge, Lexington, 1935–), VI (1940), 247–59, has value. Newton D. Mereness (ed.), *Travels in the American Colonies* (New York, 1916), contains among other items a travel journal by Lord Adam Gordon and a journal kept by Indian agent David Taitt. The Chevalier de Pontgibaud tells of his experiences in *A French Volunteer of the War of Independence* (New York, 1897); Josiah Quincy, *Memoir of the Life of Josiah Quincy, Jun.* (Boston, 1825), has descriptions of Charleston and other things Southern by Yankee Quincy. Evangeline W. Andrews and Charles M. Andrews (eds.), *Journal of a Lady of Quality* . . . [Janet Schaw] *1774 to 1776* (New Haven, 1921), has remarks about the South and Southern patriots by a Tory female. In Johann David Schoepf, *Travels in the Confederation [1783–1784]*, 2 vols., ed. and tr. by Alfred J. Morrison (Philadelphia, 1911), we are given shrewd comment on the Southern states by a German physician. William Seymour, *A Journal of The Southern Expedition, 1780–1783*, in *Historical and Biographical Papers of the Historical Society of Delaware* (Wilmington, 1879–), II (1896), tells part of the story of one Delaware soldier. John F. D. Smyth, *A Tour in the United States of America*, 1784, 2 vols. (Dublin, 1784), offers valuable description. John C. Fitzpatrick (ed.), *The Diaries of George Washington, 1748–1799*, 4 vols. (Boston, 1925), is of great importance chiefly because of its author. Richard J. Hooker (ed.), *The Carolina Backcountry on the Eve of the Revolution; The Journal and Other Writings of Charles Woodmason, Anglican Itinerant* (Chapel Hill, 1953), fascinates with its material on social and religious life in the interior of South Carolina.

MEMOIRS AND CONTEMPORARY ACCOUNTS

[James] *Adair's History of the American Indians*, ed. by Samuel C. Williams (Johnson City, Tenn., 1930), containing the observations of a veteran trader upon the Southern Indians, is a minor American classic. Thomas Anburey, *Travels Through the Interior Parts of America* (Boston, 1923), has little that is original. William Bartram, *Travels* (London, 1792), is valuable botanically and otherwise, but tinged with romanticism. In Jonathan Boucher, *A View of the Causes and Consequences of the American Revolution* (London, 1797), and Jonathan Bouchier (ed.), *Reminiscences of an American Loyalist, 1738–1789, Being the Autobiography of the Revd. Jonathan Boucher* (Boston, 1925), a Tory who knew Washington voices his opinions. William B. Willcox (ed.), *The American Rebellion; Sir Henry Clinton's Narrative of His Campaigns, 1775–1782* (New Haven, 1954), is based upon the papers of Sir Henry Clinton and describes the War of Independence as he saw it. George W. P. Custis, *Recollections and Private Memoirs of Washington* (New York, 1860), useful, is to be employed with caution. Joseph Doddridge, *Notes, on the Settlement and Indian Wars, of the Western Parts of Virginia & Pennsylvania* (Wellsburgh, Va., 1824), is valuable for frontier history, as is Willard R. Jillson (ed.), *Filson's Kentucke*, in *Filson Club Publications* (Louisville, 1884–), No. 35 (1930). [James Glen], *A Description of South Carolina* (London, 1761), is a sober contemporary work. [Alexander Hewat,] *An Historical Account of the Rise and Progress of the Colonies of South Carolina and Georgia* (London, 1779), is surprisingly mature and readable. Samuel

Kercheval, *A History of the Valley of Virginia* (4th ed., Strasburg, Va., 1925), is useful. Henry Lee, *Memoirs of the War in the Southern Department of the United States* (Philadelphia, 1812), despite occasional prejudice and error, is a classic. Hugh M'Call, *The History of Georgia*, 2 vols. (Savannah, 1811–1816), and George Milligen, *A Short Description of the Province of South Carolina* (London, 1770), are sober and helpful. William Moultrie, *Memoirs of the American Revolution*, 2 vols. (New York, 1802), gives Moultrie's view of the War of Independence. Philip Pittman, *The Present State of the European Settlements on the Mississippi,* ed. by Frank H. Hodder (Cleveland, 1906), contains good description. David Ramsay, *The History of the Revolution of South-Carolina* (Trenton, 1785), retains merit, as does the author's *The History of South-Carolina, from Its First Settlement in 1670, to the Year 1808* (Charleston, 1809); Bernard Romans, *A Concise Natural History of East and West Florida* (New York, 1775), is by a competent observer. Charles Stedman, *The History of the Origin, Progress and Termination of the American War* (London, 1794), is a bit more original than most of the contemporary histories of that conflict. Banastre Tarleton, *A History of the Campaigns of 1780 and 1781* (Dublin, 1787), tells a little about Tarleton. Samuel C. Williams (ed.), *Lieut. Henry Timberlake's Memoirs, 1756–1765* (Johnson City, Tenn., 1927), chronicles Timberlake's sojourn among the Cherokee. Elkanah Watson, *Men and Times of the Revolution* (New York, 1857), offers useful comment on the South. Arthur Young(?), *American Husbandry* (London, 1775), is a surprisingly full survey of the subject.

SPECIAL COLLECTIONS

Among the most useful special collections of documents are: Kenneth P. Bailey (ed.), *The Ohio Company Papers, 1753–1817* (San Francisco, 1947); William K. Boyd (ed.), "News, Letters and Documents concerning North Carolina and the Federal Constitution," in *Trinity College Historical Society Papers* (Durham, 1897–), XIV (1922), 75–95; William K. Boyd (ed.), *Some Eighteenth Century Tracts concerning North Carolina* (Raleigh, 1927), containing valuable papers on the Regulation; Burnett (ed.), *Letters of Members of the Continental Congress,* which throws much light on the activities of the Congress; Joseph B. Lockey, *East Florida, 1783–1785,* ed. by John W. Caughey (Berkeley and Los Angeles, 1949); Elizabeth Donnan (ed.), *Documents Illustrative of the History of the Slave Trade to America,* 4 vols. (Washington, 1930–1935); John Drayton, *Memoirs of the American Revolution,* 2 vols. (Charleston, 1821), which contains contemporary materials; Hugh E. Egerton (ed.), *The Royal Commission on the Losses and Services of the American Loyalists, 1783–1785* (Oxford, 1915); Jonathan Elliot (ed.), *The Debates in the Several State Conventions on the Adoption of the Federal Constitution,* 5 vols. (Philadelphia, 1859), an invaluable compilation of the debates over the Constitution in the state conventions; Peter Force (comp.), *American Archives,* 4th ser., 6 vols. (Washington, 1837–1846); 5th ser., 3 vols. (Washington, 1848–1853), a storehouse of documents sometimes neglected; Adelaïde L. Fries (ed.), *Records of the Moravians in North Carolina,* 7 vols. (Raleigh, 1922–1947); R. W. Gibbes (ed.), *Documentary History of the American Revolution . . . 1764–1782,* 3 vols. (New York, 1853–1857), a very useful collection; "Letters to General Greene and Others," in *South Carolina Historical and Genealogical Magazine,* XVI (1915), 97–108, 138–50; XVII (1916), 3–13, 53–57; Philip M. Hamer (ed.), "Correspondence of Henry Stuart and Alexander Cameron with the Wataugans," in *Mississippi Valley Historical Review* (Cedar Rapids, 1914–), XVII (1930–1931), 451–59; Stanislaus M. Hamilton (ed.), *Letters to Washington and Accompanying Papers,* 5 vols. (Boston and New York, 1898–1902), useful on various phases of the pre-Revolutionary period; Franklin B. Hough (ed.), *Siege of Charleston* (Albany, 1867); Franklin B. Hough (ed.), *Siege of Savannah* (Albany, 1866); Charles F. James (ed.), *Documentary History of the Struggle for Religious Liberty in Virginia* (Lynchburg, 1900); Louise P. Kellogg (ed.), *Frontier Advance on the Upper Ohio, 1778–1779* (Madison, 1916), and Louise P. Kellogg (ed.), *Frontier Retreat on the Upper Ohio, 1779–1781* (Madison, 1917), valuable for frontier history; Lawrence Kinnaird (ed.), *Spain in the Mississippi Valley, 1765–1794,* American Historical Association, *Annual Report,* 1945, II–IV (Washington, 1946); Edgar W. Knight (ed.), *A Documentary History of Education in the South before 1860,* 5 vols. (Chapel Hill, 1949–1953), a convenient collection; Hugh T. Lefler (ed.), *North Carolina History Told by Contemporaries* (Chapel Hill, 1934); Frances N. Mason (ed.), *John Norton and Sons, Merchants of London and Virginia; Being the Papers from their Counting House for the Years 1750 to 1795* (Richmond, 1937); Theodore B. Myers (ed.), *Cowpens Papers* (Charleston, 1881); Frank Moore (comp.), *Diary of the American Revolution* (New York, 1858), containing newspaper items and others not easily found elsewhere; Hezekiah Niles (ed.), *Principles and Acts of the Revolution in America* (New York, 1876), a collection still useful; Robert Purviance, *Narrative of Events Which Occurred in Baltimore Town during the Revolutionary War* (Baltimore, 1849); A. S. Salley (ed.), *Documents Relating to the History of South Carolina*

During the Revolutionary War (Columbia, 1908); Wilbur H. Siebert, *The Loyalists in East Florida, 1774–1785,* 2 vols. (De Land, 1929), offering both a narrative history and documents; Sir James E. Smith (ed.), *Selections of the Correspondence of Linnaeus and Other Naturalists* (London, 1821), helpful on American scientists; Jared Sparks (ed.), *Correspondence of the American Revolution; Being Letters of Eminent Men to George Washington,* 4 vols. (Boston, 1853), the military correspondence; Benjamin Franklin Stevens (ed.), *The Campaign in Virginia, 1781; An Exact Reprint of Six Rare Pamphlets on the Clinton-Cornwallis Controversy,* 2 vols. (London, 1888), containing Cornwallis-Clinton correspondence and other papers upon that campaign; Benjamin Franklin Stevens (ed.), *Facsimiles of Manuscripts in European Archives Relating to America, 1773–1783,* 25 vols. (London, 1889–1895), a storehouse of papers handsomely printed; Francis N. Thorpe (ed.), *The Federal and State Constitutions, Colonial Charters, and Other Organic Laws,* 7 vols. (Washington, 1909), a standard compilation of great value; Reuben G. Thwaites and Louise P. Kellogg (eds.), *Documentary History of Dunmore's War, 1774* (Madison, 1905), and Reuben G. Thwaites and Louise P. Kellogg (eds.), *Frontier Defense on the Upper Ohio, 1777–1778* (Madison, 1912), important for the trans-Allegheny West; Bernhard A. Uhlendorf (ed.), *The Siege of Charleston, with an Account of the Province of South Carolina* (Ann Arbor, 1938).

STUDIES PARTLY DEVOTED TO THE REVOLUTIONARY SOUTH

There are many works only partly concerned with the South in the Revolutionary period but valuable for phases of it. Representative of these are: John R. Alden, *The American Revolution, 1775–1783* (New York, 1954); Samuel A. Ashe, *History of North Carolina,* 2 vols. (Greensboro, 1908–1925); James C. Ballagh, *White Servitude in the Colony of Virginia* (Baltimore, 1895); James C. Ballagh, *A History of Slavery in Virginia* (Baltimore, 1902); John S. Bassett, *Slavery and Servitude in the Colony of North Carolina* (Baltimore, 1896); Charles A. Beard, *An Economic Interpretation of the Constitution of the United States* (New York, 1929), a brilliant argument for economic motivation now accepted only in part; George Louis Beer, *British Colonial Policy, 1754–1765* (New York, 1907), a solid monograph; Carl L. Becker, *The Declaration of Independence* (New York, 1922), a historical masterpiece; Samuel F. Bemis, *The Diplomacy of the American Revolution* (New York, 1935), a standard work; Frederick P. Bowes, *The Culture of Early Charleston* (Chapel Hill, 1942); Carl Bridenbaugh, *Cities in Revolt;*

Urban Life in America, 1743–1776 (New York, 1955), good social history; Carl Bridenbaugh, *Seat of Empire; The Political Role of Eighteenth-Century Williamsburg* (Williamsburg, 1950); Edmund C. Burnett, *The Continental Congress* (New York, 1941), displaying impressive scholarship; Julian A. C. Chandler, *The History of Suffrage in Virginia* (Baltimore, 1901); Julian A. C. Chandler, *Representation in Virginia* (Baltimore, 1896); Edward Channing, *A History of the United States,* 6 vols. (New York, 1905–1925), III, spotty, but still sound; Oliver P. Chitwood, *Justice in Colonial Virginia* (Baltimore, 1905); George L. Chumbley, *Colonial Justice in Virginia* (Richmond, 1938); Robert D. W. Connor, *History of North Carolina: Colonial and Revolutionary Periods* (Chicago, 1919); William K. Boyd, *History of North Carolina: The Federal Period, 1783–1860* (Chicago, 1919); David L. Corbitt, *The Formation of the North Carolina Counties, 1663–1943* (Raleigh, 1950); Robert S. Cotterill, *The Southern Indians; The Story of the Civilized Tribes before Removal* (Norman, 1954), useful and sympathetic toward the Southern tribes; E. Merton Coulter, *A Short History of Georgia* (Chapel Hill, 1933); Oliver M. Dickerson, *The Navigation Acts and the American Revolution* (Philadelphia, 1951), scholarly and thoughtful; Elisha P. Douglass, *Rebels and Democrats; The Struggle for Equal Political Rights and Majority Rule During the American Revolution* (Chapel Hill, 1955), provocative; W. E. Burghardt Du Bois, *The Suppression of the African Slave-Trade to the United States of America, 1638–1870* (New York, 1954), a standard work which could be amplified; James H. Easterby, *A History of the College of Charleston* (Charleston, 1935); Percy S. Flippin, *The Financial Administration of the Colony of Virginia* (Baltimore, 1915); Lawrence H. Gipson, *The Coming of the Revolution, 1763–1775* (New York, 1954); William C. Guess, *County Government in Colonial North Carolina,* in *James Sprunt Historical Publications,* XI (1911), 7–39; Lewis C. Gray, *History of Agriculture in the Southern United States to 1860,* 2 vols. (Washington, 1933); Fletcher M. Green, *Constitutional Development in the South Atlantic States, 1776–1860* (Chapel Hill, 1930), a very valuable monograph; Evarts B. Greene, *The Revolutionary Generation, 1763–1790* (New York, 1943); Evarts B. Greene and Virginia D. Harrington, *American Population before the Federal Census of 1790* (New York, 1932); Archibald Henderson, *North Carolina, The Old North State and the New,* 5 vols. (Chicago, 1941); Brooke Hindle, *The Pursuit of Science in Revolutionary America, 1735–1789* (Chapel Hill, 1956); Jay B. Hubbell, *The South in American Literature, 1607–1900* (Durham, 1954); J. Franklin Jameson, *The American Revolution Con-*

sidered *As a Social Movement* (Princeton, 1926), suggestive, though hardly definitive; Merrill Jensen, *The New Nation; A History of the United States during the Confederation, 1781–1789* (New York, 1950), emphasizing sociopolitical clash; Amanda Johnson, *Georgia as Colony and State* (Atlanta, 1938); Charles C. Jones, Jr., *History of Georgia*, 2 vols. (Boston, 1883); Hugh T. Lefler and Albert R. Newsome, *North Carolina; The History of a Southern State* (Chapel Hill, 1954), a scholarly history of a state; Hugh T. Lefler and Paul Wager (eds.), *Orange County—1752–1952* (Chapel Hill, 1953), valuable on the Regulators; Orin G. Libby, *The Geographical Distribution of the Vote of the Thirteen States on the Federal Constitution, 1787–8* (Madison, 1894); Paul M. McCain, *The County Court in North Carolina before 1750*, in *Trinity College Historical Society Papers*, XIII (1954); Eugene I. McCormac, *White Servitude in Maryland, 1634–1820* (Baltimore, 1904); Edward McCrady, *The History of South Carolina under the Royal Government, 1719–1776* (New York, 1899), faulty on important points, but still useful; Andrew C. McLaughlin, *The Confederation and the Constitution, 1783–1789* (New York, 1905), written from a nationalist viewpoint; Newton D. Mereness, *Maryland as a Proprietary Province* (New York, 1901); Elmer I. Miller, *The Legislature of the Province of Virginia, Its Internal Development* (New York, 1907); John C. Miller, *Origins of the American Revolution* (Boston, 1943); John C. Miller, *Triumph of Freedom, 1775–1783* (Boston, 1948); Walter H. Mohr, *Federal Indian Relations, 1774–1788* (Philadelphia, 1933); Chapman J. Milling, *Red Carolinians* (Chapel Hill, 1940); Edmund S. Morgan and Helen M. Morgan, *The Stamp Act Crisis; Prologue to Revolution* (Chapel Hill, 1953), a close study of a vitally important period; Richard B. Morris, *Government and Labor in Early America* (New York, 1946); Richard B. Morris, "Primogeniture and Entailed Estates in America," in *Columbia Law Review* (New York, 1901–), XXVII (1927), 24–51; Allan Nevins, *The American States during and after the Revolution, 1775–1789* (New York, 1924), a storehouse of information; Coralie Parker, *The History of Taxation in North Carolina during the Colonial Period, 1663–1776* (New York, 1928); Ulrich B. Phillips, *American Negro Slavery* (New York, 1918), and Ulrich B. Phillips, *Life and Labor in the Old South* (Boston, 1929), standard works; Charles Lee Raper, *North Carolina: A Study in English Colonial Government* (New York, 1904); Robert A. Rutland, *The Birth of the Bill of Rights, 1776–1791* (Chapel Hill, 1955), informative, though not detailed; Lorenzo Sabine, *The American Loyalists* (Boston, 1847); Albert B. Saye, *New Viewpoints in Georgia History* (Athens, 1943), suggestive; Albert B. Saye, *A Constitutional History of Georgia, 1732–1945* (Athens, 1948); Arthur M. Schlesinger, *The Colonial Merchants and the American Revolution, 1763–1776* (New York, 1918), dispassionate, thorough, reliable; William H. Seiler, "The Anglican Parish Vestry in Colonial Virginia," in *Journal of Southern History*, XXII (1956), 310–37; Abbot E. Smith, *Colonists in Bondage: White Servitude and Convict Labor in America, 1607–1776* (Chapel Hill, 1947); W. Roy Smith, *South Carolina as a Royal Province, 1719–1776* (New York, 1903); Julia C. Spruill, *Women's Life and Work in the Southern Colonies* (Chapel Hill, 1938), useful, dealing with a neglected subject; William B. Stevens, *A History of Georgia*, 2 vols. (New York, 1847); Stella H. Sutherland, *Population Distribution in Colonial America* (New York, 1936); John R. Swanton, *The Indians of the Southeastern United States* (Washington, 1946), a handbook containing the results of recent anthropological research; Claude H. Van Tyne, *The Causes of the War of Independence* (Boston, 1922), an older and sound study of the era 1763–1776; Claude H. Van Tyne, *The American Revolution, 1776–1783* (New York, 1905); Claude H. Van Tyne, *The Loyalists in the American Revolution* (New York, 1902), long the standard work, which ought to be replaced; David D. Wallace, *Constitutional History of South Carolina from 1725 to 1775* (Abbeville, 1899), David D. Wallace, *The History of South Carolina*, 4 vols. (New York, 1934), and David D. Wallace, *South Carolina, A Short History, 1520–1948* (Chapel Hill, 1951), the most reliable works on that state; Ethel K. Ware, *A Constitutional History of Georgia* (New York, 1947); Charles Warren, *The Making of the Constitution* (Boston, 1929); Stephen B. Weeks, *Church and State in North Carolina* (Baltimore, 1893); Stephen B. Weeks, *The Religious Development in the Province of North Carolina* (Baltimore, 1892); Thomas J. Wertenbaker, *The Old South; The Founding of American Civilization* (New York, 1942), throwing light also on the Revolutionary South; Edson L. Whitney, *Government of the Colony of South Carolina* (Baltimore, 1895); Eola Willis, *The Charleston Stage in the XVIII Century* (Columbia, 1924); and Louis B. Wright, *The First Gentlemen of Virginia; Intellectual Qualities of the Early Colonial Ruling Class* (San Marino, 1940), an enlightening study.

BIOGRAPHICAL STUDIES

The lives of many Southerners who played an important part in the Revolutionary period have not been competently described in biographical studies. Even so, only a fraction of the biographical literature can be mentioned. Among the more noteworthy studies are: William H. Masterson, *William Blount* (Baton Rouge, 1954); John Bakeless, *Daniel Boone* (New York, 1939), superior on Boone; Elisha P. Douglass, "Thomas Burke, Disillusioned Democrat," in *North Carolina Historical Review* (Raleigh, 1924–), XXVI (1949), 150–86, and Jennings B. Sanders, "Thomas Burke in the Continental Congress," *ibid.*, IX (1932), 22–37, articles which make the need for a full-length biography less pressing; Kate M. Rowland, *The Life of Charles Carroll of Carrollton, 1737–1832* (New York, 1898); Ellen Hart Smith, *Charles Carroll of Carrollton* (Cambridge, 1942); Louis Morton, *Robert Carter of Nomini Hall* (Williamsburg, 1941), a competent study of a Virginia planter; James A. James, *The Life of George Rogers Clark* (Chicago, 1928), sober, and John Bakeless, *Background to Glory; The Life of George Rogers Clark* (Philadelphia, 1957), lively; Kenneth P. Bailey, *Thomas Cresap, Maryland Frontiersman* (Boston, 1944); Aubrey C. Land, *The Dulanys of Maryland* (Baltimore, 1955), thoughtful; Bernard C. Steiner, *Life and Administration of Sir Robert Eden* (Baltimore, 1898); Robert H. Woody, "Christopher Gadsden and the Stamp Act," South Carolina Historical Association, *Proceedings* (Columbia), IX (1939), 3–12, a fragment of a projected full-length study, much needed; John R. Alden, *General Gage in America* (Baton Rouge, 1948); John W. Caughey, *Bernardo de Gálvez in Louisiana, 1776–1783* (Berkeley, 1934); Joseph W. Barnwell, ". . . Charles Garth . . . The Last Colonial Agent of South Carolina . . . ," in *South Carolina Historical and Genealogical Magazine*, XXVI (1925), 67–92; Samuel W. Patterson, *Horatio Gates, Defender of American Liberties* (New York, 1941), not well documented; George W. Greene, *Life of Nathanael Greene*, 3 vols. (New York, 1867–1871), and Francis V. Greene, *General Greene* (New York, 1893), old and incomplete; Barnhart (ed.), *Henry Hamilton and George Rogers Clark in the American Revolution*, kinder to the "Hair-Buyer" than earlier accounts of him; Robert D. W. Connor, *Cornelius Harnett* (Raleigh, 1909); Kathryn H. Mason, *James Harrod of Kentucky* (Baton Rouge, 1951); Archibald Henderson, "Richard Henderson and the Occupation of Kentucky, 1775," in *Mississippi Valley Historical Review*, I (1914–1915), 341–63, and Archibald Henderson, "The Creative Forces in Westward Expansion: Henderson and Boone," in *American Historical Review* (New York, 1895–), XX (1914–1915), 86–107, properly emphasize the major role of Henderson in the trans-Allegheny West; Moses Coit Tyler, *Patrick Henry* (Boston, 1887), and William Wirt Henry, *Patrick Henry; Life, Correspondence and Speeches*, 3 vols. (New York, 1891), should be replaced by a new scholarly study; McRee, *Life and Correspondence of James Iredell*, old and outworn; Henry S. Randall, *Life of Thomas Jefferson*, 3 vols. (New York, 1858), too sympathetic; Gilbert Chinard, *Thomas Jefferson, the Apostle of Americanism* (Boston, 1929), enlightening; Marie Kimball, *Jefferson, War and Peace, 1776 to 1784* (New York, 1943), and, by the same author, *Jefferson: The Scene of Europe, 1784–1789* (New York, 1950), excellent on the cultural side; Dumas Malone, *Jefferson the Virginian* (Boston, 1948), and *Jefferson and the Rights of Man* (Boston, 1951), the best full study, so far as it now goes; Nathan Schachner, *Thomas Jefferson* (New York, 1951); Friedrich Kapp, *The Life of John Kalb* (New York, 1884), good, but can be done again with profit; Louis R. Gottschalk, *Lafayette . . .* (Chicago, 1935–), easily the best biography of Lafayette; Edmund C. Burnett, "Edward Langworthy in the Continental Congress," in *Georgia Historical Quarterly*, XII (1928), 211–35; David D. Wallace, *The Life of Henry Laurens* (New York, 1915), sound, though possibly too generous to its subject; John R. Alden, *General Charles Lee* (Baton Rouge, 1951), tells the story of Lee and does not prove him to have been a whole-souled patriot; Burton J. Hendrick, *The Lees of Virginia* (Boston, 1935); Irving Brant, *James Madison*, 4 vols. published (Indianapolis, 1941–), a monumental work; William Gilmore Simms, *The Life of Francis Marion* (New York, 1857), should be replaced; Albert J. Beveridge, *The Life of John Marshall*, 4 vols. (Boston, 1916–1919), not a definitive work; Kate M. Rowland, *The Life of George Mason, 1725–1792* (New York, 1892); James Graham, *Life of General Daniel Morgan* (New York, 1856), old and not too reliable; Henry A. Muhlenberg, *The Life of Major-General Peter Muhlenberg* (Philadelphia, 1849); Albert Silverman, "William Paca, Signer, Governor, Jurist," in *Maryland Historical Magazine*, XXXVII (1942), 1–25; David J. Mays, *Edmund Pendleton, 1721–1803*, 2 vols. (Cambridge, 1952), a fine study; Charles C. Pinckney, *Life of General Thomas Pinckney* (Boston, 1895); William Pinkney, *The Life of William Pinkney* (New York, 1853), useful, but should be replaced; James A. James, *Oliver Pollock* (New York, 1937); Richard H. Barry, *Mr. [John] Rutledge of South Carolina* (New York, 1942); Hamilton J. Eckenrode, *The Randolphs; The Story of a Virginia Family* (Indianapolis, 1946); Moncure D. Conway, *Omitted Chapters of History Disclosed in the Life and Papers of Edmund Randolph* (New York, 1888); Thomas E. Matthews, *General James Robertson, Father of Tennessee* (Nashville, 1934); Jean Edmond Weelen, *Rochambeau* (Paris, 1934); Carl S. Driver, *John Sevier, Pioneer of the Old Southwest* (Chapel Hill, 1932); John M. Palmer, *General von Steuben* (New Haven, 1937), leaves room for further analysis of Steuben's career; Anne K. Gregorie, *Thomas*

Sumter (Columbia, 1931); Charles H. Ambler, *Washington and the West* (Chapel Hill, 1936); Hugh Cleland, *George Washington in the Ohio Valley* (Pittsburgh, 1955); John C. Fitzpatrick, *George Washington Himself* (Indianapolis, 1933), a brief and very sympathetic portrait; Douglas S. Freeman, *George Washington; A Biography*, 6 vols. (New York, 1948–1954), the best long biography; Rupert Hughes, *George Washington*, 3 vols. (New York, 1926–1930); Bernhard Knollenberg, *Washington and the Revolution* (New York, 1940), discovers some shortcomings in Washington; Curtis P. Nettels, *George Washington and American Independence* (Boston, 1951); Harry E. Wildes, *Anthony Wayne, Trouble Shooter of the American Revolution* (New York, 1941); James R. Jacobs, *Tarnished Warrior: Major-General James Wilkinson* (New York, 1938), leaves room for a judicious study of its subject; John W. Neal, *Life and Public Services of Hugh Williamson*, in *Trinity College Historical Society Papers*, XIII (1919), 62–111; William Harden, "Sir James Wright, Governor of Georgia by Royal Commission, 1760–1782," in *Georgia Historical Quarterly*, II (1918), 22–36.

POLITICAL AND SOCIAL CHANGE

There are many excellent studies of the political and social history of the Revolutionary South, including: William W. Abbot, "The Structure of Politics in Georgia: 1782–1789," in *William and Mary Quarterly*, 3d ser., XIV (1957), 47–65; Herbert B. Adams, *Maryland's Influence upon Land Cessions to the United States* (Baltimore, 1885), no longer entirely acceptable; Charles H. Ambler, *Sectionalism in Virginia from 1776 to 1861* (Chicago, 1910), a standard work; Charles A. Barker, *The Background of the Revolution in Maryland* (New Haven, 1940), a splendid study; John S. Bassett, "The Regulators of North Carolina (1765–1771)," in American Historical Association, *Annual Report*, 1894 (Washington, 1895), 141–212, a solid factual account; John S. Bassett, "The Relation between the Virginia Planter and the London Merchant," *ibid.*, 1901, I (Washington, 1902), 551–75; Beverly W. Bond, *State Government in Maryland, 1777–1781* (Baltimore, 1905); Carl Bridenbaugh, *Myths and Realities; Societies of the Colonial South* (Baton Rouge, 1952), provocative and thoughtful; Kenneth Coleman, "Restored Colonial Georgia, 1779–1782," in *Georgia Historical Quarterly*, XL (1956), 1–20; Elizabeth Cometti, "Inflation in Revolutionary Maryland," in *William and Mary Quarterly*, 3d ser., VIII (1951), 228–34; Robert D. W. Connor, "The Genesis of Higher Education in North Carolina," in *North Carolina Historical Review*, XXVIII (1951), 1–14; E. Merton Coulter, "Elijah Clarke's

Foreign Intrigues and the 'Trans-Oconee Republic,'" in *Proceedings of the Mississippi Valley Historical Association for the Year 1919–1920* (Cedar Rapids, 1907–1924), X, Pt. 2 (1919–1920), 260–79; Charles C. Crittenden, *The Commerce of North Carolina, 1763–1789* (New Haven, 1936), a careful and useful work; Philip A. Crowl, *Maryland during and after the Revolution* (Baltimore, 1943), a fine monograph; Philip G. Davidson, "The Southern Backcountry on the Eve of the Revolution," in Avery O. Craven (ed.), *Essays in Honor of William E. Dodd* (Chicago, 1935), 1–14; Robert O. DeMond, *The Loyalists in North Carolina during the Revolution* (Durham, 1940); Alonzo T. Dill, *Governor Tryon and His Palace* (Chapel Hill, 1955), a popular account; Elizabeth Donnan, "The Slave Trade into South Carolina before the Revolution," in *American Historical Review*, XXXIII (1927–1928), 804–28; Louise P. Dunbar, "The Royal Governors in the Middle and Southern Colonies on the Eve of the American Revolution: A Study in Imperial Personnel," in Richard B. Morris (ed.), *The Era of the American Revolution, Studies Inscribed to Evarts B. Greene* (New York, 1939), 214–68; Hamilton J. Eckenrode, *Separation of Church and State in Virginia* (Richmond, 1910); Max Farrand, "Compromises of the Constitution," American Historical Association, *Annual Report,* 1903, I (Washington, 1904), 71–84; E. James Ferguson, "State Assumption of the Federal Debt During the Confederation," in *Mississippi Valley Historical Review,* XXXVIII (1951–1952), 403–24, a useful study of a neglected field; Percy S. Flippin, "The Royal Government in Georgia, 1752–1776," in *Georgia Historical Quarterly,* VIII (1924), 1–37, 81–120, 243–91; IX (1925), 187–245; X (1926), 1–25, 251–76; XII (1928), 326–52; XIII (1929), 128–53; Wesley M. Gewehr, *The Great Awakening in Virginia, 1740–1790* (Durham, 1930), standard; Paul H. Giddens, "Maryland and the Stamp Act Controversy," in *Maryland Historical Magazine,* XXVII (1932), 79–98; Hugh B. Grigsby, *The History of the Virginia Federal Convention of 1788,* 2 vols., in *Collections of the Virginia Historical Society* (Richmond), new ser., IX–X (1890–1891); Hugh B. Grigsby, *The Virginia Convention of 1776* (Richmond, 1855); Isaac S. Harrell, *Loyalism in Virginia; Chapters in the Economic History of the Revolution* (Durham, 1926); Isaac S. Harrell, "North Carolina Loyalists," in *North Carolina Historical Review,* III (1926), 575–90; Freeman H. Hart, *The Valley of Virginia in the American Revolution, 1763–1789* (Chapel Hill, 1942); C. Robert Haywood, "The Mind of the North Carolina Opponents of the Stamp Act," in *North Carolina Historical Review,* XXIX (1952), 317–43; Archibald Henderson, "The Mecklenburg Declaration of Independence," in *Mis-*

sissippi Valley Historical Review, V (1918–1919), 207–15, argues for the Mecklenburg Declaration; Archibald Henderson (ed.), "The Origin of the Regulation in North Carolina," in *American Historical Review,* XXI (1915–1916), 320–32; Richard J. Hooker (ed.), *The Carolina Backcountry on the Eve of the Revolution: The Journal and Other Writings of Charles Woodmason, Anglican Itinerant* (Chapel Hill, 1953), offers thoughtful comment on the South Carolina frontier; William H. Hoyt, *The Mecklenburg Declaration of Independence* (New York, 1907), remains valuable; Wilfred B. Kerr, "The Stamp Act in the Floridas, 1765–1766," in *Mississippi Valley Historical Review,* XXI (1934–1935), 463–70; William T. Laprade, "The Stamp Act in British Politics," in *American Historical Review,* XXXV (1929–1930), 735–57, a careful analysis; James M. Leake, *The Virginia Committee System and the American Revolution* (Baltimore, 1917); Charles L. Lingley, *The Transition in Virginia from Colony to Commonwealth* (New York, 1910); Ella Lonn, *The Colonial Agents of the Southern Colonies* (Chapel Hill, 1945); W. A. Low, "The Farmer in Post-Revolutionary Virginia, 1783–1789," in *Agricultural History* (Chicago, Baltimore, Evansville, Wis., 1927–), XXV (1951), 122–27, and W. A. Low, "Merchant and Planter Relations in Post-Revolutionary Virginia, 1783–1789," in *Virginia Magazine of History and Biography,* LXI (1953), 308–18, valuable analyses; Henry R. McIlwaine, *The Struggle of Protestant Dissenters for Religious Toleration in Virginia* (Baltimore, 1894); Jackson T. Main, "Sections and Politics in Virginia, 1781–1787," in *William and Mary Quarterly,* 3d ser., XII (1955), 96–112, a thoughtful essay; Miles S. Malone, "Falmouth and the Shenandoah: Trade before the Revolution," in *American Historical Review,* XL (1934–1935), 693–703; Elmer I. Miller, "The Virginia Committee of Correspondence, 1759–1770," in *William and Mary Quarterly,* 1st ser., XXII (1913), 1–19; Albert R. Newsome, "North Carolina's Ratification of the Federal Constitution," in *North Carolina Historical Review,* XVII (1940), 287–301; Edgar L. Pennington, "East Florida in the American Revolution, 1775–1778," in *Florida Historical Society Quarterly* (Gainesville, 1923–), IX (1930–1931), 24–46; Eunice R. Perkins, "The Progress of the Revolution in Georgia," in *Georgia Historical Quarterly,* XVII (1933), 259–75; Nelson Rightmyer, "The Anglican Church in Maryland: Factors Contributing to the American Revolution," in *Church History* (Scottsdale, Pa., New York, Chicago, 1932–), XIX (1950), 187–98; Alexander S. Salley, Jr., "The Mecklenburg Declaration: The Present Status of the Question," in *American Historical Review,* XIII (1907–1908), 16–43, a fascinating analysis, still worthy of study; William A. Schaper, *Sectionalism and Representation in South Carolina,* American Historical Association, *Annual Report,* 1900, I (Washington, 1901), 237–463; Leila Sellers, *Charleston Business on the Eve of the American Revolution* (Chapel Hill, 1934); Wilbur H. Siebert, *Loyalists in East Florida, 1774 to 1785* (De Land, 1929); Enoch W. Sikes, *The Transition of North Carolina from Colony to Commonwealth* (Baltimore, 1898); Charles G. Singer, *South Carolina in the Confederation* (Philadelphia, 1941), useful, though not complete enough to stand indefinitely; John A. Silver, *The Provisional Government of Maryland (1774–1777)* (Baltimore, 1895); St. George L. Sioussat, "The North Carolina Cession of 1784 in Its Federal Aspects," in *Proceedings of the Mississippi Valley Historical Association for the Year 1908–1909,* II (1910), 35–62; Bernard C. Steiner, *Western Maryland in the Revolution* (Baltimore, 1902); Reba C. Strickland, *Religion and the State in Georgia in the Eighteenth Century* (New York, 1939), a good study in an area deserving greater attention; Kathryn Sullivan, *Maryland and France, 1774–1789* (Philadelphia, 1936); Charles S. Sydnor, *Gentlemen Freeholders; Political Practices in Washington's Virginia* (Chapel Hill, 1952), scholarly and charming, and sympathetic; Louise I. Trenholme, *The Ratification of the Federal Constitution in North Carolina* (New York, 1932), leaves little to be said; William F. Zornow, "The Tariff Policies of Virginia, 1775–1789," in *Virginia Magazine of History and Biography,* LXII (1954), 306–19, sober and thoughtful.

MILITARY STUDIES

Of books about the War of Independence there is and perhaps should be no end. The following studies dealing at least in part with the war in the South by no means exhaust the subject: Gardner W. Allen, *A Naval History of the American Revolution* (Boston, 1913); Albert S. Britt, Jr., "The Battle of the Cowpens: an Application of Certain Principles of War," in *Military Review* (Fort Leavenworth, 1934–), XXX (1951), 47–50; Henry B. Dawson, *Battles of the United States by Sea and Land,* 2 vols. (New York, 1858); Lyman C. Draper, *King's Mountain and Its Heroes* (Cincinnati, 1881), old and deserves replacement; John W. Fortescue, *A History of the British Army,* 13 vols. in 14 (New York, 1899–1930), often unreliable, but not to be ignored; Henry P. Johnston, *The Yorktown Campaign and the Surrender of Cornwallis, 1781* (New York, 1881); Joseph S. Jones, *A Defense of the Revolutionary History of the State of North Carolina from the Aspersions of Mr. Jefferson* (Boston, 1834); H. L. Landers,

The Battle of Camden (Washington, 1929); H. L. Landers, *The Virginia Campaign and the Blockade and Siege of Yorktown, 1781* (Washington, 1931); Alexander A. Lawrence, *Storm over Savannah; The Story of Count d'Estaing and the Siege of the Town in 1779* (Athens, 1951), a fine monograph; Benson J. Lossing, *Pictorial Field Book of the Revolution,* 2 vols. (New York, 1859–1860), still useful; Edward McCrady, *The History of South Carolina in the Revolution, 1775–1780* (New York, 1901), and Edward McCrady, *The History of South Carolina in the Revolution, 1780–1783* (New York, 1902), retain value; Alfred T. Mahan, *The Major Operations of the Navies in the War of American Independence* (Boston, 1913), thoughtful and not entirely outdated; Louis Van A. Naisawald, "Robert Howe's Operations in Virginia, 1775–1776," in *Virginia Magazine of History and Biography,* LX (1952), 437–41; Hugh F. Rankin, "Cowpens: Prelude to Yorktown," in *North Carolina Historical Review,* XXXI (1954), 336–69; Eric Robson, "The Expedition to the Southern Colonies, 1775–1776," in *English Historical Review* (London, 1886–), LXVI (1951), 535–60; David Schenck, *North Carolina. 1780–'81. Being a History of the Invasion of the Carolinas by the British Army under Lord Cornwallis* (Raleigh, 1889); Willard M. Wallace, *Appeal to Arms: A Military History of the American Revolution* (New York, 1951), brief and very good; Christopher Ward, *The War of the Revolution,* 2 vols., ed. by John R. Alden (New York, 1952), readable and generally sound; William B. Willcox, "British Strategy in America, 1778," in *Journal of Modern History* (Chicago, 1929–), XIX (1947), 97–121, William B. Willcox, "Rhode Island in British Strategy, 1780–1781," *ibid.,* XVII (1945), 304–31, and William B. Willcox, "British Road to Yorktown: A Study in Divided Command," *American Historical Review,* LII (1946), 1–35, careful studies based in part on new evidence.

THE SOUTHERN FRONTIER

Studies in frontier advance, land speculation, Indian troubles, and international rivalry in the Old Southwest during the Revolutionary period are almost surprisingly numerous, although much work remains to be done. A representative selection must include: Thomas P. Abernethy, *From Frontier to Plantation in Tennessee* (Chapel Hill, 1932), Thomas P. Abernethy, *Three Virginia Frontiers* (Baton Rouge, 1940), and Thomas P. Abernethy, *Western Lands and the American Revolution* (New York, 1937), thought-provoking studies by a veteran student of frontier history; George H. Alden, *New Governments West of the Alleghenies before 1780* (Madison, 1897); John R. Alden, *John*

Stuart and the Southern Colonial Frontier . . . *1754–1775* (Ann Arbor, 1944), a sober work containing some information difficult to find elsewhere; Clarence W. Alvord, *The Mississippi Valley in British Politics,* 2 vols. (Cleveland, 1917), a pioneer work which has been assailed at various points by later scholars; Kenneth P. Bailey, *The Ohio Company of Virginia and the Westward Movement, 1748–1792* (Glendale, 1939); John P. Brown, *Old Frontiers; The Story of the Cherokee Indians from Earliest Times to* . . . *1838* (Kingsport, 1938), deals with early Cherokee history; Clarence E. Carter, "The Beginnings of British West Florida," in *Mississippi Valley Historical Review,* IV (1917–1918), 314–41; Clarence E. Carter, "Some Aspects of British Administration in West Florida," *ibid.,* I (1914–1915), 364–75; John W. Caughey, "Willing's Expedition down the Mississippi, 1778," in *Louisiana Historical Quarterly* (New Orleans, 1917–), XV (1932), 5–36; Randolph C. Downes, "Dunmore's War: An Interpretation," in *Mississippi Valley Historical Review,* XXI (1934–1935), 311–30, thoughtful; Randolph C. Downes, *Council Fires on the Upper Ohio* (Pittsburg, 1940); Robert S. Cotterill, *History of Pioneer Kentucky* (Cincinnati, 1917), superior in interpretation; W. Neil Franklin, "Virginia and the Cherokee Indian Trade, 1753–1775," in the East Tennessee Historical Society *Publications* (Knoxville, 1929–), No. 5 (1933), 22–38; Philip M. Hamer, "John Stuart's Indian Policy during the Early Months of the American Revolution," in *Mississippi Valley Historical Review,* XVII (1930–1931), 351–66, a logical analysis; Archibald Henderson, *The Conquest of the Old Southwest* . . . *1740–1790* (New York, 1920), colorful and brief; Archibald Henderson, "Dr. Thomas Walker and the Loyal Company," in *Proceedings of the American Antiquarian Society* (Worcester, 1880–), new ser., XVI (1931), 77–178; Archibald Henderson, "A Pre-Revolutionary Revolt in the Old Southwest," in *Mississippi Valley Historical Review,* XVII (1930–1931), 191–212; Cecil Johnson, *British West Florida, 1763–1783* (New Haven, 1943), a standard work; Shaw Livermore, *Early American Land Companies* (New York, 1939); Robert L. Meriwether, *The Expansion of South Carolina, 1729–1765* (Kingsport, 1940), a careful study; Charles L. Mowat, *East Florida As a British Province, 1763–1784* (Berkeley and Los Angeles, 1943), brief and useful; Howard H. Peckham, *Pontiac and the Indian Uprising* (Princeton, 1947), adds valuably to Francis Parkman's account; Paul C. Phillips, *The West in the Diplomacy of the American Revolution* (Champaign, 1913); Wilbur H. Siebert, "The Loyalists in West Florida and the Natchez District," in *Mississippi Valley Historical Review,* II (1915–1916), 465–83; Helen Louise Shaw, *British Administration of the*

Southern Indians, 1756–1783 (Lancaster, 1931); St. George L. Sioussat, "The Breakdown of the Royal Management of Lands in the Southern Provinces, 1773–1775," in *Agricultural History*, III (1929), 67–98; Garland Taylor, "Colonial Settlement and Early Revolutionary Activity in West Florida up to 1779," in *Mississippi Valley Historical Review*, XXII (1935–1936), 351–60; Frederick J. Turner, "Western State-Making in the Revolutionary Era," in *American Historical Review*, I (1895–1896), 70–87, 251–69; Dale Van Every, *Men of the Western Waters* (Boston, 1956), a popular history of the Revolutionary West; George O. Virtue, *British Land Policy and the American Revolution* (Lincoln, 1955), thoughtful, but does not take all the evidence into account; Arthur P. Whitaker, *The Spanish-American Frontier, 1783–1795* (Boston, 1927), reliable and thorough; Samuel C. Williams, *Beginnings of West Tennessee . . . 1541–1841* (Johnson City, Tenn. 1930); Samuel C. Williams, *History of the Lost State of Franklin* (Johnson City, Tenn. 1924); Samuel C. Williams, *Tennessee during the Revolutionary War* (Nashville, 1944).

INDEX

Abbeville District, 9
Actaeon, H.M.S., 205
Adams, John, 189, 207, 217, 304, 308, 309, 337, 339, 372; on American Revolution, 1; quoted, 175
Adams, Samuel, 95, 107, 165, 176
Adamses, the, 209
Address to the People of Granville County, An, 156
Admiralty courts, 61, 103–104
Alamance, battle of the, 159–61
Albemarle region, the, 18, 38, 203
Alexandria, 28
Allston, Jonathan, 33
American nationality, rise of, 207–208
Amherst, Sir Jeffrey, 52, 55
"Amicable Society," the, 113
Anglican church, 146, 153; in South Carolina, 36; in Virginia, 29, 67–68, 145, 320–22
Angus, George, stamp distributor for Georgia, 96, 97
Annapolis, 80, 111, 116
Annapolis convention, 378–79
Anson, Admiral George, 124
Antigua, 21, 33
Arbuthnot, Admiral Marriot, 239, 242, 260, 292, 293
Aristocracy in the South, 26–37
Arnold, Benedict, 188, 228, 256, 260, 292–93
Articles of Confederation, 336, 354, 381, 391; making and adoption of, 214–23; proposed amendments to, 223–25, 377–78
Asbury, Bishop Francis, 341
Ashe, Colonel John, 88, 182, 196, 198
Ashe, Lieutenant John, 160
Association, Continental, 173, 178, 347; vigorously enforced, 178–80; not carried out in Georgia, 183

Atkin, Edmund, 58
Atlanta, 25
Attakullakulla (Little Carpenter), 124, 135
Attmore, William, quoted, 40n
Augusta, 25, 235; surrender of, 263; treaty of, 274; academy at, 342

Bacon, Nathaniel, 143
Bahamas, the, 53
Baldwin, Abraham, 342, 379, 387
Baltimore, 17, 25, 110, 116
Baltimore, Frederick, Lord, 46, 78, 79
Baptists, 39, 145, 147, 153, 156, 335; in Virginia, 320, 321
Barbados, 7, 33
Barnwell, Captain, 199
Barnwell, Robert, 391; quoted, 392
Barras, Admiral De, 294, 295, 297
Barré, Colonel Isaac, 62
Baton Rouge, 277
Bell, Thomas, 150
"Benevolus," quoted, 344n
Berkeley, Sir William, 143, 162
Bernard, Governor Francis, 74, 115, 116
Bill of Rights, in Southern states, 317–19; federal, 395, 397, 399
Bird, Colonel Henry, 287
Birmingham (Ala.), 18, 25
Blair, John, 107
Blair, John, 379
Blake, William, 42
Bland, Richard, 68, 84, 107, 175, 176; his *An Inquiry into the Rights of the British Colonies*, 77
Bloodworth, Timothy, 398
Blount, William, 351, 379
Blue Licks, battle of, 288
Boardman, Timothy, quoted, 34, 42n
Bond servants, 40

427

Boone, Daniel, 6, 127, 137, 279

Boone, Governor Thomas, 91, 92

Boston, 1, 24, 35n, 74, 170; Massacre, 57, 116; Tea Party, 166, 169, 170, 172; Port Bill, 173

Botetourt, Governor Lord, 109, 129, 133, 134

Bougainville, Louis-Antoine De, 237

Bourbon County, 352, 353, 359

Brant, Joseph, 287

Braxton, Carter, 210

Brétigny, Marquis De, 236

Brewton, Miles, 34

British colonial policy, 47–63, 100–105, 115–16, 123–24, 131, 132–33, 134–35, 137–38, 164–66, 169–71, 186–88; see Cabinet; Parliament

British customs service in America, 61

British standing army in America, 51–56, 59, 60, 61, 63, 64–65, 99, 104–105, 108, 109, 115–16, 186–87

British West Indies, 7, 20, 21, 52, 59, 171, 178, 187

Brodhead, General Daniel, 281–82

Browne, Colonel Thomas, 193, 200, 263, 275

Brunswick, N.C., 86, 88, 114, 153

Bryan, Jonathan, 113, 114

Bryan's Station, 288

Bull, II, Lieutenant Governor William, 23n, 35, 92, 93, 98, 148, 151, 152, 159, 167, 174, 183, 185, 238n, 327, 341

Bunker Hill, 195

Burgoyne, General John, 229, 241

Burke, Judge Aedanus, 337, 339

Burke, Edmund, 186

Burke, Governor Thomas, 216, 300, 302, 325

Burnaby, Andrew, quoted, 64

Bute ministry, 51–52

Butler, Pierce, 379, 383, 388, 393n

Butler, William, 157, 158, 161

Byrd, William, II, 26, 30

Byrd, William, III, 323

Byron, Lord, quoted, 67

Cabinet, British, 48, 51, 55, 56, 59, 61, 66, 100, 101, 102, 103, 104, 109, 110, 111, 115, 121, 133, 134, 164, 169, 170, 186, 202, 230, 280; see Parliament

Cahokia, 53

Caldwell, the Reverend Mr. David, 160, 398

Calhoun, John, 219

Calhoun, Patrick, 150

Calhoun, William, 150

Calhouns, the, 9

Calvert, Cecilius, 78

Calverts, the, 3, 6, 46, 78–79, 82

Cambridge, S.C., college at, 341

Camden, Lord, 84n, 136n

Camden, S.C., 25, 261, 263; battle of, 242–46

Cameron, Alexander, 140, 280

Campbell, Lieutenant Colonel Archibald, 232–33

Campbell, Colonel Arthur, 274, 366

Campbell, Dougal, 94

Campbell, General John, 277–78

Campbell, Colonel William, 249, 250

Campbell, Governor Lord William, 201

Canada, 49, 50

Cape Fear region, the, 86–87

Captain Will, 127

Carleton, General Sir Guy, 202, 228, 266, 269, 299

Carlisle Mission, 230

Carroll, Daniel, 379

Carroll of Carrollton, Charles, 221, 224, 344, 374

Carrolls, the, of Carrollton, 27, 30

Carter, Landon, 28; quoted, 28n

Carter, Robert, 28

Carters, the, 27, 30

Cary, Mr., 152

Cary, Archibald, 107

Caswell, Richard, 198, 301, 351, 398

Catawba nation, 5, 140n, 272; description of, 12–13

Cattle industry, 12–13

Charles III of Spain, 49, 50

Charleston, 6, 10, 17, 21, 32, 34, 35, 36, 37, 114, 153; economy of, 24–25; Chamber of Commerce of, 168, 169; British capture of, 239–42; abandoned by British, 266–67

Charleston *Courier*, quoted, 341–42

Chase, Samuel, 217, 221, 344, 391
Cherokee, H.M.S., 201
Cherokee, the, 5, 43, 58, 124, 125, 126, 192, 199, 203, 206, 227, 279, 351, 352, 356; description of, 13; boundaries of, with colonists, 132-41; attitude of, toward colonists, 141; warfare of, with Americans, 270-74, 357-58; *see also* Chickamauga
Chickamauga, the, 273, 278, 356-59
Chickasaw, the, 5, 121, 271, 275, 278, 286, 287, 351, 352, 356, 359, 360; description of, 14-15
Chillicothe town, 287, 288
Chippewa tribe, 285
Choctaw, the, 5, 121, 123, 125, 142, 271, 275, 278, 286, 287, 352, 356, 359, 360; description of, 14
Choiseul, Etienne François, Duc De, 50
Choisy, General De, 298, 299
Choté, 273, 274, 358
Christian, Colonel William, **273**
Christophe, Henri, 237
Churchill, John, 30n
Cincinnati, Order of the, 337
Clark, George Rogers, 1, 353; campaigns of, in the West, 283-89, 357
Clarke, General Elijah, 263, 267
Clay, Joseph, 370-71
Clinton, Governor George, 339, 397
Clinton, General Sir Henry, 231, 295, 296, 297, 299; in attack upon Sullivan's Island, 202-206; operations of, in Georgia and South Carolina, 232-42; relations of, with Cornwallis, 248-49, 259-61, 290-91, 293-94
Coats, Captain William, 93
Cockspur Island, 97
Coercive (Intolerable) Acts, 170-71
Coffell, Joseph, 151, 152
Cokesbury College, 341
Colbert, Comte De, 237
College of Charleston, 341
College of South Carolina, 35
Collier, Admiral Sir George, 291
"Committee of the Revisors," 331-32
Committees of correspondence, 165, 171
Common Sense, 209
Conciliatory Resolution, 187, 202

Concord, fighting at, 188
Congarees, the, 151
Congregationalists, 39
Congress, 179, 180, 183, 306, 307; First Continental, 171, 172, 187; assumes authority, 188-89; declares independence, 212-14; makes Articles of Confederation, 214-23; Indian policy of, 269, 354-56; debates place terms, 299-304; and Ordinance of 1785, p. 322n; and slavery in the West, 344-45; challenged by Georgia, 356; the Mississippi question in, 362-63
Connolly, Dr. John, 269, 270, 279
Conservatives, 314, 315, 329; defined, 311-12; favor stronger central government, 376
Constitution, Federal, of 1787, 336; making of, 378-89; ratification by Southern states of, 390-400
Constitutions, making of, in Southern states, 307-308, 316-17; *see* names of states
Convicts, transported, 40
Corbin, Richard, 323
Cornstalk, Chief, 280
Cornwallis, Charles, Lord, 202, 265; campaigns of, in the Carolinas, 244-61; campaign of, in Virginia, 290, 293-99
Cowpens, battle of the, 252-54
Crawford, Colonel William, 288
Creeks, the, 5, 18, 43, 121, 123, 125, 174, 227, 355; description of, 13-14; attitude of, toward colonists, 141-42; behavior of, in the War of Independence, 271, 273, 274, 275, 278; post-war troubles with, 359-60
Cross Creek (Fayetteville), 86, 196, 197
Cruger, Lieutenant Colonel John Harris, 264
Cruizer, H.M.S., 196
Cumberland, Richard, 148, 149
Cunningham, Patrick, 200
Cunningham, Robert, 200
Cunningham, William, 328
Curling, Captain Alexander, 166-67, 168
Currency Acts, 61, 65
Customs Commissioners, Board of, 103, 107-109

Dart, Benjamin, 167
Dartmouth, Earl of, 135, 136, 164, 187, 270
Davie, William R., 379, 384
Dealy, James, 199
Debts paid to British merchants, 371–72
Declaration of Independence, 207–14, 347
Declaration of Rights, Virginia, 317–18, 320, 334–35
Declaratory Act, 101, 102, 105
Defense, the, 201
"Defense of the Constitutions," 339
Delaware, abolishes slave trade, 347
Delawares, the, 278, 279, 287, 288
Democrats, 312, 314n, 315, 327, 328, 329, 374; defined, 311–12
DeRosset, Moses John, 88, 89
Destouches, Captain Sochet, 292, 295
Detroit, 53, 280–84
Dewitt's Corner, treaty of, 273
Dickinson, John, 106, 189, 210, 214, 215, 222
Diligence, H.M.S., 87
Dinwiddie, Lieutenant Governor Robert, 129
Dixon, Jeremiah, 2
Dobbs, Governor Arthur, 85
Donaldson, Thomas, 161
Donelson, Colonel John, 135, 273, 274, 351
Dragging Canoe, 272, 273, 274, 357–59
Drayton, John, 167
Drayton, William Henry, 35, 140n, 225, 314n, 300–301, 302; defends British authority, 108, 113; leads South Carolina patriots, 183, 185, 199; expedition of, to Upcountry, 200; views of, concerning declaration of independence, 211n; proposes substitute for Articles of Confederation, 219–20
Duane, James, 176
Dulany, Daniel, 83–84
Dulany, Daniel, the Elder, 84n
Dumfries, 28, 75
Dundas, Colonel Thomas, 292
Dunkards, 153
Dunmore, Earl of, 135, 136, 137, 138, 173, 191, 228, 269, 270; seizes powder, 184–85; harries Virginia coast, 194–95

Dunmore's War, Lord, 136
Durnford, Elias, 277

East Florida, 3, 58; Stamp Act crisis in, 97–98; boundaries of, 121; growth of, 121–22
East India Company, 165, 166, 168, 169, 173
Eaton's Station, 272
Eden, Governor Sir Robert, forced to leave Maryland, 193–94
Edenton, 86
Education, advances in, as result of the Revolution, 333, 339–43
Edwards, Jonathan, 37
Ellis, Governor Henry, 95
Ellsworth, Oliver, 386
Emistisiguo, 142, 278
English element in South, 6–7, 38, 146, 153, 323
Entail, abolition of, 330–31, 332n, 335–36
Escotchabie, 123
Estaing, Comte D', 231, 232, 295; repulsed at Savannah, 236–39
Eutaw Springs, battle of, 264–66
Evans, Major John, 358

Fairfax, Thomas, Lord, 27, 33
Fairfax County resolutions, 180–81
Family Compact, Bourbon, 51
Fanning, David, 325
Fanning, Edmund, 89; and the Regulators, 154–62
Fanshawe, Captain, 97
Fauquier, Lieutenant Governor Francis, 72, 73, 127; defends Mercer, 75–76; and Virginia expansion, 131–32
Federal Convention of 1787, p. 3, 376, 377n, 379–89
Federalists (party), 337
Fenwick family, 124n
Ferguson, Major Patrick, 240–41, 249, 250
Few, James, 161
Few, William, 379
First Continental Congress, 175–79
Fiske, John, 349
Fithian, Philip, 30
Fitzhughs, the, 129
Fletchall, Colonel Thomas, 200, 201

Flint Creek, battle of, 358
Floridas, the, 24, 301–305
Fort Bute, 123
Fort Charlotte (Mobile), 277
Fort Charlotte (S.C.), 199
Fort Chartres, 53
Fort George (Georgia), 97
Fort George (Pensacola), 278
Fort Granby, 261, 263
Fort Jefferson, 287
Fort Johnson (S.C.), 93, 94, 199, 201
Fort Johnston (N.C.), 88, 89, 182, 240
Fort Loudoun (Tenn.), 124
Fort Motte, 261, 263
Fort Moultrie, 240, 241
Fort Nelson, 287
Fort Panmure, 123
Fort Pitt, 53
Fort Prince George, 53
Fort Sackville, 284, 285, 286
Fort St. Joseph, 287
Fort Stanwix, treaty of, 133, 134
Fovey, H.M.S., 185, 194
Fox tribe, the, 285
France, 46, 49, 50, 51, 53, 54, 209; enters war as American ally, 229–30
Franklin, Benjamin, 66, 77, 79n, 100, 169, 170, 187, 188, 207, 209, 295, 304, 305, 311n, 366, 379
Franklin, state of, 354, 364, 366
Franklin College, 342
Frederick Town, 25, 28
French in America, 38, 39, 52–53, 57, 98, 119, 123, 146, 284–86
French West Indies, 21, 49–50, 60, 232, 295
Frohock, John, 155
Frohock, Thomas, 155
Frohock, William, 155
Frohocks, the, 155–56

Gadsden, Christopher, 33, 91, 92, 108, 112, 113, 117, 174, 175, 176, 177, 189, 209, 240, 241, 249, 326; in Stamp Act Congress, 93; characterized, 94–95; and Continental Association, 178
Gage, General Thomas, 52, 55, 59, 65, 112, 115, 124, 132, 135, 170, 171, 176, 182, 184, 186, 187, 192, 197, 202, 227,

270; and Stamp Act crisis, 74, 81, 99–100
Galloway, Joseph, 188; his plan, 176–77
Galphin, George, 141, 275
Galvez, Governor Bernardo De, 275, 276–78, 304
Garden, Alexander, 37
Gardoqui, Don Diego De, negotiates with Jay, 361–63
Garth, Charles, 92
Gaspée incident, the, 164, 165
Gates, General Horatio, 27, 232n, 251, 335; campaign of, in South, 243–46
George III, 15, 49, 100, 102, 105, 112, 115, 164, 186, 213, 230
Georgetown, 261; evacuated by British, 262–63
Georgia, settlement of, 5; population of, 7, 9, 10; economy of, 16–18, 20–22; political system in 1763 of, 46–47, 95; Stamp Act crisis in, 95–97; in Townshend crisis, 108, 113–14; extended to St. Mary's River, 120; expansion of, 123, 128, 130, 140–41; no sectionalism in, 145; crisis of 1774–1775 in, 174, 179, 183–84; closing years of war in, Chaps. XIII–XIV; constitutions, 307, 310, 312, 314–15; movement of capital of, 317; Bill of Rights in, 317, 319; religious freedom in, 319, 322; punishment of Tories by, 325–26; social reform in, 335, 336, 342, 347–48; expansion of, 351–54; defies Congress, 356, 359; troubles of, with the Creeks, 359–60; postwar conditions in, 370–71, 374, 375; delegation of, in federal convention, 379; ratification of Constitution by, 390
Gérard, Conrad Alexandre, 303
Germain, Lord George, 201, 248, 270
Germans in the South, 6, 7, 9, 38, 39, 145, 146, 153, 196, 200, 323
Gerry, Elbridge, 386
Gibault, Father Pierre, 284
Gibert, Jean Louis, 9
Gibraltar, 230, 299
Gillespie's Station, 358
Gillon, Commodore Alexander, 327n, 328n

Gilman, Nicholas, 385, 386
Girty, Simon, 286, 287
Glen, Governor James, 148
Goldsmith, Oliver, quoted, 16
Gordon, Adam, Lord, quoted, 35n
Gorham, Nathanael, 386
Gosport, 194
Grafton, Duke of, as first minister, 102–103, 115
Grand Ohio Company, 134, 135, 136, 140
Grant, Governor Sir James, 122, 127; in Stamp Act crisis, 97–98
Granville, Earl of, 156
Grasse, Admiral De, 237; in Yorktown campaign, 294–99
Graves, Admiral Samuel, 192
Graves, Admiral Thomas, 296, 297
Grayson, Colonel William, 229, 394, 395, 399
Great Bridge, battle of, 194–95
Great Compromise, 382
Great Lakes, the, 53, 54
Greenbrier Company, 133
Greene, General Nathanael, 209, 226, 232n, 243, 294, 328n, 367; estimate of, 250–51, 267; campaigns of, in the South, 251–67
Grenville, George, 79, 83, 84, 100, 101, 103; colonial policy of, 49–63
Grimké, John F., 339
Guadeloupe, 49
Guilford Court House, battle of, 256–59
Gunby, Colonel John, 262
Gunston Hall, 28
Gwinnett, Button, 35n, 281

Habersham, James, 96
Habersham, Joseph, 192, 193
Haddrell's Point, 205
Hall, Governor Lyman, 342
Hamilton, Alexander, 223, 224, 378
Hamilton, Lieutenant Governor Henry, 280, 284–86
Hamilton, Ninian, 158
Hampton, Wade, 351
Hancock, John, 24, 176
Hand, Brigadier General Edward, 280
Hanover county court, 68

Hanover Courthouse, 42
Hard Labor boundary, 133, 134
Harford, Henry, 79
Harnett, Cornelius, 88, 114, 196, 320n
Harrison, Benjamin, 175, 181, 217, 224
Hart, Benjamin, 149
Hart, Thomas, 158
Hawkins, Benjamin, 355
Helm, Captain Leonard, 284, 285
Henderson, Judge Richard, 130, 158, 159, 273–74, 282, 283; and settlement of Kentucky, 136–37
Henry, Patrick, 15, 77, 107, 172, 175, 176, 177, 209, 210, 212, 284, 321, 324, 344, 353, 372, 400; abilities of, 67; in Parson's Cause, 67–68; leads in struggle against stamp tax, 67–72; his oration against the Stamp Act, 68–69; political behavior of, 143–44; quoted, 181; and defense of Virginia, 181–82; opposes ratification of the Constitution, 391, 393–97, 399–400
Henry VIII, treason statute of, 110
Hessians, 232, 236, 242, 257, 258, 259
Hewitt, Mr., 29n
Heyward, Nathaniel, 42, 43
Highwaymen, 29n
Hill, Whitmell, 300
Hillsboro, 157, 158, 160, 161
Hillsborough, Earl of, 107, 133, 135
Hobkirk's Hill, battle of, 262–63
Hogg, James, 282
Holston River, settlements on, 128, 135, 350
Holt, Michael, 158
Hood, Admiral Sir Samuel, 296, 297
Hood, Zachariah, Maryland stamp collector, 80; resigns, 81
Hooper, William, 217, 315, 398
Hopewell, treaties signed at, 356
Hornet, H.M.S., 80
Horry, Daniel, 327n
Horry, Peter, 237
Horse racing, 16–17
Houston, county of, 351
Houston, Dr. William, stamp collector for North Carolina, 86; resigns, 89
Houstoun, William, 379
Howard, John Eager, 374

Howe, Richard, Lord Admiral, 228, 231, 232

Howe, General Robert, 182, 196, 232, 235

Howe, General Sir William, 162, 202, 228, 229, 231

Howell, Rednap, 143, 155; in the Regulator movement, 157–61

Howley, Richard, 303

Huger, General Isaac, 35n, 225, 226, 237, 240, 252, 255, 267, 353

Hume, David, 37

Hunter, James, 157, 158, 161, 162

Hunting, 17

Husband, Hermon, 143; in the Regulator movement, 157–62

Hutchinson, Governor Thomas, 74, 116, 166

Iberville River, scheme to open, 123

Illinois country, in the War of Independence, 282–86

India, 49, 50

Indian boundaries, 130–42

Indian policy, British, 57–59

Indian superintendents, British, 55, 57–59, 65

Indian trade, 63, 121, 125–26, 140–41, 359–60; importance of, 15; regulation of, 59, 65, 104, 126–27

Indian traders, 53–54

Indians, 3, 6, 31n, 38, 45, 53, 55, 123, 125, 193, 269, 270, 276, 278, 286, 354, 356; in South, description of, 12–15; see also names of tribes

Indigo culture, 16, 21–22, 119, 338, 368, 369

Internal Revolution, 306

Intolerable Acts, 177; see also Coercive Acts

Iredell, James, 311, 344, 399

Irish element in America, 6, 7, 323

Iron Act of 1750, p. 48

Iron mining, 17–18

Iroquois (Six Nations), 12, 132, 133, 251n, 279

Irvine, General William, 288

Izard, Ralph, 42, 43

Jack, Major Samuel, 272

Jamestown Ford, 294

Jay, John, 210, 303, 304, 305, 339, 364; negotiations of, with Gardoqui, 362–63

Jay treaty, 372

Jefferson, Thomas, 2, 16, 30, 36, 71, 77, 139, 172, 221, 222, 283, 284, 286, 294, 304, 316, 337, 372, 379, 400; quoted, concerning Patrick Henry, 67; and Declaration of Independence, 212–14; as reformer, 308, 311, 320–22, 330–35, 336, 339, 340n, 343, 345

Jenifer, Daniel of St. Thomas, 379

Jerry, slave, 199

Jews in South, 7, 38

Johnson, Sir William, 57, 58, 65, 124, 126, 132, 133, 354

Johnston, Samuel, 315

Johnstone, Governor George, 98, 121

Johnstone, McKewn, 20

Jones, Joseph, 222

Jones, Robert, 88

Jones, Willie, 311, 398

Jonesborough, 366

Joyner, Captain, 199

Kalb, Baron De, 243, 245, 246

Kanawha River settlements, 128, 129, 131–32, 133, 134

Kaskaskia, 53; Clark's capture of, 284

Kentucky, 4, 8, 9; settlement of, 128, 136–38, 139, 282, 349–50; War of Independence in, 279–88; border warfare after 1783 in, 356–57; and Mississippi question, 361–64; movement for statehood in, 364–65

Kershaw, Joseph, 150

King, Rufus, 362, 378

"King's Friends," 112

King's Mountain, battle of, 249–50

Kirk, John, Jr., 358

Kirkland, Moses, 149, 200

Knox, General Henry, 355

Knox, William, 95, 96

Knyphausen, General von, 239, 248n

Lafayette, Marquis De, in Virginia, 292, 294, 295, 296

Lancaster, Pa., 99

Land redistribution as result of the Revolution, 337–38

Laurens, Henry, 24, 33, 225, 300–301, 304, 344; in Stamp Act troubles, 92–94; views of, concerning declaration of independence, 211n

Laurens, Colonel John, 35, 225, 226, 229, 237, 295, 344

Lea, John, 158

League of Armed Neutrality, 230

Lee, Dr. Arthur, 30, 128

Lee, General Charles, 6, 180, 192, 193, 232n; defense of Charleston by, 203–206

Lee, Light-Horse Henry, 1, 229, 252, 256, 257, 258, 259, 261, 263, 264, 265, 394; quoted, 395

Lee, Richard Henry, 30, 39, 66, 75, 76n, 128, 144, 172, 175, 176, 177, 185, 212, 222, 283, 300, 321, 344, 399

Lee, Robert E., 400

Lee, Colonel Thomas, 30, 128

Lee, Thomas Ludwell, 330, 331

Lees, the, 28, 128, 129

Lemprière, Captain Clement, 199

Leslie, General Alexander, 250, 251, 291, 292

Lewis, Andrew, 133–34, 136

Lexington, battle of, 188

Liberals, 312, 315, 321, 329, 375; defined, 311–12; favor stronger central government, 376–77

"Liberty Boys," 183, 192

Liberty Hall, 343

Lillington, Colonel Alexander, 88, 198

Lincoln, Abraham, 345

Lincoln, General Benjamin, 232n, 298; campaigns of, in South, 235–41

Lining, John, 37

Linn, Benjamin, 283

Liverpool, 10, 115

Livingston, William, 208

Lloyd, Caleb, 93

Lloyd, Thomas, 88

Lobb, Captain Jacob, 87–89

Lochaber Indian boundary, 135, 136

Logan, Benjamin, 357

London, the, 167, 168

Long Island, treaty of, 273

Long Island (S.C.), 204, 205

Louis XV, 50

Louis XVI, 230

Louisa Company, 137

Louisiana, 3, 5, 14, 15, 45, 50, 118–19, 123, 360–64

Low Country, the, 19–22, 32–37, 38n, 42–43, 90, 191, 312–16, 327–28, 338, 341, 347, 369, 393; see Regulation; Regulators

Lowndes, Rawlins, 167, 168, 327n; opposes ratification of Constitution, 391–92

Lowndeses, the, 91, 314

Loyal Company, 129, 133

Loyalists, 11, 194, 199–201, 242, 248; see also Tories

Lucas, Eliza, 21–22

Lutherans, 39, 145, 320

Lynch, Thomas, 112, 117, 175, 177, 189, 217; in Stamp Act Congress, 93

McClurg, Dr. James, 379–400

McCulloh, Henry, 86

McDonald, Donald, 197, 198

McDowell, Charles, 249

McGillivray, Alexander, king of the Creeks, 355, 359–60

McGillivray, Lachlan, 141, 359

McHenry, James, 379

Machenry's Tavern, 96

McIntosh, General Lachlan, 35, 237, 240, 281, 355

Mackenzie, John, 113

Maclaine, Archibald, 398

McLeod, Donald, 197, 198

Madeira wine, 65

Madison, James, 2, 30, 36, 222, 224, 225, 303, 374, 378, 399, 400; as reformer, 311, 318, 320–22, 339; in federal convention, 379–86; leads in fight for ratification of Constitution in Virginia, 394–97

Madison, James, of William and Mary, 30

Magdalen, H.M.S., 185

"Maham Tower," 263, 264

Maitland, Lieutenant Colonel John, 236, 238, 239

Manchac, 277
Manigault, Gabriel, 24, 33
Manigaults, the, 91
Mann, Andrew, 39n
Mansfield, Lord, 137n
Manufacturing in South, 23
Manumission of slaves, 335, 344
Marion, General Francis, 1, 237, 242, 252, 259, 261, 263, 264, 265, 267
Marjoribanks, Major John, 266
Marshall, Judge John, 30, 394
Marshall, Thomas, 37, 39
Martin, Alexander, 158, 379
Martin, Joseph, 351, 355, 358
Martin, Governor Josiah, 136, 137, 162, 174, 180, 182, 198, 201, 202, 203; driven from North Carolina, 195–96
Martin, Laughlin, 199
Martin, Luther, 379, 381, 386, 389, 390–91
Martinique, 49
Martin's Station, 287
Maryland, part of the South, 3; population of, 6, 8, 10; economy of, 16–19, 24; aristocracy of, 26–32; slavery in, 40; political system in 1763 of, 46–47, 48, 78–79; in Stamp Act crisis, 79–84; in Townshend crisis, 107–108, 110–11, 116–17; sectionalism in, 145; crisis of 1774–1775 in, 172, 180; patriots seize control of, 193–94; and western lands, 220–23; constitution of, 307, 309, 312; Bill of Rights in, 317, 318; religious freedom in, 319, 322; punishment of Tories by, 324; social reform in, 335, 336, 339, 340–41, 344, 347; post-war conditions in, 368–70, 373–75; delegation of, in federal convention, 379; ratification of Constitution by, 390–91
Maryland, University of, 340–41
Maryland Gazette, the, 80, 82, 324
Mason, Charles, 2
Mason, George, 2, 28, 110, 114, 283, 311, 315, 317, 320, 330, 331, 344, 379, 380, 382, 386, 389, 394, 395; quoted concerning Patrick Henry, 67; quoted, 361
Mason, Thomson, 173
Massachusetts Circular Letter, 107, 108, 110
Mathew, General Edward, 291

Mathews, Governor George, 328n
Mathews, Governor John, 267
Maury, the Reverend Mr. James, 68
Mecklenburg Declaration of Independence, 196n
Mecklenburg resolutions, 196
Mercer, George, 80; stamp distributor for Virginia, 66; resigns, 75–76
Mercer, John Francis 379, 389, 391
Merchants in the South, 24–25, 33, 75, 90–91, 105–106, 111, 114, 116, 117, 166, 168, 171, 174, 179–80
Methodists, 335
Miami tribe, the, 285
Middle class, in the South, 53
Middleton, Arthur, 35, 189
Middleton, Henry, 175, 327n
Middletons, the, 91
Mingos, the, 271, 278, 279
Mining, 17–18
Miró, Governor Esteban, 353, 360
Mississippi Company, 129
Mississippi River navigation question, 300, 301–305, 360–64
Mobile, 14, 25, 53, 98, 120, 121; Spanish capture of, 277
Molasses Act, 48, 60
Moncrief, James, 238
Monroe, James, 229, 362, 394, 395, 399
Montagu, Governor Lord Charles, 108, 112, 149, 151, 167
Montgomery, General Richard, 192
Monticello, 32
Moore, Colonel James, at Moore's Creek Bridge, 197–98
Moore, John (Tory), 242
Moore, Maurice, 89
Moore, Samuel, 283
Moore's Creek Bridge, battle of, 197–98, 203
Moravians, 153
Morgan, General Daniel, 38, 228, 229, 255, 257; his victory at the Cowpens, 252–54
Morgan, George, 276, 281
Morris, Gouverneur, 382, 383, 384
Morris, Robert, 251
Mortar, The, killed, 142
Mosquito Inlet, 122

Moultrie, Colonel William, 2, 236, 241; defends Sullivan's Island, 203–206
Mount Pleasant, 122
Mount Vernon, 28, 32
Mowbray, Lieutenant, 80
Murdock, William, 82
Murray, William Vans, quoted, 26n
Muscle Shoals, 353, 359, 366
Muscle Shoals Company, 351–52
Mutiny Act. *See* Quartering Act

Nash, Abner, 229
Nash, Francis, 155
Nashville, 351, 357–58; founding of, 274
Natchez, 123, 276, 277, 352, 363
Naval stores, production of, 22–23
Navigation Acts, 48, 61, 89, 177, 210
Negroes, 3, 6, 7, 19, 20, 21, 22, 24, 25, 26, 28, 90, 111, 119, 122, 145, 146, 173, 199, 209, 216, 217, 218, 219, 220, 233, 237, 238, 267, 271, 323, 329, 349, 370; numbers of, in Southern states, 6, 10–12; status of, 41–43; on plantations, 42–43; in West Florida, 121; use of slaves as patriot soldiers, 191, 225–26; with Dunmore, 194–95; counting of, in representation and taxation, 382–84
New Bern, 86, 114
Newfoundland fisheries question, 300–301
New Orleans, 15, 50, 53, 54
Newport, 10
"New Purchase," the Georgia, 140–41
New Smyrna, 122
New York, 21, 53; lower house of, condemns Sugar Act, 66
Niagara, 53, 356
Nicholas, George, 321, 396
Nicholas, Robert Carter, 68, 144, 181, 185, 212, 321
Nicholas, Wilson Cary, 321
Ninety-Six, 200, 261, 263, 271; siege and evacuation of, 264
Noailles, Vicomte De, 237
Nolichucky River settlements, 135
Nomini Hall, 28, 30
Norfolk, 25, 28
North, Frederick, Lord, 115, 116, 187, 230; and Tea Act of 1773, pp. 164–66

North Carolina, 46; population of, 6, 7, 9, 10; economy of, 16–18, 22–23; political system in 1763 of, 46–47, 84–85; opposes Sugar Act, 66, 85; in Stamp Act crisis, 84–89; in Townshend crisis, 106, 114–15, 116; expansion of, 123, 128, 130, 349–51; Regulator movement in, 152–63; in crisis of 1774–1775, p. 174, 180, 182–83; patriots seize control of, 195–96; early fighting in, 197–98; aids South Carolina, 204; attacks Cherokee, 206; delegates in Congress authorized to vote for independence, 210–11; constitution of, 307, 309–310, 312, 315; movement of capital of, 317; Bill of Rights in, 317, 318–19; struggle for religious freedom in, 318, 322; punishment of Tories by, 324–26; social reform in, 335, 336, 338, 343, 347; challenges authority of Congress, 356; consents to statehood for Tennessee, 366; post-war conditions in, 368, 369, 373, 375; delegation of, in federal convention, 379; ratification of Constitution by, 398–99
North-Carolina Gazette, the, 86
Northwest Ordinance, 350
Nutbush, 157

O'Hara, General, 298
Ohio Company of Virginia, 128–29
Old Northwest, 131, 138
Old Southwest, 4, Chaps. VIII, XV, XXL
Old Tassel, 358
Oliver, Andrew, 74
Orangeburg, 261, 263
Ordinance of 1784, p. 345
Ordinance of 1785, p. 322n
O'Reilly, General Alexander, 119
Otis, James, 77
Ottawa nation, the, 285, 355
Ouconnostotah, 274

Paine, Thomas, 209
Panton, Leslie, and Company, 357, 359, 360
Paper money, post-war struggles over, 372–74

Paris, Peace of, 1763, p. 45; of 1783, p. 305

Parker, Commodore Hyde, 232, 233

Parker, Sir Peter, 201, 296; attack of, upon Sullivan's Island, 202–206

Parliament, British, 22, 44, 47, 48, 49, 54, 56, 60, 62, 73, 77, 83–84, 85, 91, 95, 100–101, 102, 103, 106, 108, 109, 112, 115, 166, 169–70, 171, 176, 177, 178, 187, 230, 299

Parson's Cause, 67–68, 143

Paterson, William, 381, 382, 384

Patton, James, 129, 131

Pearis, Richard, 140

Peggy Stewart, the, 172

Pendleton, Edmund, 30, 107, 144, 175, 181, 185, 189, 212, 311, 321, 330, 331, 332, 334, 344, 394, 396; quoted, concerning Patrick Henry, 67

Pendleton, Henry, 339

Pendleton, Nathaniel, quoted, 329, 353

Penn, John, 300

Pensacola, 14, 25, 53, 98, 120, 121, 124, 271, 273, 275, 357; Spanish capture, 277–78

Peronneau, Henry, 167

Peronneau, Isaac, 311, 327, 328

Pérouse, Comte De La, 237

Person, Thomas, 161, 162, 311, 398

Petersburg, 17, 153, 261, 291, 293

Phi Beta Kappa, founding of, 333–34n

"Philanthropos," 88

Phillips, General William, 293

Phipps, Captain Constantine, 87–89

Pickens, General Andrew, 2, 235, 242n, 250, 253, 254, 261, 263, 264, 265, 267, 328n, 355

Piedmont, the, 1, 5, 6, 9, 17, 18, 23, 25, 143, 144, 145, 196, 313–16, 369, 370, 392, 398; see Regulation; Regulators

Pierce, William, 379

Pinckney, Governor Charles, 3, 336, 379, 382, 388, 391, 392

Pinckney, Charles, loyalist, 199, 327n, 379

Pinckney, Charles Cotesworth, 35, 237, 241, 379, 383, 386–88, 391, 392

Pinckney, Roger, 151

Pinckney, General Thomas, 237, 311

Pinckneys, the, 2, 91, 314, 400

Pinkney, William, 344

Pitt, William, Earl of Chatham, 83, 84n, 100, 101, 115, 186, 230; and ministry of "All the Talents," 102–103

Pittsburgh, 81; see Fort Pitt

Piqua town, 287

"Plan for the Future Management of Indian Affairs," 59, 126

Planter's Adventure, the, 93

Poe, Edgar Allen, 37

Pollock, Oliver, 276, 277, 285

Pontiac's War, 55, 58, 64

"Poor white trash," 40–41

Pope, Alexander, 162

Population of South, 5–14

Portsmouth, 194, 291, 292, 293

Portugal, 21, 50

Powell, George Gabriel, 168

Powell, Thomas, 168

Presbyterians, 38, 39, 67, 68, 145, 147, 153, 156, 320, 321

Prevost, General Augustine, 232, 235

Primogeniture, abolition of, 330–31, 332, 335–36

Privy council, British, 47, 48, 149, 170

Proclamation of October 7, 1763, p. 104, 120–21, 131, 139; terms of, and reasons for, 58–59

Prohibitory Act, 202

Pulaski, Count Casimir, 237, 239

Purviance, Samuel, 193

Pyle, Colonel John, 256

Quakers, 196

Quartering Act of 1765, p. 56, 102, 104; as grievance, 104, 112

Quartering Act of 1774, p. 170

Quebec, province of, 52, 58, 98

Quebec Act, 138–39, 170, 171

Queen's College, 343

Quincy, Josiah, Jr., quoted, 25, 33n

Radicals; see Democrats

Raleigh Tavern, 173

Randolph, Edmund, 379, 380, 383, 386, 389, 394, 396, 397

Randolph, Attorney General John, 323

Randolph, Peter, 76

Randolph, Peyton, 68, 175, 185

Randolphs, the, 27

Rattletrap, The, 276

Rawdon, General, Lord, 244, 265; British commander in the far South, 260–64

Regulation, the, in North Carolina, 108

Regulators, 182, 196; of North Carolina, 143, 153–63; of South Carolina, 145–52, 154

Religion, struggle for freedom of, 321; in Virginia, 318, 320–22; in North Carolina, 318; in Georgia, 319; in Maryland, 319; in South Carolina, 319, 320

Republicans (party), 337

Reynolds, Sir Joshua, 37

Rhode Island, 21, 35; opposes Stamp Act, 72

Rice culture, 16, 20–21, 178, 183

Richardson, Colonel Richard, crushes South Carolina Tories, 200–201

Richmond, 291, 294

Ringgold, Thomas, 82

Robertson, James, 272, 273, 274, 351, 357, 363, 364

Robinson, John, 65, 68, 69, 144

Rochambeau, General Comte De, 291, 294, 295, 296

Rocheblave, Chevalier De, 284

Rockingham, Marquis of, first ministry of, 100–102

Rodney, Admiral Sir George, 293n, 296

Rolle, Denys, 122

Rollestown, 122

Rouverie, Armand De La, 243

Royle, Joseph, 72

Ruddle's Station, 287

Rush, Dr. Benjamin, 339

Rutherford, General Griffith, 273, 311, 326, 351

Rutledge, Edward, 168, 175, 176, 177, 191, 210, 216, 217, 241, 328

Rutledge, John, 2, 35, 93, 108, 150, 175, 177, 203, 204, 224, 225, 235, 236, 239, 241, 326, 379, 382, 383, 386, 388, 391; tribute to, 242; champions Constitution, 392–93

Rutledges, the, 91, 189, 199, 314, 392, 400

Sabine Hall, 28

St. Asaph, 282

St. Augustine, 14, 53, 97, 112, 120, 122, 124, 206, 227, 362

St. Clair, General Arthur, 266

St. Johns, the, 184

St. John's College, 340

St. Louis, 286

St. Lucia, 49, 231

St. Marks, 120

Saint-Simon, Marquis De, 295–96

Salem, N.C., 38

Salisbury, 25

Saluy, 134

Sandusky, 53

Savannah, 21, 96, 97; British capture of, 232–34; Franco-American repulse at, 236–39; British evacuation of, 266

Saxby, George, stamp distributor for South Carolina, 93–94

Schaw, Janet, quoted, 11n

Schoepf, Johann David, quoted, 29, 31n, 42

Schuyler, Philip, 232n

Scorpion, H.M.S., 196, 201

Scotch-Irish in the South, 6–7, 9, 38, 39, 145, 146, 153, 200, 323

Scots in the South, 6, 7, 32, 38, 110, 146, 182, 196, 200, 323; beaten at Moore's Creek Bridge, 197–98

Scott, John, 149

Sedgwick, Theodore, 378

Seminole Indians, 12, 275, 360

Senatus Academicus, 342

"Sentry, A," quoted, 324

Seven Years' War, results of, 49–50; expense of, 51

Sevier, John, 1, 249, 272, 274, 351, 353, 358, 363, 364, 366

Sharpe, Lieutenant Governor Horatio, 107; and Stamp Act crisis, 80–82

Shawnee nation, the, 127, 136, 142, 271, 278, 279, 280, 287, 288, 355, 357

Shelburne, Earl of, 127, 132

Shelby, Evan, 273

Shelby, Isaac, 1, 249

Shenandoah Valley, 6, 26, 38, 49, 144

Sheridan, Major Henry, 266

Sheridan, Richard B., 37
Sherman, Roger, 386
Shinner, Chief Justice Charles, 94, 148
Simcoe, Colonel John Graves, 292
Sims, George, 156–57
Slave trade, 10, 213–14; abolition of, 335, 346–48, 387–88
Slavery, 214, 225, 226; views of patriot leaders concerning, 334–35, 343–44; abolition of, 334, 344–46; *see* Negroes
Smallwood, General William, 245
Social reformation, Chap. XVIII
Sodom, 34
"Sons of Liberty," 82, 96, 97, 114
South, role of, in the Revolution, 1–2; emergence of, 2–3; population of, 5–15; economy of, 15–25; aristocracy of, 26–37; middle class in, 37–40; political situation of, in 1763, pp. 45–49; opposes Grenville program, Chap. V, Chap. VI; in the Townshend crisis, 106–17; ill-feeling against North in colonial, 172; supports the American cause in 1775, p. 188; sectional feeling against North in 1775, pp. 190–91; as a military district, 191–92; first British attacks upon, 192–206; attitude of, toward Articles of Confederation, 216–20; quarrel of, with the North over Congressional requisitions, 224–25; contest of, with North over peace terms, 299–304; tension between, and North, 304; struggles for opening of the Mississippi, 362–63; return to prosperity in, 367–70; post-war exports of, 368–69; post-war troubles of, 370–75; disputes between North and, 378–79, 383–88; enters the federal union, Chap. XXII
South Carolina, population of, 9, 10; economy of, 16–18, 20–22, 23–24; aristocracy of, 32–37; education in, 35–36; political system in 1763 of, 46–47, 89–92; Stamp Act crisis in, 92–95; planters of, 90–91; in Townshend crisis, 108, 111–13, 115, 116–17; expansion of, 123, 128, 130, 139–40, 350; and Indian trade, 126; Regulator move-

ment in, 145–52; grievances of Piedmont, 146–47; quarrel between Commons House and council of, 164, 167–69; crisis of 1774–1775 in, 172, 174–79, 183, 185; early fighting in, 198–206; closing years of war in, Chaps. XIII–XIV; fear of powerful central government in, 219–20; constitutions of, 307, 312, 313–14; movement of capital, 317; Bill of Rights in, 317, 318; struggle for religious freedom in, 319, 320, 322; punishment of Tories by, 325, 326–28; social reform in, 335–36, 339, 341–42, 346–47, 347–48; post-war conditions in, 368, 369, 370, 371, 373, 375; delegation of, in federal convention, 379, 380–81; ratification of Constitution by, 391–93
South Carolina Gazette, the, 38, 168; quoted, 11–12, 36
Southerners, serve in campaigns in North, 188, 227–29
Spaight, Richard Dobbs, 379
Spain, 21, 51, 53, 54; cedes Florida to Britain, 50; declares war on Britain, 230; and Mississippi question, 301–305; post-war quarrels of, with the United States, 360–64
Spanish in America, 5, 9, 14, 15, 45, 53, 54, 118–19, 123, 274–78, 283, 287
Spanish West Indies, 21, 60
Speedwell, H.M.S., 97
Spencer, Samuel, 398
Sphinx, H.M.S., 205
"Squaw Campaign," the, 281
Stamp Act, 109, 132; passage of, 61–62; terms of, 62–63; crisis, Chaps. IV–VI; repeal of, 99–102, 105
Stamp Act Congress, 73, 96
Stamp tax, 56; American opposition to, Chaps. V–VI
Stanleys, the, 27
Statute of Religious Liberty, 321–22, 330; quoted, 322
Sterne, Laurence, 37
Steuart, Andrew, 86
Steuben, General von, 292, 336–37
Stevens, General Edward, 244, 245, 258

439

Stuart, Lieutenant Colonel Alexander, commands British in far South, 264–66

Stuart, John, Indian superintendent, 58, 65, 123, 273, 275, 280, 354; sketch of, 124; Indian policy of, 125–26; tries to protect Indian lands, 130–37, 140–41; flees from patriots, 192, 199; and use of Indians against patriots, 268–70

Suffrage, in Maryland, 312; in South Carolina, 312–13; in Georgia, 315; in North Carolina, 315; in Virginia, 316

Suffren, Pierre André De, 237

Sugar Act, 56, 59–60, 61, 64, 65, 72, 92; condemned by Stamp Act Congress, 73; modified, 101–102

Sullivan's Island, battle of, 202–206

Sumner, General Jethro, 265

Sumter, General Thomas, 1, 242, 244, 250, 252, 259, 265, 267, 392

Sunbury, 97; academy at, 342

Swiss in the South, 7

Sycamore Shoals congress, 137

Syren, H.M.S., 205

Taitt, David, 275

Tamar, H.M.S., 201

Tammany, Saint, 172

Tarleton, Lieutenant Colonel Banastre, 240–41, 245, 246, 250, 252, 257, 258, 259, 294, 298; routed at the Cowpens, 253–54

Tennent, the Reverend Mr. William, 200

Tennessee, 4, 9; settlement of, 128, 135, 136–38, 273–74, 349–51; War of Independence in, 271–74; border warfare after 1783 in, 357–59, 360; Mississippi question and, 361–64, 366; movement for statehood in, 364–66

Ternay, Chevalier De, 291, 292

Texas, 5

Thirteen Colonies, 24, 52, 53, 54, 66, 90, 95, 99

Thomas, Lieutenant John, 123

Thompson, Colonel William, 204, 205, 237

Tidewater, 16, 17, 19–22, 26, 32–37, 38, 42–43, 69, 143–44, 145, 196, 313–16,

327–28, 338, 341, 347, 369, 392, 393, 398; see Regulation; Regulators

Tilghman, Edward, 82

Timothy, Peter, 38, 111, 174

Titles of nobility, movement against, 336–37

Tobacco culture, 16, 18–20, 31–32, 368–70

Tollemache, Captain, 201

Tories, 33n, 162, 179, 195, 209, 232, 236, 249, 250, 253, 262, 264, 270, 271, 280, 286, 287, 288, 314; of North Carolina, 196–97, 198, 235, 242, 248, 249, 255, 256; of South Carolina, 206, 241; of Georgia, 235; description of, 323; punishment of, 323–28; see also Loyalists

Townshend, Charles, 100, 102, 103, 104, 105, 115

Townshend crisis, Chap. VII

Townshend duties, 103–104, 107, 108, 109, 114, 165, 166; repeal of, 111–12, 115–17

Townshend measures, 102–104

Transylvania, colony of, 282

Transylvania Company, 137

Tryon, Governor William, 98, 108; and Stamp Act crisis, 85–89; in Townshend crisis, 114; and the Regulators, 154, 157–62; burial place of, 162

Turnbull, Dr. Andrew, 122

Tybee Island, 97

Tyler, John, 394; quoted, 395

Ulloa, Governor Juan Antonio De, 119

University of Georgia, 342

University of North Carolina, 343

University of South Carolina, 341

University of Virginia, 333

Unzaga y Amezaga, Governor Luis De, 123

Upcountry of South Carolina, 25, 200–201, 239, 313–16, 392; see Regulation; Regulators

Usteneka, 134

Vandalia, proposed colony of, 135–36, 137

Vaudreuil, Marquis De, 237

Vergennes, Comte De, 229

Vermont, 304, 307

Vincennes, 283, 357; capture of, 284–86
Viper, H.M.S., 87
Virginia, 5, 46, 49; likeness of Maryland and, 3; population of, 6, 8–9, 10; economy of, 16–19, 24; planters of, 19, 24, 31–32; aristocracy of, 26–32; slavery in, 41–42; political system in 1763 of, 45–47; reaction in, against Grenville program, Chap. V; in Townshend crisis, 106, 107–108, 109–110, 116; expansion of, 123, 127–30, 132–39; and regulation of Indian trade, 126; sectionalism in, 143–45; county government in, 154; crisis of 1774–1775 in, 172–73, 175–76, 180–82; patriots of, struggle against Dunmore, 195–96; aids South Carolina, 204; attacks Cherokee, 206; delegates in Congress ordered to propose declaration of independence, 211–12; convention of, asserts independence, 212; in quarrel with Maryland over Western lands, 220–23; cedes claim to Old Northwest, 222–23; raided by British, 250, 260; asserts control over Kentucky, 282–83; supports George Rogers Clark, 283–84; British invasions of, 290–99; constitution of, 307, 309, 312, 315–16; movement of capital of, 317; Bill of Rights in, 317–18; struggle for religious freedom, 318, 320–22; punishment of Tories by, 323–24; social reform in, 330–35, 344–46; Revolutionary expansion of, 349–50; consents to statehood for Kentucky, 365; post-war conditions in, 368–70, 371–75; delegation of, in federal convention, 379–80; ratification of Constitution by, 393–98, 399–400
Virginia Company, 353
Virginia Gazette (Royle), 72
Virginia Plan, 380–81

Waddell, General Hugh, 88, 160, 161
Walker, Captain John, 160
Walker, Dr. Thomas, 129, 133–34
Waltho, Mr., 69
Walton, George, 303
Warren, Dr. Joseph, 176
Washington, George, 1, 2, 27, 31, 33, 76, 110, 165, 175, 180, 181, 185, 191, 209, 231, 232, 236, 240, 243, 251, 252, 293, 321, 337n, 344, 368, 369, 378, 379, 380, 386, 391, 394; speculator in Western lands, 129–30, 138–39; quoted, 173; chosen commander in chief, 189–90; in Yorktown campaign, 294–99; American worship of, 399–400
Washington, Lawrence, 128
Washington, Colonel William, 42, 43, 228–29, 253, 254, 257, 258, 262, 263, 265, 328
Washington College, 340
Washingtons, the, 129
Watauga settlements, 135, 350; Indian attacks upon, 271–72
Watts, John, 358
Wayne, General Anthony, 266, 294
Webster, Lieutenant Colonel James, 258, 259
Wedderburn, Alexander, 170
Weedon, George, 229
Welsh element in the South, 153
Wentworths, the, 27
West, the, British policy regarding, 123–24, 131–42; *see* Proclamation of October 7, 1763
West Florida, 3, 58; Stamp Act crisis in, 98; boundaries of, 121; growth of, 121–22; American attempts to secure, 276, 302–303, 305–306; Spanish acquisition of, 276–78, 305; post-war boundary of, 360–61, 363
Westsylvania, 365
West Virginia, settlement of, 350; movement for statehood in, 365–66
Wheat growing, 368, 369
White, James, 356
Whitney, Eli, 16
Wilkes, John, 112, 113, 167
Wilkinson, Edward, 140
Wilkinson, James, 353, 363, 364, 365n
William and Mary, College of, 30, 35, 333
Williams, James, 249
Williams, John, 158
Williams, Colonel Otho Holland, 255
Williamsburg, 65, 66, 69, 72, 75, 109, 129, 134, 135, 144, 173, 184, 185, 282, 316, 317

Williamson, General Andrew, 150, 200, 237, 242, 272, 273, 328n
Williamson, Dr. Hugh, 379, 382
Willing, Captain James, 276–77
Wilmington, 25, 86, 114, 153, 293
Wilson, James, 217, 224, 382, 386
Winchester, 25
Winnsboro, college at, 341
Wirt, William, 69
Witherspoon, John, 217
Womble, Mr., 40n
Woodford, Colonel William, 194, 229
Woodmason, the Reverend Mr. Charles, 39, 147, 152; quoted, 150
Woodward, Thomas, 149
Wormeley, Ralph, 323
Wragg, William, 92, 108, 113

Wright, Governor Sir James, 98, 108, 174, 184, 202, 238, 326; characterized, 95; in Stamp Act crisis, 95–97; and "New Purchase," 141; driven from Georgia, 192–93
Wyandots, the, 271, 279, 355
Wythe, George, 68, 330, 331, 332, 334, 379

Yankees, 49
Yazoo Company, 353
Yorke, Charles, 136
Yorkers, 49
Yorktown, siege of, 294–99

Zubly, the Reverend Mr. John Joachim, 323